NORAGAMI
STRAY GOD

ADACHITOKA

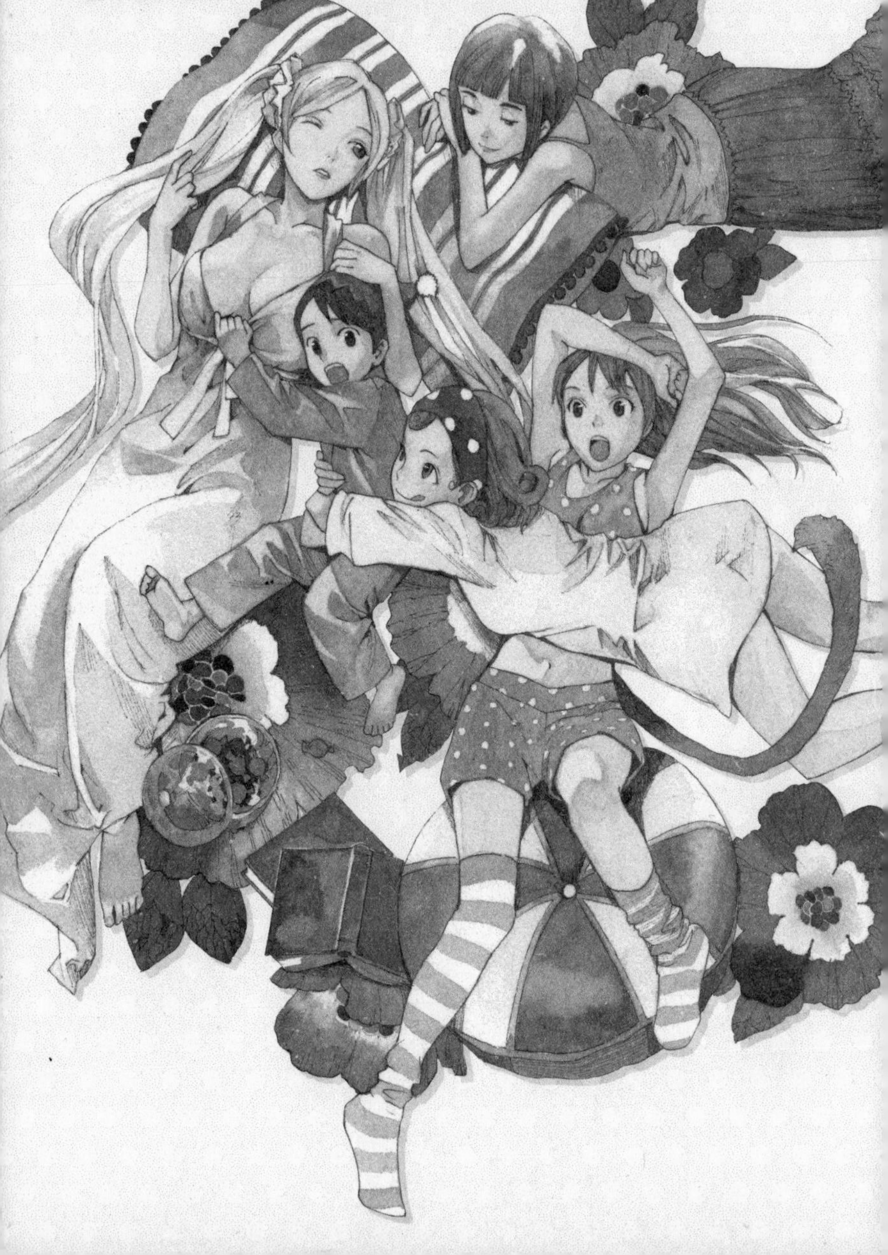

CHAPTER 40: WE NOT-SO-HUMBLY PRAY   5

CHAPTER 41: A PICTURE TOGETHER   51

CHAPTER 42: CAUSES NOTHING BUT DISASTER   97

CHAPTER 43: SECRETS   143

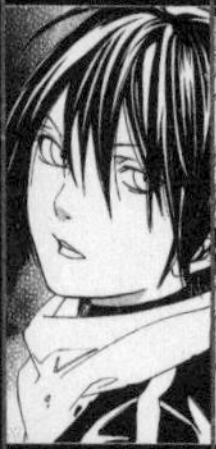

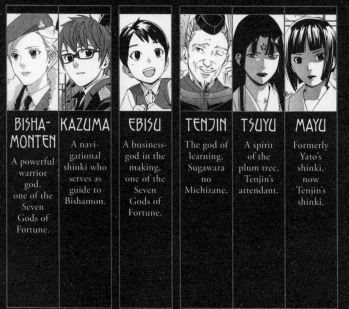

YATO

A minor deity who always wears a sweatsuit.

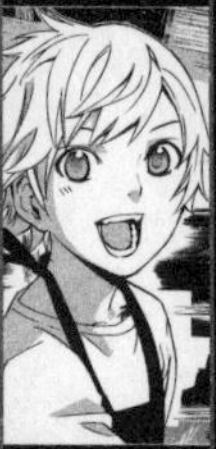

YUKINÉ

Yato's shinki who turns into swords.

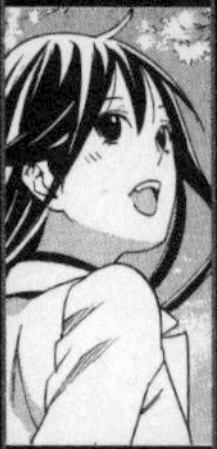

HIYORI IKI

A high school student who has become half-ayakashi.

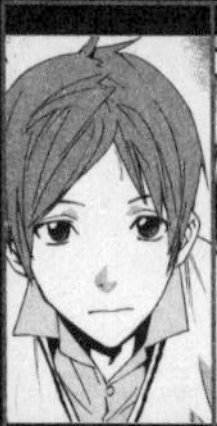

KÔTO FUJISAKI

Yato's "father."

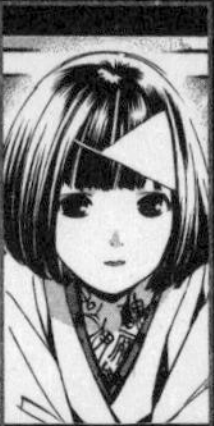

STRAY

A shinki who serves an unspecified number of deities.

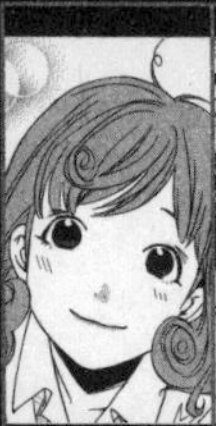

KOFUKU

A goddess of poverty who calls herself Ebisu, after the god of fortune.

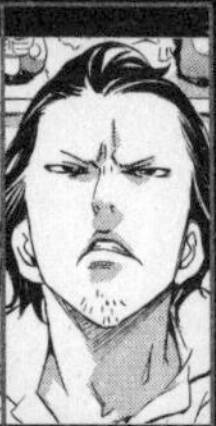

DAIKOKU

Kofuku's shinki who summons storms.

characters

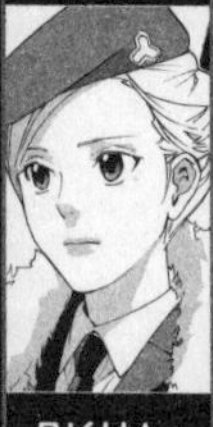

BISHAMONTEN

A powerful warrior god, one of the Seven Gods of Fortune.

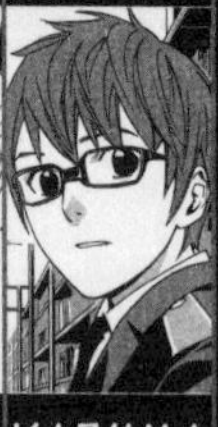

KAZUMA

A navigational shinki who serves as guide to Bishamon.

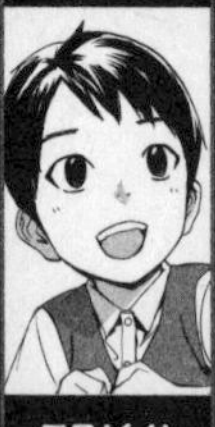

EBISU

A business-god in the making, one of the Seven Gods of Fortune.

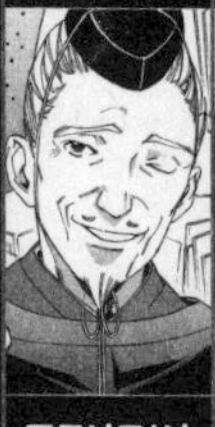

TENJIN

The god of learning, Sugawara no Michizane.

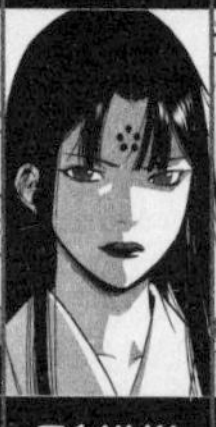

TSUYU

A spirit of the plum tree, Tenjin's attendant.

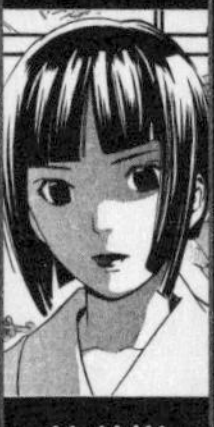

MAYU

Formerly Yato's shinki, now Tenjin's shinki.

野

夏

師

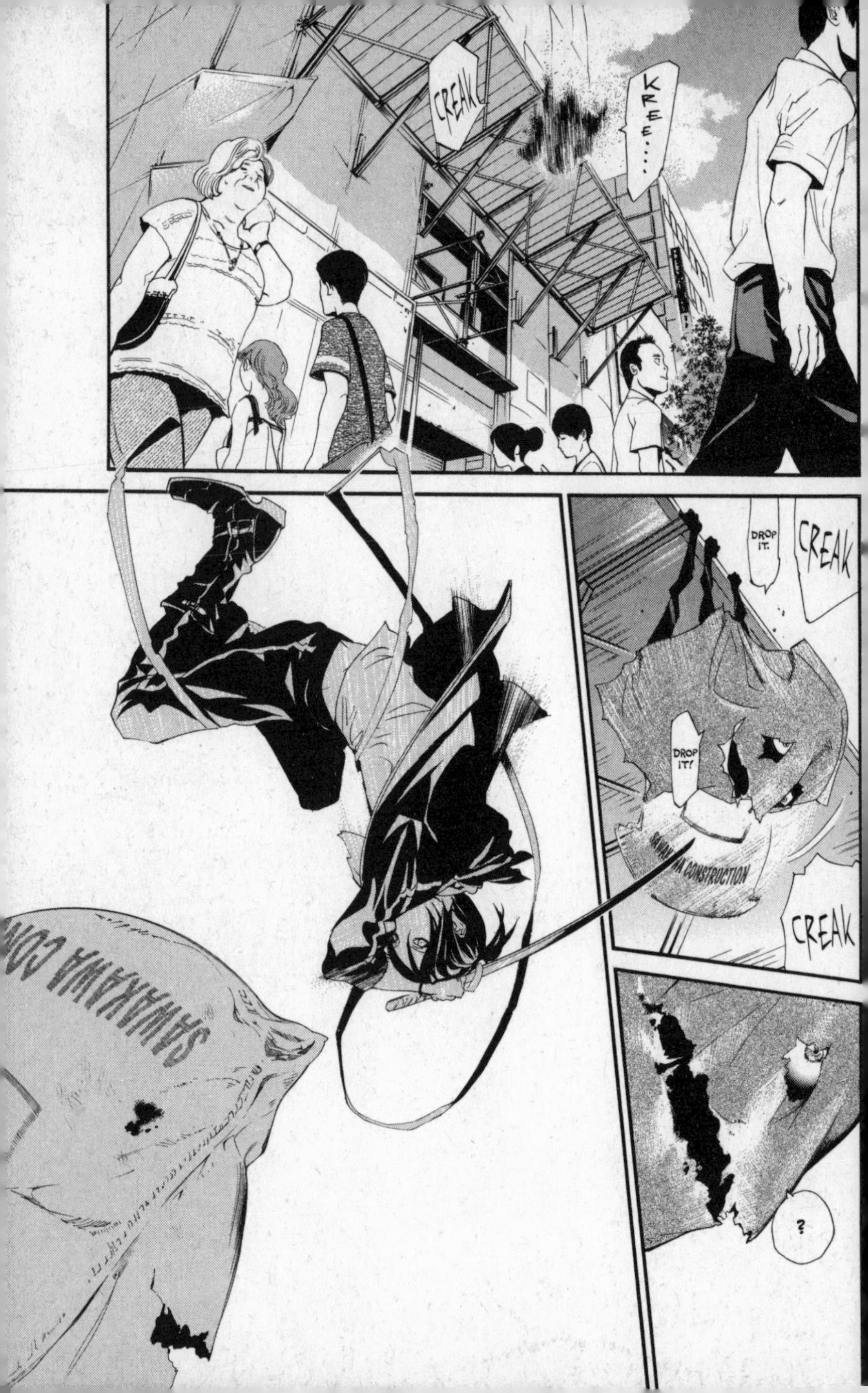
KREE.....
CREAK
CREAK
DROP IT.
DROP IT!
SAWAYAMA CONSTRUCTION
CREAK
?
SAWAYAMA CON

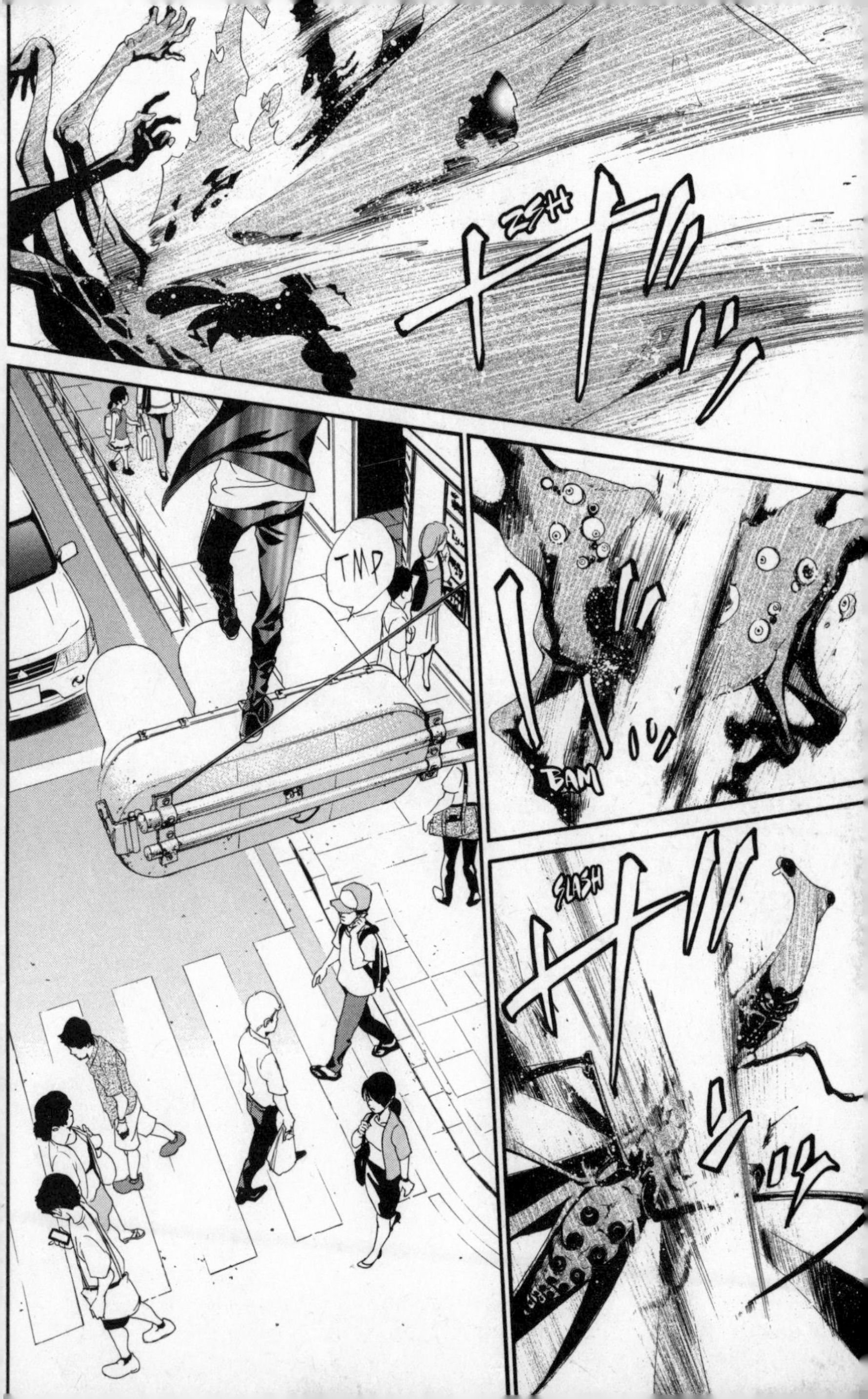
ZSH
BAM
TMP
SLASH

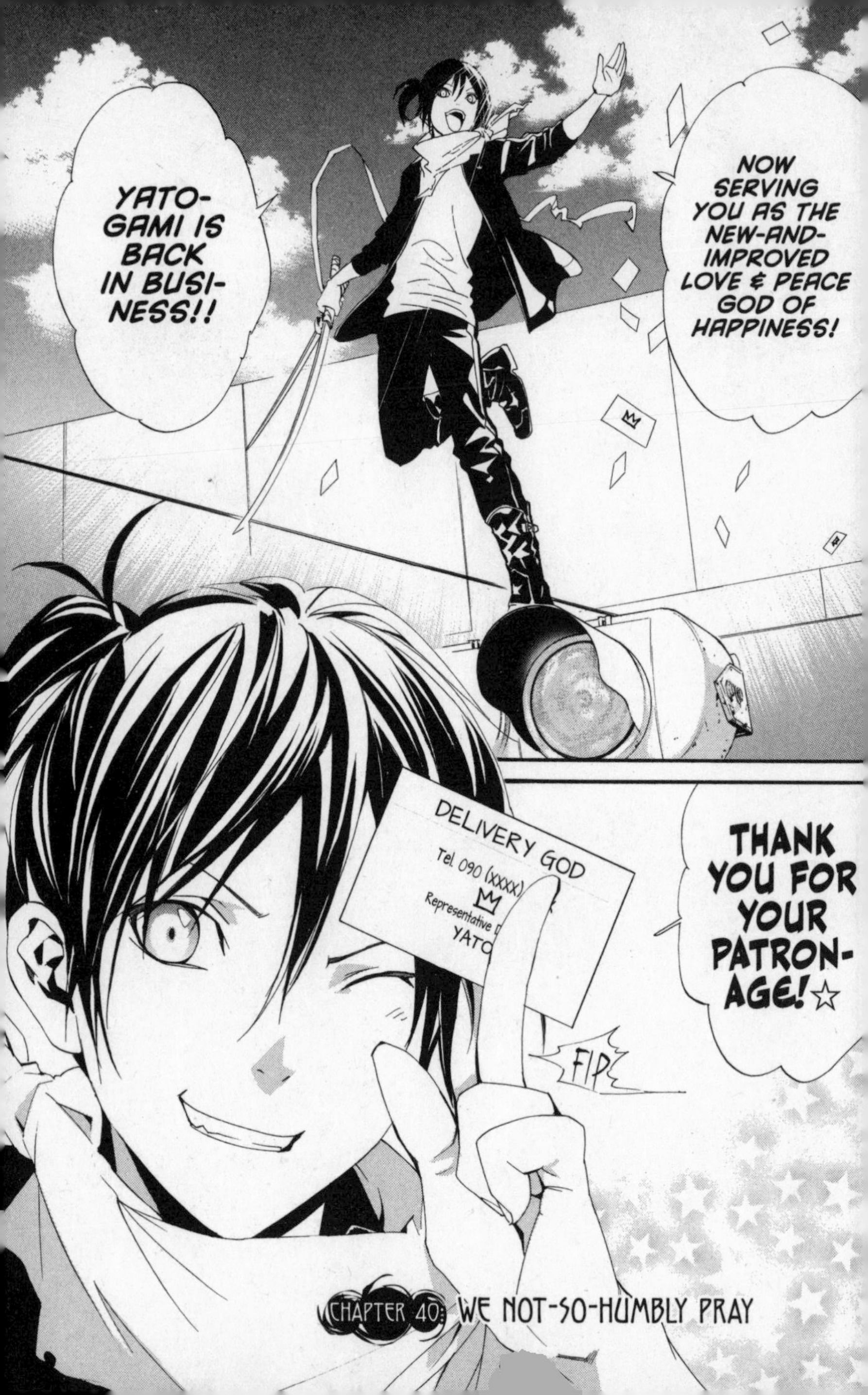
NOW SERVING YOU AS THE NEW-AND-IMPROVED LOVE & PEACE GOD OF HAPPINESS!
YATO-GAMI IS BACK IN BUSINESS!!
DELIVERY GOD
Tel. 090 (xxxx)
Representative
YATO
THANK YOU FOR YOUR PATRONAGE!☆
FIP
CHAPTER 40: WE NOT-SO-HUMBLY PRAY

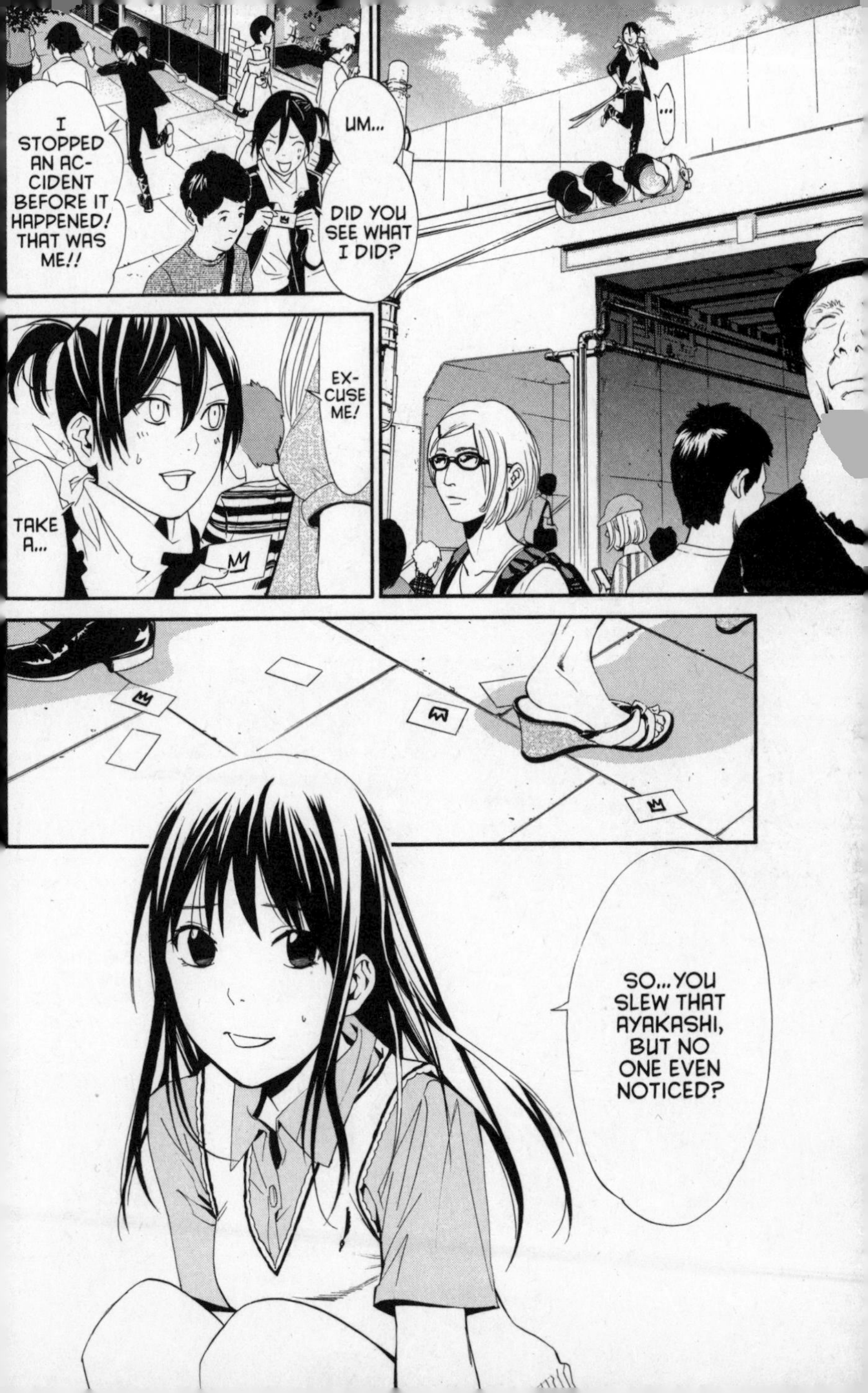
...
UM...
DID YOU SEE WHAT I DID?
I STOPPED AN ACCIDENT BEFORE IT HAPPENED! THAT WAS ME!!
EX-CUSE ME!
TAKE A...
SO...YOU SLEW THAT AYAKASHI, BUT NO ONE EVEN NOTICED?

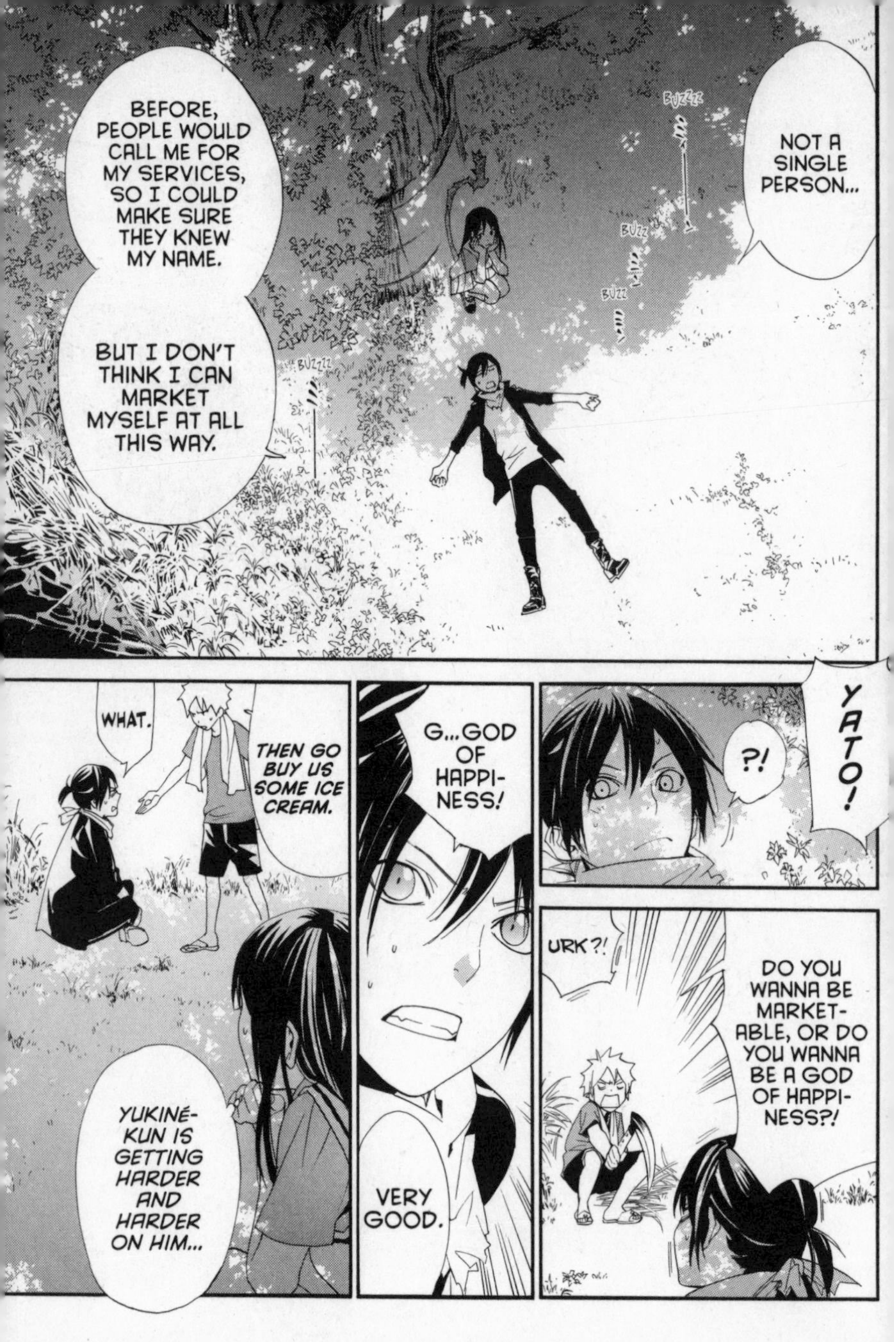
NOT A SINGLE PERSON...
BUZZZ
BUZZ
BUZZ
BEFORE, PEOPLE WOULD CALL ME FOR MY SERVICES, SO I COULD MAKE SURE THEY KNEW MY NAME.
BUT I DON'T THINK I CAN MARKET MYSELF AT ALL THIS WAY.
YATO!
?!
DO YOU WANNA BE MARKET-ABLE, OR DO YOU WANNA BE A GOD OF HAPPI-NESS?!
URK?!
G...GOD OF HAPPI-NESS!
VERY GOOD.
WHAT.
THEN GO BUY US SOME ICE CREAM.
YUKINÉ-KUN IS GETTING HARDER AND HARDER ON HIM...

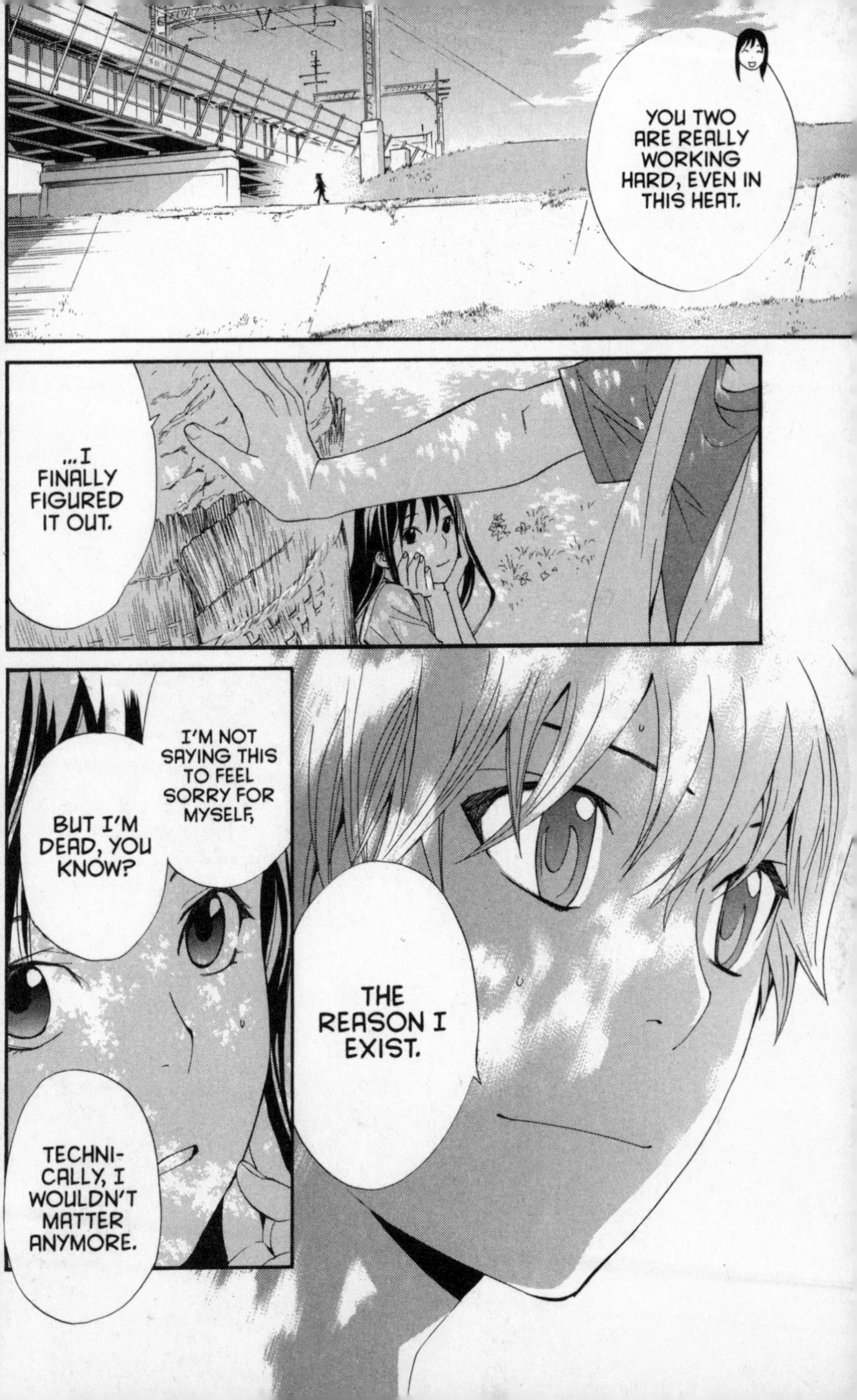
YOU TWO ARE REALLY WORKING HARD, EVEN IN THIS HEAT.
...I FINALLY FIGURED IT OUT.
THE REASON I EXIST.
I'M NOT SAYING THIS TO FEEL SORRY FOR MYSELF,
BUT I'M DEAD, YOU KNOW?
TECHNICALLY, I WOULDN'T MATTER ANYMORE.

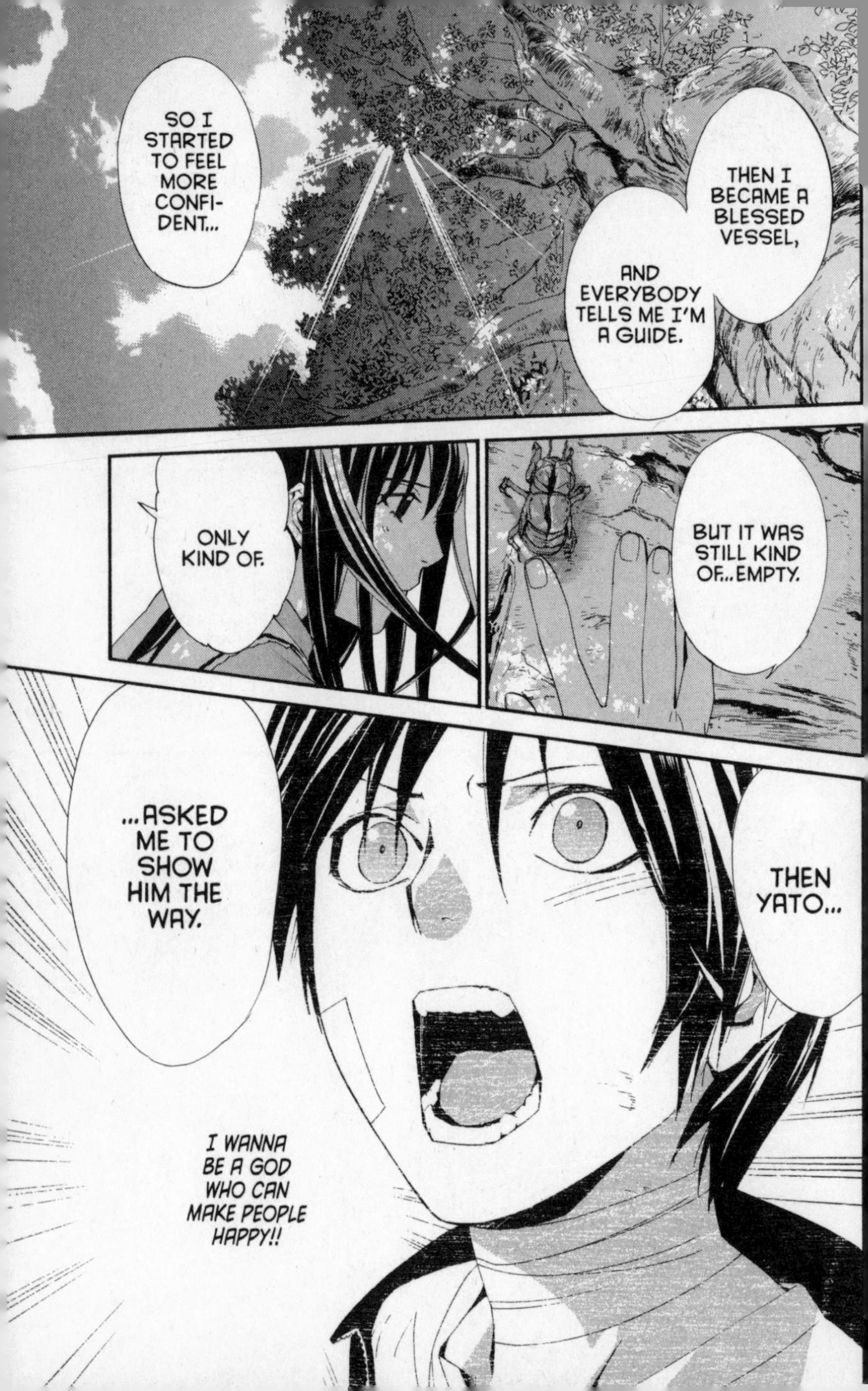
THEN I BECAME A BLESSED VESSEL,
AND EVERYBODY TELLS ME I'M A GUIDE.
SO I STARTED TO FEEL MORE CONFI-DENT...
BUT IT WAS STILL KIND OF...EMPTY.
ONLY KIND OF.
THEN YATO...
...ASKED ME TO SHOW HIM THE WAY.
I WANNA BE A GOD WHO CAN MAKE PEOPLE HAPPY!!

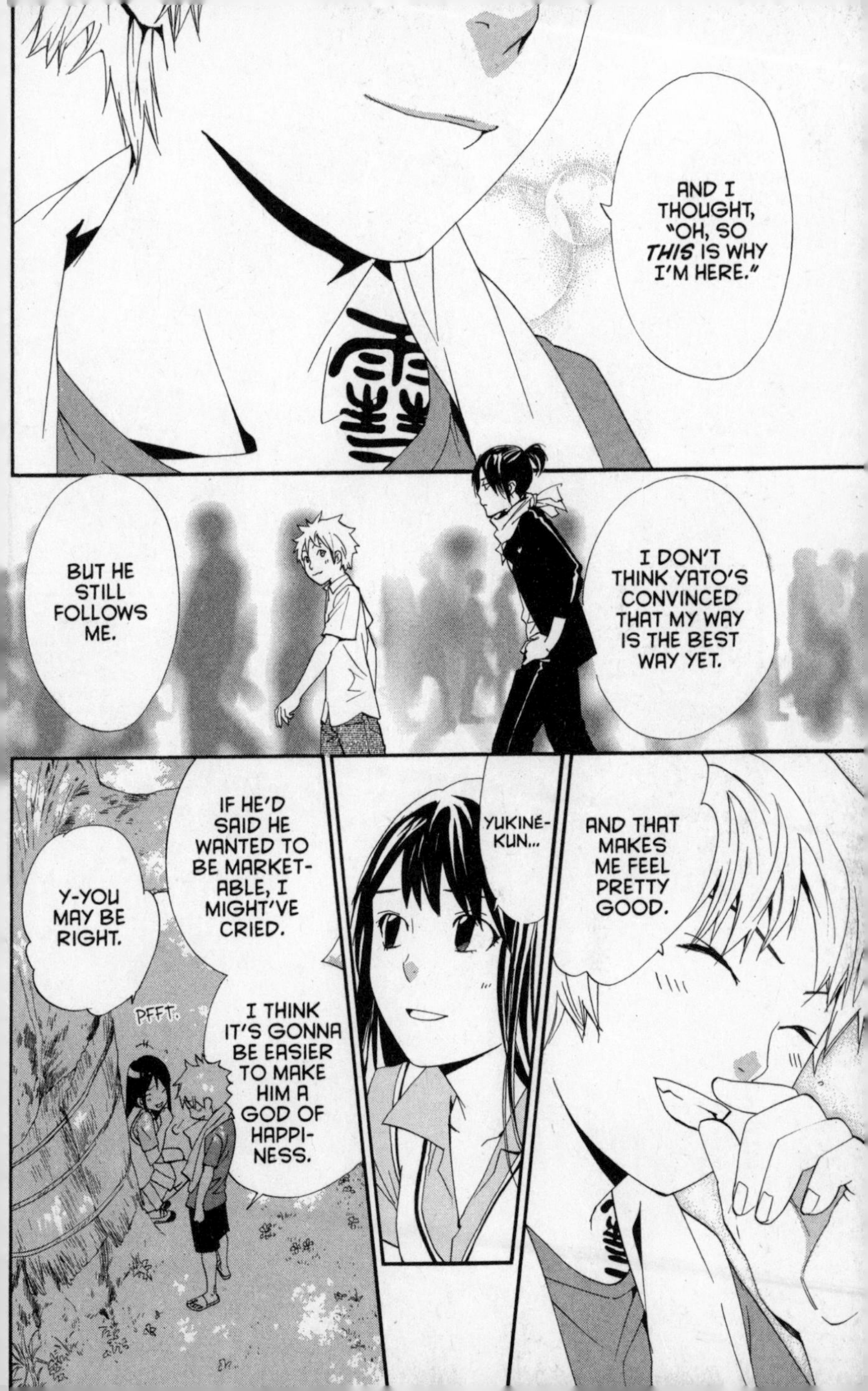

AND I THOUGHT, "OH, SO *THIS* IS WHY I'M HERE."
I DON'T THINK YATO'S CONVINCED THAT MY WAY IS THE BEST WAY YET.
BUT HE STILL FOLLOWS ME.
AND THAT MAKES ME FEEL PRETTY GOOD.
YUKINÉ-KUN...
IF HE'D SAID HE WANTED TO BE MARKETABLE, I MIGHT'VE CRIED.
Y-YOU MAY BE RIGHT.
I THINK IT'S GONNA BE EASIER TO MAKE HIM A GOD OF HAPPINESS.
PFFT.

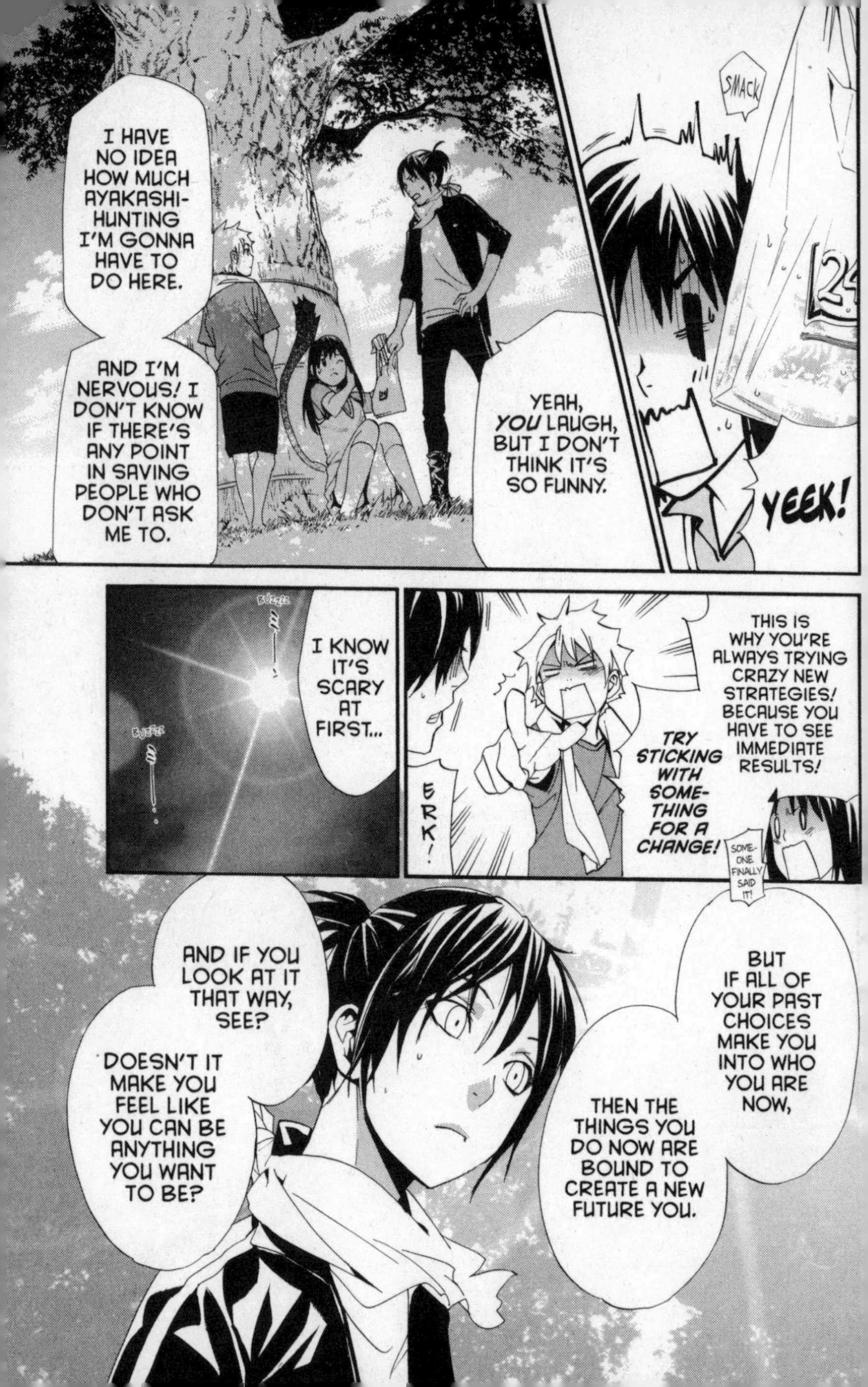

SMACK
YEEK!
I HAVE NO IDEA HOW MUCH AYAKASHI-HUNTING I'M GONNA HAVE TO DO HERE.
AND I'M NERVOUS! I DON'T KNOW IF THERE'S ANY POINT IN SAVING PEOPLE WHO DON'T ASK ME TO.
YEAH, *YOU* LAUGH, BUT I DON'T THINK IT'S SO FUNNY.
THIS IS WHY YOU'RE ALWAYS TRYING CRAZY NEW STRATEGIES! BECAUSE YOU HAVE TO SEE IMMEDIATE RESULTS!
TRY STICKING WITH SOMETHING FOR A CHANGE!
SOMEONE FINALLY SAID IT!
ERK!
I KNOW IT'S SCARY AT FIRST...
BUT IF ALL OF YOUR PAST CHOICES MAKE YOU INTO WHO YOU ARE NOW,
THEN THE THINGS YOU DO NOW ARE BOUND TO CREATE A NEW FUTURE YOU.
AND IF YOU LOOK AT IT THAT WAY, SEE?
DOESN'T IT MAKE YOU FEEL LIKE YOU CAN BE ANYTHING YOU WANT TO BE?

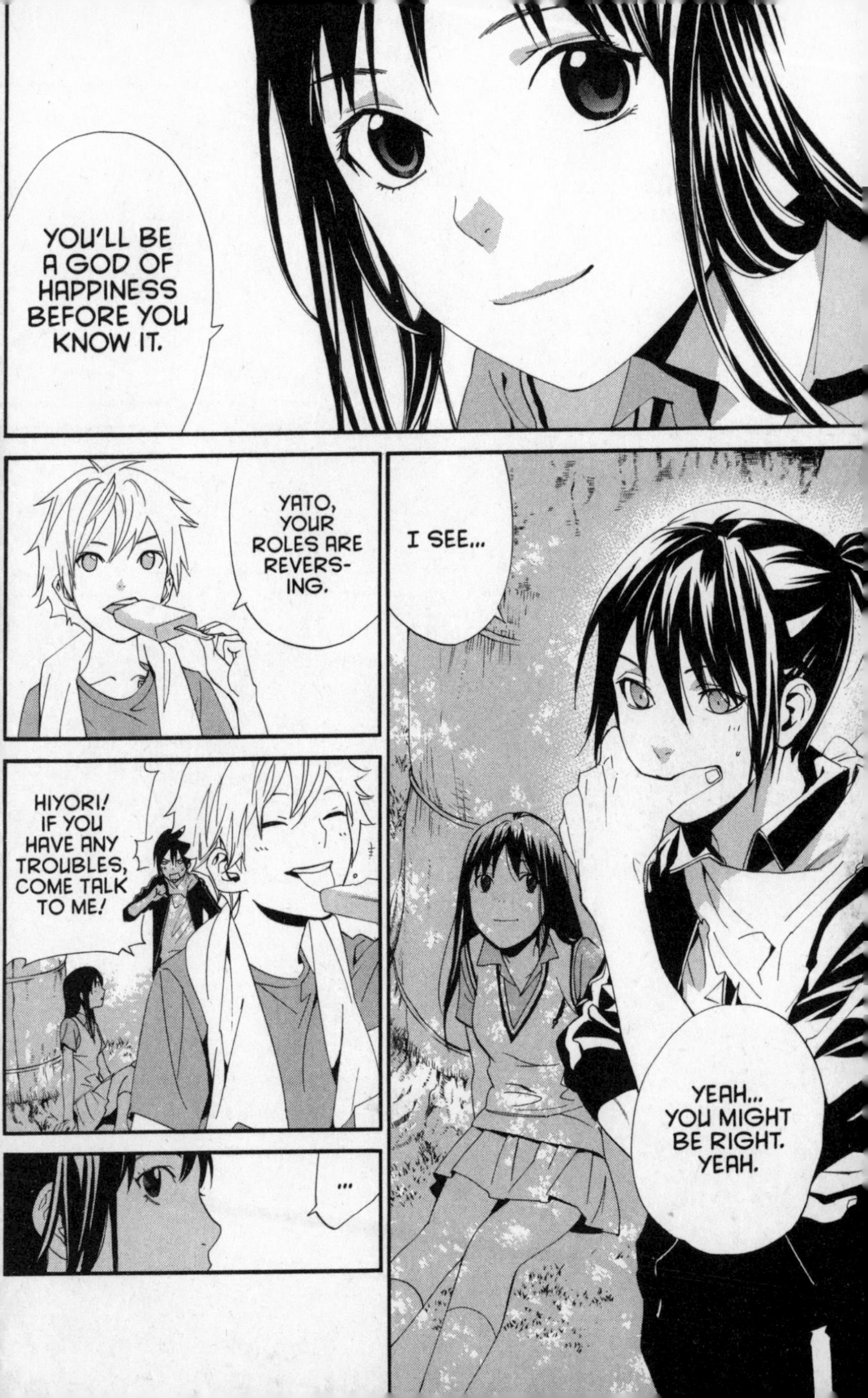
YOU'LL BE A GOD OF HAPPINESS BEFORE YOU KNOW IT.
I SEE...
YEAH... YOU MIGHT BE RIGHT. YEAH.
YATO, YOUR ROLES ARE REVERS-ING.
HIYORI! IF YOU HAVE ANY TROUBLES, COME TALK TO ME!
...

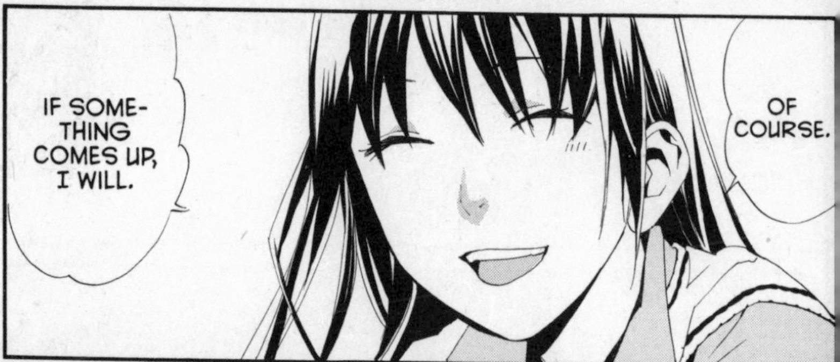
OF COURSE.
IF SOME-THING COMES UP, I WILL.
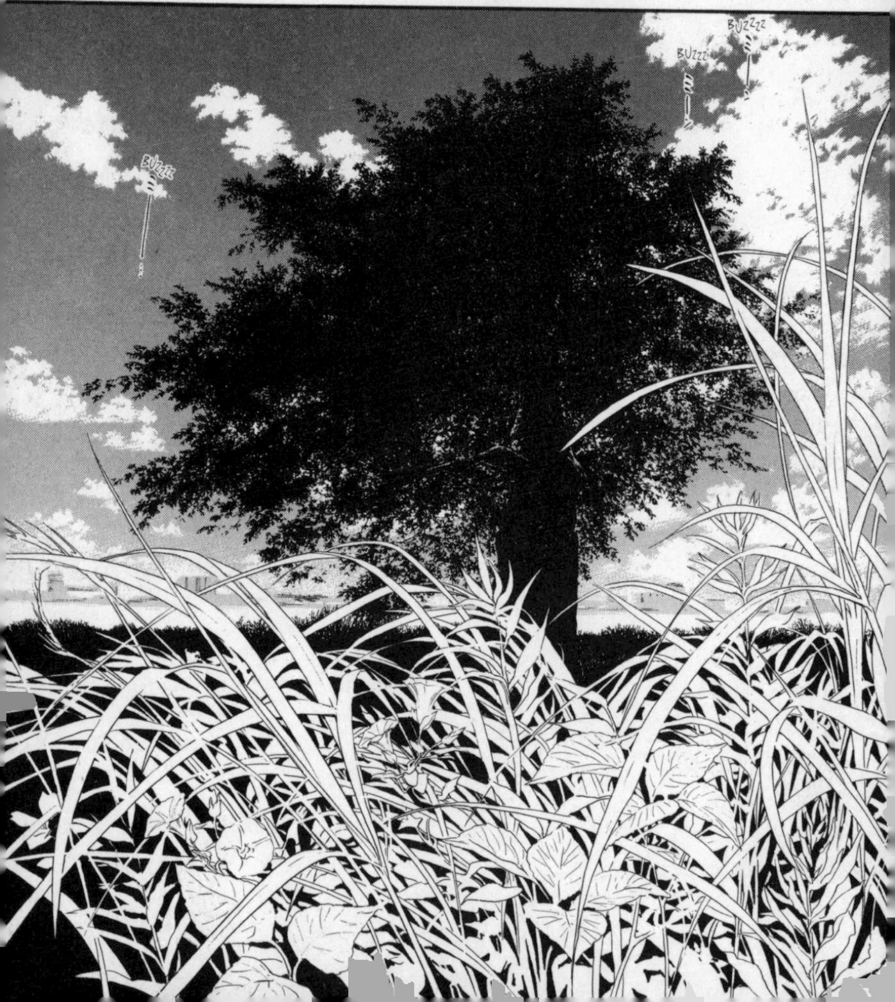
BUZZZZ
BUZZZ
BUZZZZ

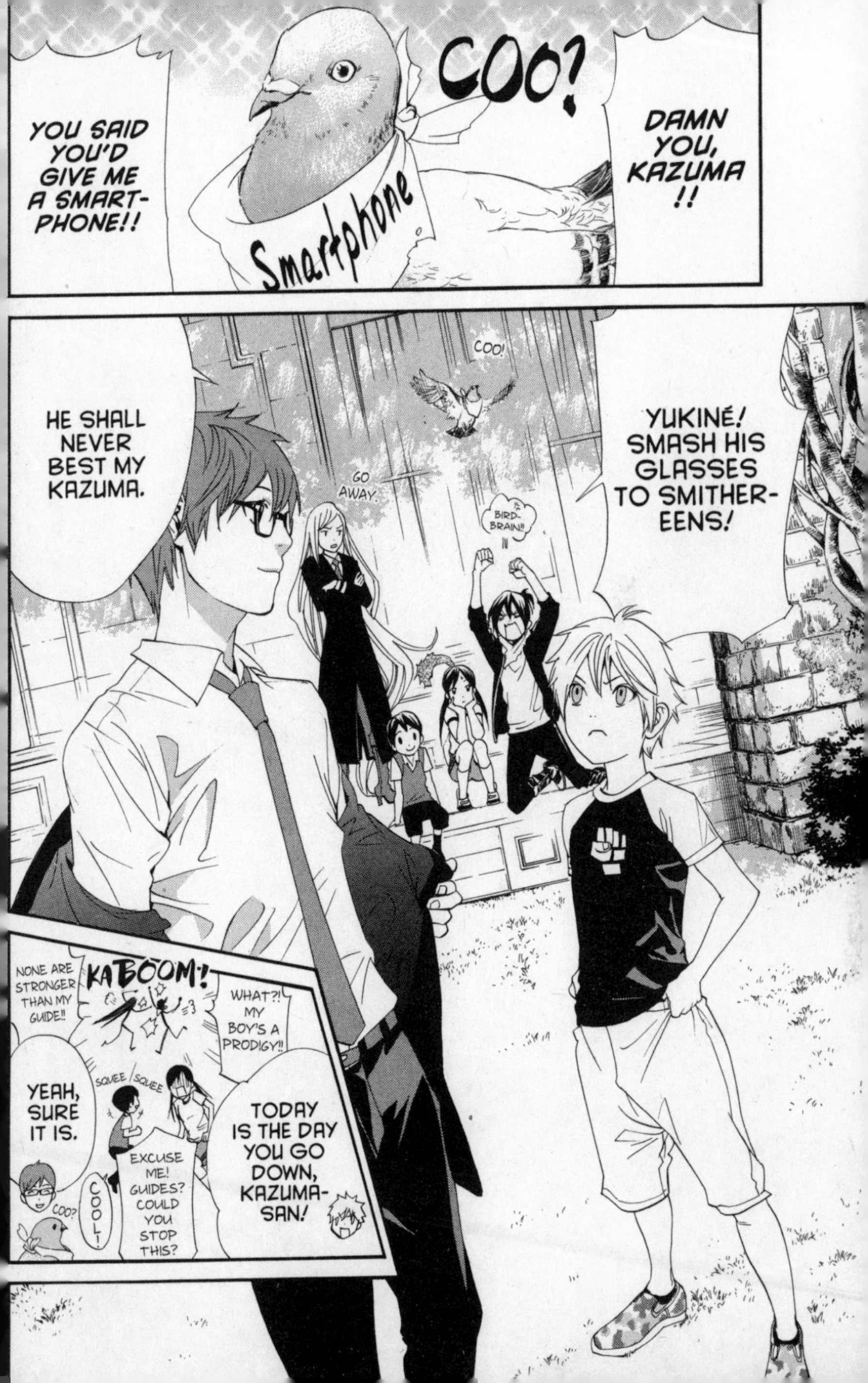
DAMN YOU, KAZUMA!!
COO?
YOU SAID YOU'D GIVE ME A SMART-PHONE!!
Smartphone
YUKINÉ! SMASH HIS GLASSES TO SMITHER-EENS!
COO!
BIRD-BRAIN!!
GO AWAY.
HE SHALL NEVER BEST MY KAZUMA.
TODAY IS THE DAY YOU GO DOWN, KAZUMA-SAN!
WHAT?! MY BOY'S A PRODIGY!!
KABOOM!
NONE ARE STRONGER THAN MY GUIDE!!
SQUEE SQUEE
YEAH, SURE IT IS.
EXCUSE ME! GUIDES? COULD YOU STOP THIS?
COOL!
COO?

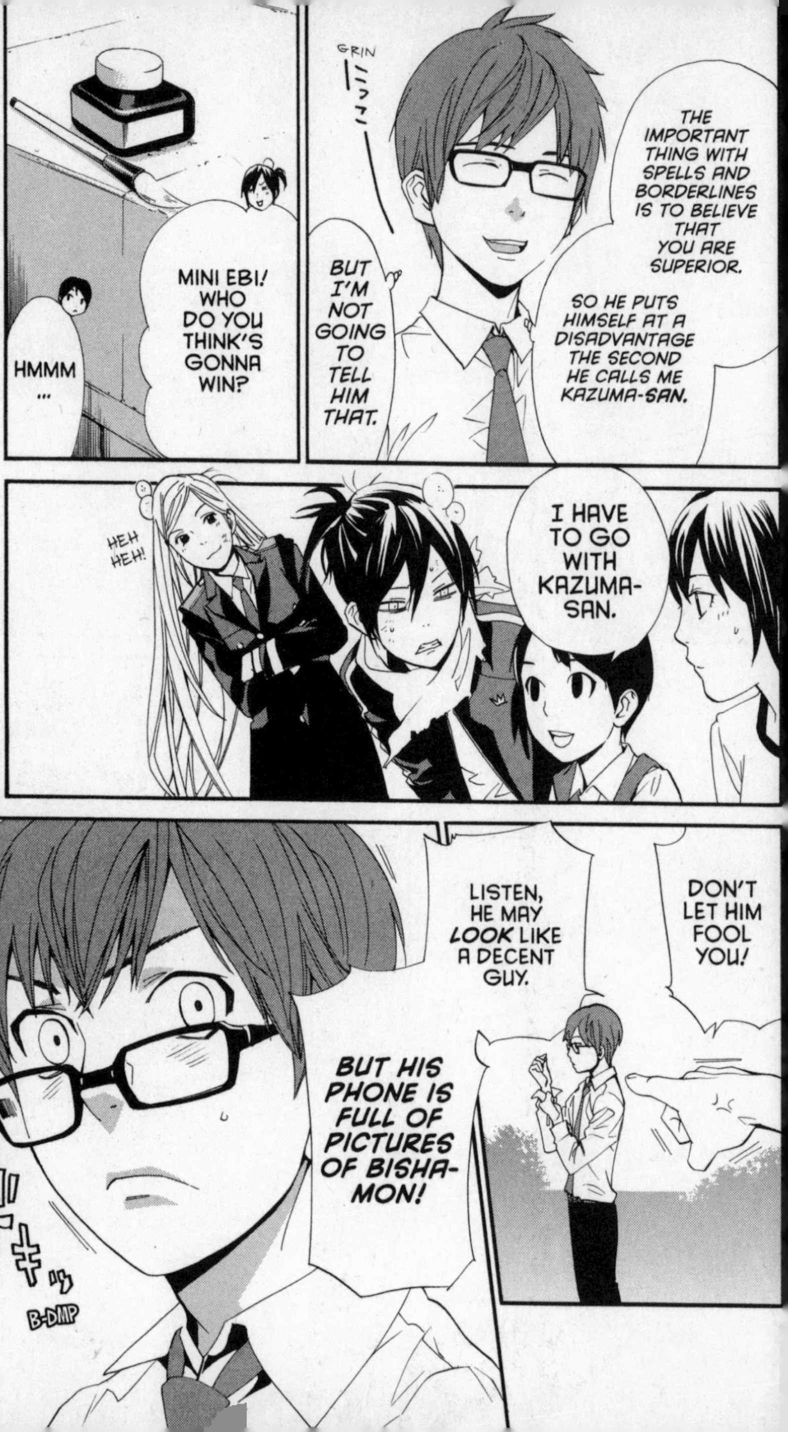
GRIN
THE IMPORTANT THING WITH SPELLS AND BORDERLINES IS TO BELIEVE THAT YOU ARE SUPERIOR.
SO HE PUTS HIMSELF AT A DISADVANTAGE THE SECOND HE CALLS ME KAZUMA-SAN.
BUT I'M NOT GOING TO TELL HIM THAT.
MINI EBI! WHO DO YOU THINK'S GONNA WIN?
HMMM...
I HAVE TO GO WITH KAZUMA-SAN.
HEH HEH!
DON'T LET HIM FOOL YOU!
LISTEN, HE MAY LOOK LIKE A DECENT GUY.
BUT HIS PHONE IS FULL OF PICTURES OF BISHAMON!
B-DMP

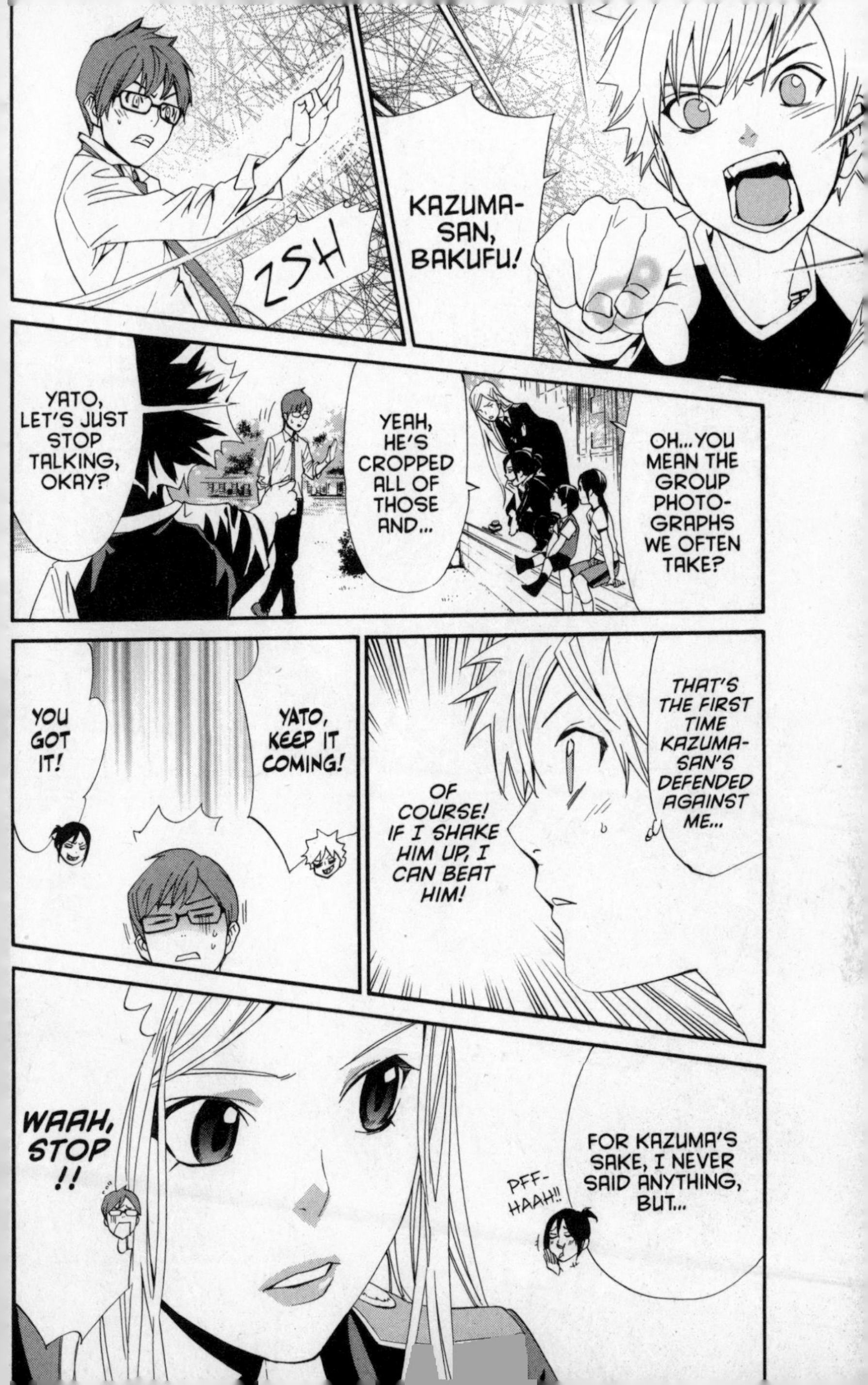
KAZUMA-SAN, BAKUFU!
ZSH
OH...YOU MEAN THE GROUP PHOTOGRAPHS WE OFTEN TAKE?
YEAH, HE'S CROPPED ALL OF THOSE AND...
YATO, LET'S JUST STOP TALKING, OKAY?
THAT'S THE FIRST TIME KAZUMA-SAN'S DEFENDED AGAINST ME...
OF COURSE! IF I SHAKE HIM UP, I CAN BEAT HIM!
YATO, KEEP IT COMING!
YOU GOT IT!
FOR KAZUMA'S SAKE, I NEVER SAID ANYTHING, BUT...
PFF-HAAH!!
WAAH, STOP!!

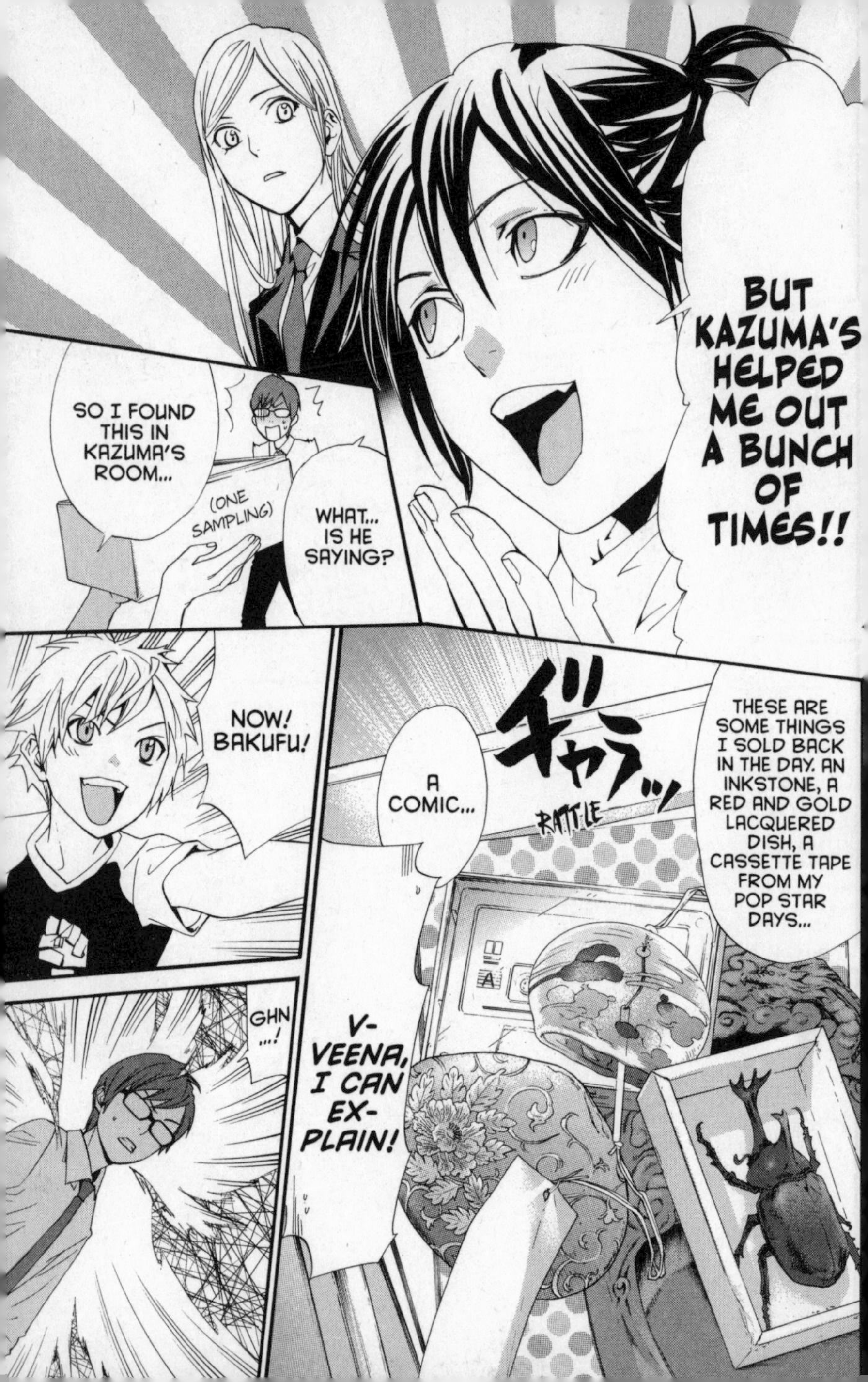
BUT KAZUMA'S HELPED ME OUT A BUNCH OF TIMES!!
SO I FOUND THIS IN KAZUMA'S ROOM...
(ONE SAMPLING)
WHAT... IS HE SAYING?
THESE ARE SOME THINGS I SOLD BACK IN THE DAY. AN INKSTONE, A RED AND GOLD LACQUERED DISH, A CASSETTE TAPE FROM MY POP STAR DAYS...
ギャラッ
RATTLE
A COMIC...
V-VEENA, I CAN EX-PLAIN!
NOW! BAKUFU!
GHN ...!

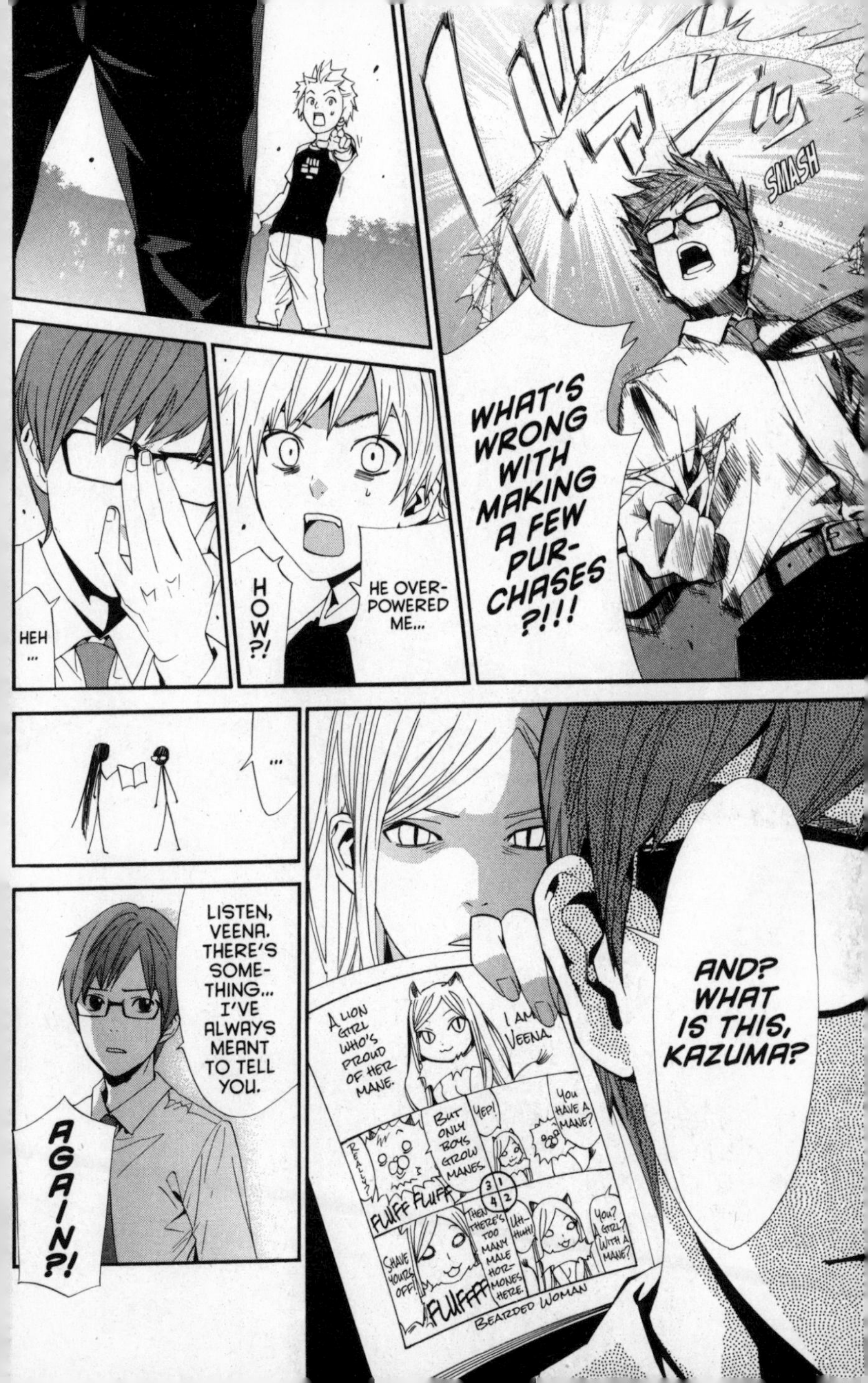
SMASH
WHAT'S WRONG WITH MAKING A FEW PUR-CHASES?!!!
HE OVER-POWERED ME...
HOW?!
HEH...
AND? WHAT IS THIS, KAZUMA?
A LION GIRL WHO'S PROUD OF HER MANE.
I AM VEENA.
YOU HAVE A MANE?
YEP!
BUT ONLY BOYS GROW MANES.
REALLY?
FLUFF FLUFF
YOU? GIRL WITH A MANE?
UH-HUH!
THEN THERE'S TOO MANY MALE HOR-MONES HERE.
SHAVE YOURS OFF!
FLUFFFF
BEARDED WOMAN
...
LISTEN, VEENA. THERE'S SOME-THING... I'VE ALWAYS MEANT TO TELL YOU.
AGAIN?!

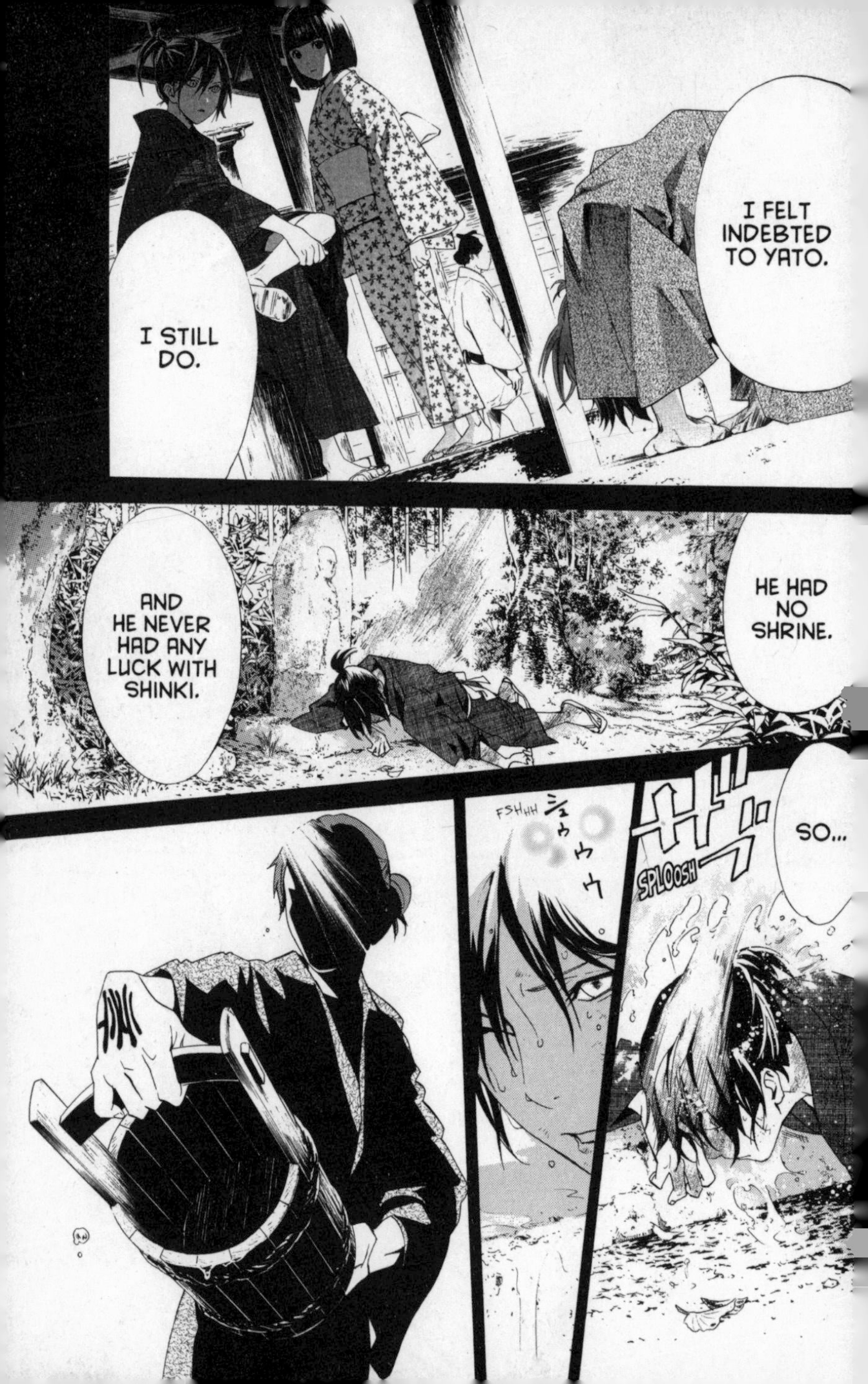
I FELT INDEBTED TO YATO.
I STILL DO.
HE HAD NO SHRINE.
AND HE NEVER HAD ANY LUCK WITH SHINKI.
SO...
SPLOOSH
FSHHH

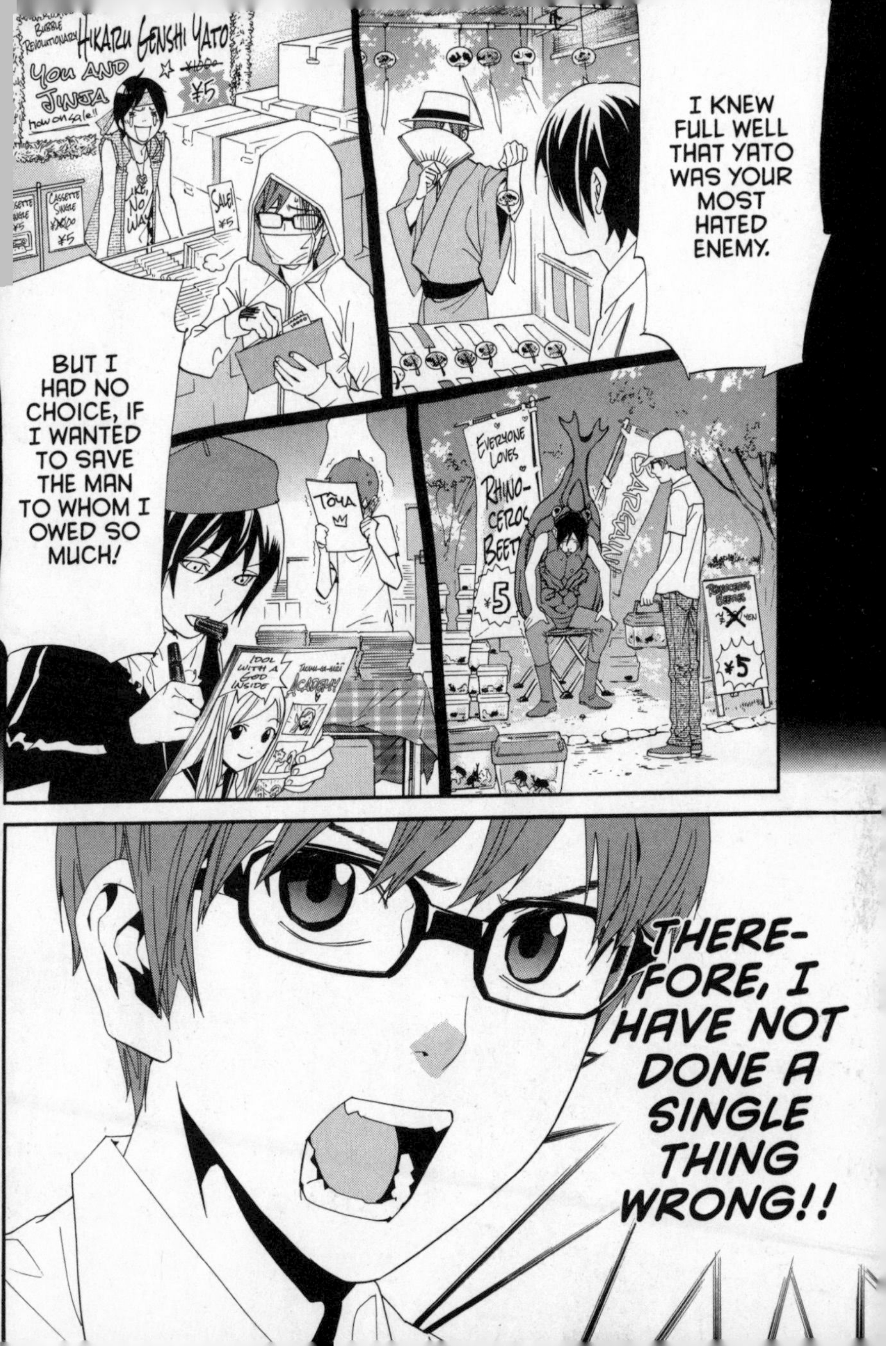
I KNEW FULL WELL THAT YATO WAS YOUR MOST HATED ENEMY.
BUBBLE REVOLUTIONARY HIKARU GENSHI YATO
YOU AND JINJA
now on sale!!
¥1000 ¥5
CASSETTE SINGLE ¥1000 ¥5
SALE! ¥5
EVERYONE LOVES RHINO-CEROS BEET
¥5
¥5
BUT I HAD NO CHOICE, IF I WANTED TO SAVE THE MAN TO WHOM I OWED SO MUCH!
TÔYA
IDOL WITH A GOD INSIDE
ACADEMY!
THERE-FORE, I HAVE NOT DONE A SINGLE THING WRONG!!

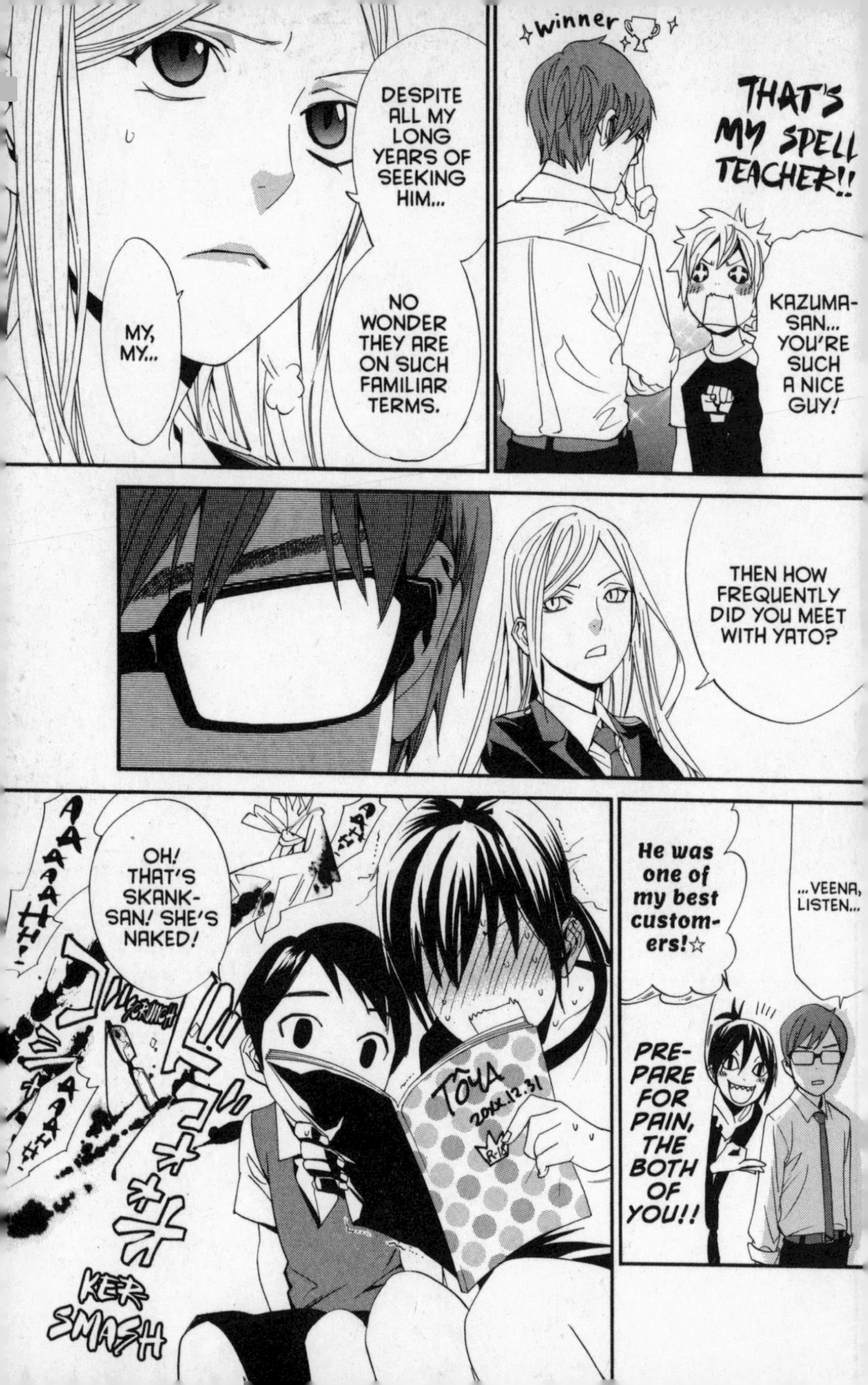
Winner
THAT'S MY SPELL TEACHER!!
KAZUMA-SAN... YOU'RE SUCH A NICE GUY!
DESPITE ALL MY LONG YEARS OF SEEKING HIM...
NO WONDER THEY ARE ON SUCH FAMILIAR TERMS.
MY, MY...
THEN HOW FREQUENTLY DID YOU MEET WITH YATO?
...VEENA, LISTEN...
He was one of my best customers!☆
PRE-PARE FOR PAIN, THE BOTH OF YOU!!
OH! THAT'S SKANK-SAN! SHE'S NAKED!
TŌYA
R-18
AAAAAHH!
KER SMASH

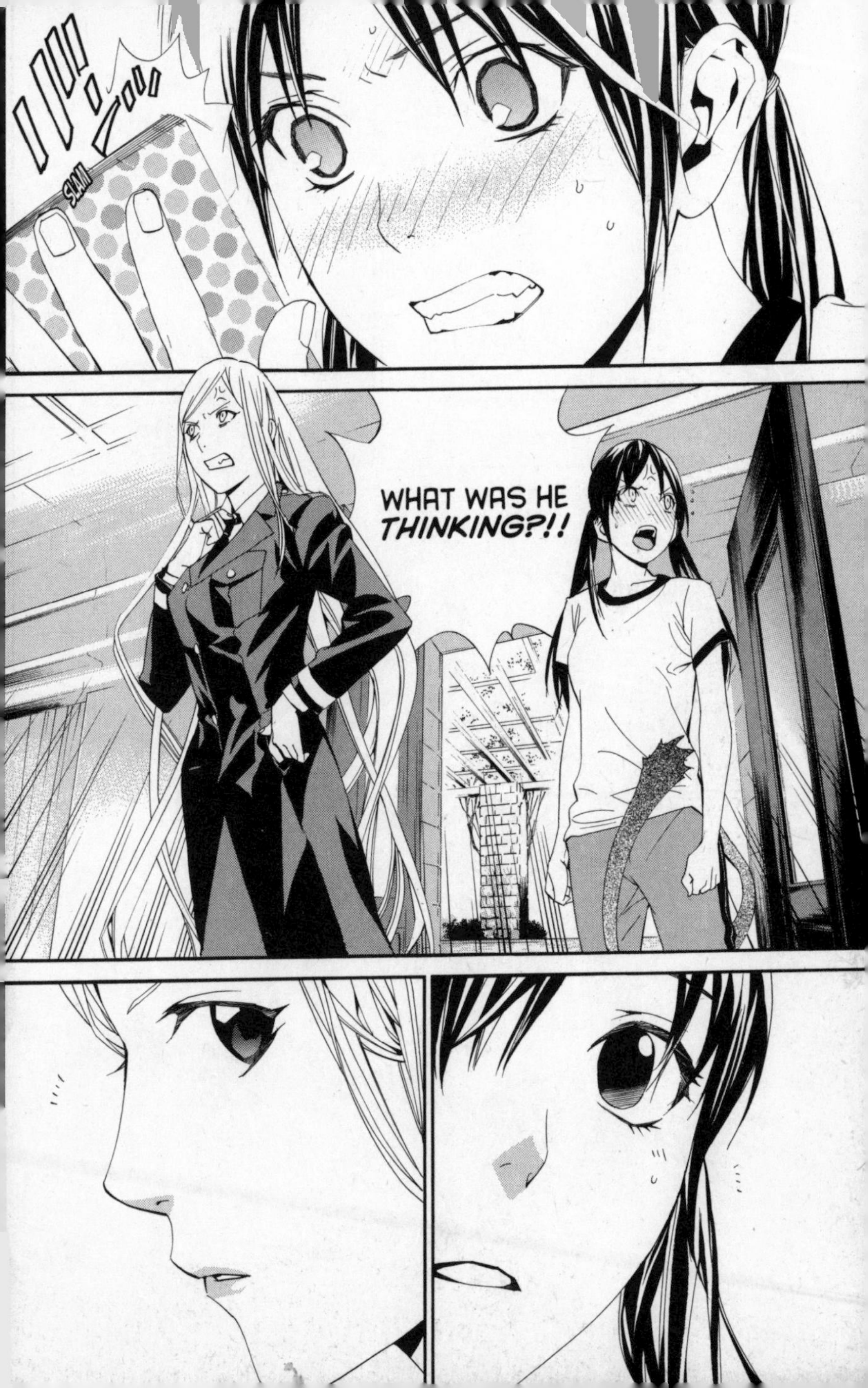
SLAM
WHAT WAS HE THINKING?!!

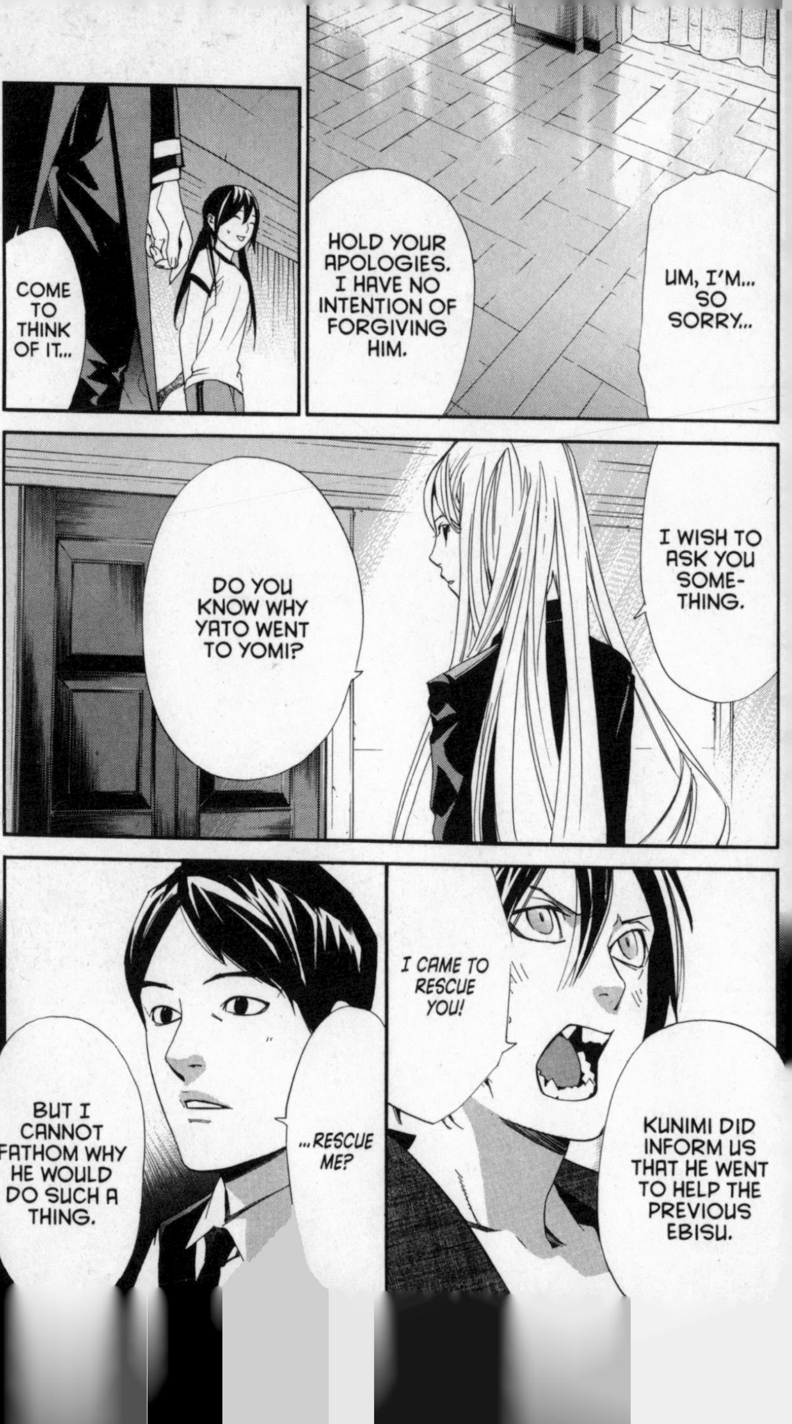
UM, I'M... SO SORRY...
HOLD YOUR APOLOGIES. I HAVE NO INTENTION OF FORGIVING HIM.
COME TO THINK OF IT...
I WISH TO ASK YOU SOME-THING.
DO YOU KNOW WHY YATO WENT TO YOMI?
KUNIMI DID INFORM US THAT HE WENT TO HELP THE PREVIOUS EBISU.
I CAME TO RESCUE YOU!
...RESCUE ME?
BUT I CANNOT FATHOM WHY HE WOULD DO SUCH A THING.

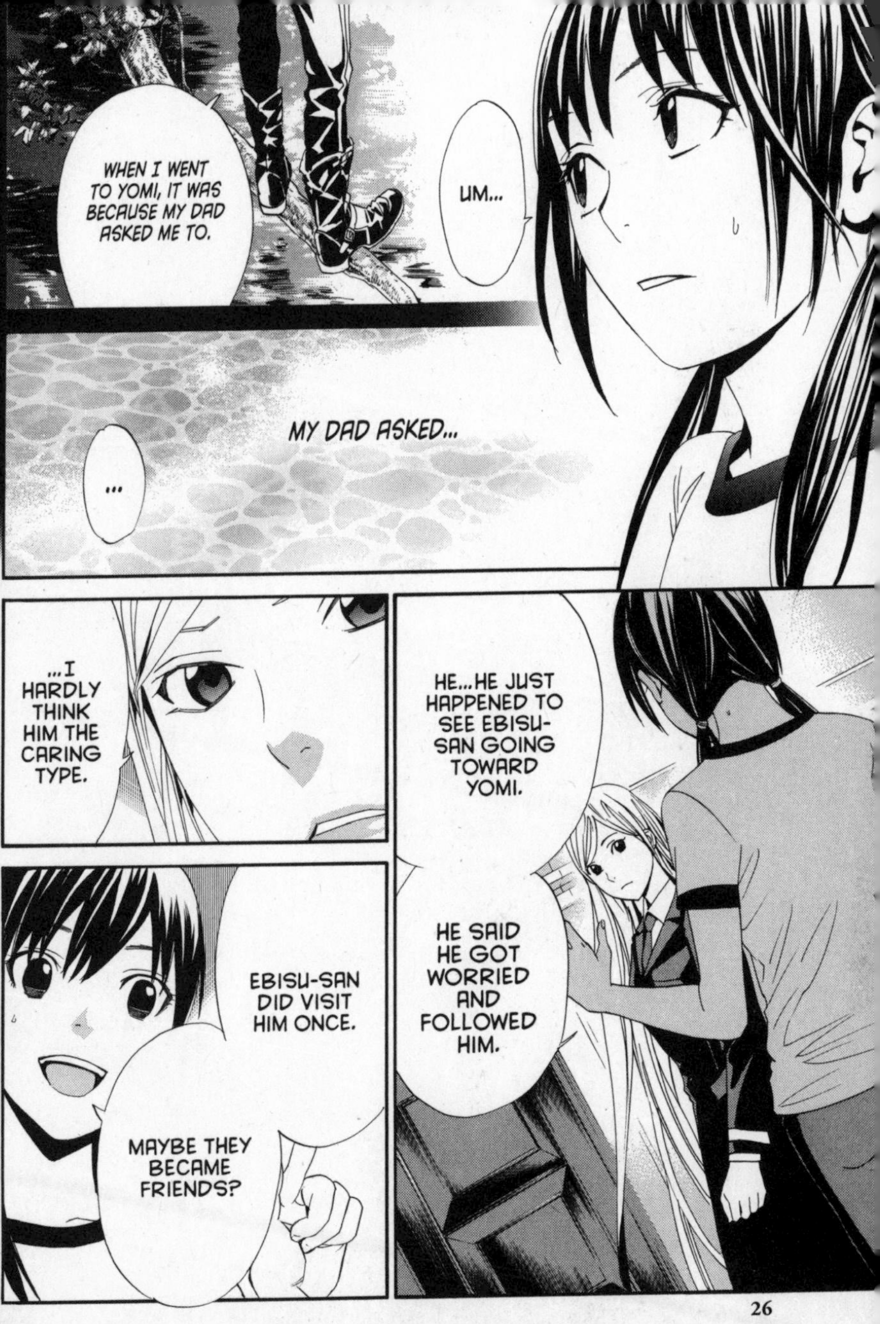
UM...
WHEN I WENT TO YOMI, IT WAS BECAUSE MY DAD ASKED ME TO.
MY DAD ASKED...
...
HE...HE JUST HAPPENED TO SEE EBISU-SAN GOING TOWARD YOMI.
HE SAID HE GOT WORRIED AND FOLLOWED HIM.
...I HARDLY THINK HIM THE CARING TYPE.
EBISU-SAN DID VISIT HIM ONCE.
MAYBE THEY BECAME FRIENDS?

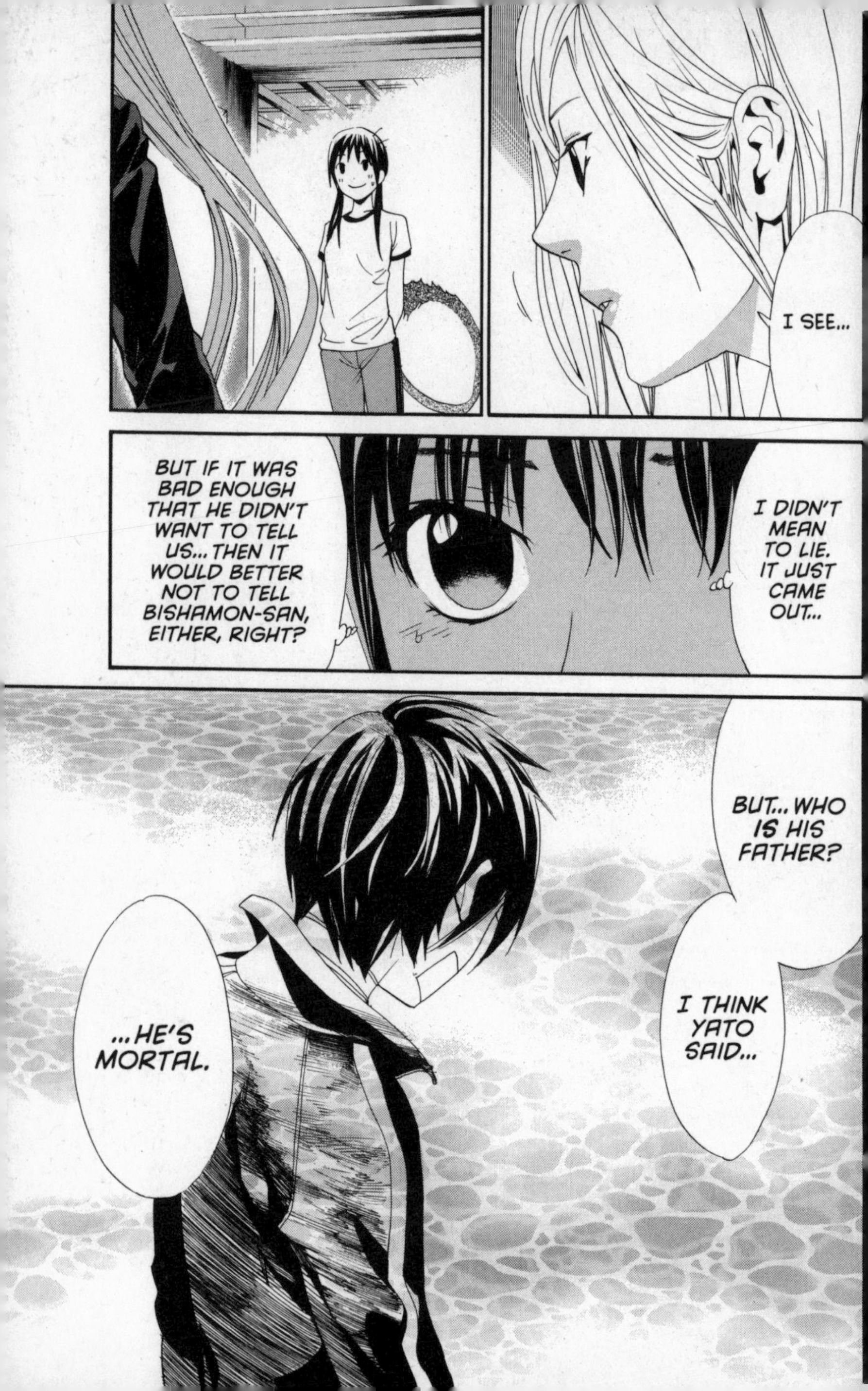
I SEE...
I DIDN'T MEAN TO LIE. IT JUST CAME OUT...
BUT IF IT WAS BAD ENOUGH THAT HE DIDN'T WANT TO TELL US... THEN IT WOULD BETTER NOT TO TELL BISHAMON-SAN, EITHER, RIGHT?
BUT... WHO IS HIS FATHER?
I THINK YATO SAID...
...HE'S MORTAL.

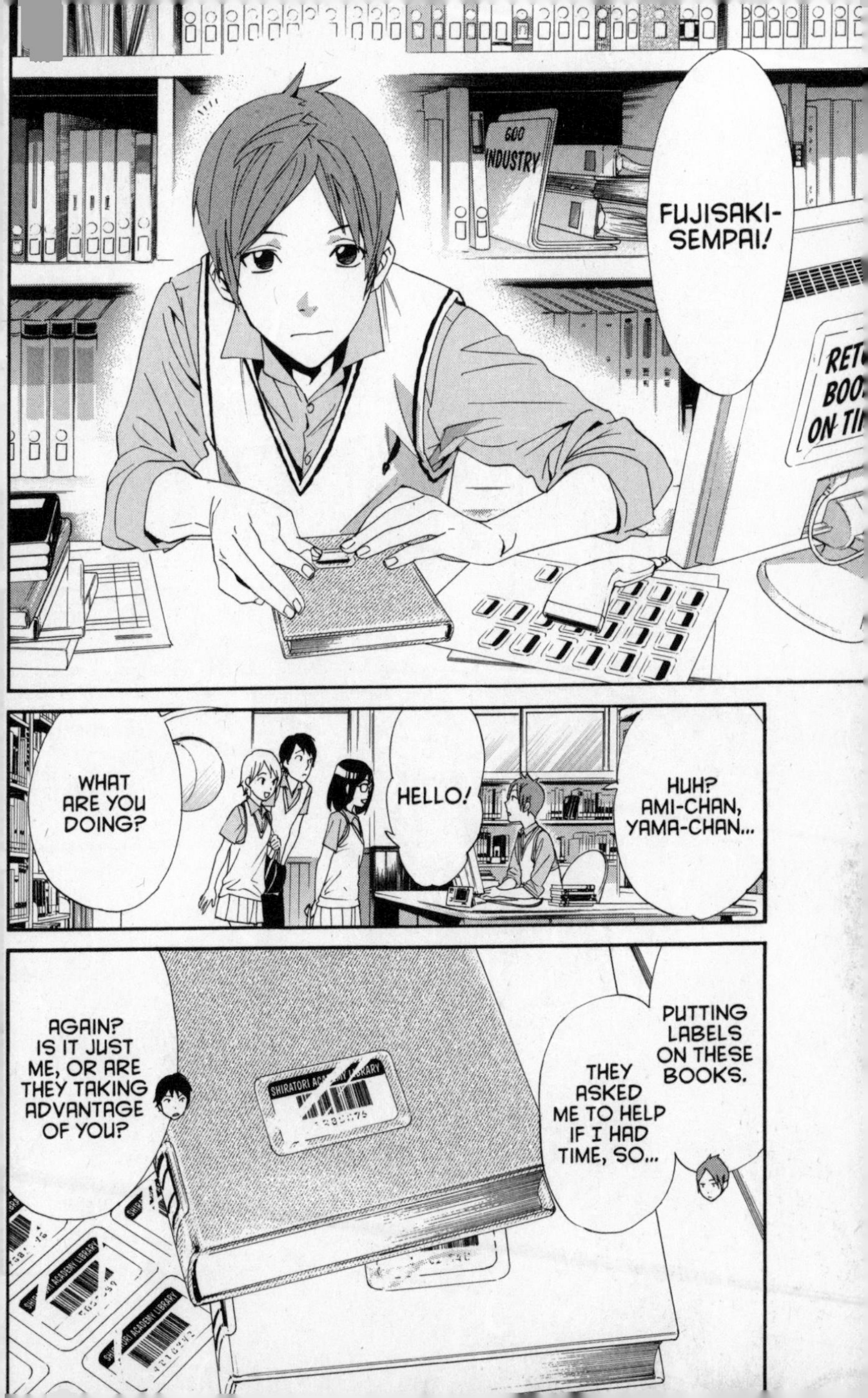
INDUSTRY
FUJISAKI-SEMPAI!
HUH? AMI-CHAN, YAMA-CHAN...
HELLO!
WHAT ARE YOU DOING?
PUTTING LABELS ON THESE BOOKS.
THEY ASKED ME TO HELP IF I HAD TIME, SO...
SHIRATORI ACADEMY LIBRARY
AGAIN? IS IT JUST ME, OR ARE THEY TAKING ADVANTAGE OF YOU?

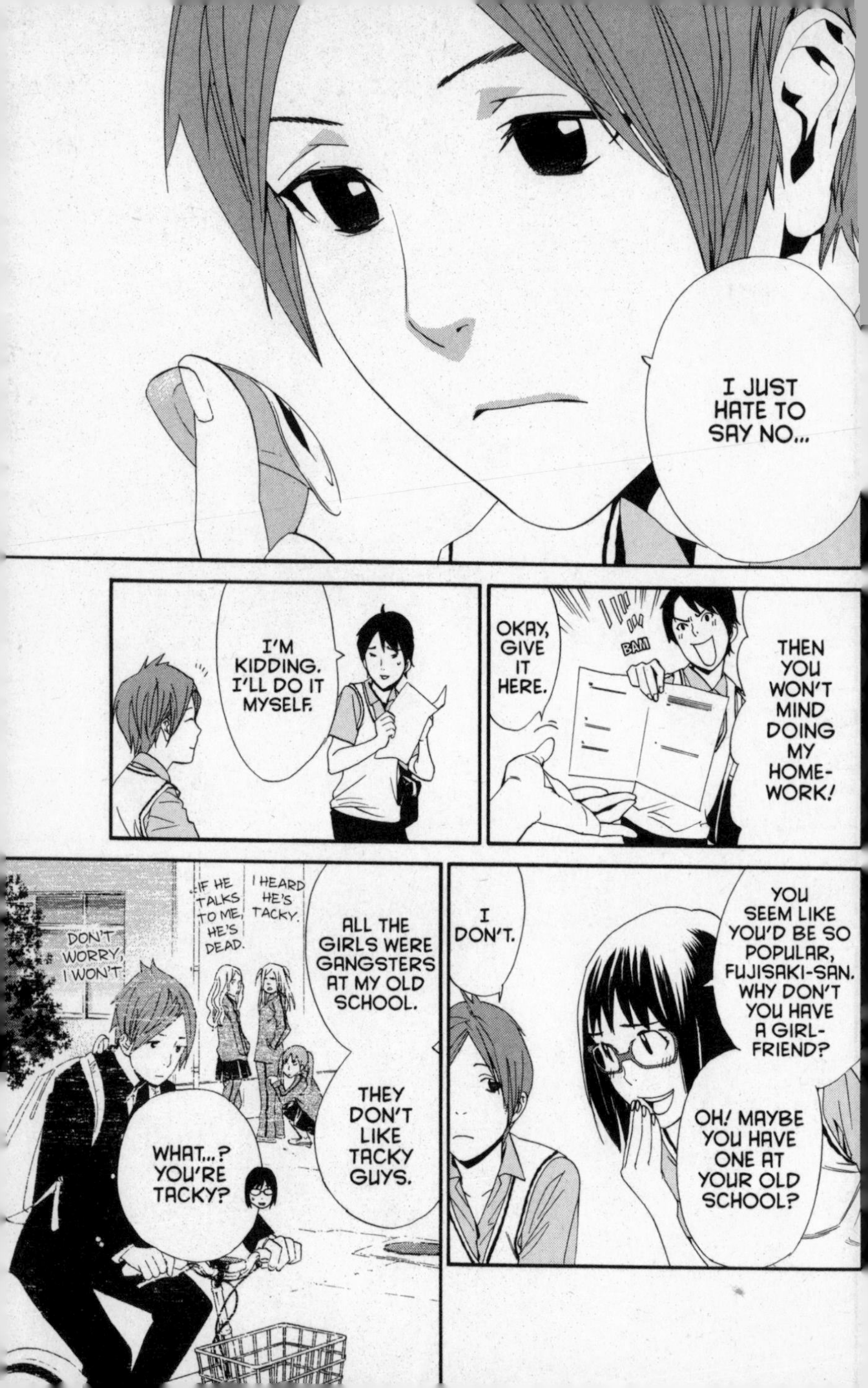
I JUST HATE TO SAY NO...
THEN YOU WON'T MIND DOING MY HOMEWORK!
BAM
OKAY, GIVE IT HERE.
I'M KIDDING. I'LL DO IT MYSELF.
YOU SEEM LIKE YOU'D BE SO POPULAR, FUJISAKI-SAN. WHY DON'T YOU HAVE A GIRLFRIEND?
OH! MAYBE YOU HAVE ONE AT YOUR OLD SCHOOL?
I DON'T.
ALL THE GIRLS WERE GANGSTERS AT MY OLD SCHOOL.
THEY DON'T LIKE TACKY GUYS.
I HEARD HE'S TACKY.
IF HE TALKS TO ME, HE'S DEAD.
DON'T WORRY, I WON'T.
WHAT...? YOU'RE TACKY?

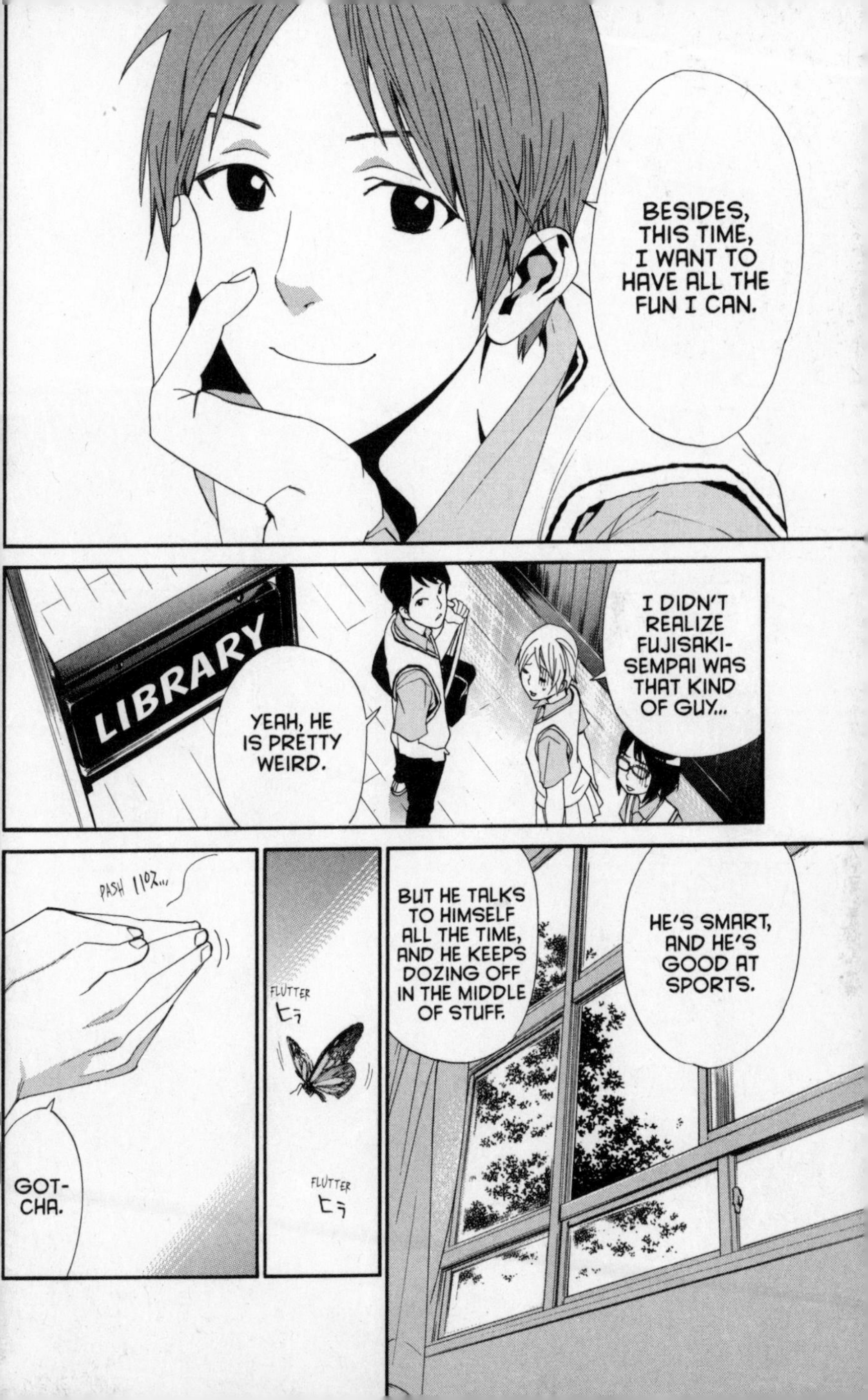
BESIDES, THIS TIME, I WANT TO HAVE ALL THE FUN I CAN.
I DIDN'T REALIZE FUJISAKI-SEMPAI WAS THAT KIND OF GUY...
LIBRARY
YEAH, HE IS PRETTY WEIRD.
HE'S SMART, AND HE'S GOOD AT SPORTS.
BUT HE TALKS TO HIMSELF ALL THE TIME, AND HE KEEPS DOZING OFF IN THE MIDDLE OF STUFF.
FLUTTER ヒラ
FLUTTER ヒラ
PASH パス...
GOT-CHA.

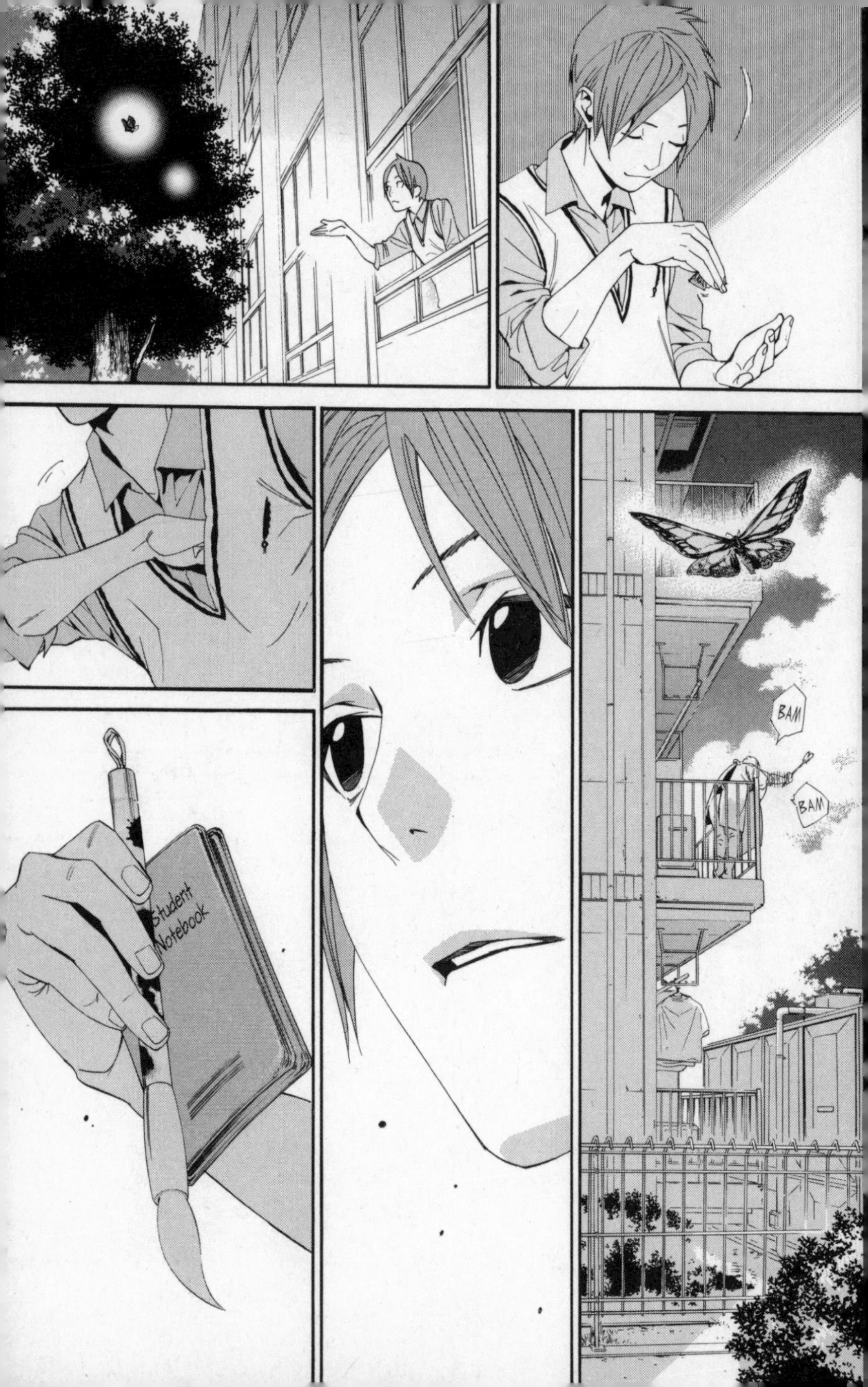
BAM
BAM
Student Notebook

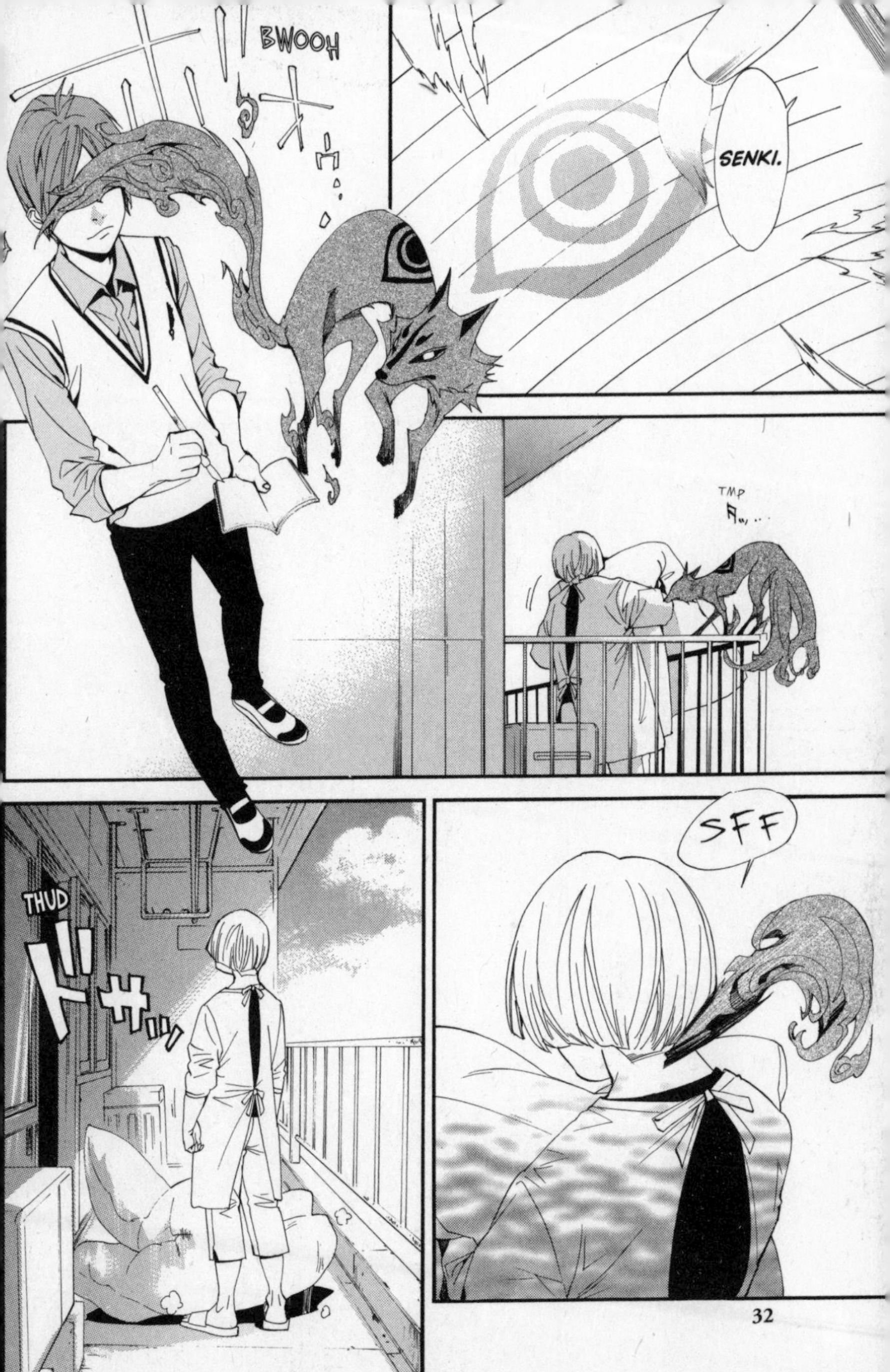
SENKI.
TMP
BWOOH
SFF
THUD

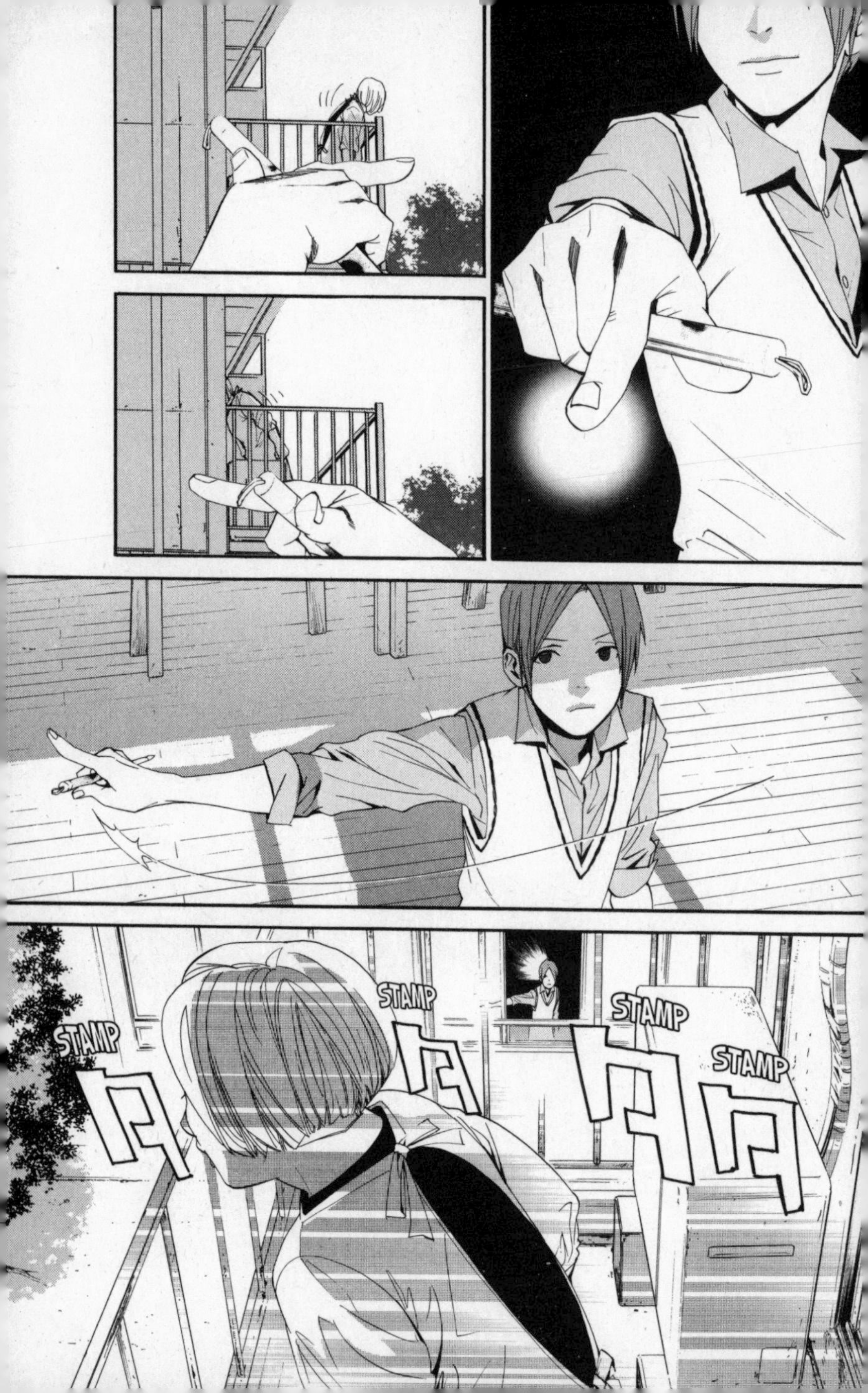
STAMP
STAMP
STAMP
STAMP

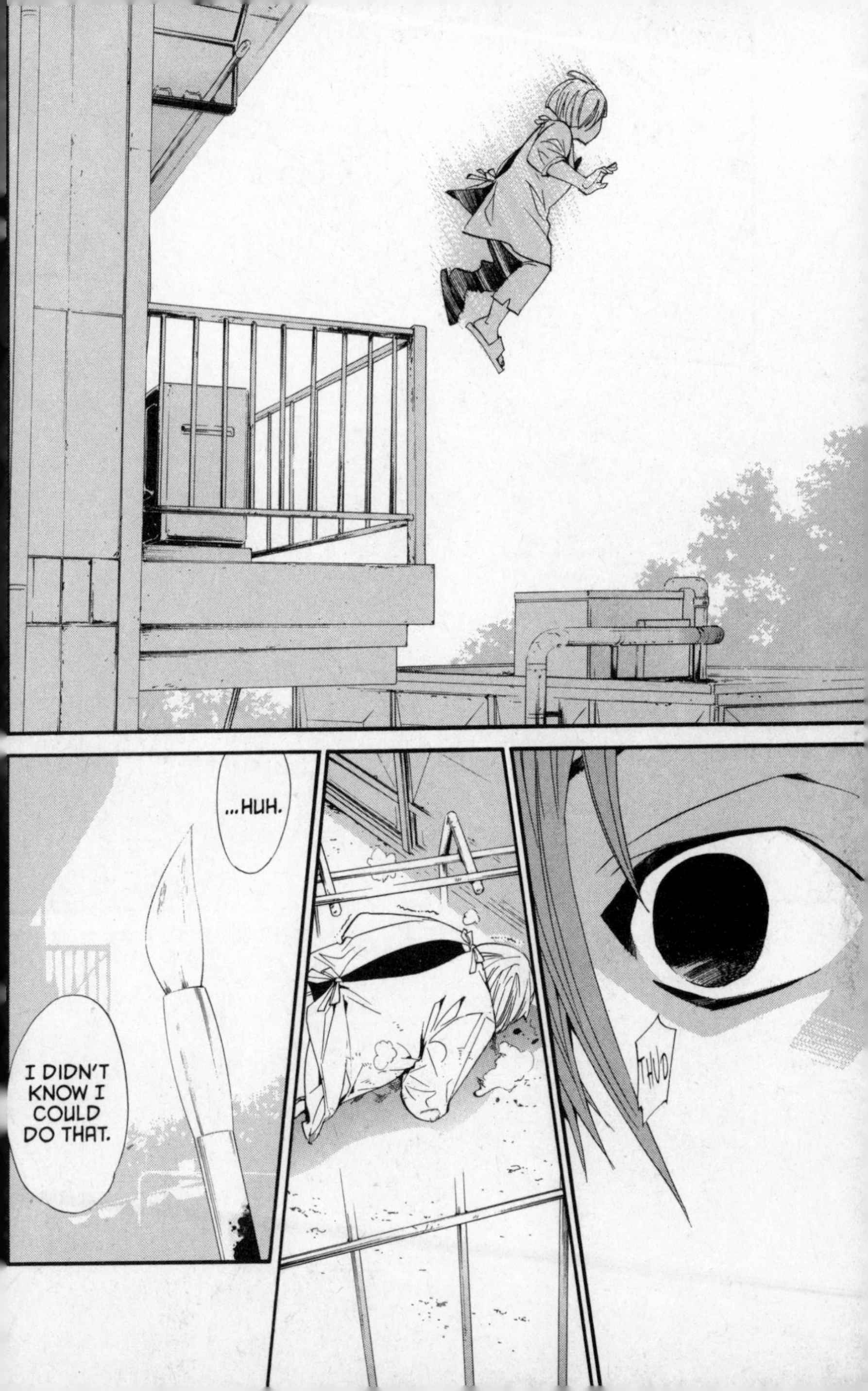
THUD
...HUH.
I DIDN'T KNOW I COULD DO THAT.

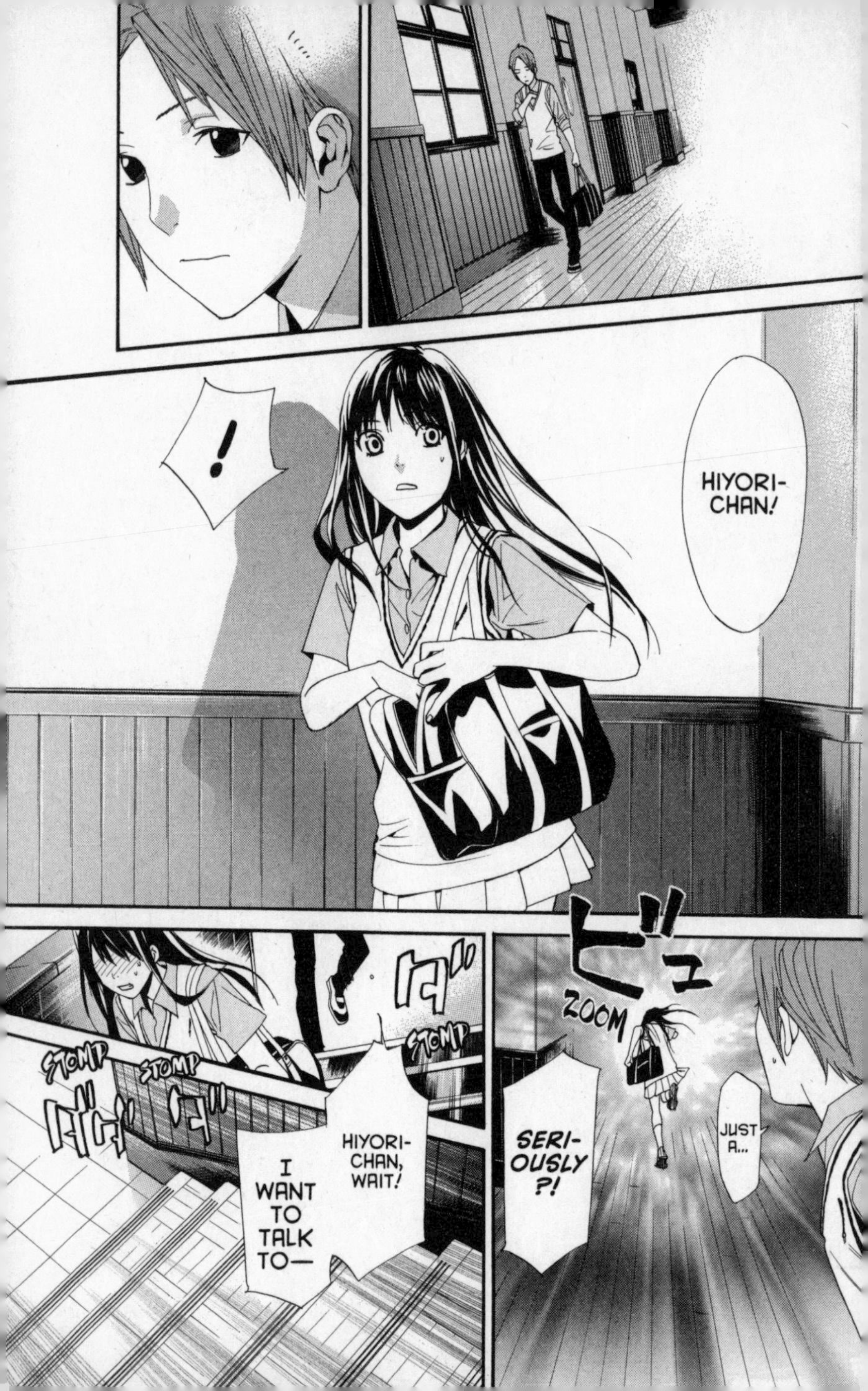

HIYORI-CHAN!
!
ビュ
ZOOM
JUST A...
SERI-OUSLY ?!
STOMP
HIYORI-CHAN, WAIT!
I WANT TO TALK TO—
STOMP
STOMP

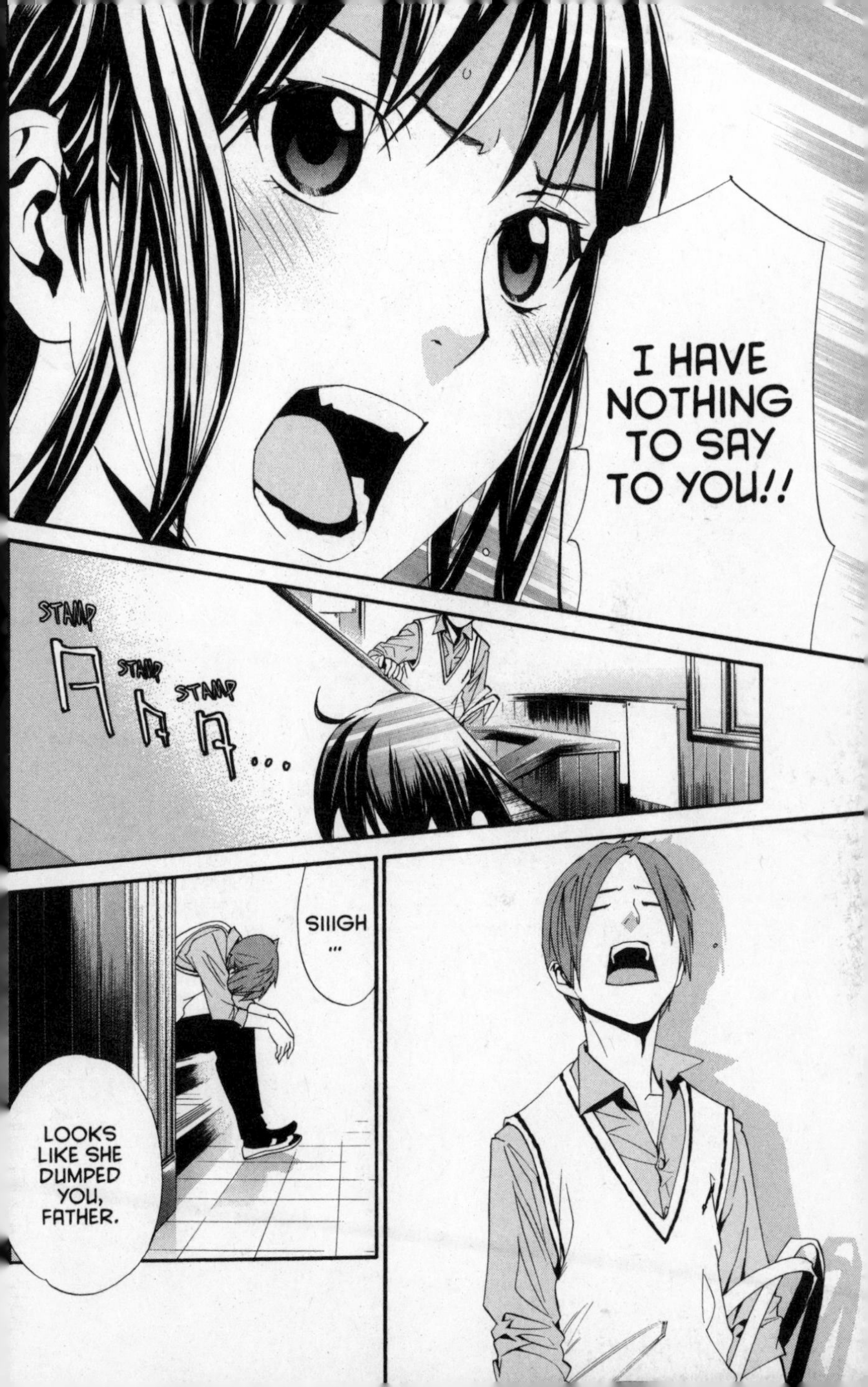
I HAVE NOTHING TO SAY TO YOU!!
STAMP
STAMP
STAMP
SIIIGH ...
LOOKS LIKE SHE DUMPED YOU, FATHER.

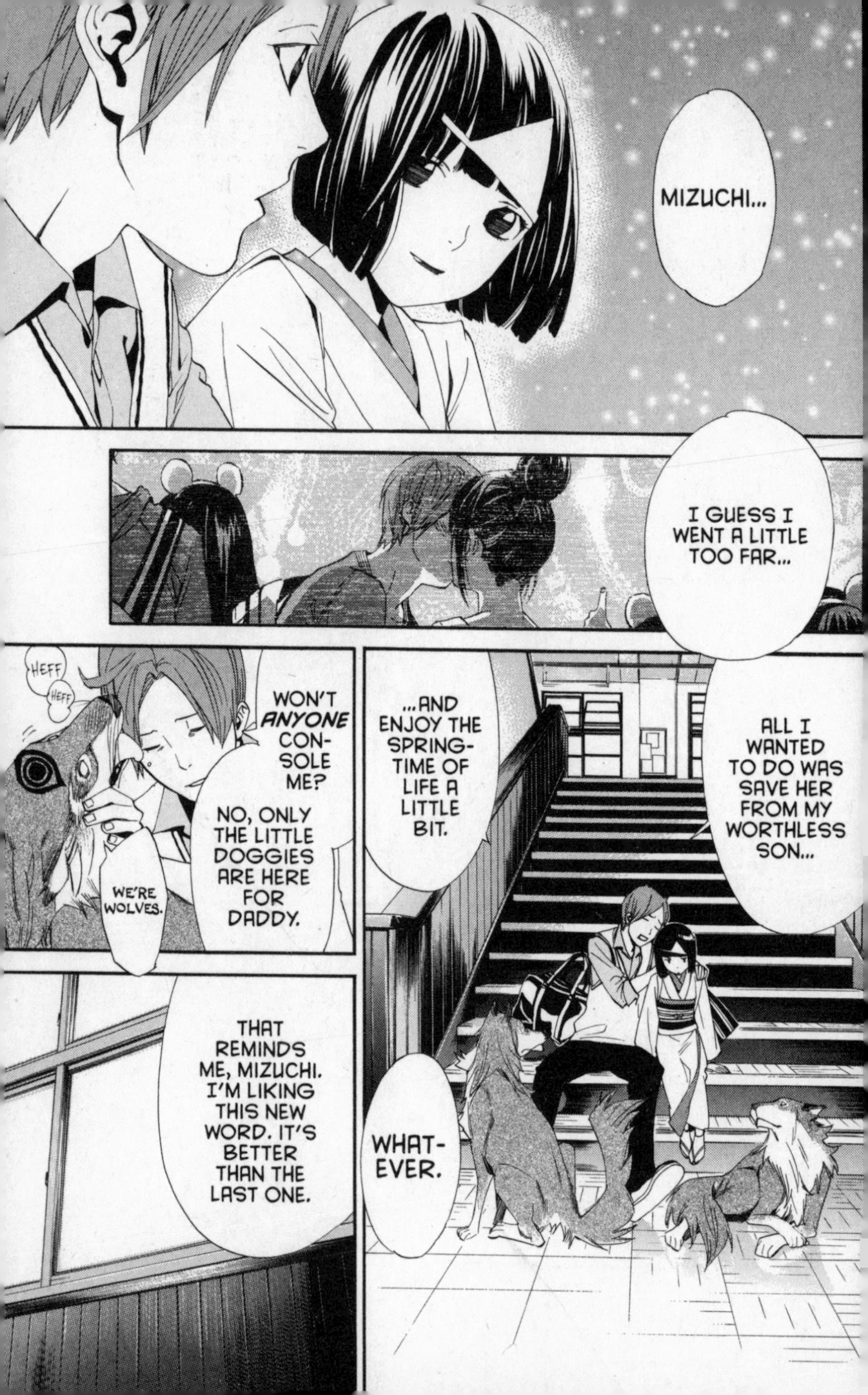
MIZUCHI...
I GUESS I WENT A LITTLE TOO FAR...
ALL I WANTED TO DO WAS SAVE HER FROM MY WORTHLESS SON...
...AND ENJOY THE SPRING-TIME OF LIFE A LITTLE BIT.
WHAT-EVER.
HEFF
HEFF
WON'T *ANYONE* CON-SOLE ME?
NO, ONLY THE LITTLE DOGGIES ARE HERE FOR DADDY.
WE'RE WOLVES.
THAT REMINDS ME, MIZUCHI. I'M LIKING THIS NEW WORD. IT'S BETTER THAN THE LAST ONE.

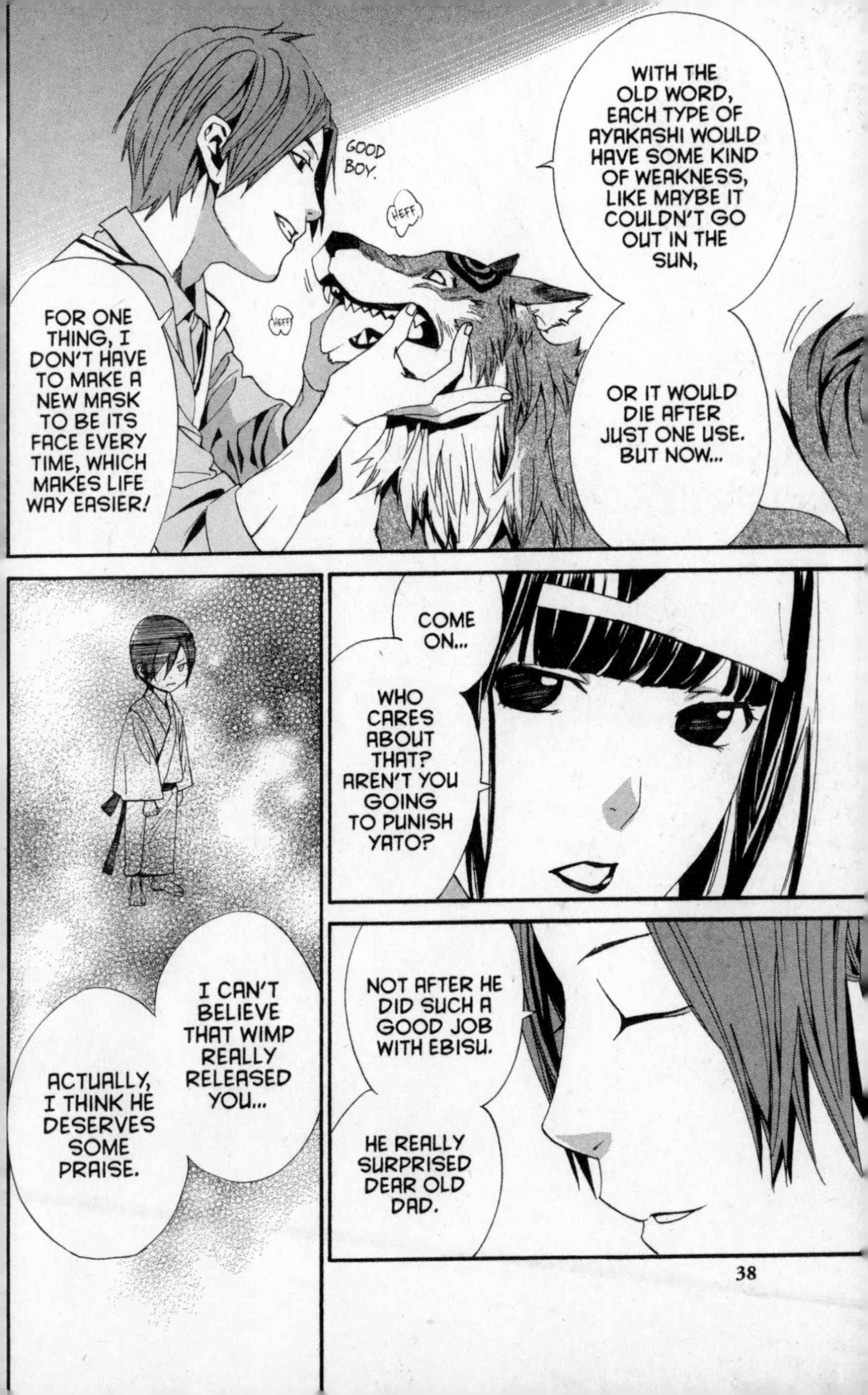
WITH THE OLD WORD, EACH TYPE OF AYAKASHI WOULD HAVE SOME KIND OF WEAKNESS, LIKE MAYBE IT COULDN'T GO OUT IN THE SUN,
OR IT WOULD DIE AFTER JUST ONE USE. BUT NOW...
GOOD BOY.
HEFF
HEFF
FOR ONE THING, I DON'T HAVE TO MAKE A NEW MASK TO BE ITS FACE EVERY TIME, WHICH MAKES LIFE WAY EASIER!
COME ON...
WHO CARES ABOUT THAT? AREN'T YOU GOING TO PUNISH YATO?
NOT AFTER HE DID SUCH A GOOD JOB WITH EBISU.
HE REALLY SURPRISED DEAR OLD DAD.
I CAN'T BELIEVE THAT WIMP REALLY RELEASED YOU...
ACTUALLY, I THINK HE DESERVES SOME PRAISE.

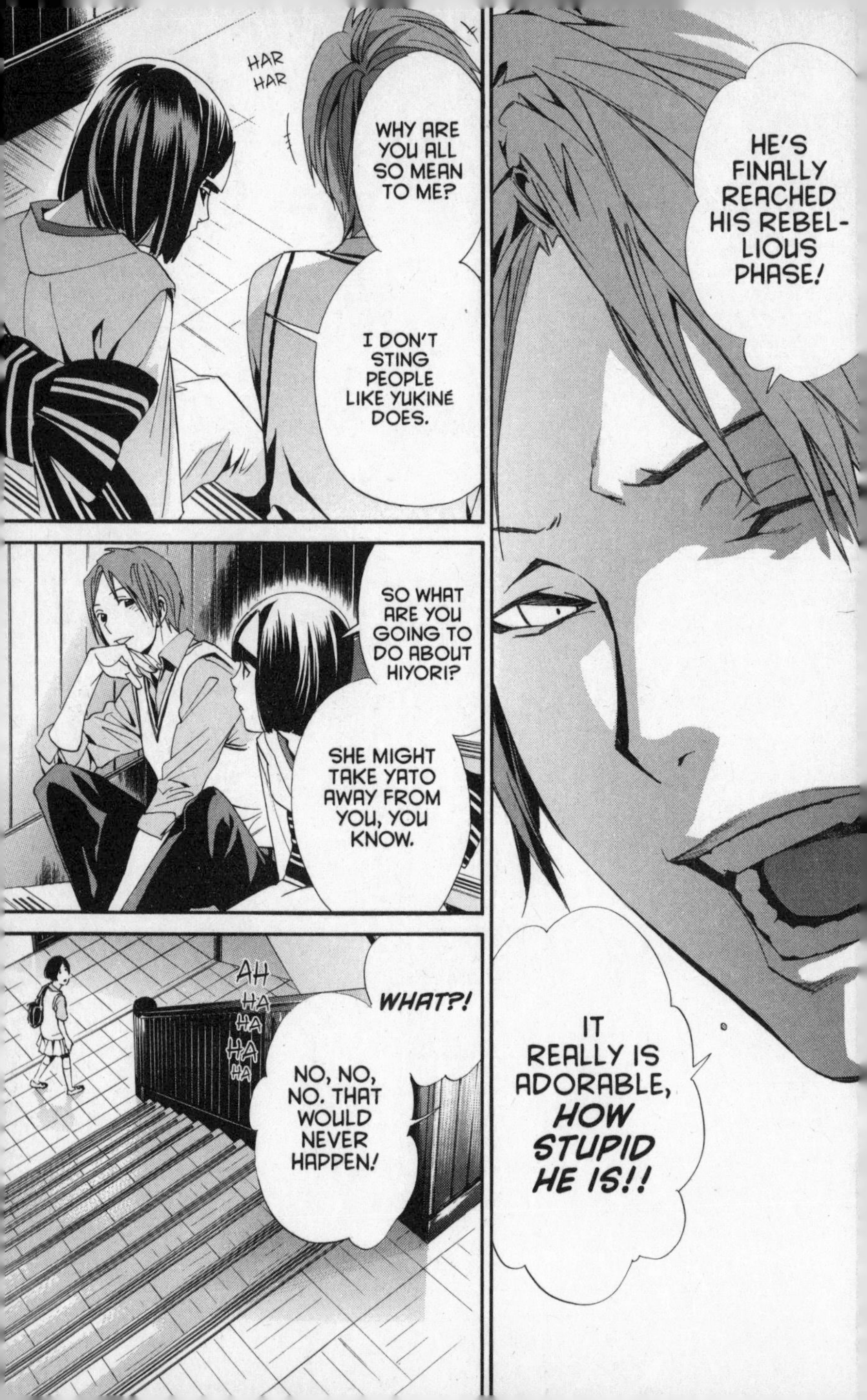
HE'S FINALLY REACHED HIS REBEL-LIOUS PHASE!
IT REALLY IS ADORABLE, HOW STUPID HE IS!!
WHY ARE YOU ALL SO MEAN TO ME?
HAR HAR
I DON'T STING PEOPLE LIKE YUKINÉ DOES.
SO WHAT ARE YOU GOING TO DO ABOUT HIYORI?
SHE MIGHT TAKE YATO AWAY FROM YOU, YOU KNOW.
WHAT?!
AH HA HA HA HA
NO, NO, NO. THAT WOULD NEVER HAPPEN!

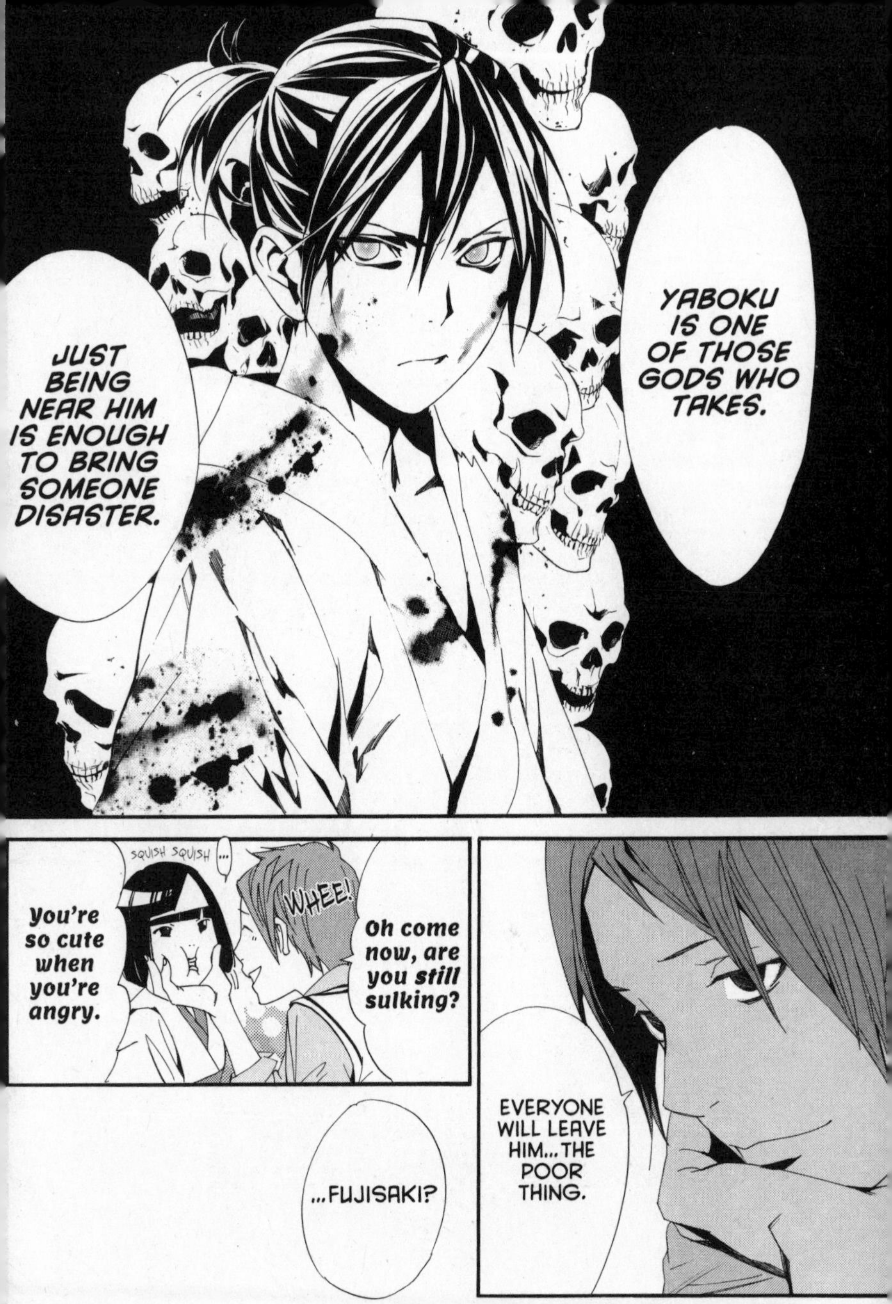
YABOKU IS ONE OF THOSE GODS WHO TAKES.
JUST BEING NEAR HIM IS ENOUGH TO BRING SOMEONE DISASTER.
EVERYONE WILL LEAVE HIM...THE POOR THING.
Oh come now, are you *still* sulking?
WHEE!
SQUISH SQUISH
...
You're so cute when you're angry.
...FUJISAKI?

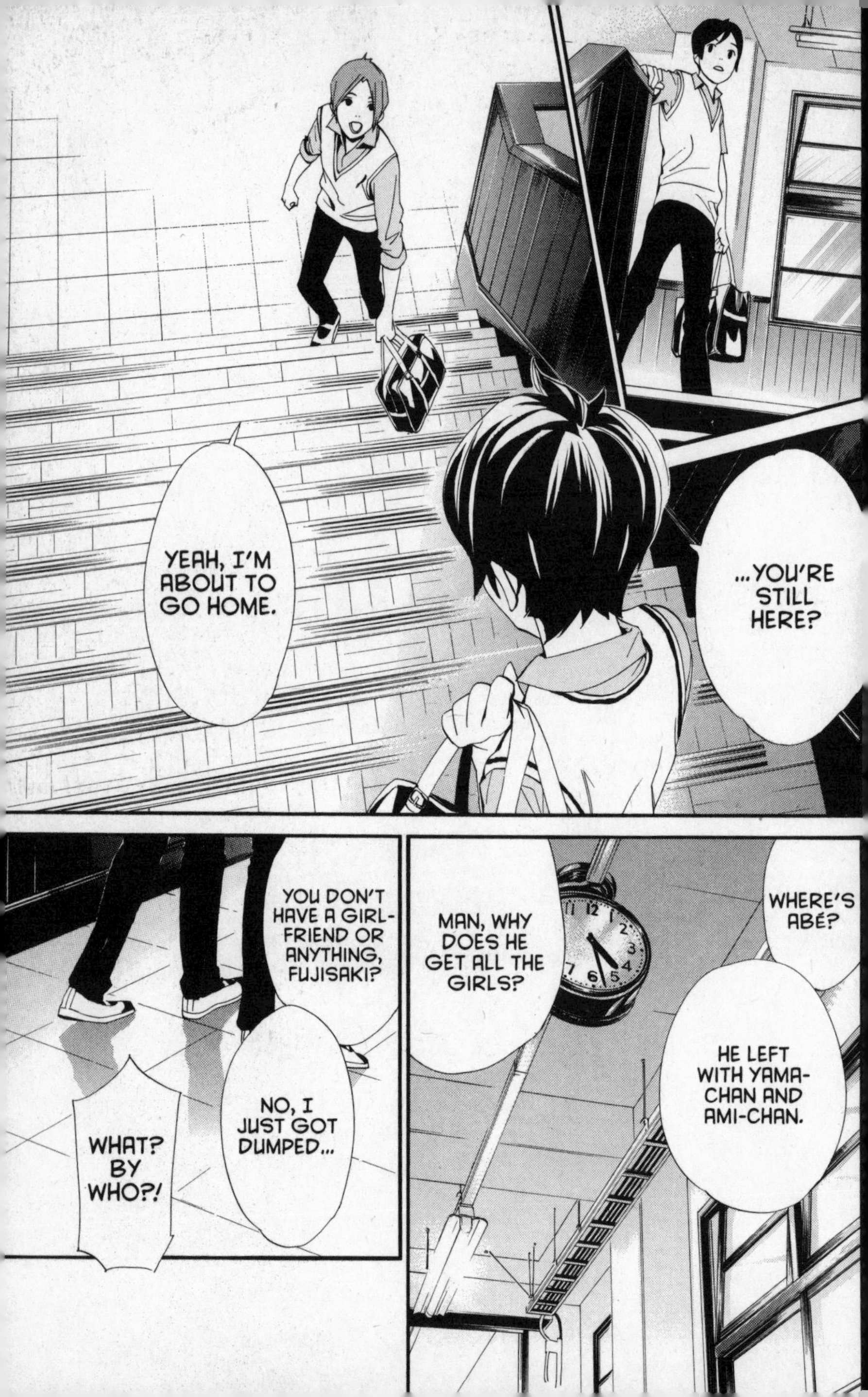
...YOU'RE STILL HERE?
YEAH, I'M ABOUT TO GO HOME.
WHERE'S ABÉ?
HE LEFT WITH YAMA-CHAN AND AMI-CHAN.
MAN, WHY DOES HE GET ALL THE GIRLS?
YOU DON'T HAVE A GIRL-FRIEND OR ANYTHING, FUJISAKI?
NO, I JUST GOT DUMPED...
WHAT? BY WHO?!

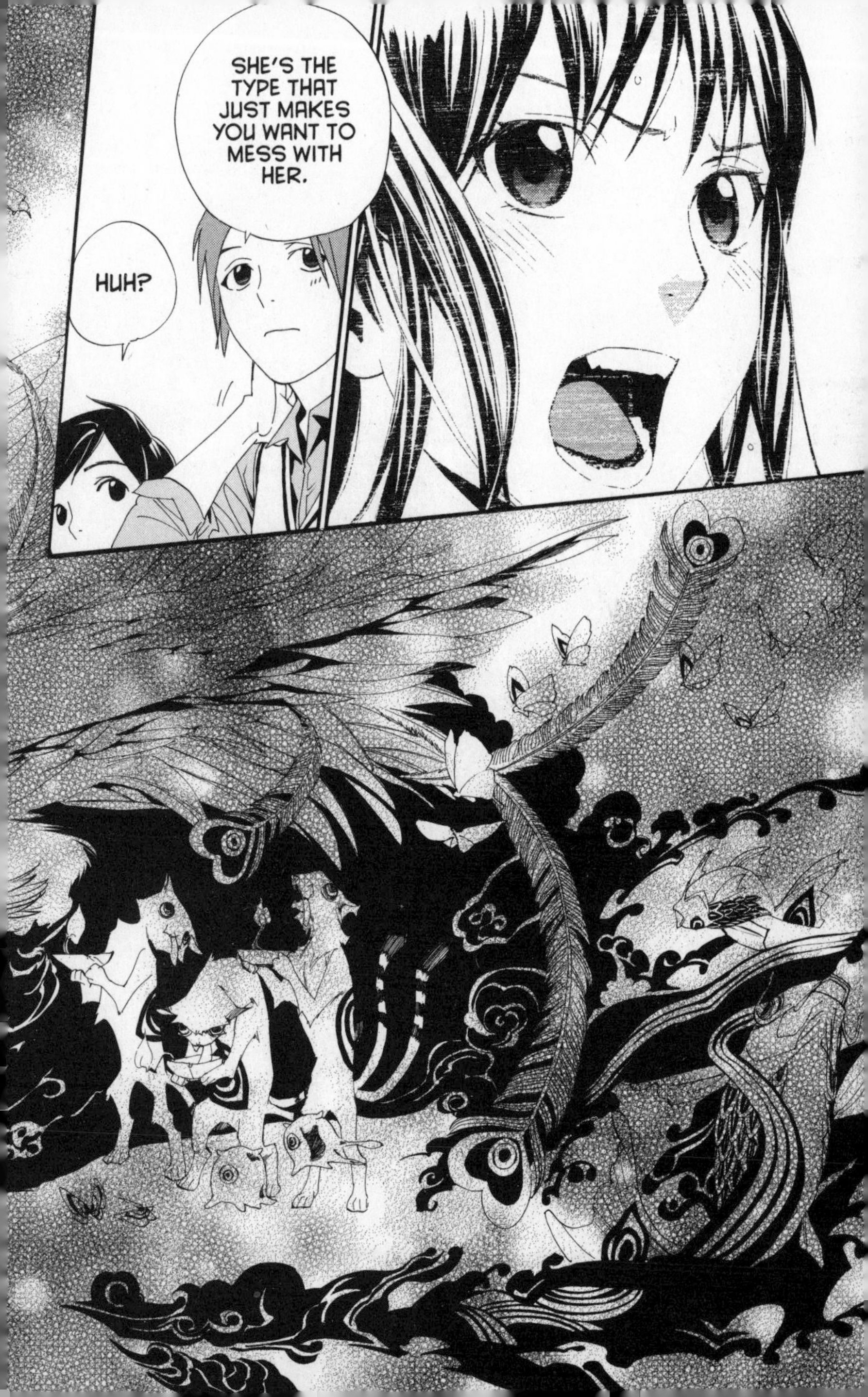
SHE'S THE TYPE THAT JUST MAKES YOU WANT TO MESS WITH HER.
HUH?

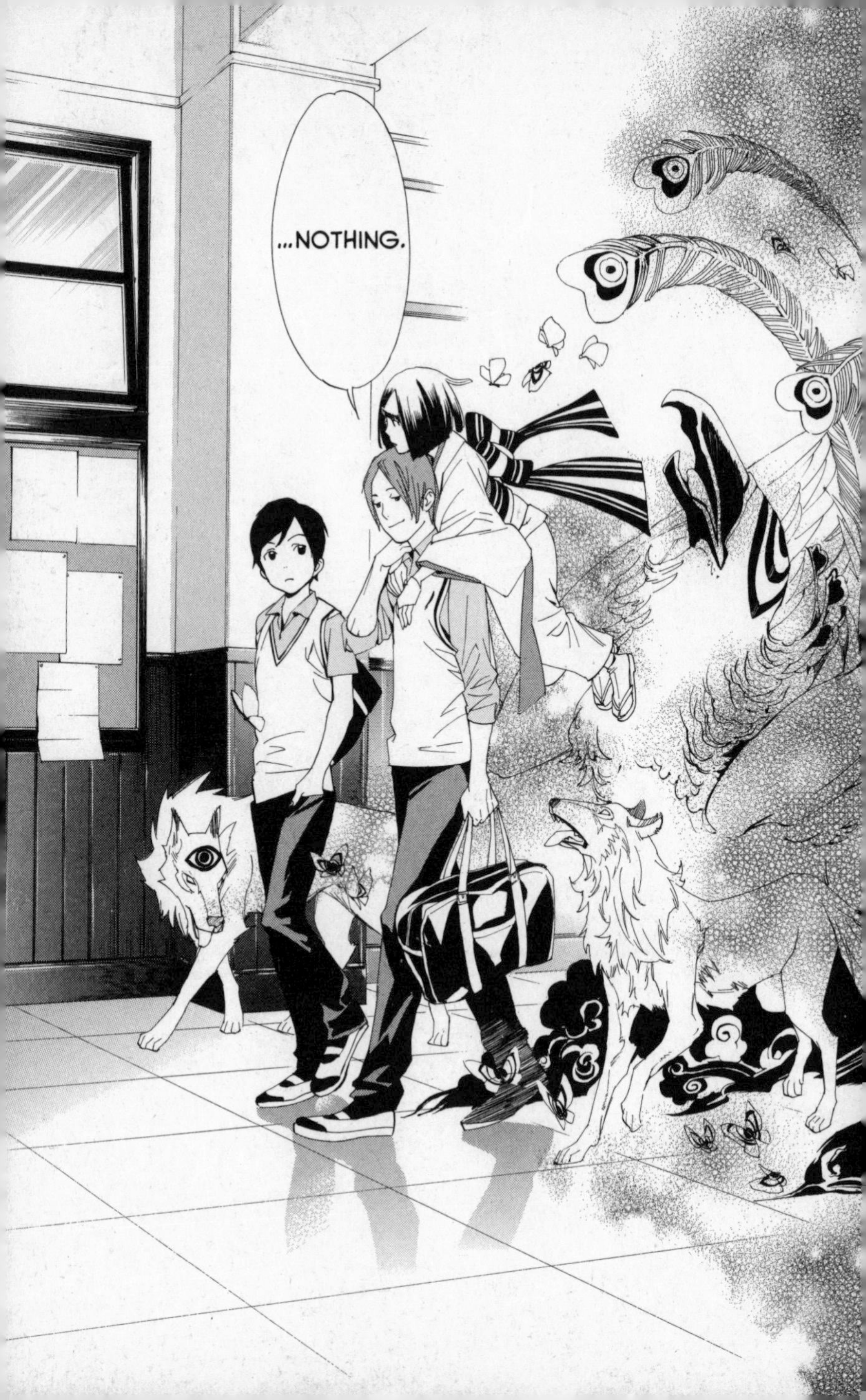
...NOTHING.

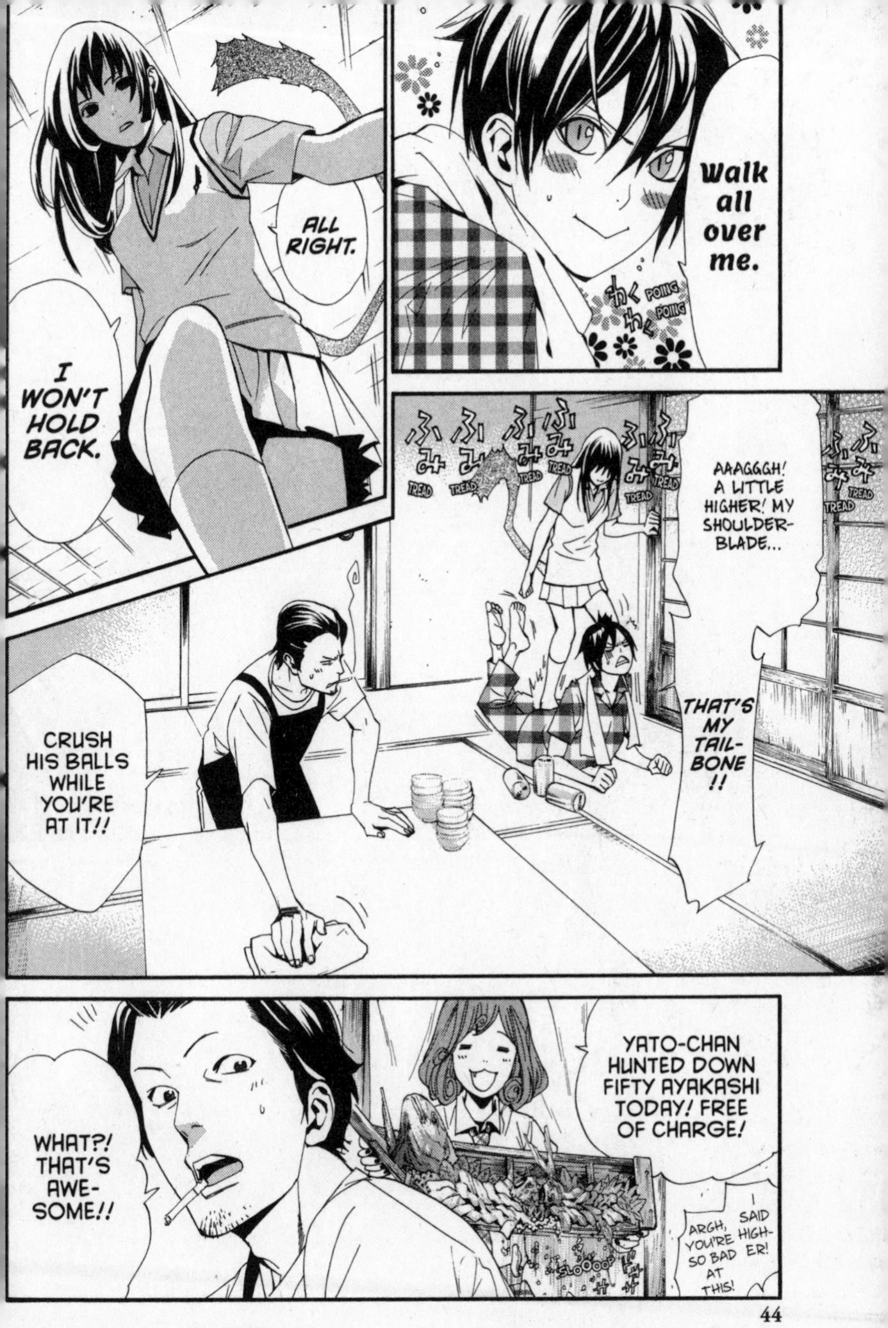
Walk all over me.
わくわく
POING POING
ALL RIGHT.
I WON'T HOLD BACK.
ふみふみ
TREAD TREAD TREAD TREAD TREAD TREAD TREAD
AAAGGGH! A LITTLE HIGHER! MY SHOULDER-BLADE...
THAT'S MY TAIL-BONE !!
CRUSH HIS BALLS WHILE YOU'RE AT IT!!
YATO-CHAN HUNTED DOWN FIFTY AYAKASHI TODAY! FREE OF CHARGE!
I SAID HIGH-ER!
ARGH, YOU'RE SO BAD AT THIS!
SLOOOOP
WHAT?! THAT'S AWE-SOME!!

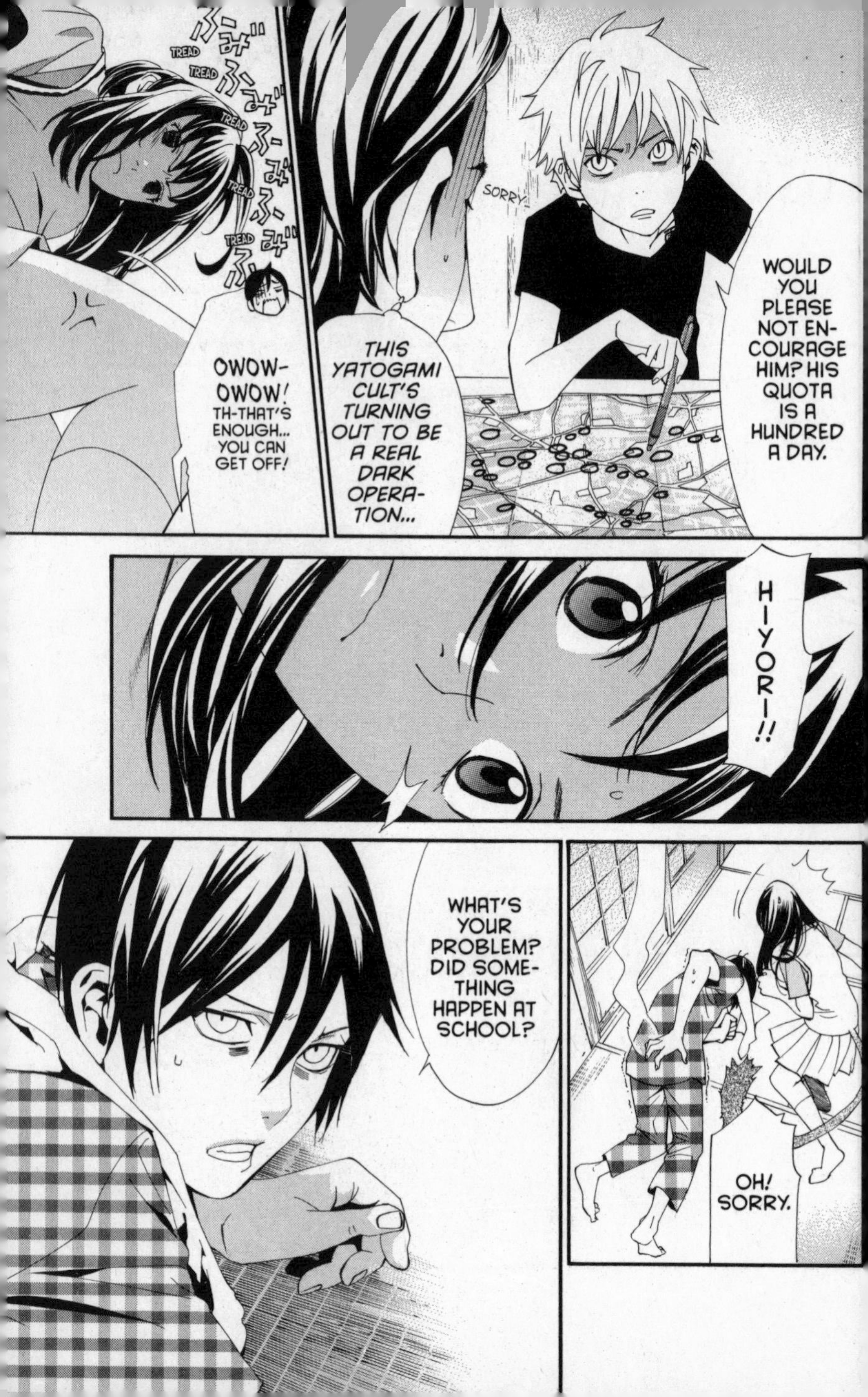

WOULD YOU PLEASE NOT EN-COURAGE HIM? HIS QUOTA IS A HUNDRED A DAY.
SORRY.
THIS YATOGAMI CULT'S TURNING OUT TO BE A REAL DARK OPERA-TION...
TREAD TREAD TREAD TREAD TREAD
OWOW-OWOW! TH-THAT'S ENOUGH... YOU CAN GET OFF!
HIYORI!!
OH! SORRY.
WHAT'S YOUR PROBLEM? DID SOME-THING HAPPEN AT SCHOOL?

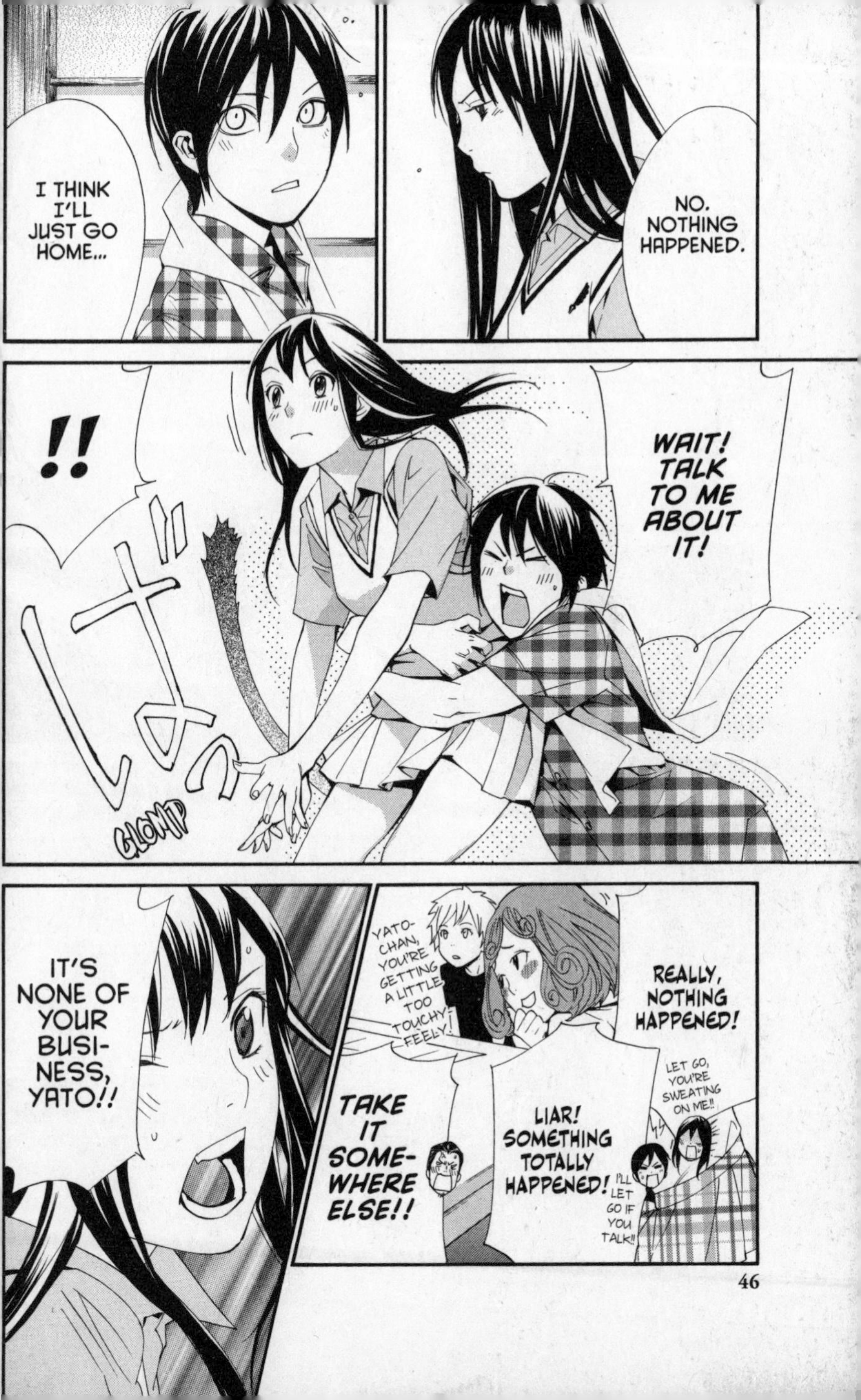
NO. NOTHING HAPPENED.
I THINK I'LL JUST GO HOME...
WAIT! TALK TO ME ABOUT IT!
!!
GLOMP
REALLY, NOTHING HAPPENED!
LET GO, YOU'RE SWEATING ON ME!!
YATO-CHAN, YOU'RE GETTING A LITTLE TOO TOUCHY-FEELY!
LIAR! SOMETHING TOTALLY HAPPENED!
I'LL LET GO IF YOU TALK!!
TAKE IT SOMEWHERE ELSE!!
IT'S NONE OF YOUR BUSINESS, YATO!!

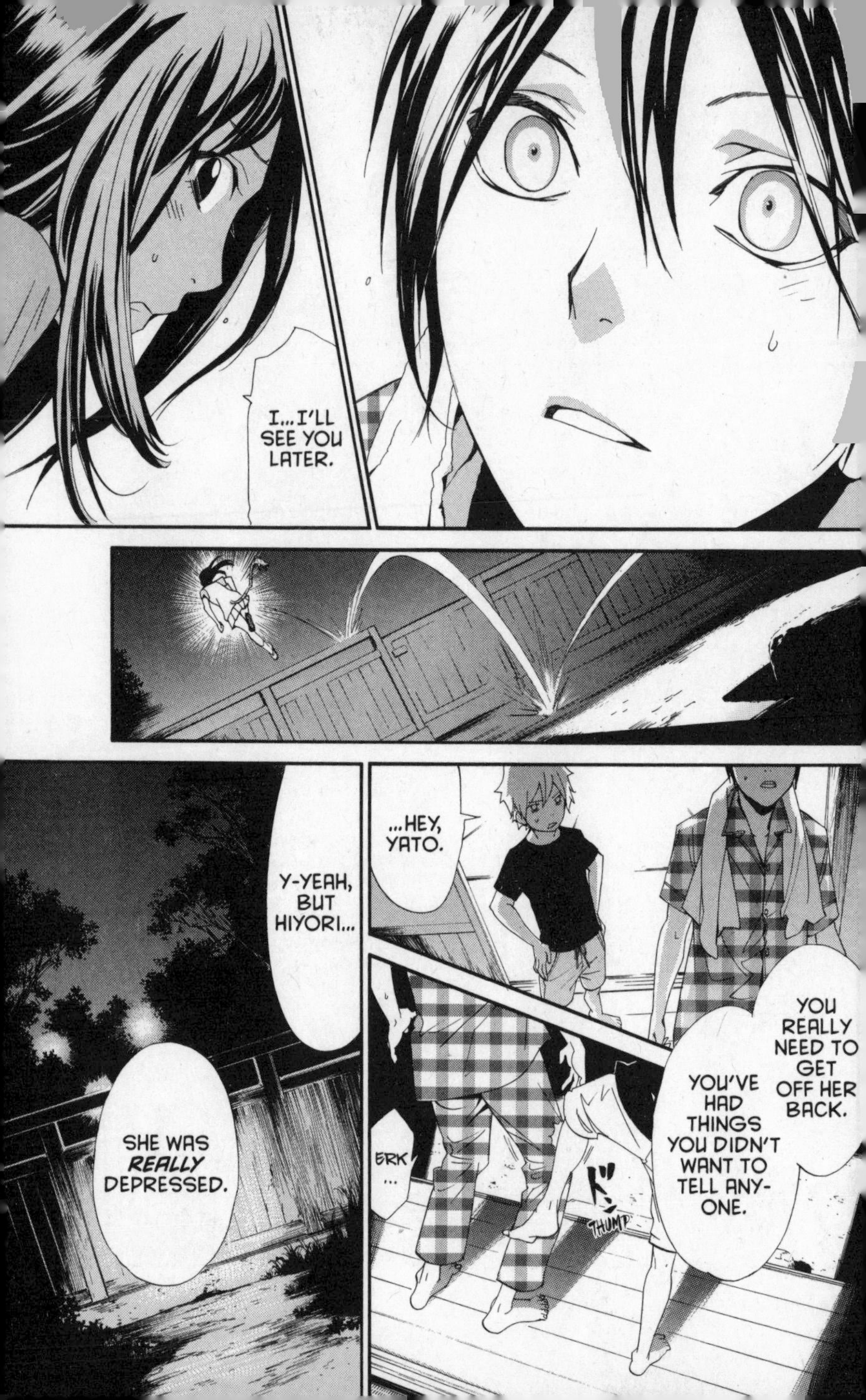

I...I'LL SEE YOU LATER.
...HEY, YATO.
YOU REALLY NEED TO GET OFF HER BACK.
YOU'VE HAD THINGS YOU DIDN'T WANT TO TELL ANY-ONE.
ERK...
THUMP
Y-YEAH, BUT HIYORI...
SHE WAS *REALLY* DEPRESSED.

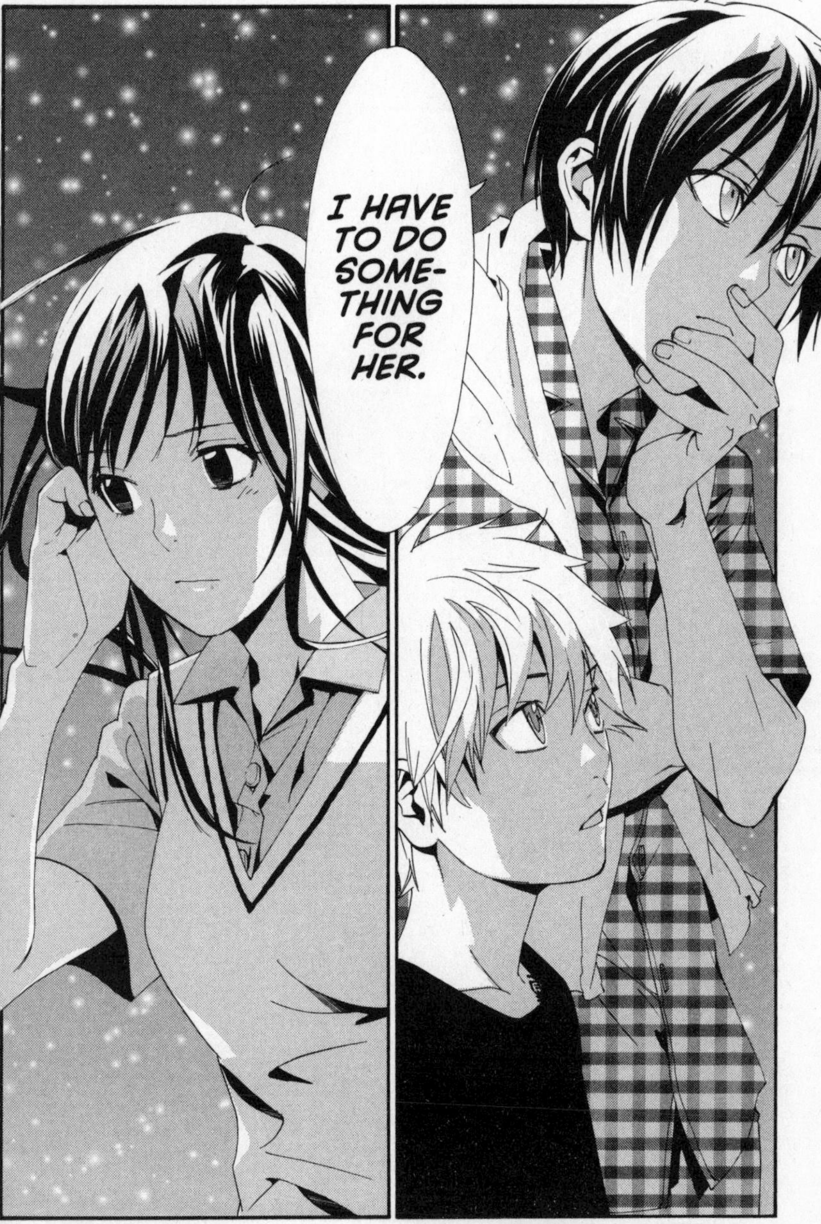
I HAVE TO DO SOME-THING FOR HER.

CHAPTER 40 / END

野

息

神

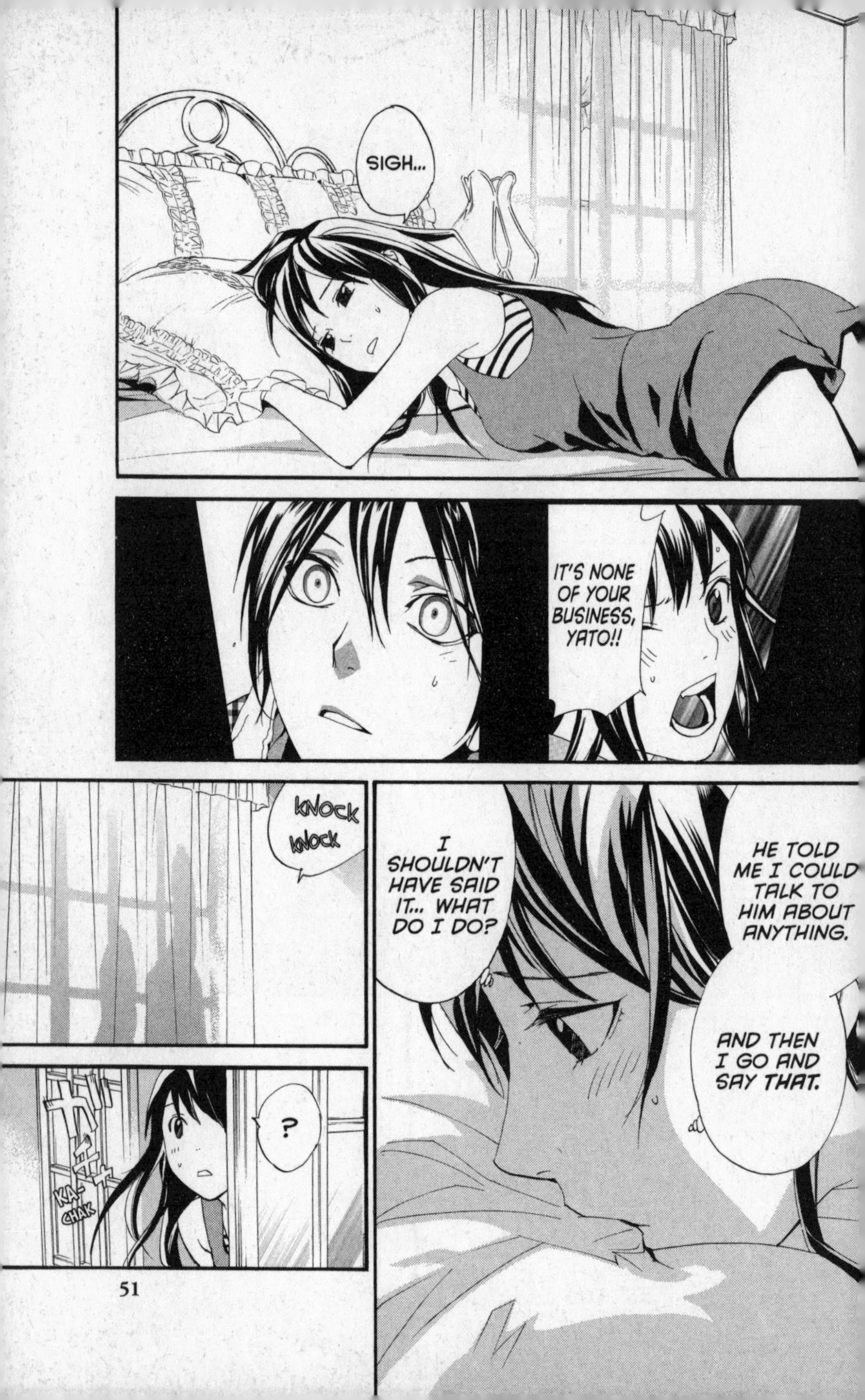
SIGH...
IT'S NONE OF YOUR BUSINESS, YATO!!
HE TOLD ME I COULD TALK TO HIM ABOUT ANYTHING.
AND THEN I GO AND SAY THAT.
I SHOULDN'T HAVE SAID IT... WHAT DO I DO?
KNOCK KNOCK
?
KA-CHAK

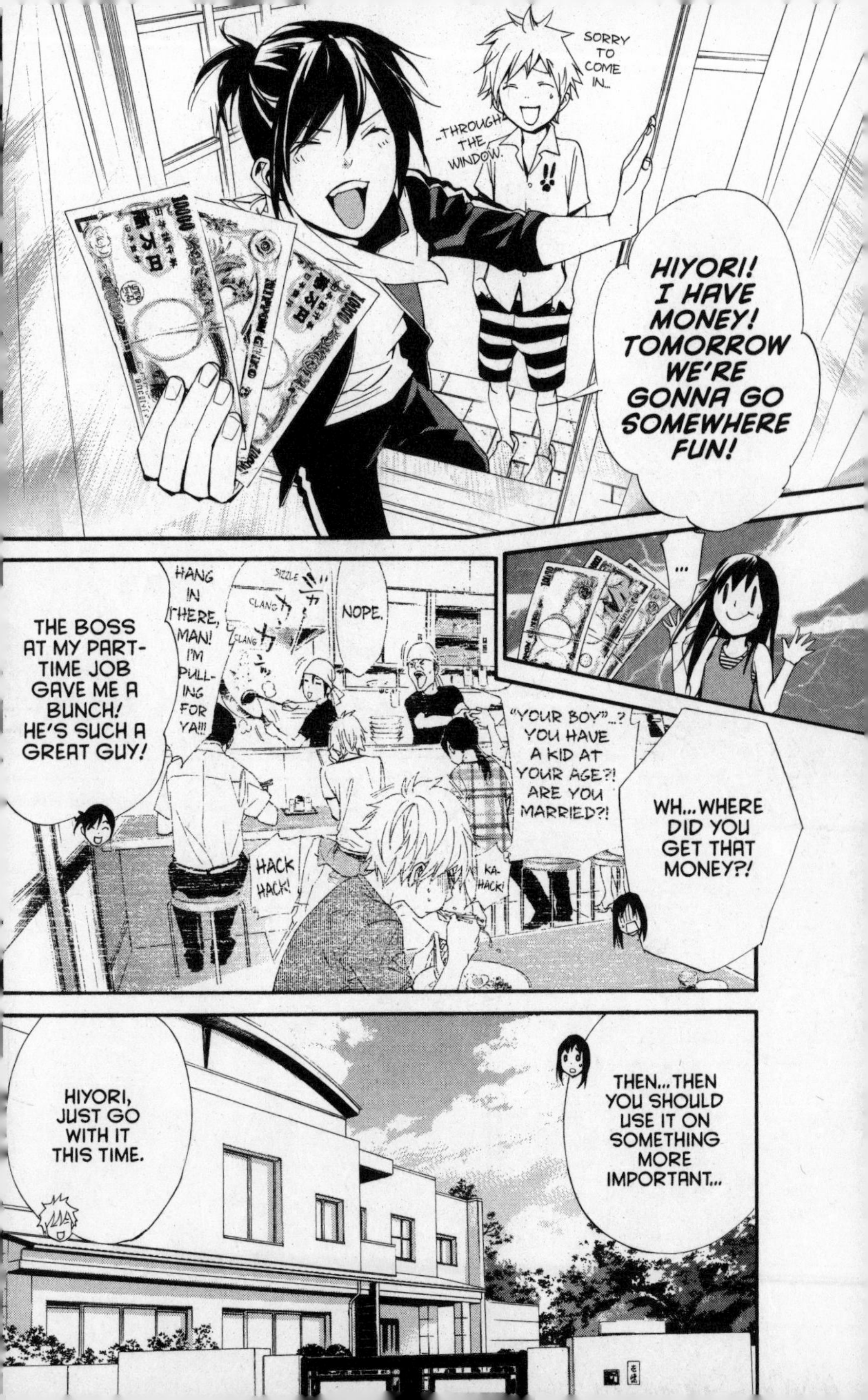
SORRY TO COME IN...
...THROUGH THE WINDOW.
HIYORI! I HAVE MONEY! TOMORROW WE'RE GONNA GO SOMEWHERE FUN!
...
WH...WHERE DID YOU GET THAT MONEY?!
NOPE.
SIZZLE
CLANG
CLANG
HANG IN THERE, MAN! I'M PULLING FOR YA!!!
"YOUR BOY"...? YOU HAVE A KID AT YOUR AGE?! ARE YOU MARRIED?!
THE BOSS AT MY PART-TIME JOB GAVE ME A BUNCH! HE'S SUCH A GREAT GUY!
KA-HACK!
HACK HACK!
THEN...THEN YOU SHOULD USE IT ON SOMETHING MORE IMPORTANT...
HIYORI, JUST GO WITH IT THIS TIME.

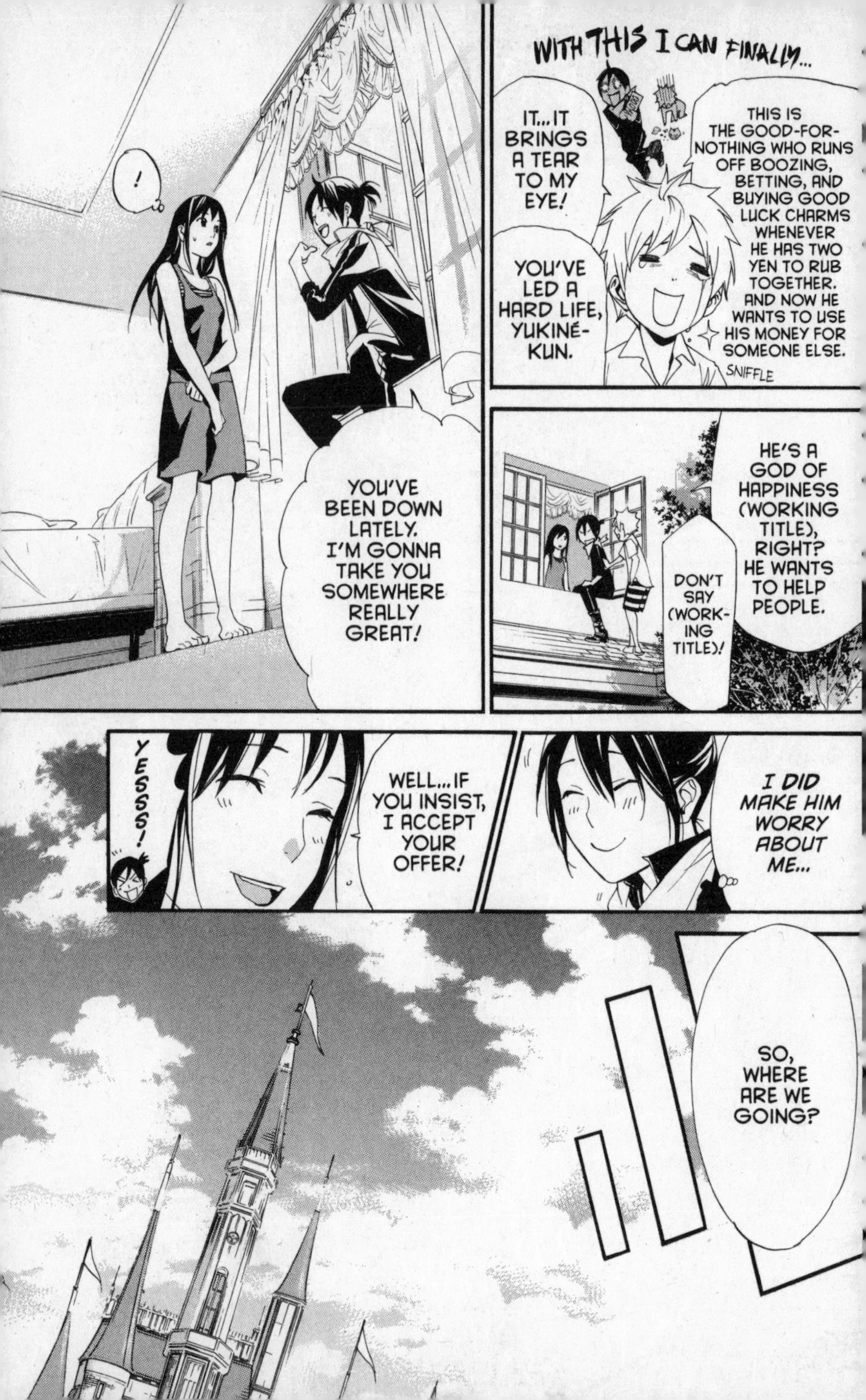
WITH THIS I CAN FINALLY...
THIS IS THE GOOD-FOR-NOTHING WHO RUNS OFF BOOZING, BETTING, AND BUYING GOOD LUCK CHARMS WHENEVER HE HAS TWO YEN TO RUB TOGETHER. AND NOW HE WANTS TO USE HIS MONEY FOR SOMEONE ELSE.
SNIFFLE
IT... IT BRINGS A TEAR TO MY EYE!
YOU'VE LED A HARD LIFE, YUKINÉ-KUN.
HE'S A GOD OF HAPPINESS (WORKING TITLE), RIGHT? HE WANTS TO HELP PEOPLE.
DON'T SAY (WORKING TITLE)!
!
YOU'VE BEEN DOWN LATELY. I'M GONNA TAKE YOU SOMEWHERE REALLY GREAT!
I DID MAKE HIM WORRY ABOUT ME...
WELL... IF YOU INSIST, I ACCEPT YOUR OFFER!
YESSS!
SO, WHERE ARE WE GOING?

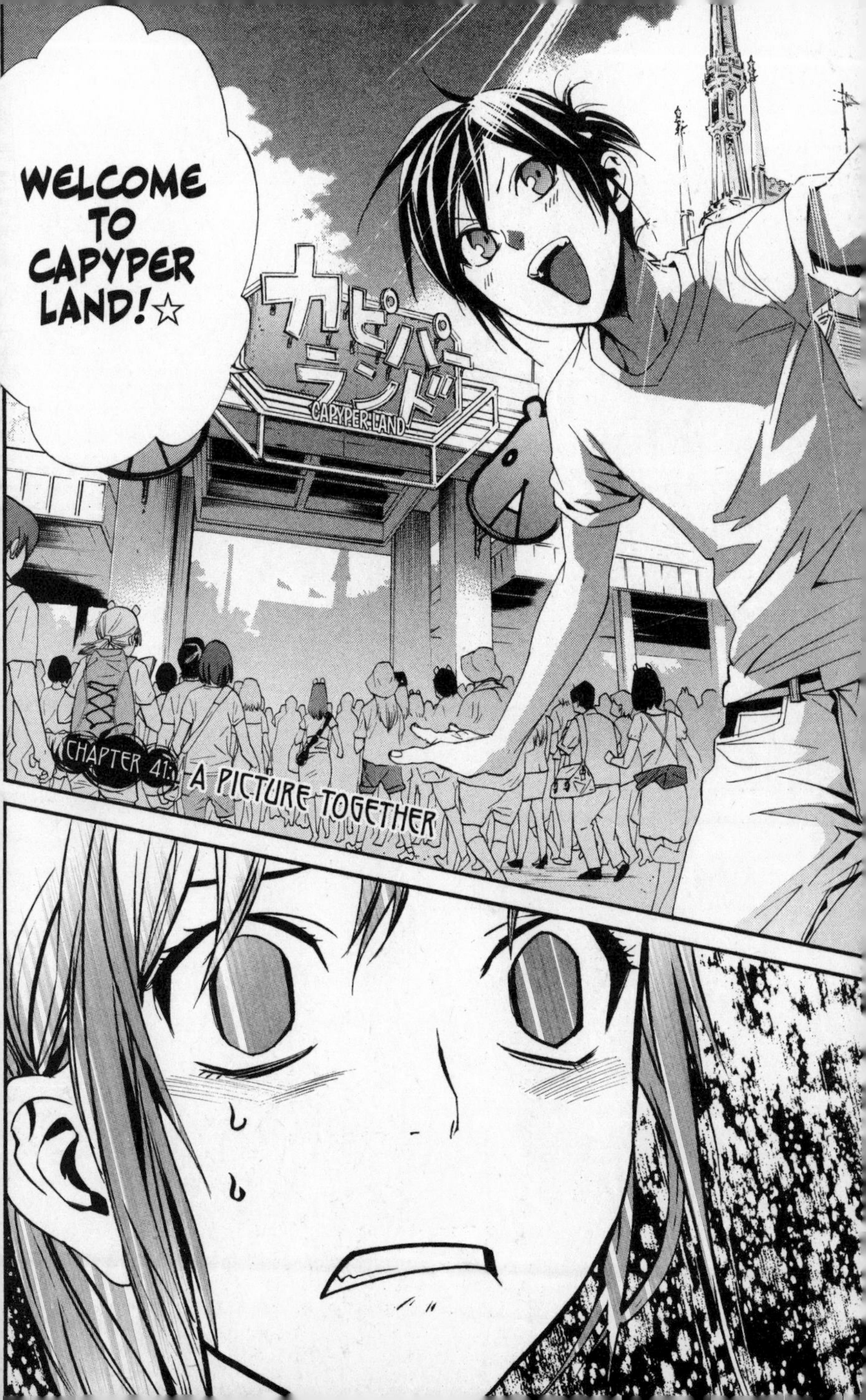
WELCOME TO CAPYPER LAND!☆
カピパーランド
CAPYPER LAND
CHAPTER 41: A PICTURE TOGETHER

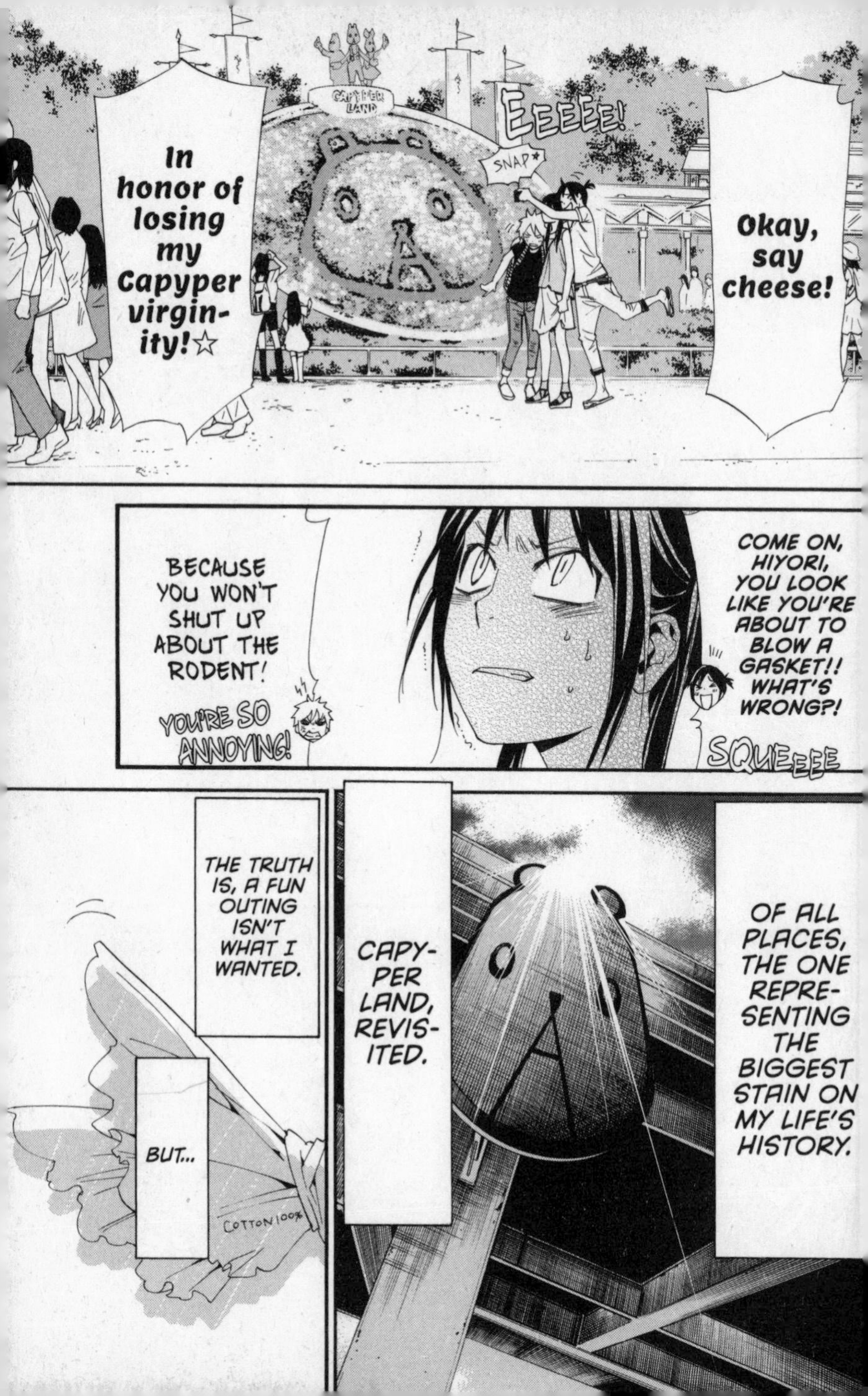
Okay, say cheese!
EEEEE!
SNAP*
CAPYPER LAND
In honor of losing my Capyper virgin-ity!☆
COME ON, HIYORI, YOU LOOK LIKE YOU'RE ABOUT TO BLOW A GASKET!! WHAT'S WRONG?!
SQUEEEE
BECAUSE YOU WON'T SHUT UP ABOUT THE RODENT!
YOU'RE SO ANNOYING!
OF ALL PLACES, THE ONE REPRESENTING THE BIGGEST STAIN ON MY LIFE'S HISTORY.
CAPY-PER LAND, REVIS-ITED.
THE TRUTH IS, A FUN OUTING ISN'T WHAT I WANTED.
BUT...
COTTON 100%

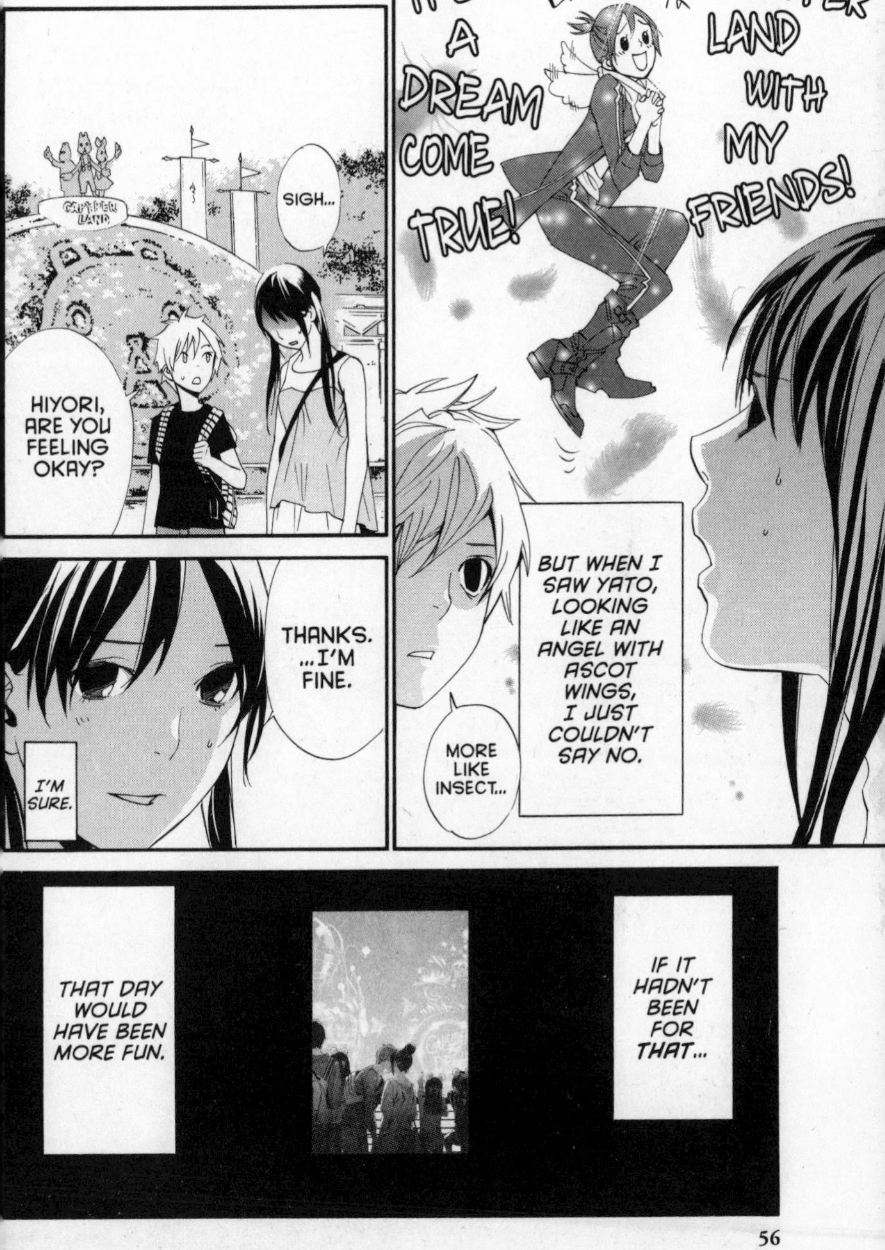
CAPYPER LAND WITH MY FRIENDS!
FLAP FLAP FLAP FLAP FLAP
しばばばばばば
IT'S A DREAM COME TRUE!
BUT WHEN I SAW YATO, LOOKING LIKE AN ANGEL WITH ASCOT WINGS, I JUST COULDN'T SAY NO.
MORE LIKE INSECT...
SIGH...
CAPYPER LAND
HIYORI, ARE YOU FEELING OKAY?
THANKS. ...I'M FINE.
I'M SURE.
IF IT HADN'T BEEN FOR THAT...
THAT DAY WOULD HAVE BEEN MORE FUN.

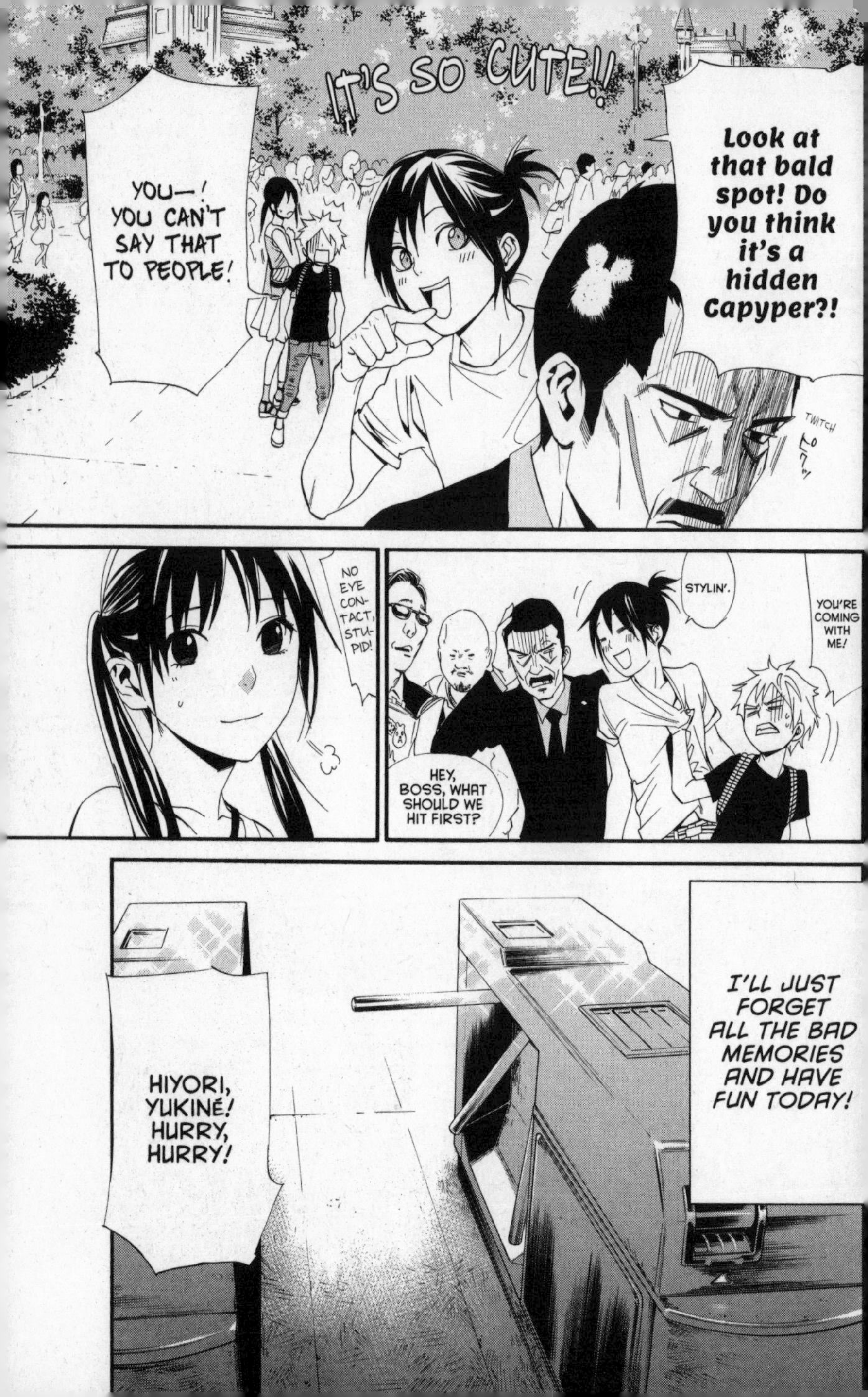
IT'S SO CUTE!!
Look at that bald spot! Do you think it's a hidden Capyper?!
YOU—! YOU CAN'T SAY THAT TO PEOPLE!
TWITCH
STYLIN'.
YOU'RE COMING WITH ME!
HEY, BOSS, WHAT SHOULD WE HIT FIRST?
NO EYE CONTACT, STUPID!
I'LL JUST FORGET ALL THE BAD MEMORIES AND HAVE FUN TODAY!
HIYORI, YUKINÉ! HURRY, HURRY!

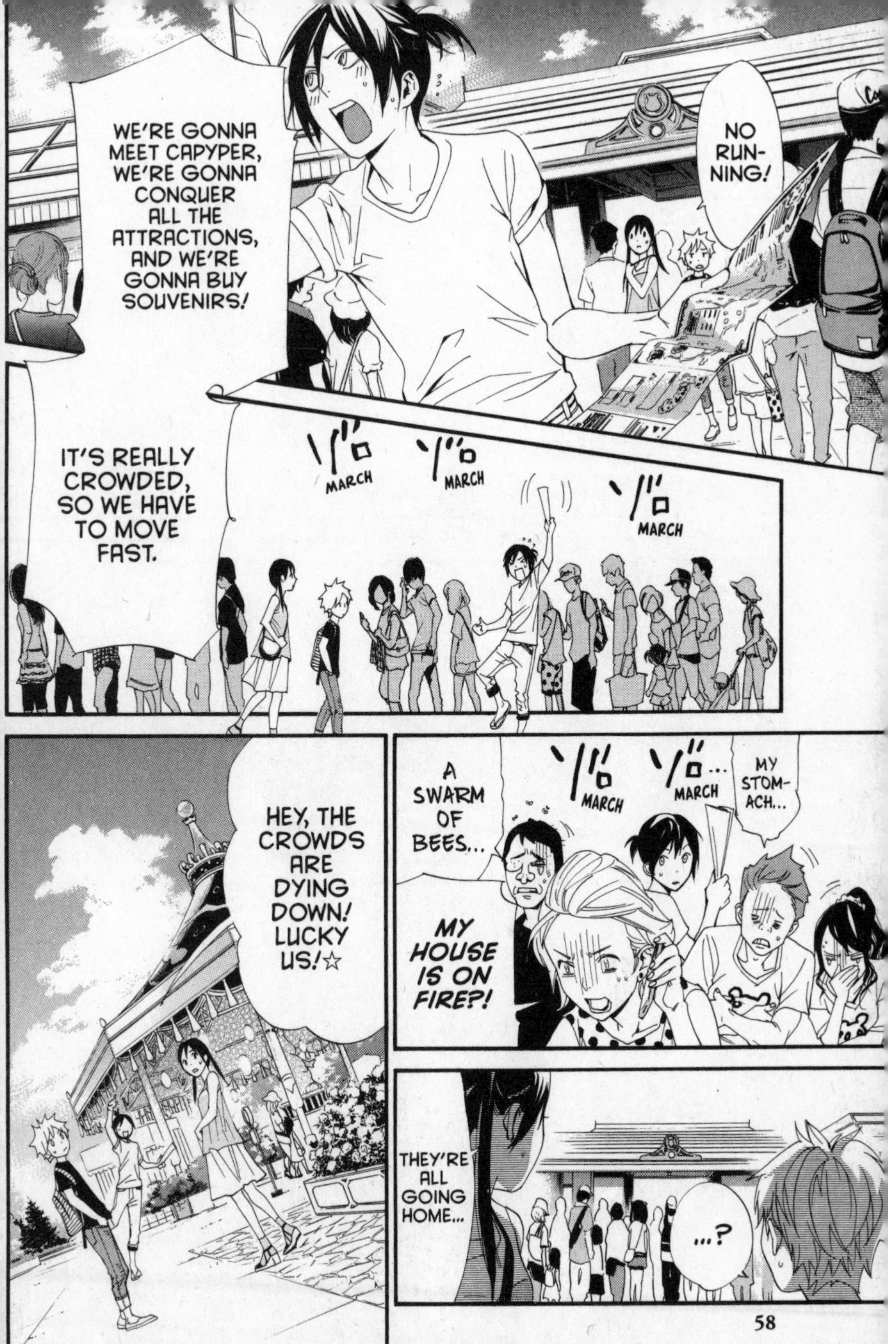
NO RUN-NING!
WE'RE GONNA MEET CAPYPER, WE'RE GONNA CONQUER ALL THE ATTRACTIONS, AND WE'RE GONNA BUY SOUVENIRS!
ゾロ MARCH
ゾロ MARCH
ゾロ MARCH
IT'S REALLY CROWDED, SO WE HAVE TO MOVE FAST.
MY STOM-ACH...
ゾロ... MARCH
ゾロ MARCH
A SWARM OF BEES...
MY HOUSE IS ON FIRE?!
...?
THEY'RE ALL GOING HOME...
HEY, THE CROWDS ARE DYING DOWN! LUCKY US!☆

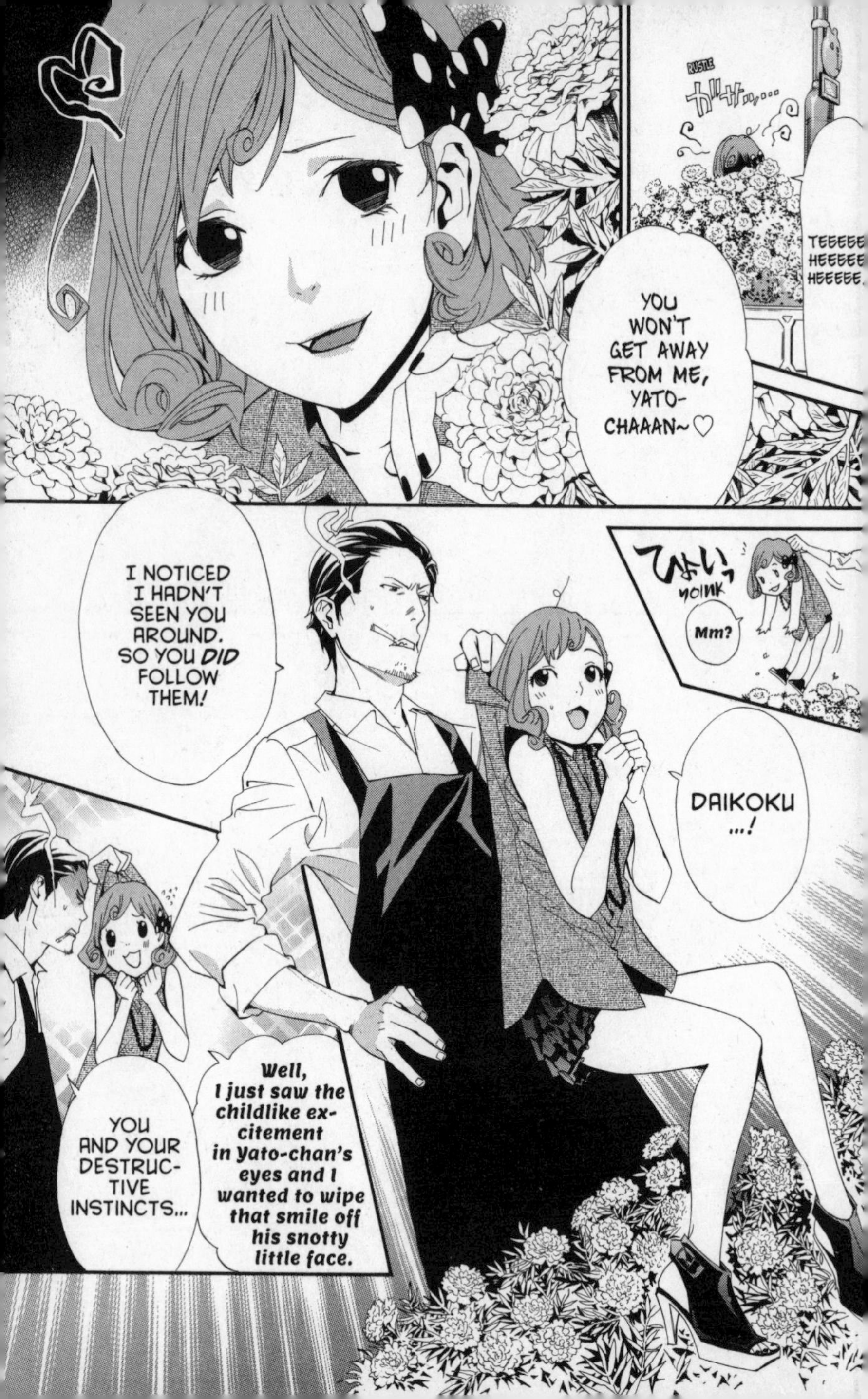
RUSTLE
ガサッ…
TEEEEE HEEEEE HEEEEE.
YOU WON'T GET AWAY FROM ME, YATO-CHAAAN~♡
ひょいっ
YOINK
Mm?
DAIKOKU ...!
I NOTICED I HADN'T SEEN YOU AROUND. SO YOU *DID* FOLLOW THEM!
Well, I just saw the childlike ex-citement in Yato-chan's eyes and I wanted to wipe that smile off his snotty little face.
YOU AND YOUR DESTRUC-TIVE INSTINCTS...

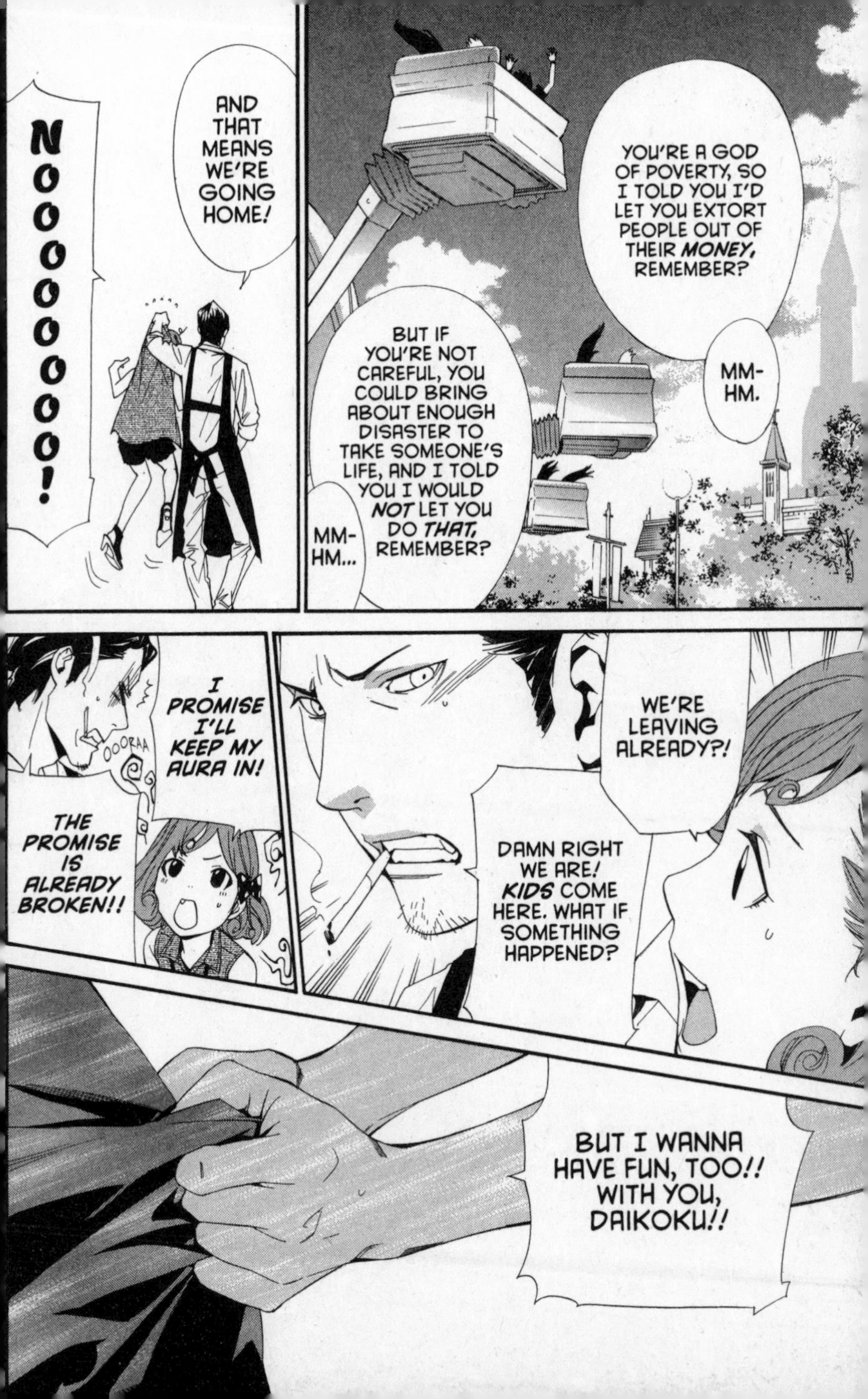
YOU'RE A GOD OF POVERTY, SO I TOLD YOU I'D LET YOU EXTORT PEOPLE OUT OF THEIR *MONEY*, REMEMBER?
MM-HM.
BUT IF YOU'RE NOT CAREFUL, YOU COULD BRING ABOUT ENOUGH DISASTER TO TAKE SOMEONE'S LIFE, AND I TOLD YOU I WOULD *NOT* LET YOU DO *THAT*, REMEMBER?
MM-HM...
AND THAT MEANS WE'RE GOING HOME!
NOOOOOOOOO!
WE'RE LEAVING ALREADY?!
DAMN RIGHT WE ARE! *KIDS* COME HERE. WHAT IF SOMETHING HAPPENED?
I PROMISE I'LL KEEP MY AURA IN!
OOORAA
THE PROMISE IS ALREADY BROKEN!!
BUT I WANNA HAVE FUN, TOO!! WITH YOU, DAIKOKU!!

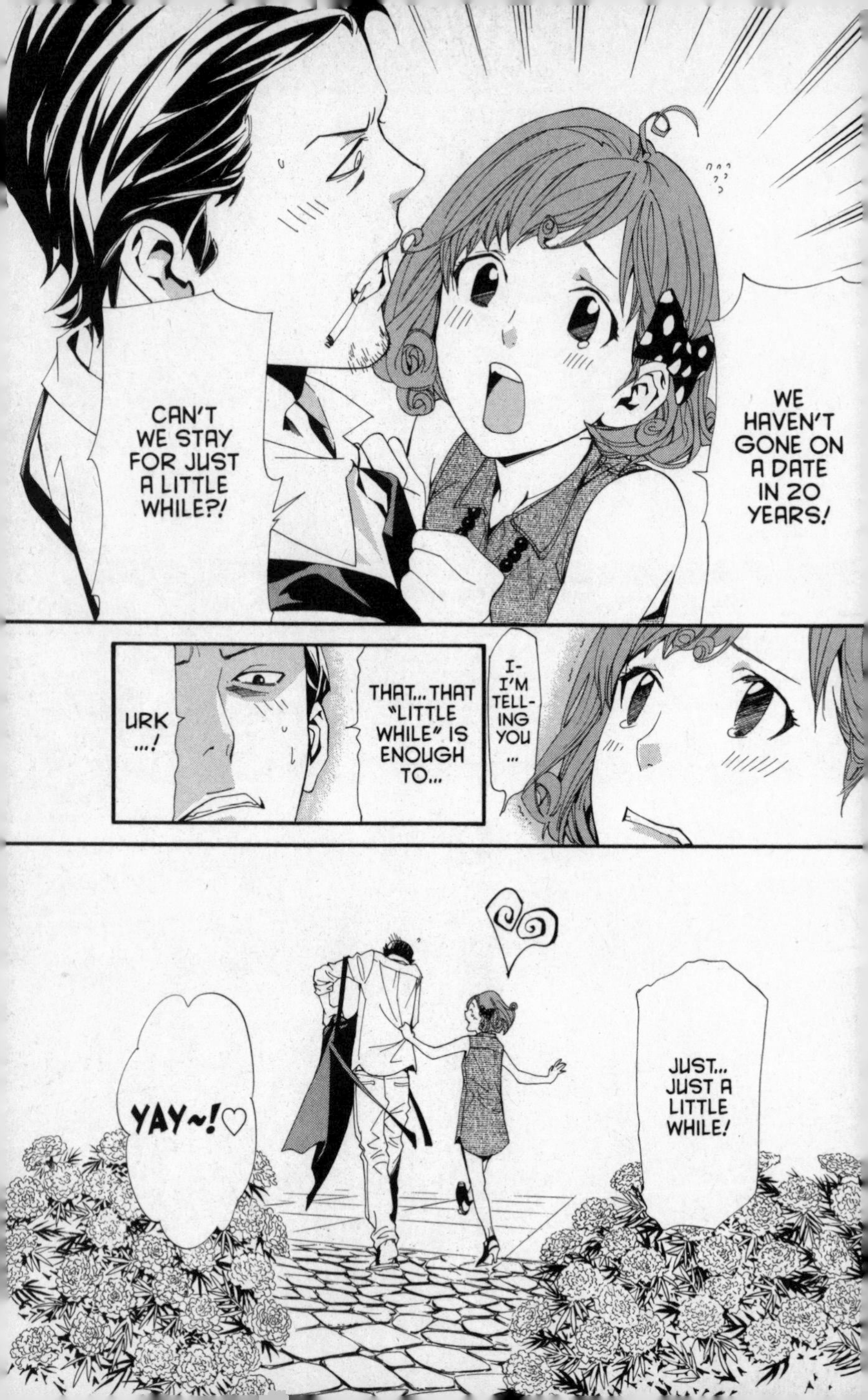
WE HAVEN'T GONE ON A DATE IN 20 YEARS!
CAN'T WE STAY FOR JUST A LITTLE WHILE?!
I- I'M TELLING YOU...
THAT... THAT "LITTLE WHILE" IS ENOUGH TO...
URK...!
JUST... JUST A LITTLE WHILE!
YAY~!♡

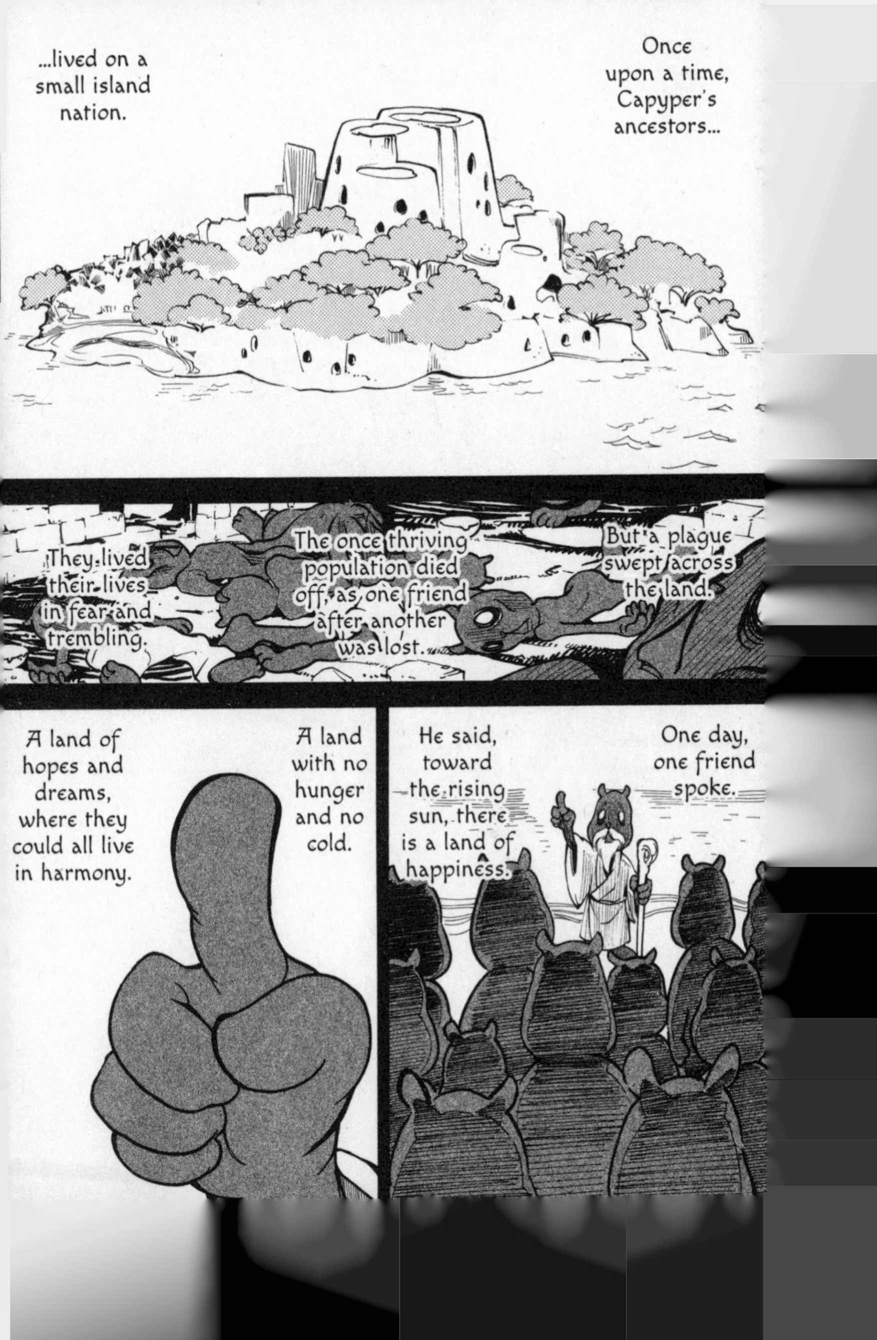
Once upon a time, Capyper's ancestors...
...lived on a small island nation.
But a plague swept across the land.
The once thriving population died off, as one friend after another was lost.
They lived their lives in fear and trembling.
One day, one friend spoke.
He said, toward the rising sun, there is a land of happiness.
A land with no hunger and no cold.
A land of hopes and dreams, where they could all live in harmony.

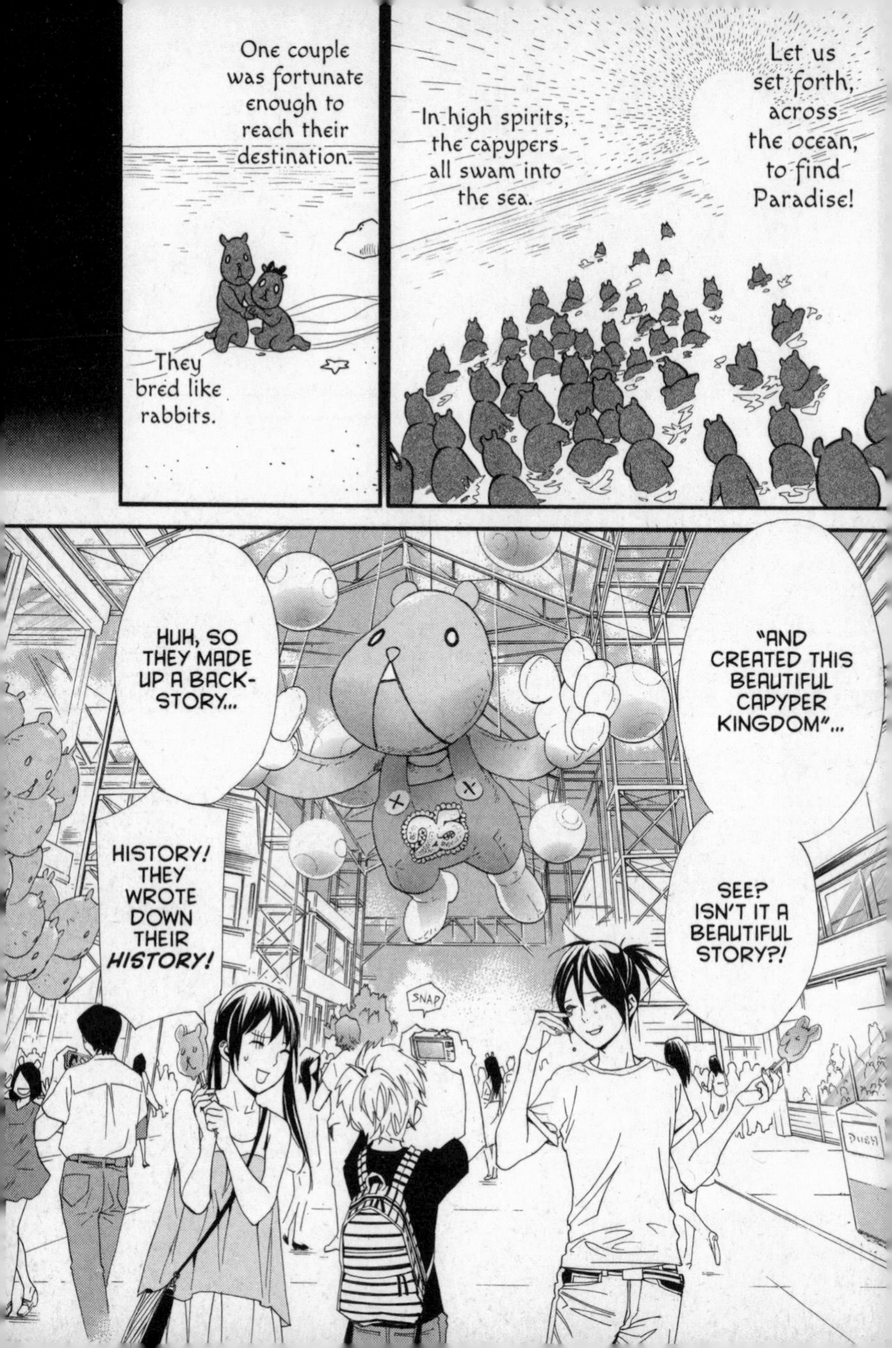
Let us set forth, across the ocean, to find Paradise!
In high spirits, the capypers all swam into the sea.
One couple was fortunate enough to reach their destination.
They bred like rabbits.
"AND CREATED THIS BEAUTIFUL CAPYPER KINGDOM"...
HUH, SO THEY MADE UP A BACK-STORY...
SEE? ISN'T IT A BEAUTIFUL STORY?!
SNAP
HISTORY! THEY WROTE DOWN THEIR *HISTORY*!
PUSH

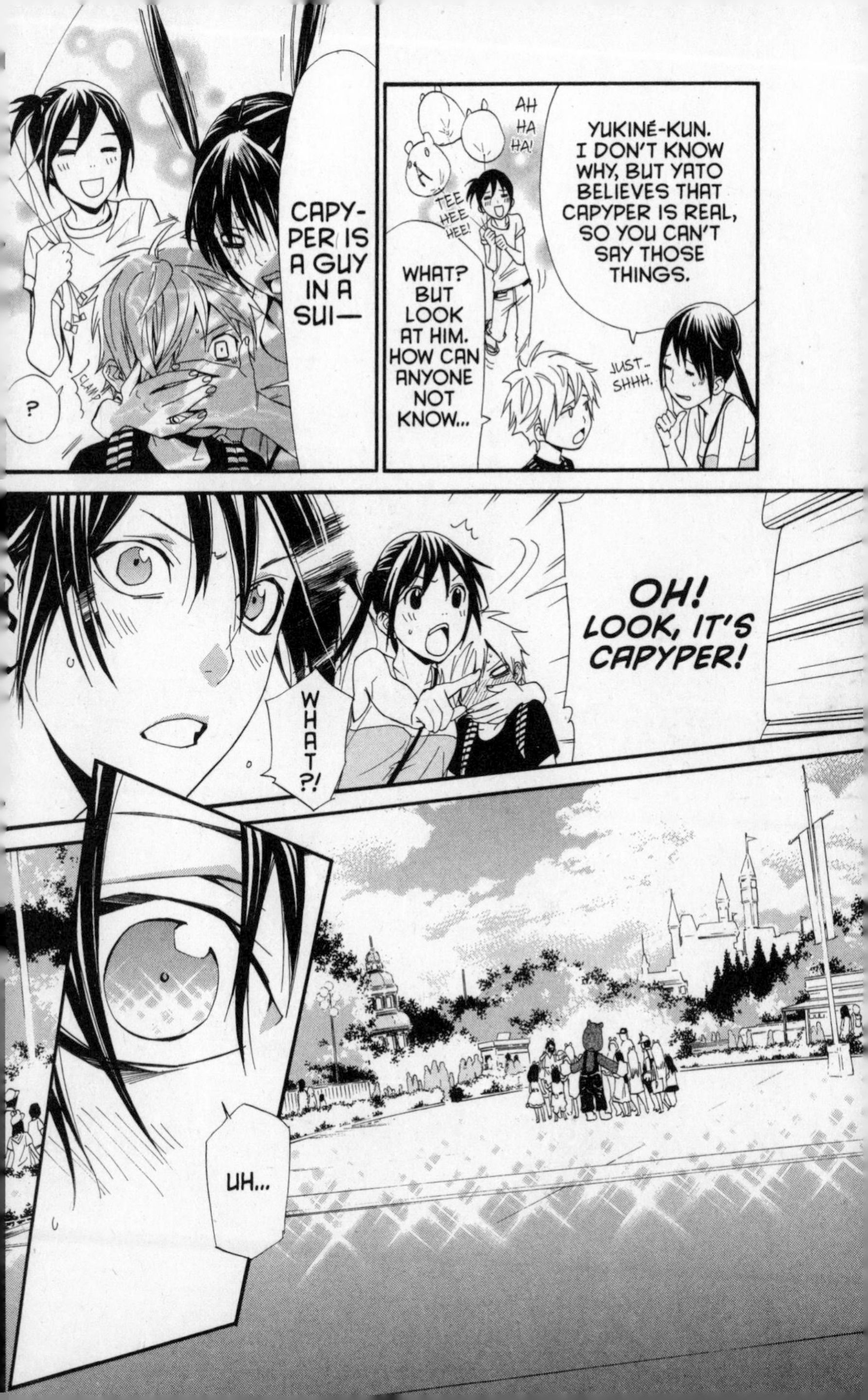
YUKINÉ-KUN. I DON'T KNOW WHY, BUT YATO BELIEVES THAT CAPYPER IS REAL, SO YOU CAN'T SAY THOSE THINGS.
AH HA HA!
TEE HEE HEE!
WHAT? BUT LOOK AT HIM. HOW CAN ANYONE NOT KNOW...
JUST.. SHHH.
CAPY-PER IS A GUY IN A SUI—
CLAMP
?
OH! LOOK, IT'S CAPYPER!
WHAT?!
UH...

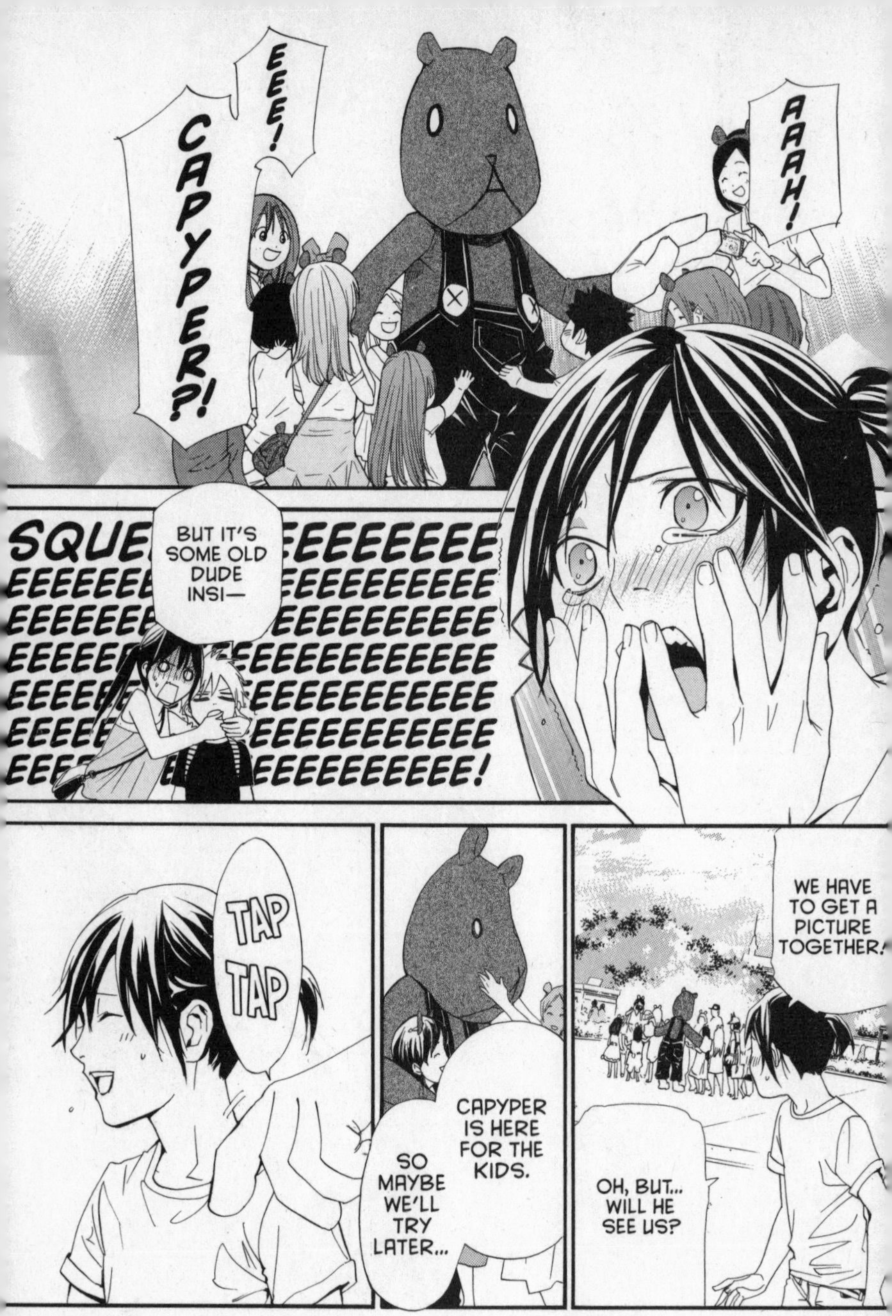
AAAH!
EEE! CAPYPER?!
SQUEEEEEEEEEEEEEEEEEEEEEEEEEEEEEEEEEEEEEEEEEEEEEEEEEEEEEEEEEEEEEEEEEEEEEEEEEEEEEEEEEEEEEEEEEEEEEEEEEEEEEEEEEEEEEEE!
BUT IT'S SOME OLD DUDE INSI—
WE HAVE TO GET A PICTURE TOGETHER!
OH, BUT... WILL HE SEE US?
CAPYPER IS HERE FOR THE KIDS.
SO MAYBE WE'LL TRY LATER...
TAP TAP

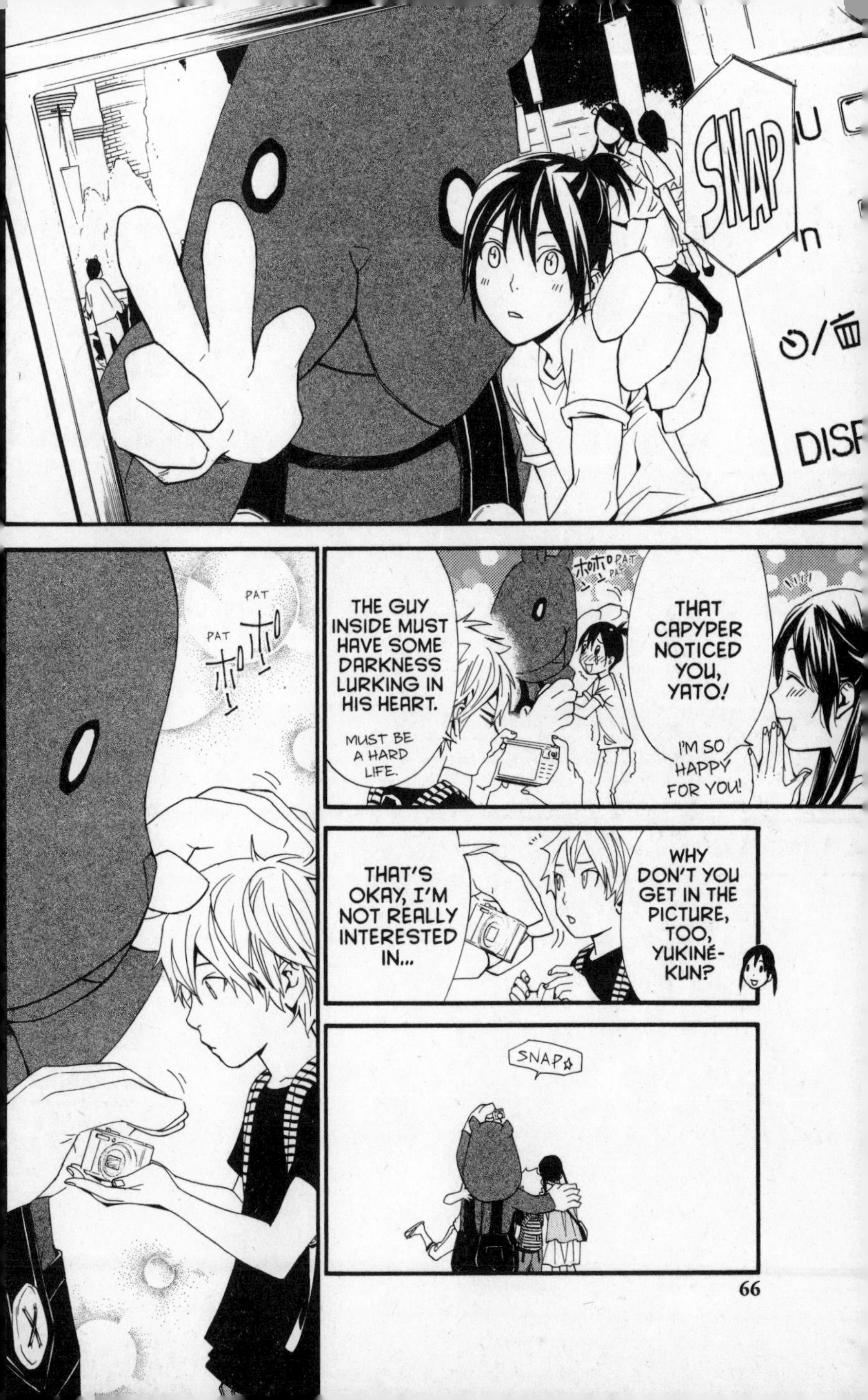
SNAP
DISP
THAT CAPYPER NOTICED YOU, YATO!
I'M SO HAPPY FOR YOU!
PAT PAT
THE GUY INSIDE MUST HAVE SOME DARKNESS LURKING IN HIS HEART.
MUST BE A HARD LIFE.
WHY DON'T YOU GET IN THE PICTURE, TOO, YUKINÉ-KUN?
THAT'S OKAY, I'M NOT REALLY INTERESTED IN...
SNAP
PAT
PAT

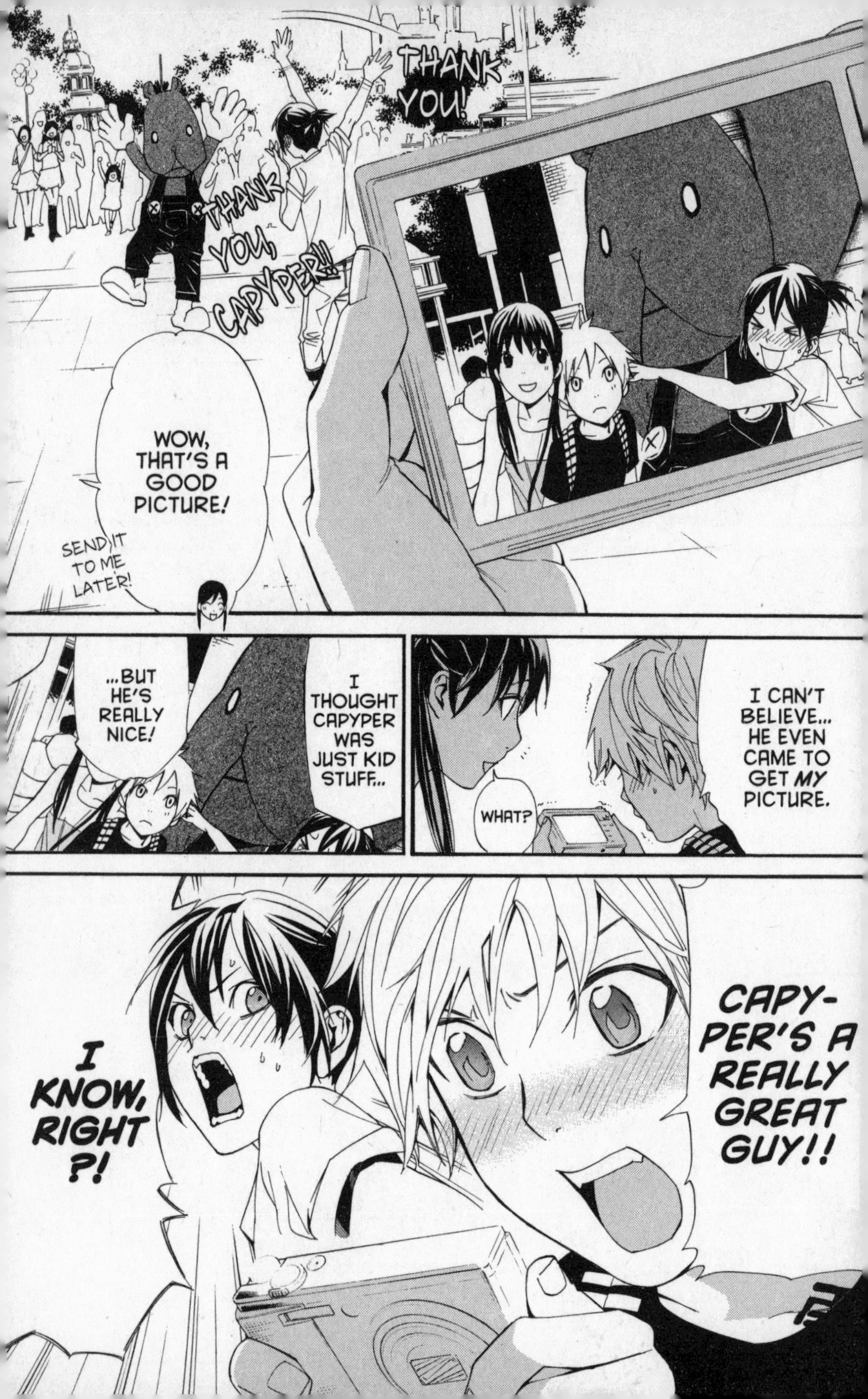
THANK YOU!
THANK YOU, CAPYPER!!
WOW, THAT'S A GOOD PICTURE!
SEND IT TO ME LATER!
I CAN'T BELIEVE... HE EVEN CAME TO GET MY PICTURE.
WHAT?
I THOUGHT CAPYPER WAS JUST KID STUFF...
...BUT HE'S REALLY NICE!
CAPY-PER'S A REALLY GREAT GUY!!
I KNOW, RIGHT?!

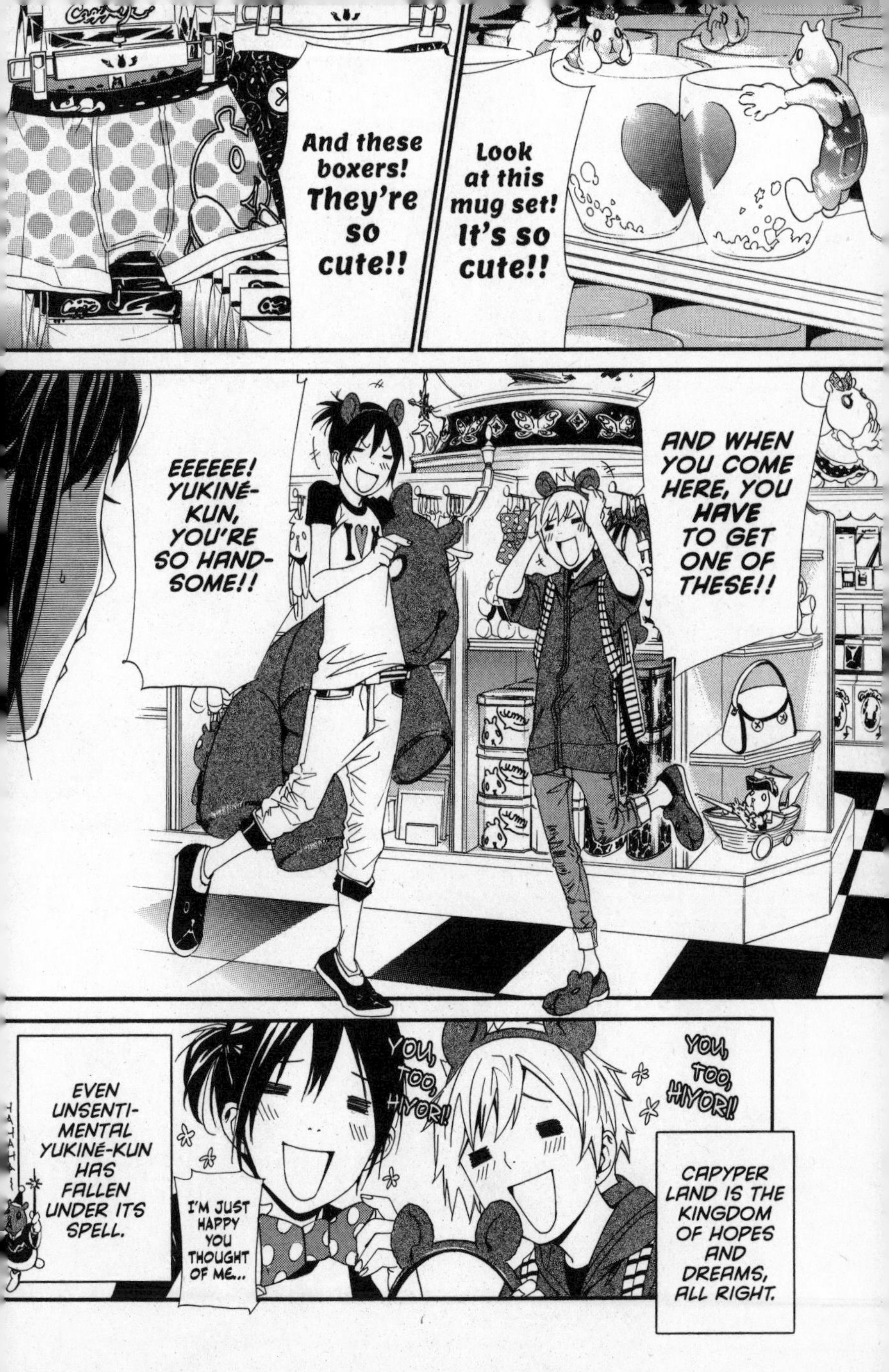
Look at this mug set! It's so cute!!
And these boxers! They're so cute!!
AND WHEN YOU COME HERE, YOU HAVE TO GET ONE OF THESE!!
EEEEEE! YUKINÉ-KUN, YOU'RE SO HAND-SOME!!
YOU, TOO, HIYORI!
CAPYPER LAND IS THE KINGDOM OF HOPES AND DREAMS, ALL RIGHT.
YOU, TOO, HIYORI!
EVEN UNSENTI-MENTAL YUKINÉ-KUN HAS FALLEN UNDER ITS SPELL.
I'M JUST HAPPY YOU THOUGHT OF ME...

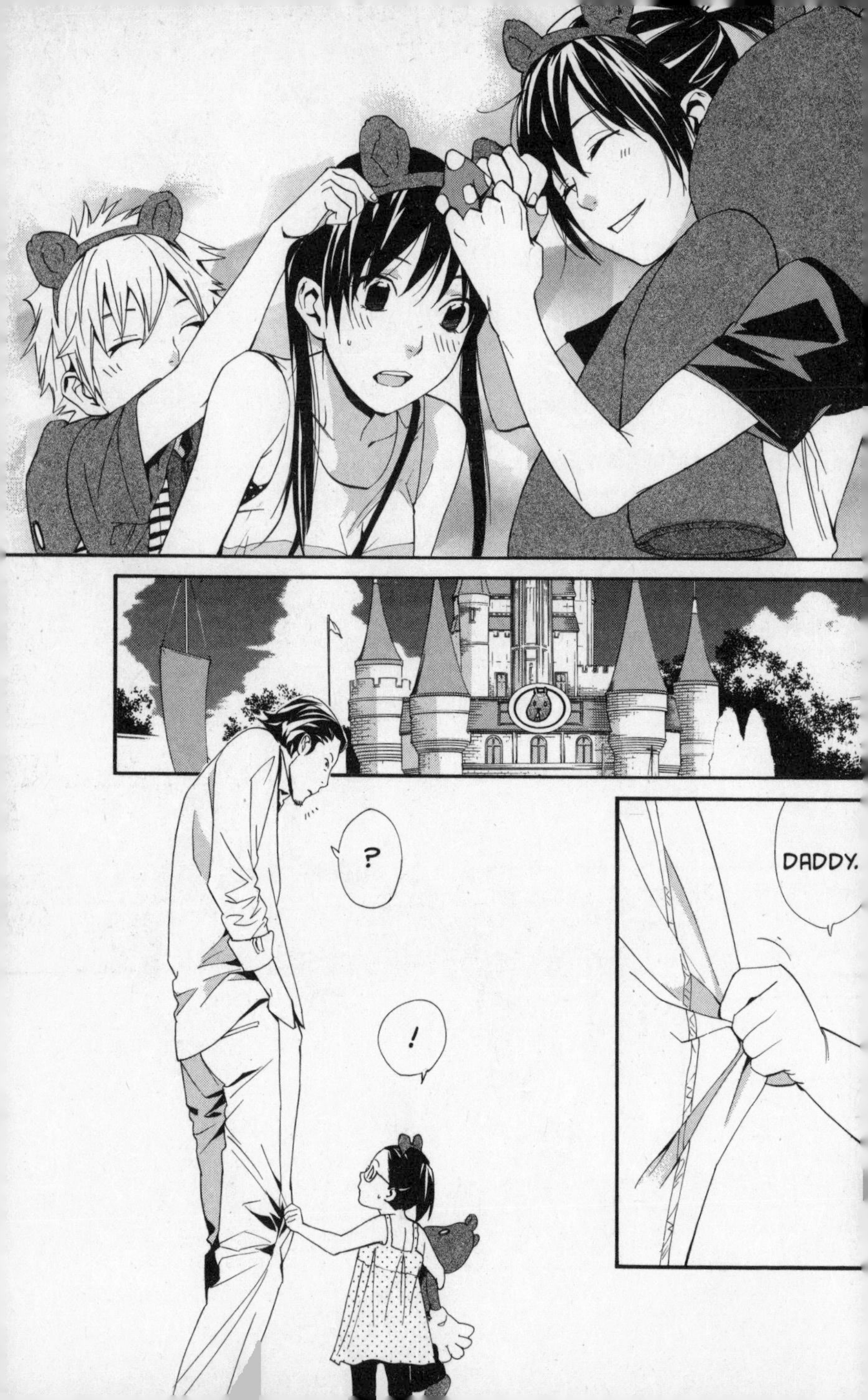
DADDY.
?
!

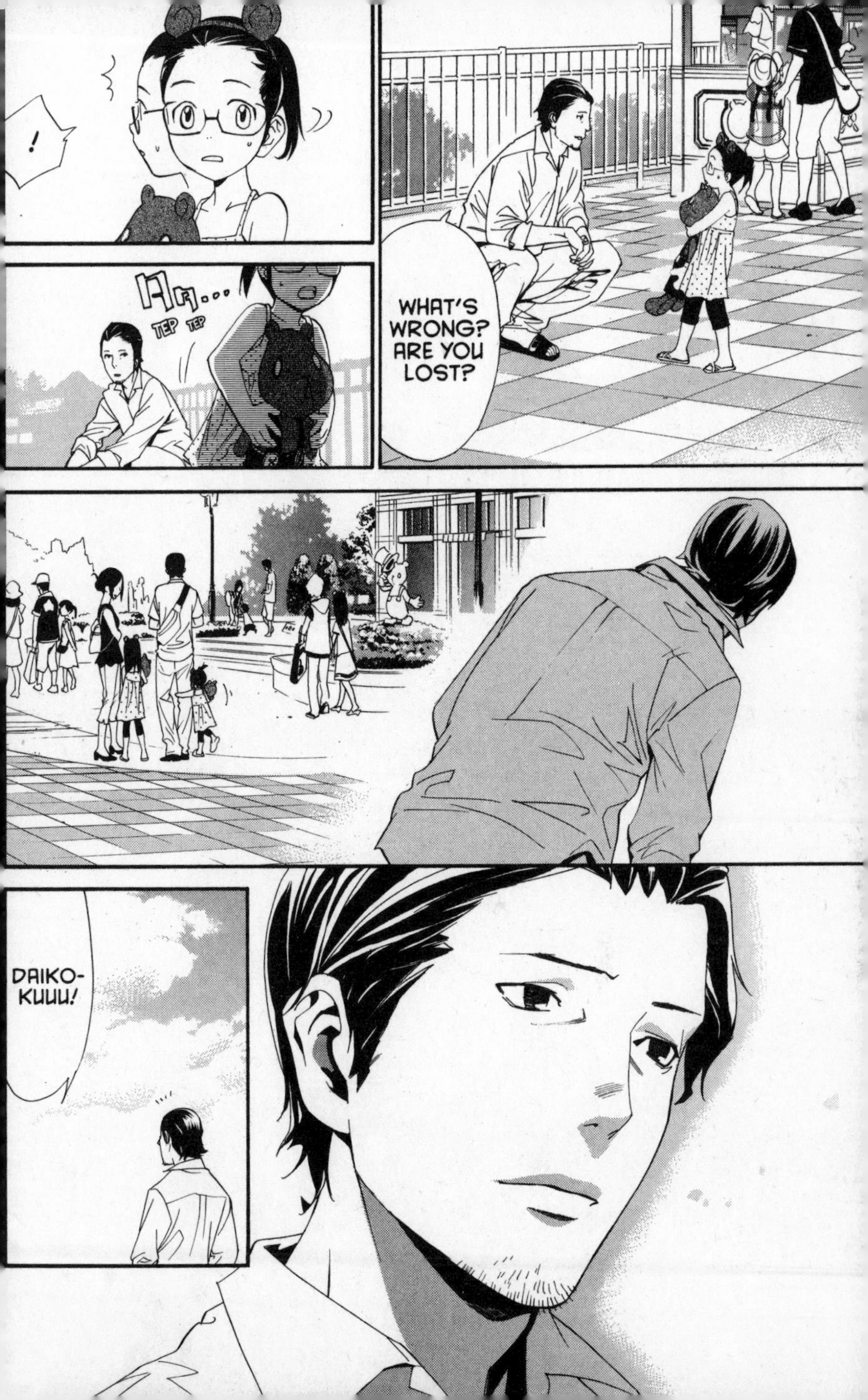
WHAT'S WRONG? ARE YOU LOST?
!
AH...
TEP TEP
DAIKO-KUUU!

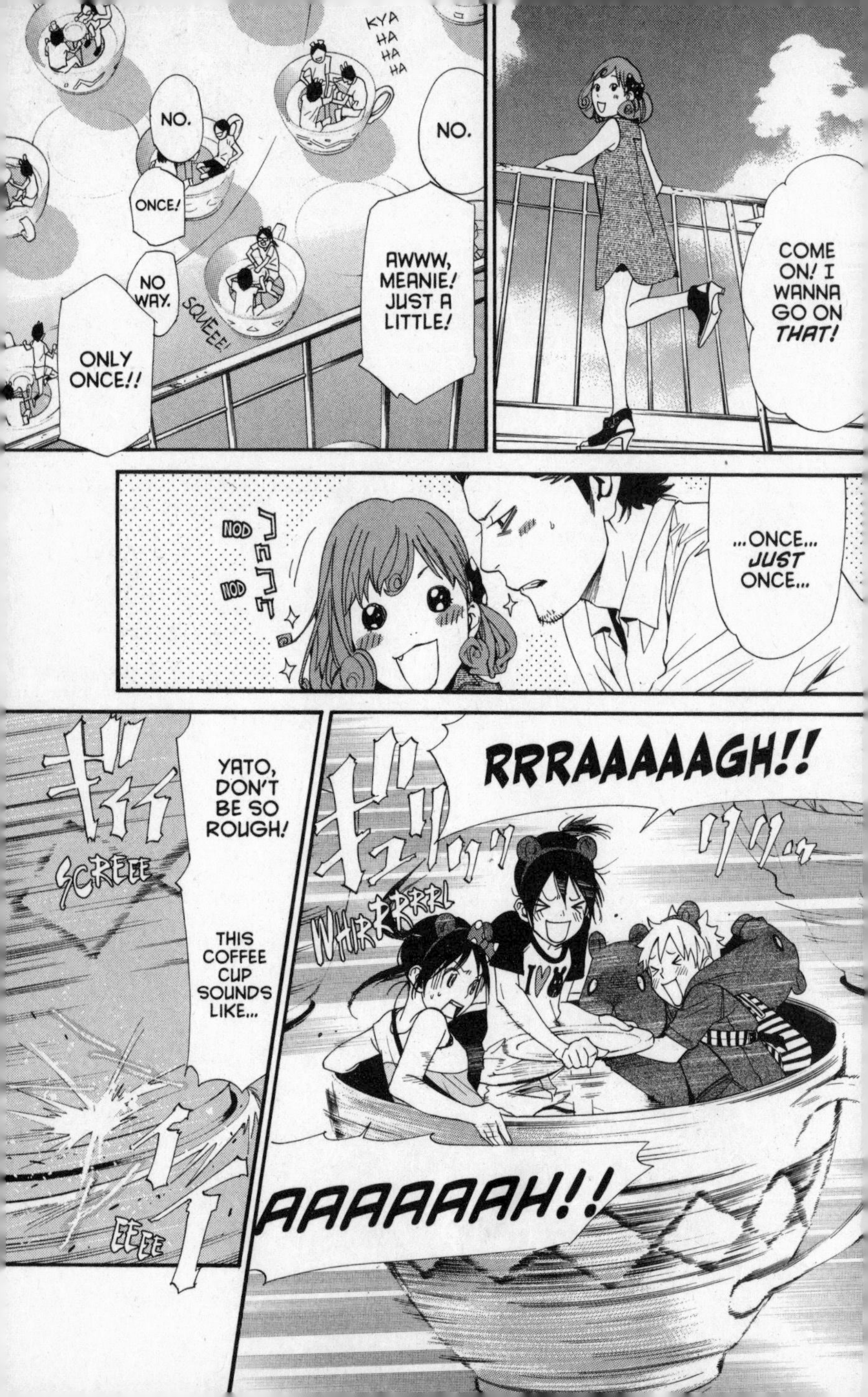
COME ON! I WANNA GO ON THAT!
KYA HA HA HA
NO.
AWWW, MEANIE! JUST A LITTLE!
NO.
ONCE!
NO WAY.
SQUEEE!
ONLY ONCE!!
...ONCE... JUST ONCE...
NOD NOD
RRRAAAAAGH!!
WHRRRRRL
AAAAAAH!!
YATO, DON'T BE SO ROUGH!
SCREEE
THIS COFFEE CUP SOUNDS LIKE...
EEEE

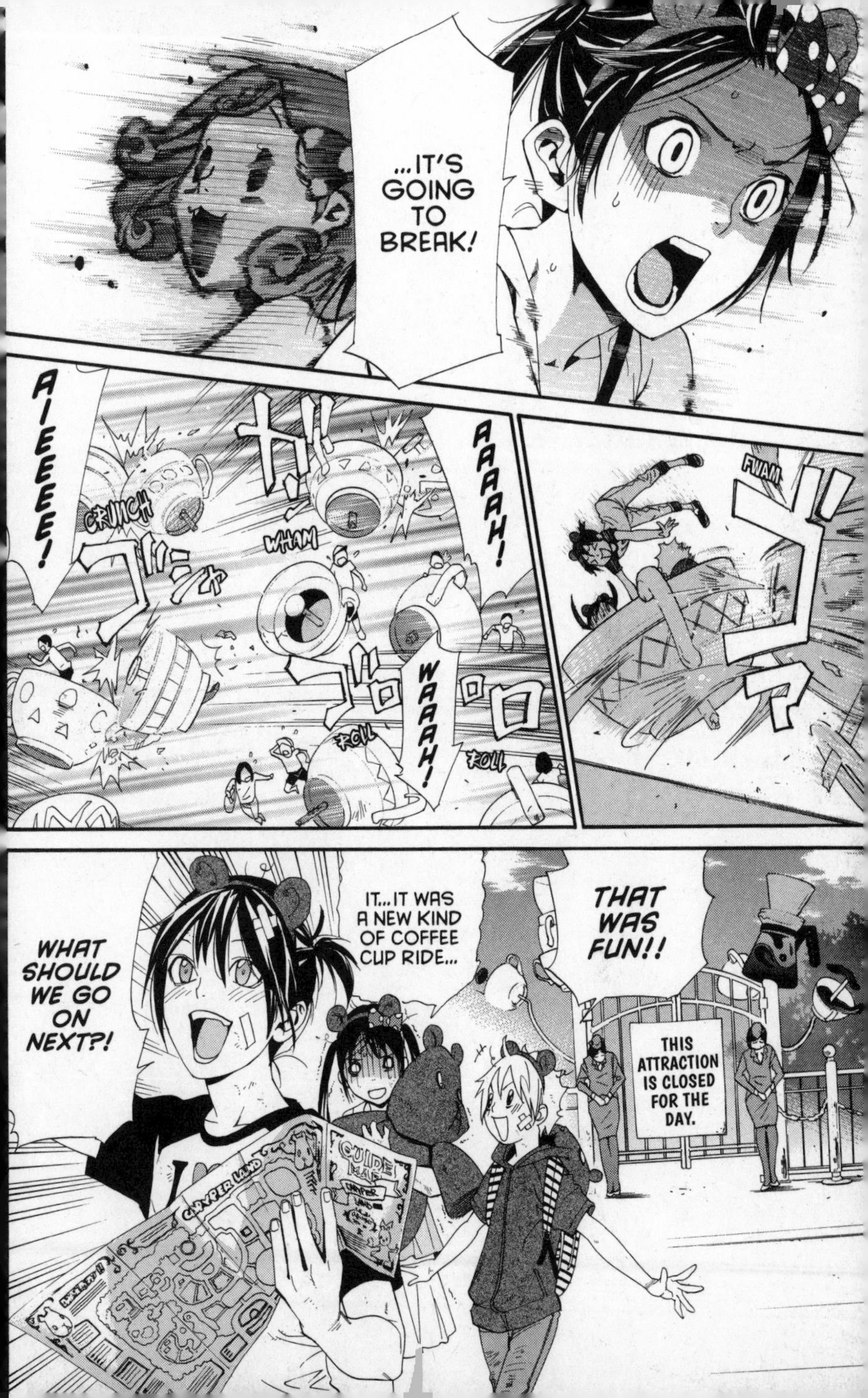
...IT'S GOING TO BREAK!
FWAM
AAAAAH!
AIEEEEE!
CRUNCH
WHAM
WAAAAH!
ROLL
ROLL
THAT WAS FUN!!
THIS ATTRACTION IS CLOSED FOR THE DAY.
IT...IT WAS A NEW KIND OF COFFEE CUP RIDE...
WHAT SHOULD WE GO ON NEXT?!

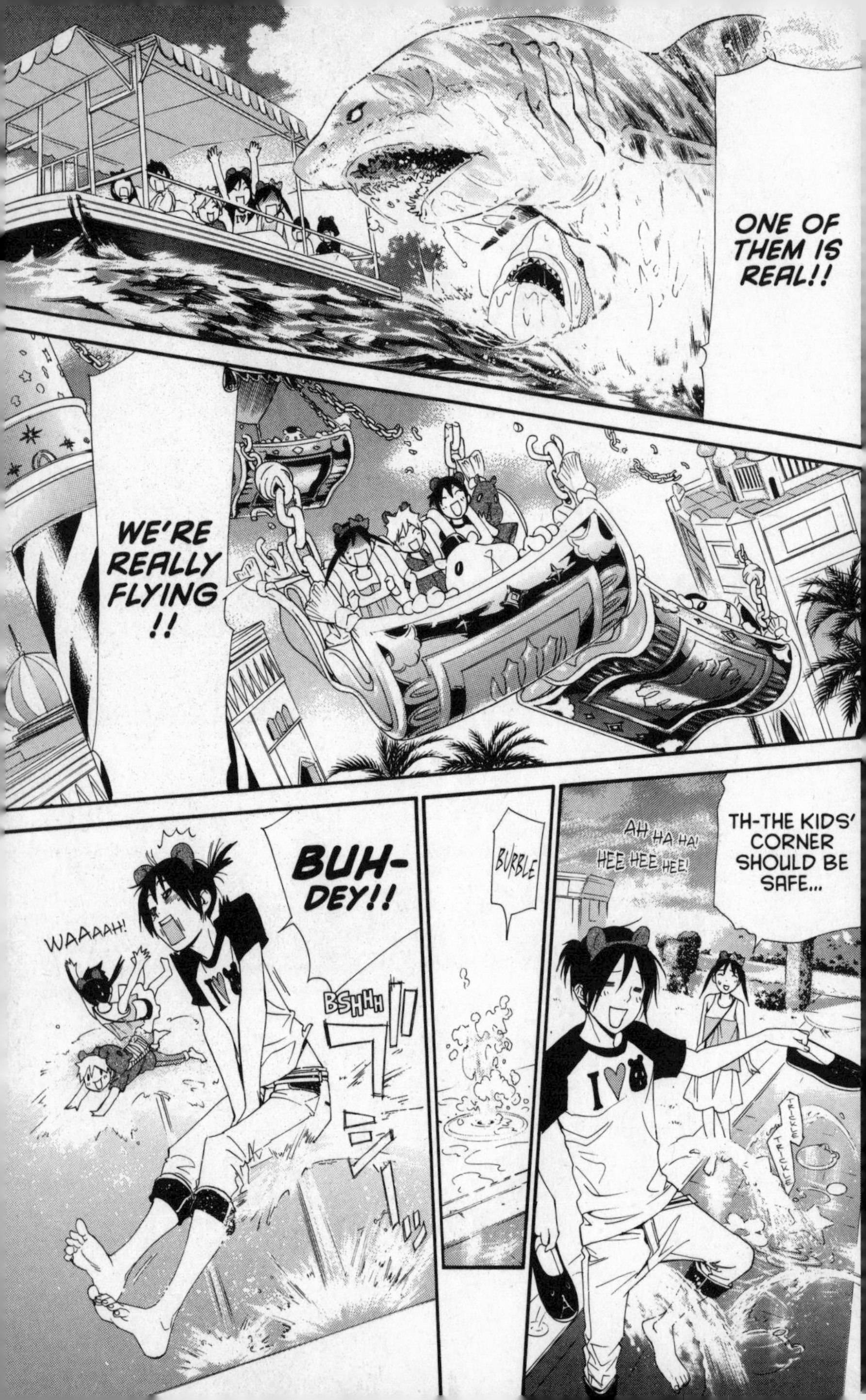
ONE OF THEM IS REAL!!
WE'RE REALLY FLYING !!
TH-THE KIDS' CORNER SHOULD BE SAFE...
AH HA HA! HEE HEE HEE!
TRICKLE TRICKLE
BURBLE
BUH-DEY!!
BSHHH
WAAAAH!

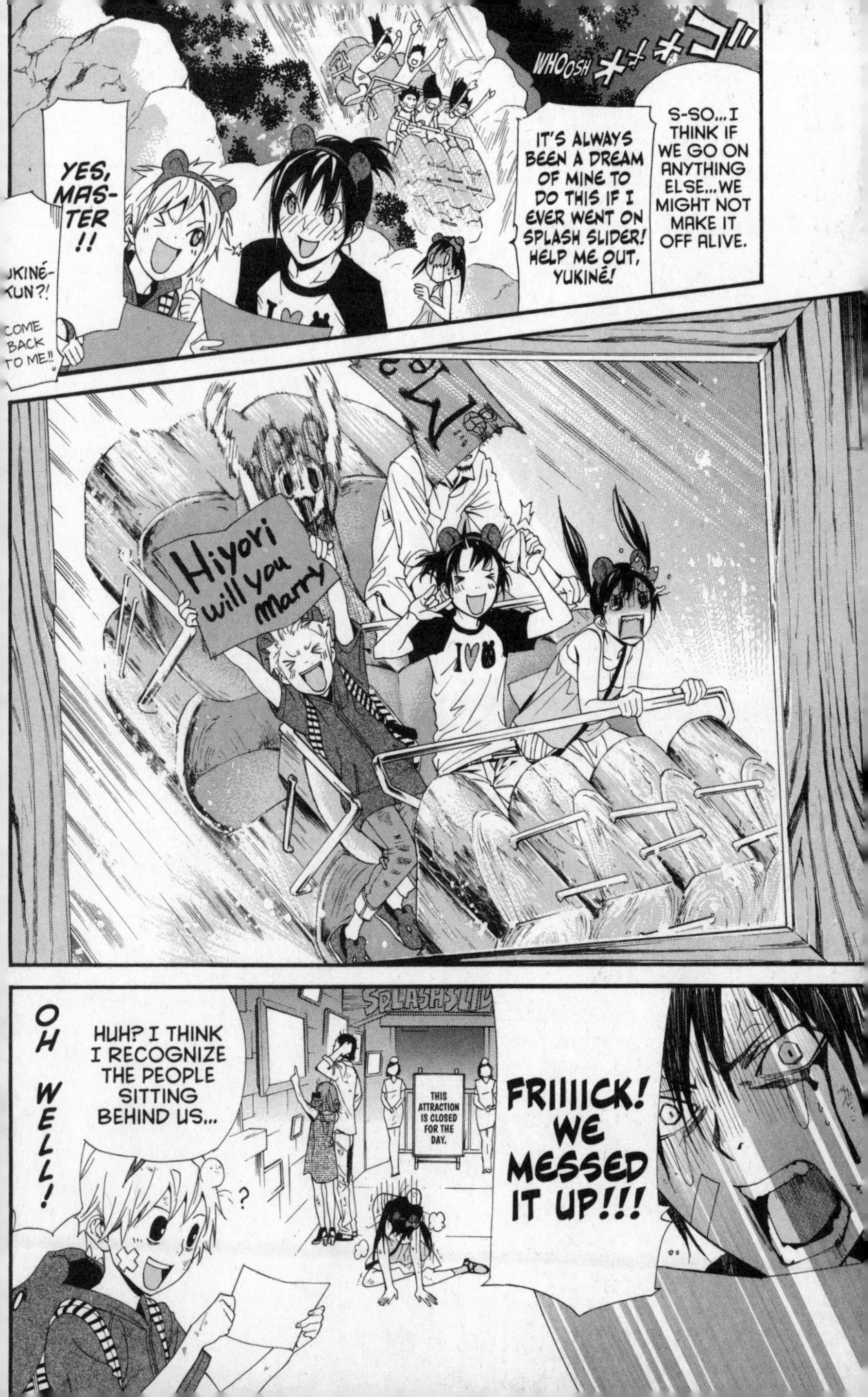
WHOOSH
S-SO...I THINK IF WE GO ON ANYTHING ELSE...WE MIGHT NOT MAKE IT OFF ALIVE.
IT'S ALWAYS BEEN A DREAM OF MINE TO DO THIS IF I EVER WENT ON SPLASH SLIDER! HELP ME OUT, YUKINÉ!
YES, MASTER!!
UKINÉ-KUN?!
COME BACK TO ME!!
Hiyori will you marry
FRIIIICK! WE MESSED IT UP!!!
SPLASH SLID
THIS ATTRACTION IS CLOSED FOR THE DAY.
HUH? I THINK I RECOGNIZE THE PEOPLE SITTING BEHIND US...
OH WELL!

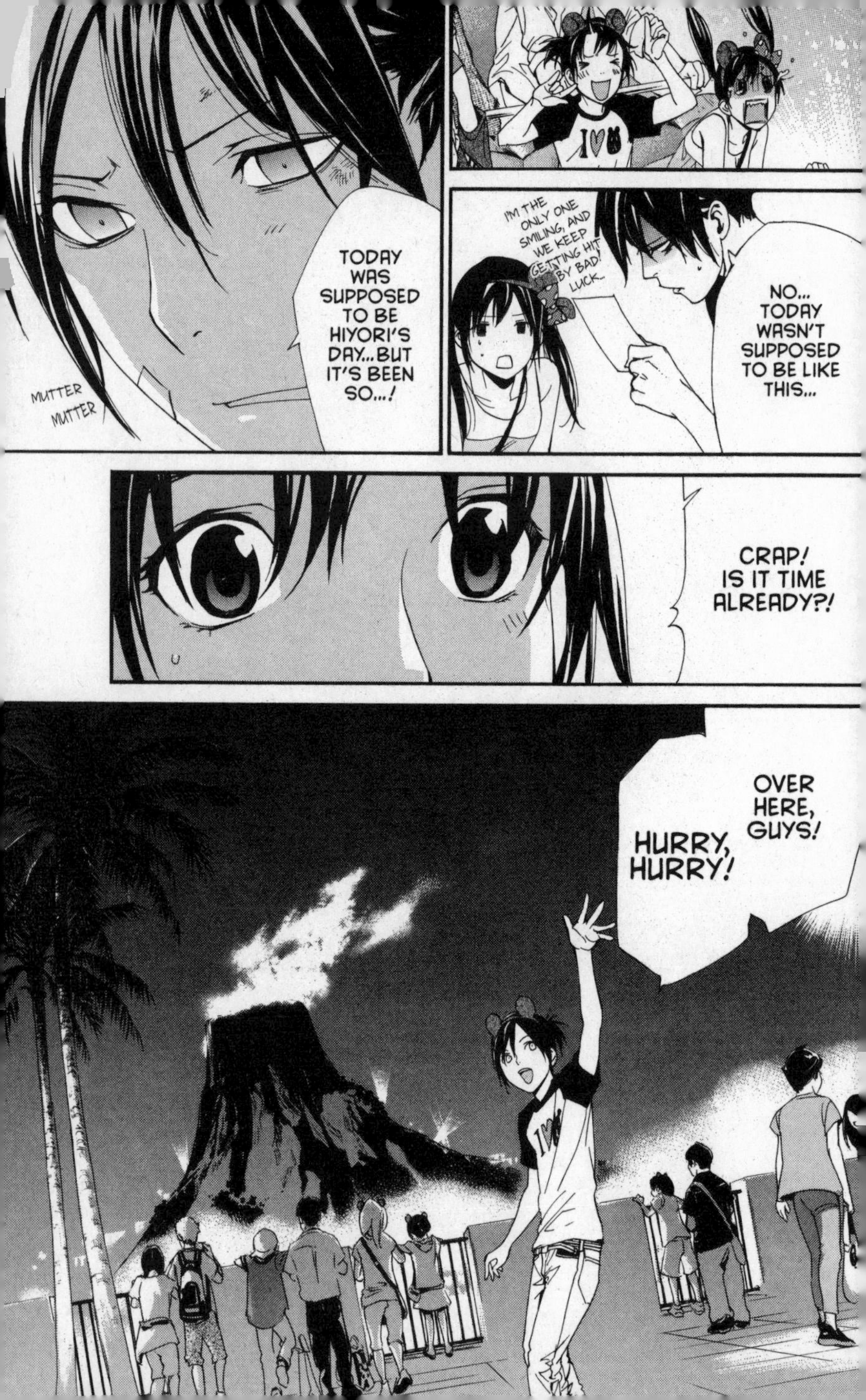
NO... TODAY WASN'T SUPPOSED TO BE LIKE THIS...
I'M THE ONLY ONE SMILING, AND WE KEEP GETTING HIT BY BAD LUCK...
TODAY WAS SUPPOSED TO BE HIYORI'S DAY...BUT IT'S BEEN SO...!
MUTTER MUTTER
CRAP! IS IT TIME ALREADY?!
OVER HERE, GUYS!
HURRY, HURRY!

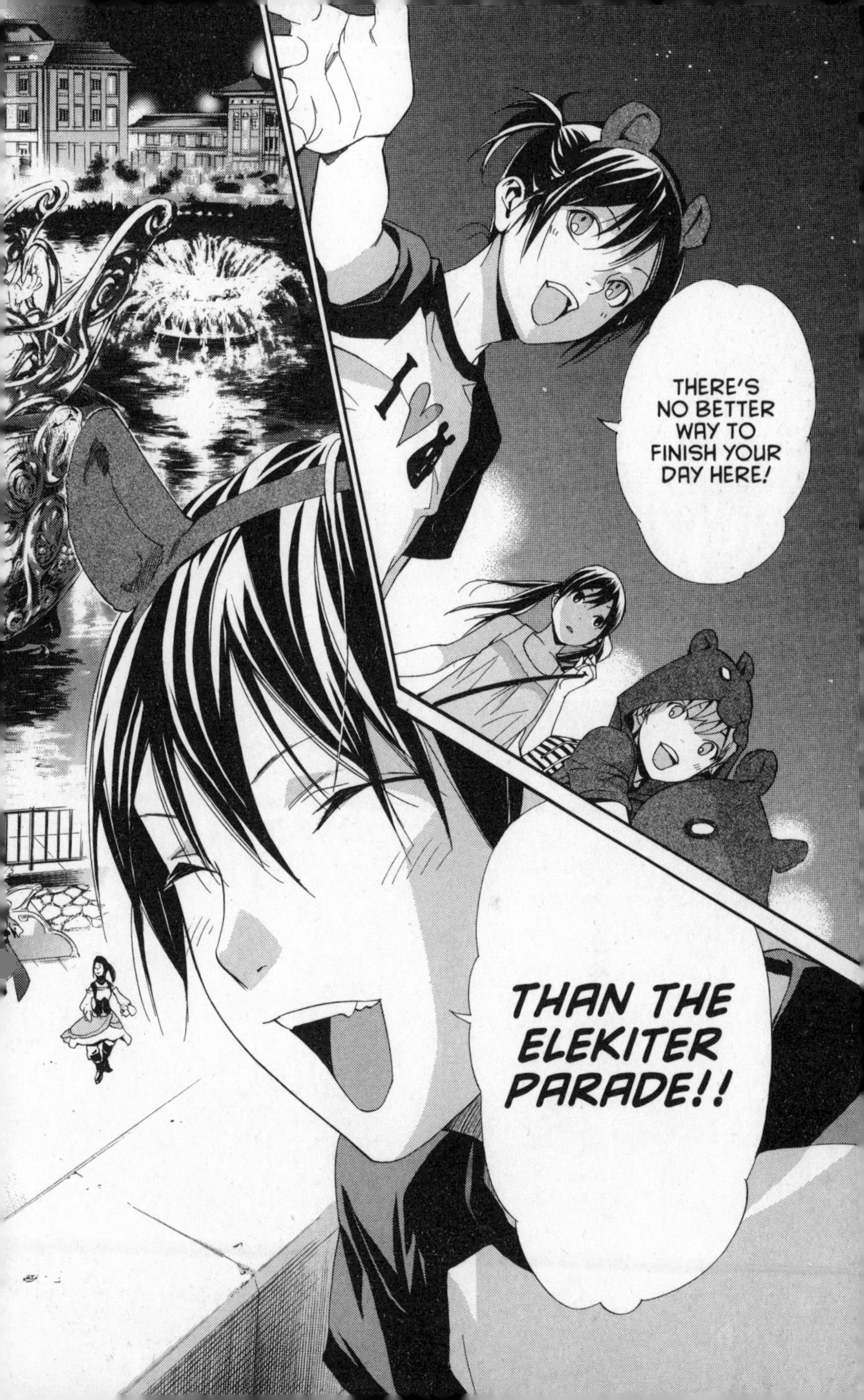
THERE'S NO BETTER WAY TO FINISH YOUR DAY HERE!
THAN THE ELEKITER PARADE!!

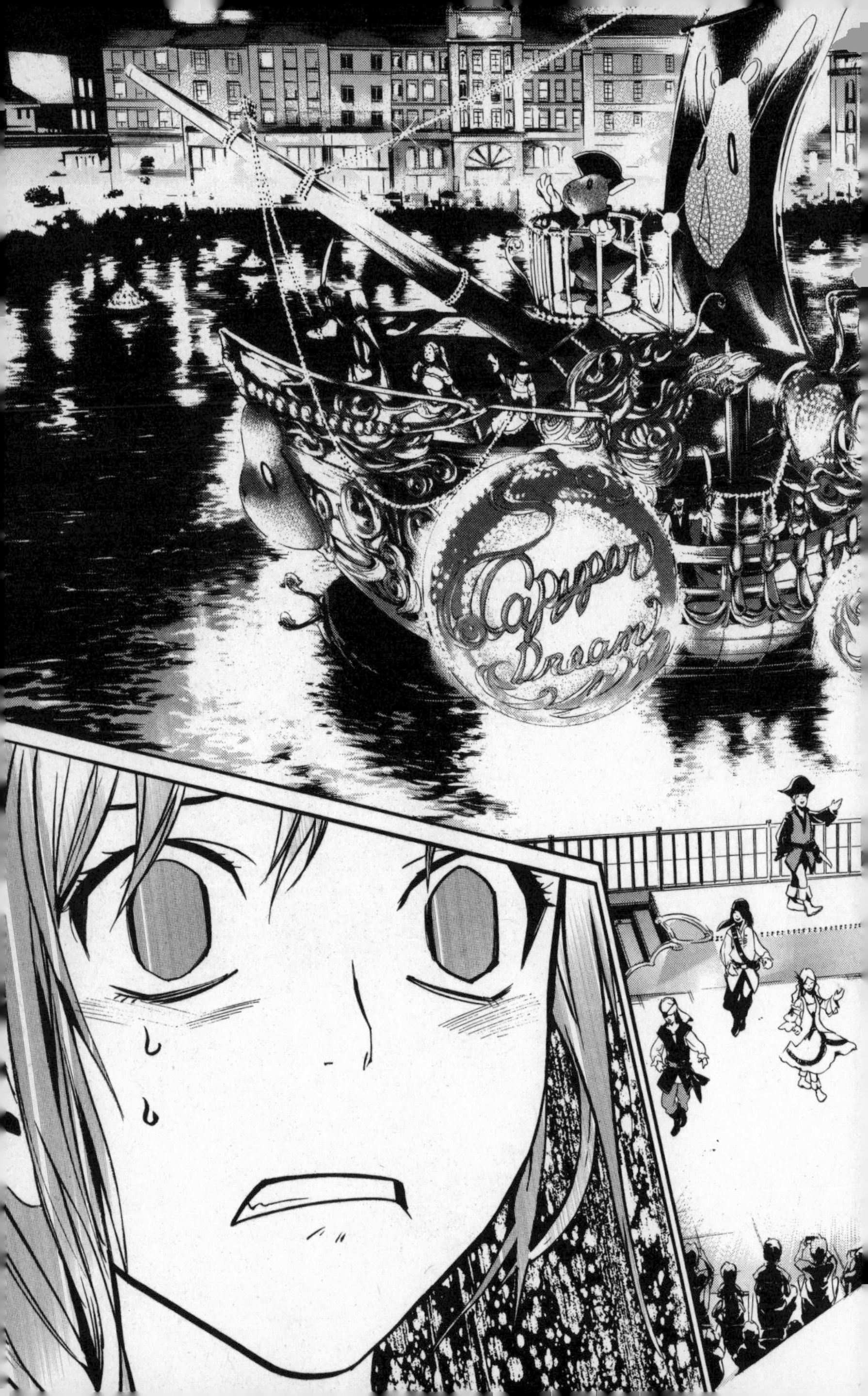

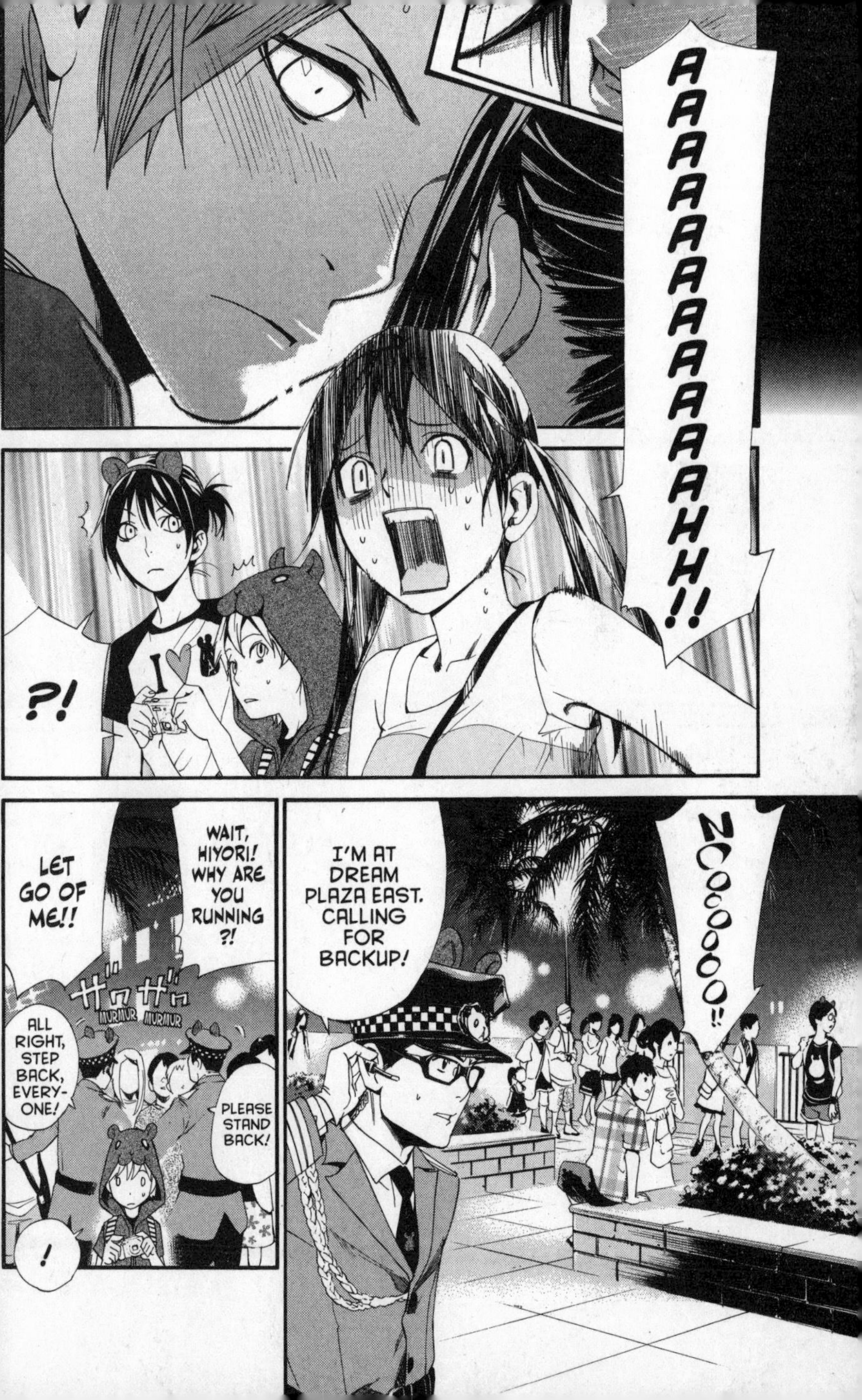
AAAAAAAAAAAHH!!
?!
NOOOOOOO!!
I'M AT DREAM PLAZA EAST. CALLING FOR BACKUP!
WAIT, HIYORI! WHY ARE YOU RUNNING?!
LET GO OF ME!!
ザワザワ
MURMUR MURMUR
PLEASE STAND BACK!
ALL RIGHT, STEP BACK, EVERYONE!
!

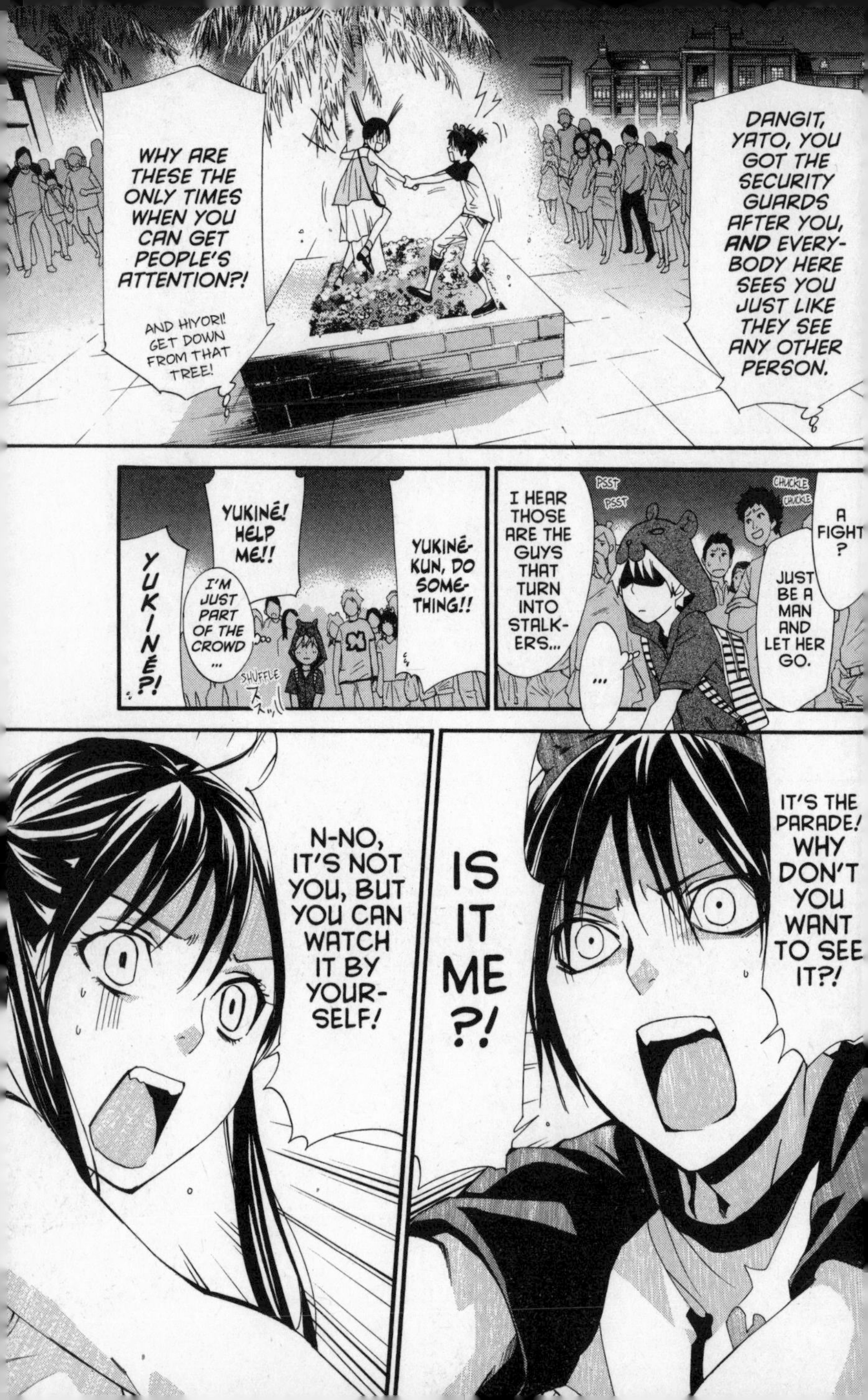
DANGIT, YATO, YOU GOT THE SECURITY GUARDS AFTER YOU, AND EVERYBODY HERE SEES YOU JUST LIKE THEY SEE ANY OTHER PERSON.
WHY ARE THESE THE ONLY TIMES WHEN YOU CAN GET PEOPLE'S ATTENTION?!
AND HIYORI! GET DOWN FROM THAT TREE!
CHUCKLE CHUCKLE
A FIGHT?
JUST BE A MAN AND LET HER GO.
PSST PSST
I HEAR THOSE ARE THE GUYS THAT TURN INTO STALKERS...
...
YUKINÉ-KUN, DO SOMETHING!!
YUKINÉ! HELP ME!!
YUKINÉ?!
I'M JUST PART OF THE CROWD ...
SHUFFLE
IT'S THE PARADE! WHY DON'T YOU WANT TO SEE IT?!
IS IT ME?!
N-NO, IT'S NOT YOU, BUT YOU CAN WATCH IT BY YOURSELF!

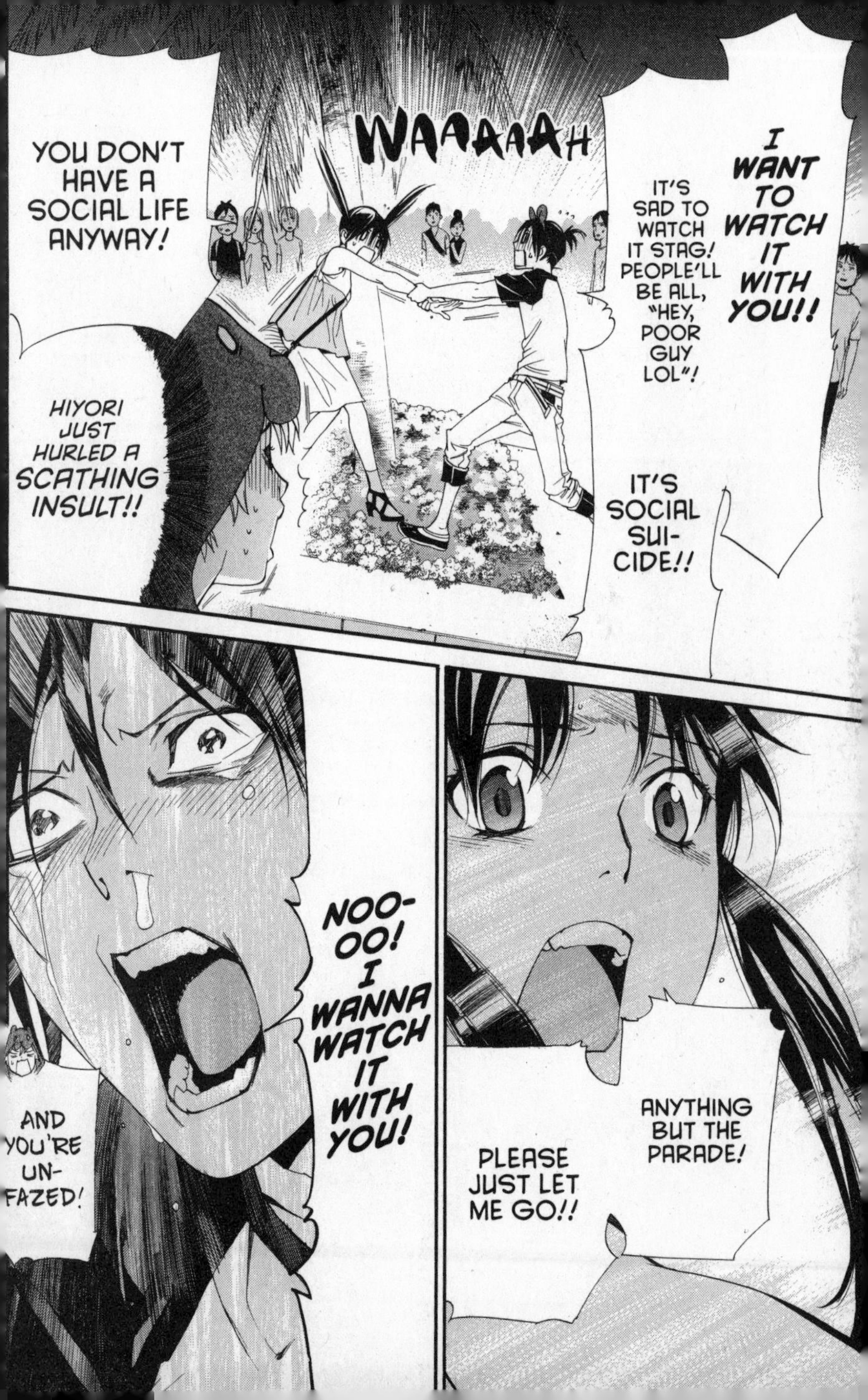
I WANT TO WATCH IT WITH YOU!!
IT'S SAD TO WATCH IT STAG! PEOPLE'LL BE ALL, "HEY, POOR GUY LOL"!
IT'S SOCIAL SUI-CIDE!!
WAAAAAH
YOU DON'T HAVE A SOCIAL LIFE ANYWAY!
HIYORI JUST HURLED A SCATHING INSULT!!
ANYTHING BUT THE PARADE!
PLEASE JUST LET ME GO!!
NOO-OO! I WANNA WATCH IT WITH YOU!
AND YOU'RE UN-FAZED!

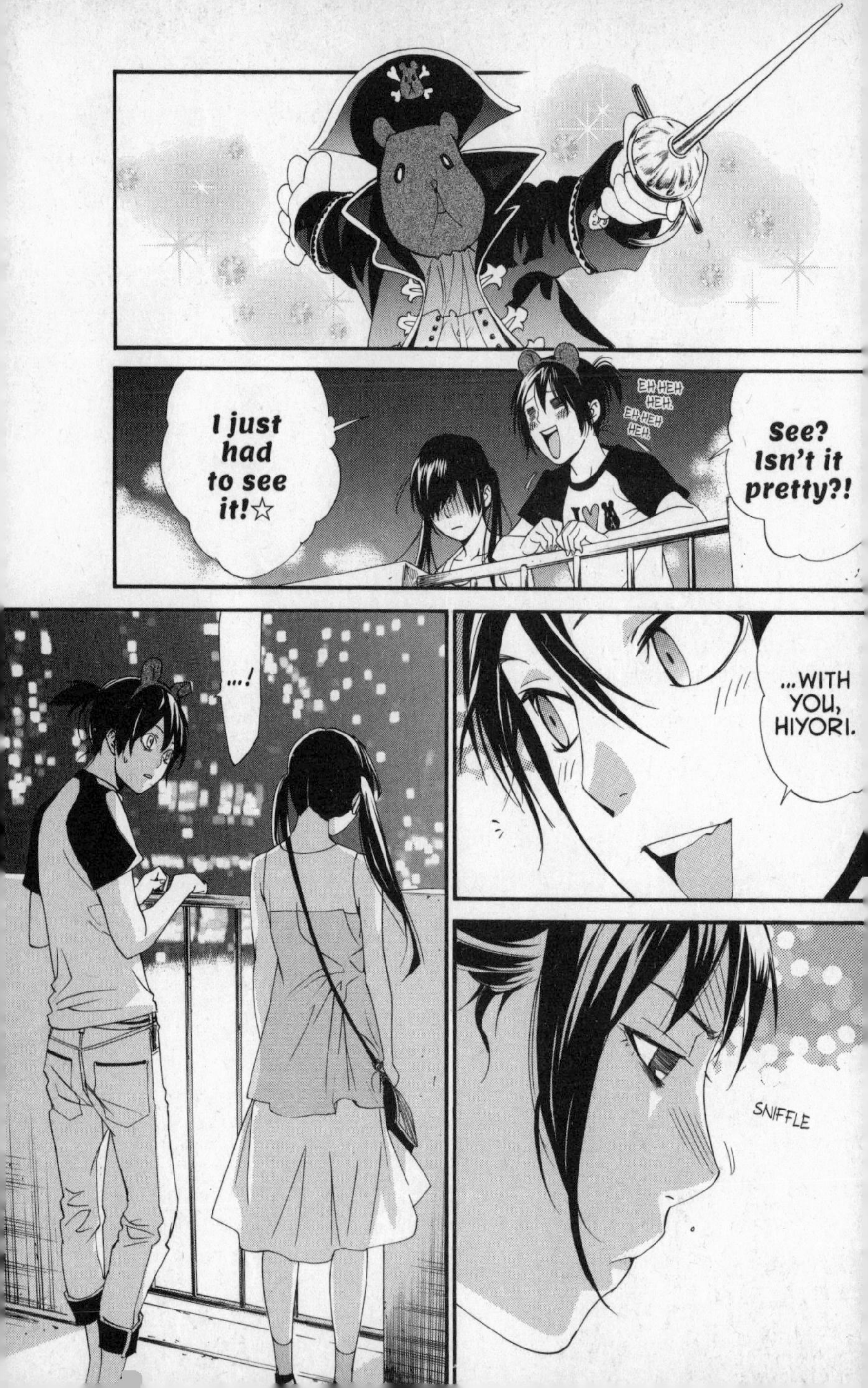
See? Isn't it pretty?!
EH HEH HEH. EH HEH HEH.
I just had to see it!☆
...WITH YOU, HIYORI.
SNIFFLE
...!

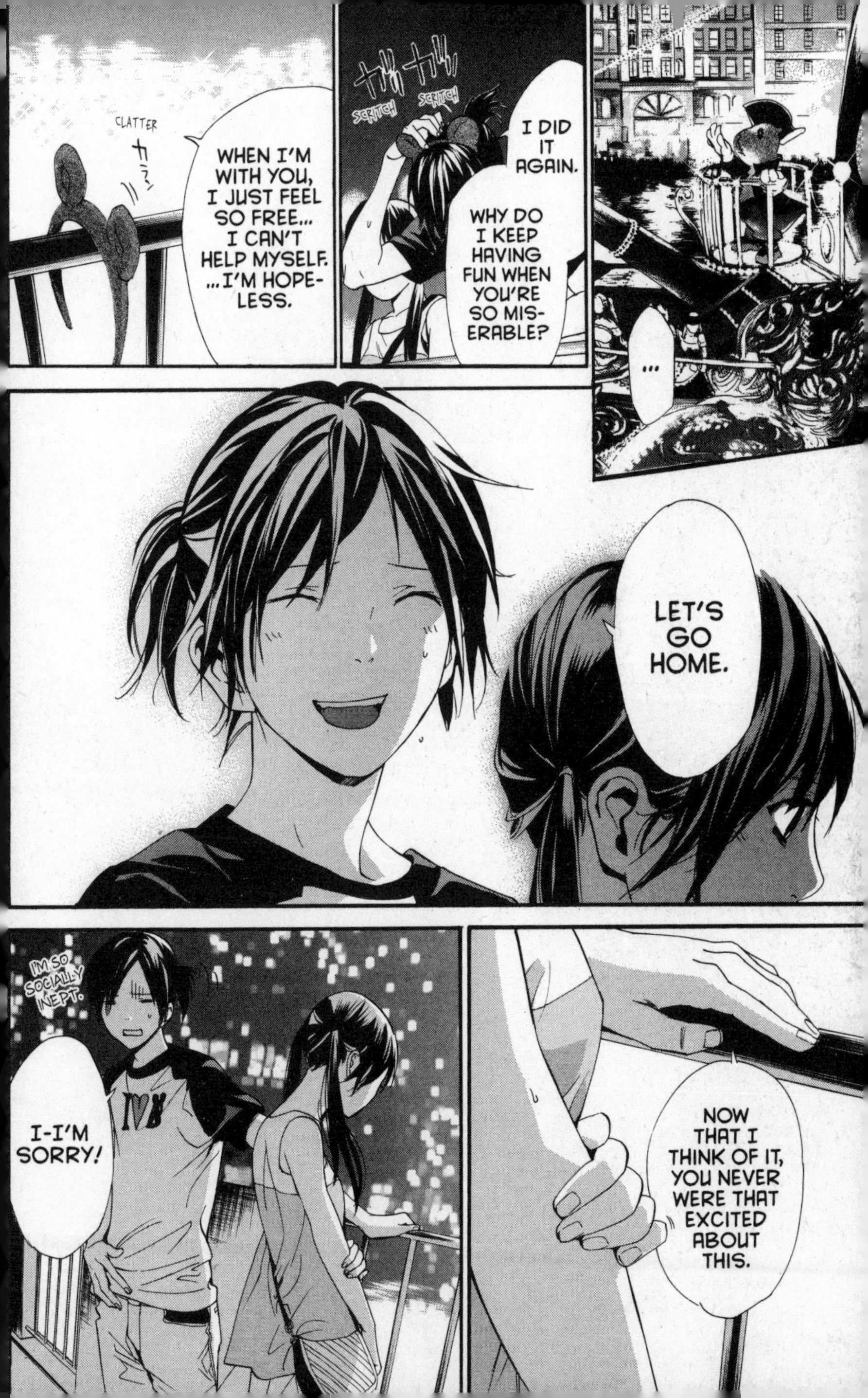
...
SCRATCH SCRATCH
I DID IT AGAIN.
WHY DO I KEEP HAVING FUN WHEN YOU'RE SO MISERABLE?
CLATTER
WHEN I'M WITH YOU, I JUST FEEL SO FREE... I CAN'T HELP MYSELF. ...I'M HOPELESS.
LET'S GO HOME.
NOW THAT I THINK OF IT, YOU NEVER WERE THAT EXCITED ABOUT THIS.
I'M SO SOCIALLY INEPT.
I-I'M SORRY!

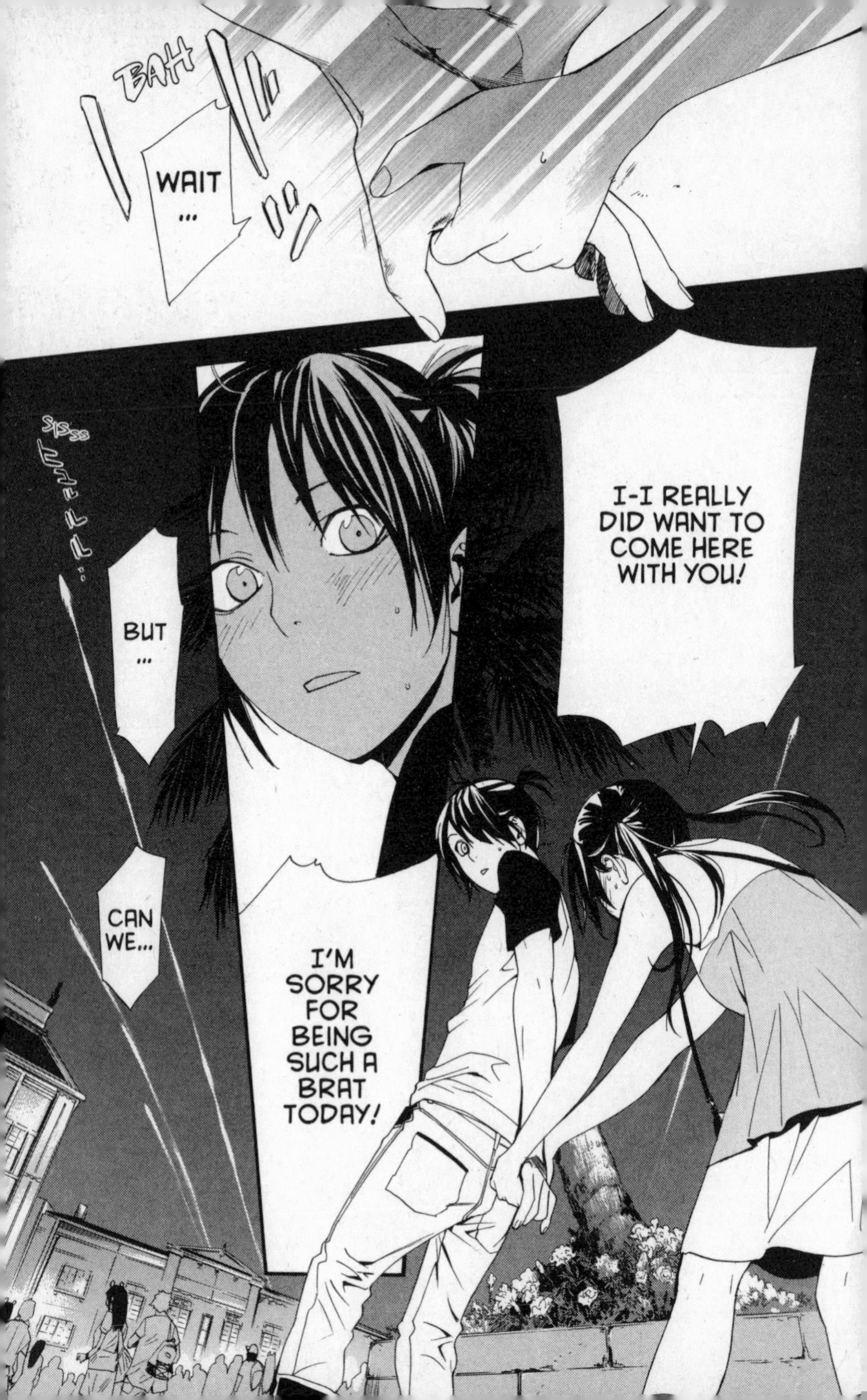
BAH
WAIT ...
I-I REALLY DID WANT TO COME HERE WITH YOU!
I'M SORRY FOR BEING SUCH A BRAT TODAY!
SISSS
BUT ...
CAN WE...

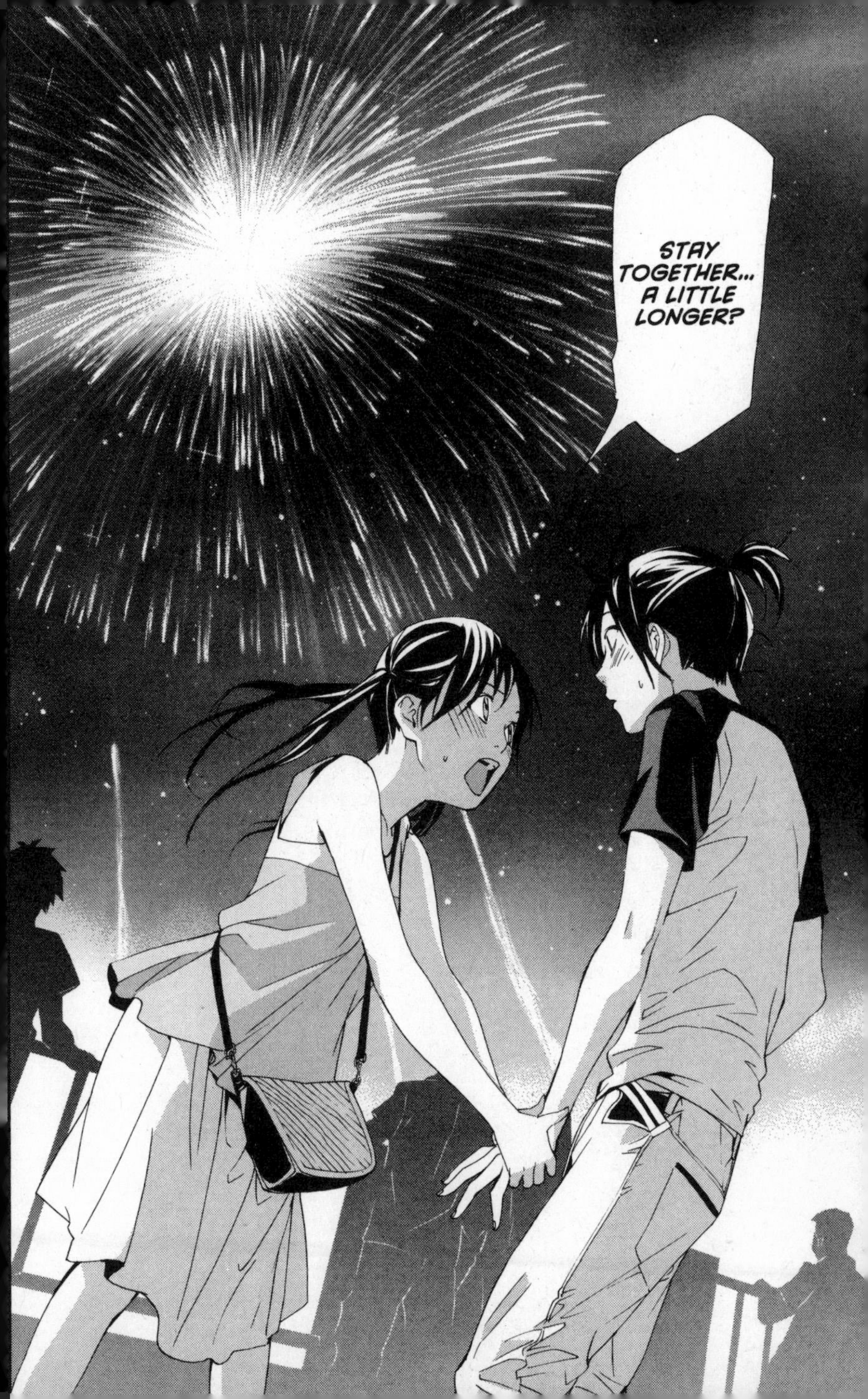
STAY TOGETHER... A LITTLE LONGER?

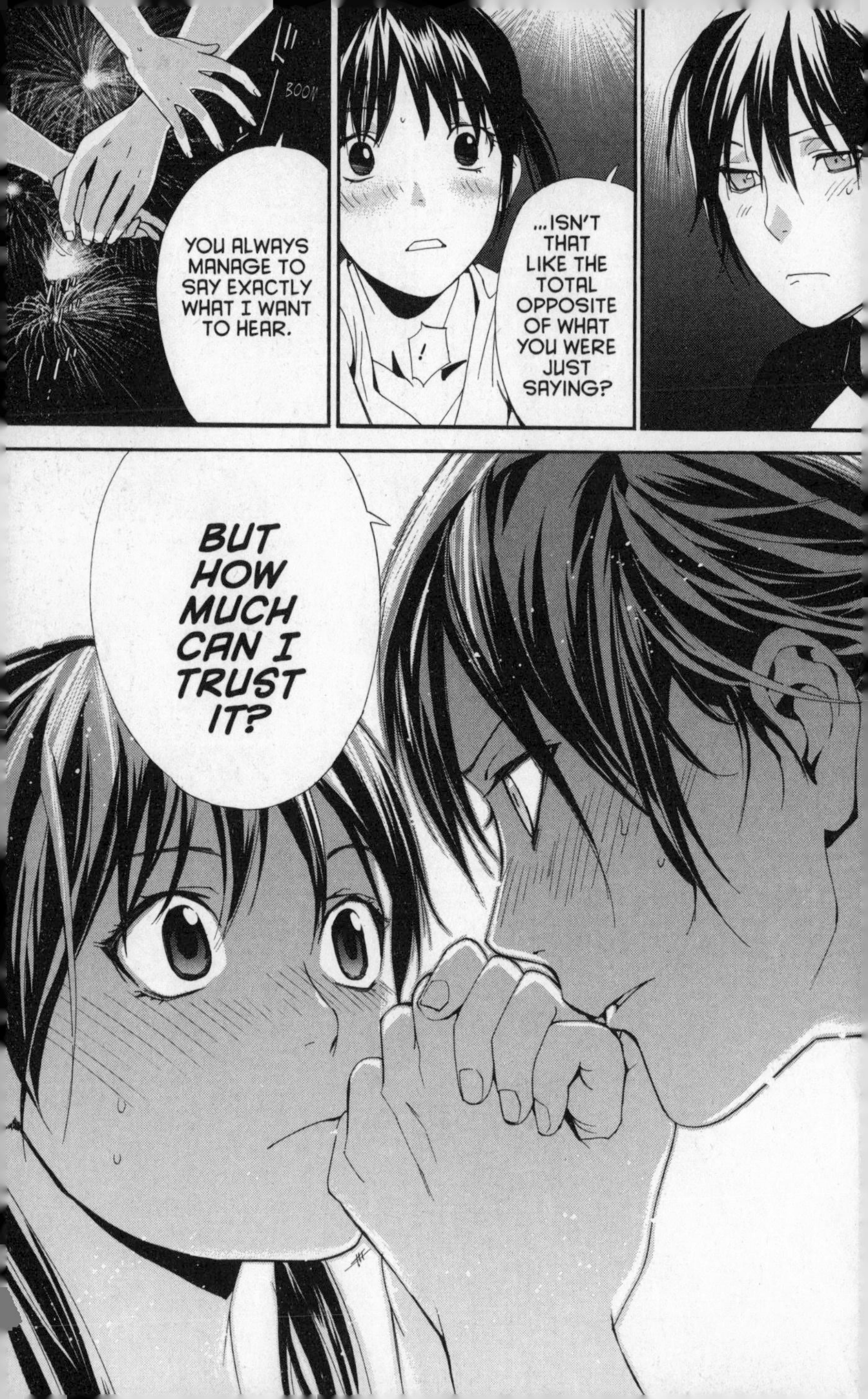
...ISN'T THAT LIKE THE TOTAL OPPOSITE OF WHAT YOU WERE JUST SAYING?
BOOM
YOU ALWAYS MANAGE TO SAY EXACTLY WHAT I WANT TO HEAR.
BUT HOW MUCH CAN I TRUST IT?

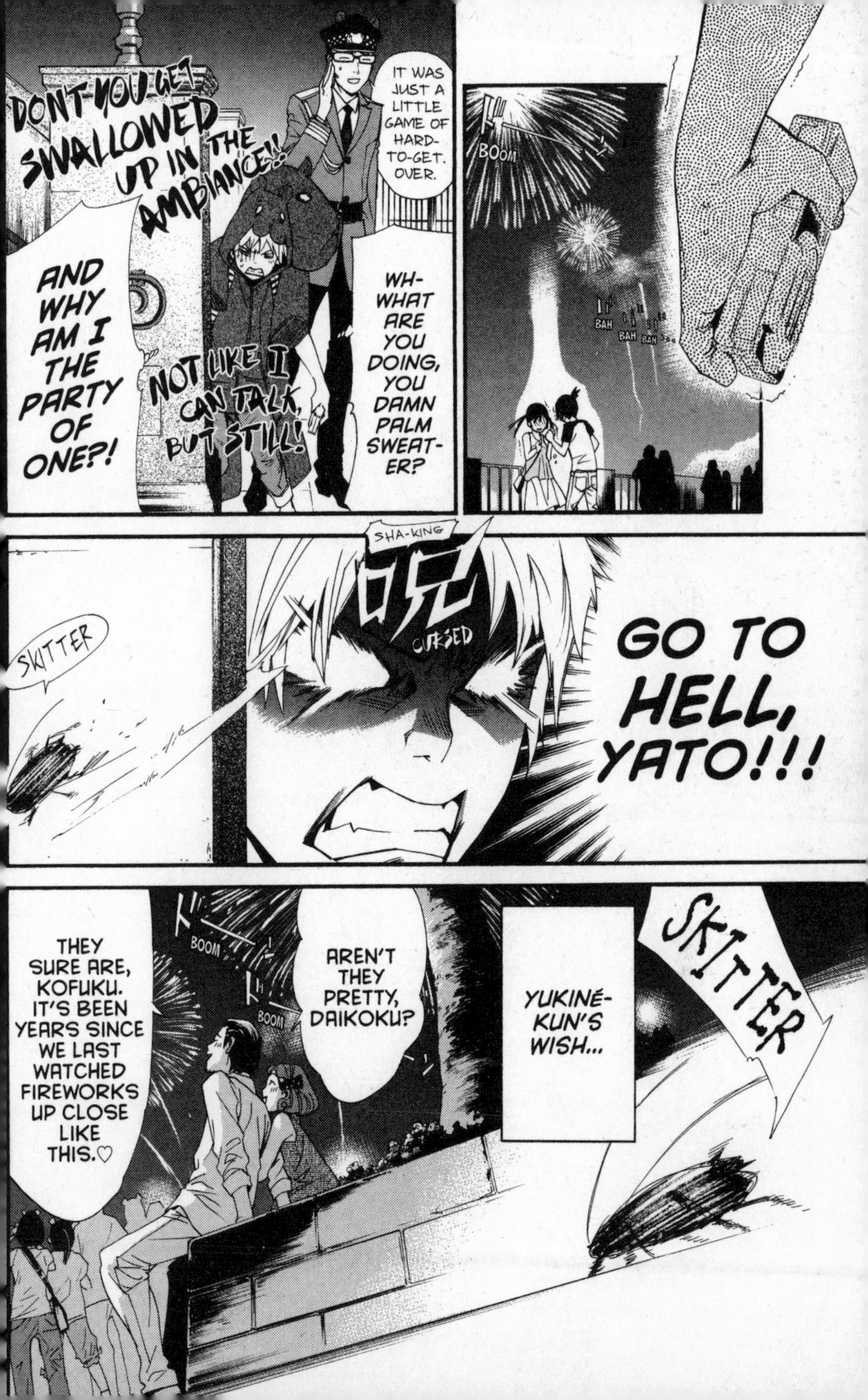
BOOM
BAH
BAH
BAH
IT WAS JUST A LITTLE GAME OF HARD-TO-GET. OVER.
WH-WHAT ARE YOU DOING, YOU DAMN PALM SWEATER?
DON'T YOU GET SWALLOWED UP IN THE AMBIANCE!!
NOT LIKE I CAN TALK, BUT STILL!
AND WHY AM I THE PARTY OF ONE?!
GO TO HELL, YATO!!!
SHA-KING
CURSED
SKITTER
SKITTER
YUKINÉ-KUN'S WISH...
AREN'T THEY PRETTY, DAIKOKU?
BOOM
BOOM
THEY SURE ARE, KOFUKU. IT'S BEEN YEARS SINCE WE LAST WATCHED FIREWORKS UP CLOSE LIKE THIS.♡

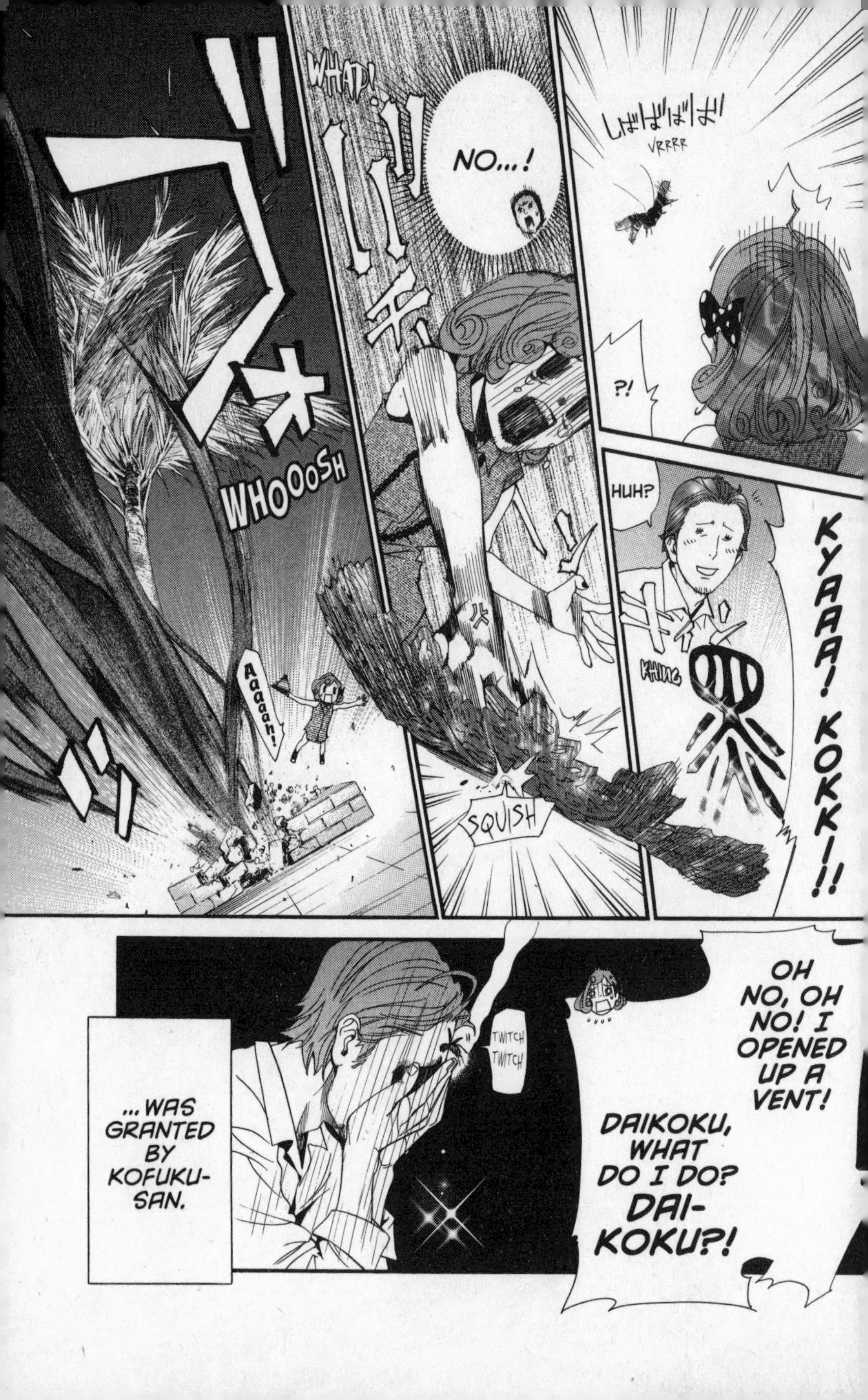
VRRRR
?!
HUH?
KHING
KYAAA! KOKKI!!
WHAT?!
NO...!
SQUISH
WHOOOSH
Aaaaah!
OH NO, OH NO! I OPENED UP A VENT!
DAIKOKU, WHAT DO I DO? DAI-KOKU?!
TWITCH TWITCH
...WAS GRANTED BY KOFUKU-SAN.

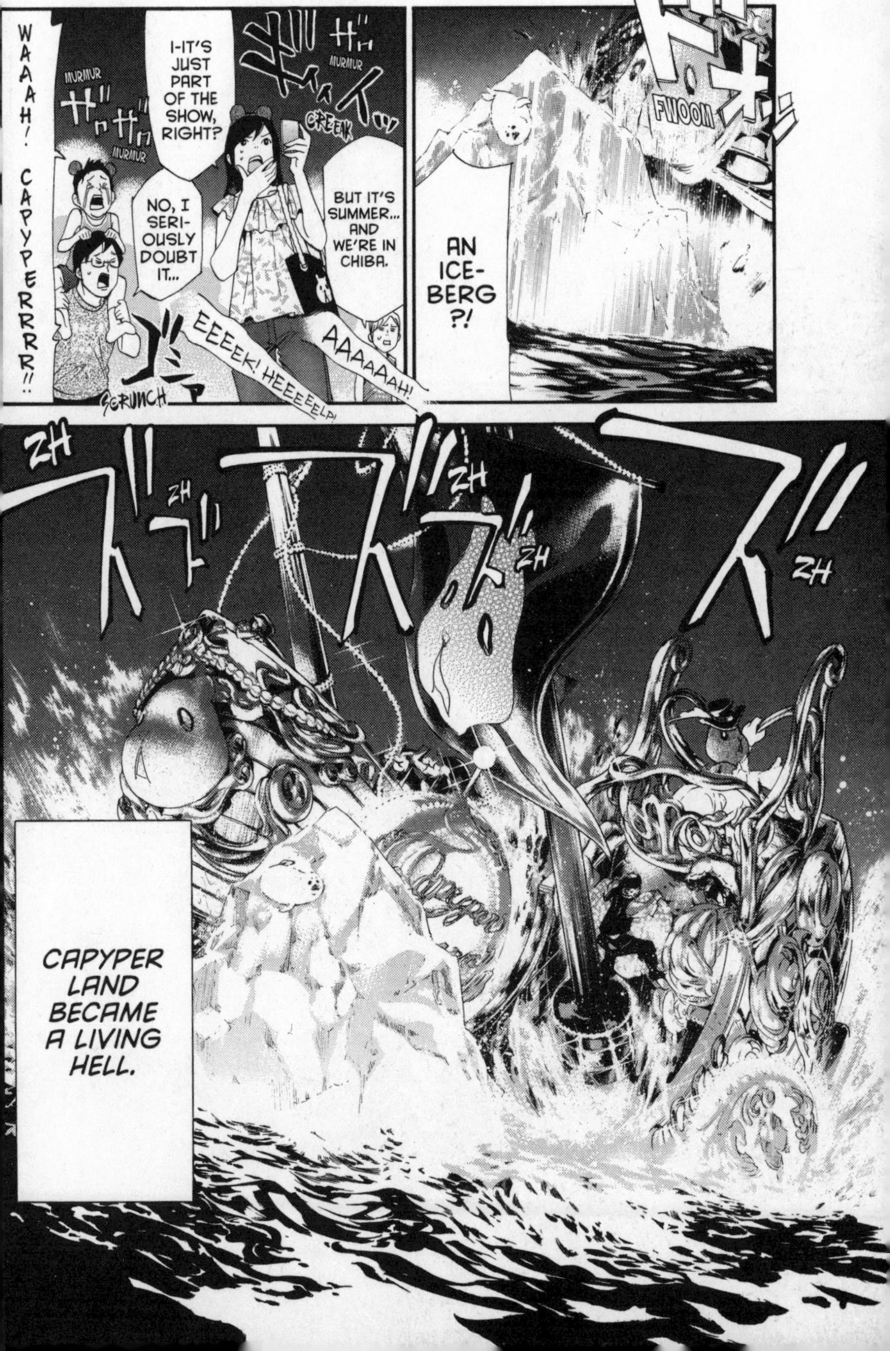
FWOOM
AN ICE-BERG?!
I-IT'S JUST PART OF THE SHOW, RIGHT?
MURMUR
CREEAK
BUT IT'S SUMMER... AND WE'RE IN CHIBA.
NO, I SERIOUSLY DOUBT IT...
MURMUR
MURMUR
WAAAAH! CAPYPERRRR!!
AAAAAAAH!
EEEEEK! HEEEEEELP!
SCRUNCH
ZH
ZH
ZH
ZH
ZH
CAPYPER LAND BECAME A LIVING HELL.

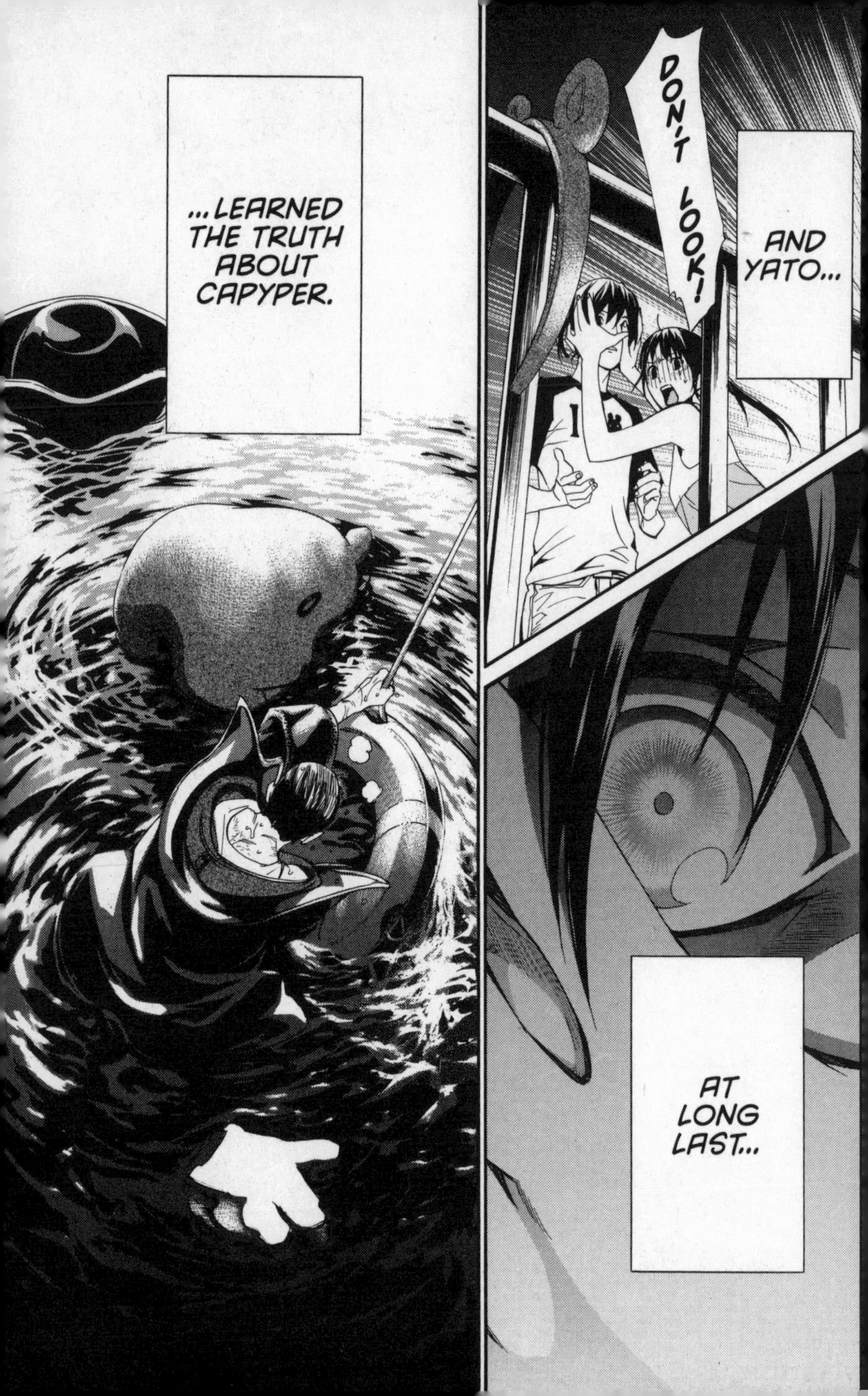
DON'T LOOK!
AND YATO...
AT LONG LAST...
...LEARNED THE TRUTH ABOUT CAPYPER.

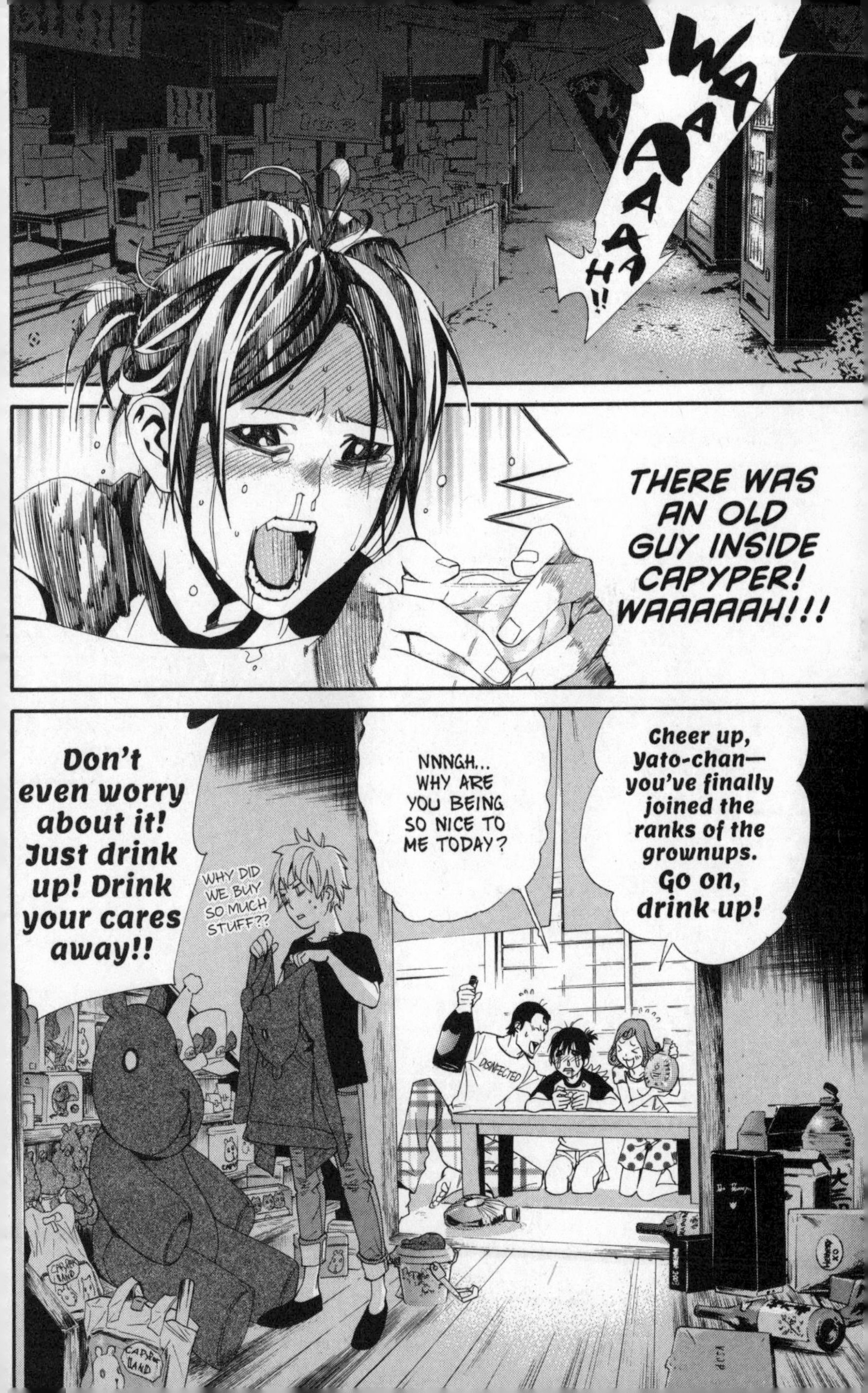
WAAAAAAH!!
THERE WAS AN OLD GUY INSIDE CAPYPER! WAAAAAH!!!
Cheer up, Yato-chan—you've finally joined the ranks of the grownups. Go on, drink up!
NNNGH... WHY ARE YOU BEING SO NICE TO ME TODAY?
Don't even worry about it! Just drink up! Drink your cares away!!
WHY DID WE BUY SO MUCH STUFF??
DISINFECTED

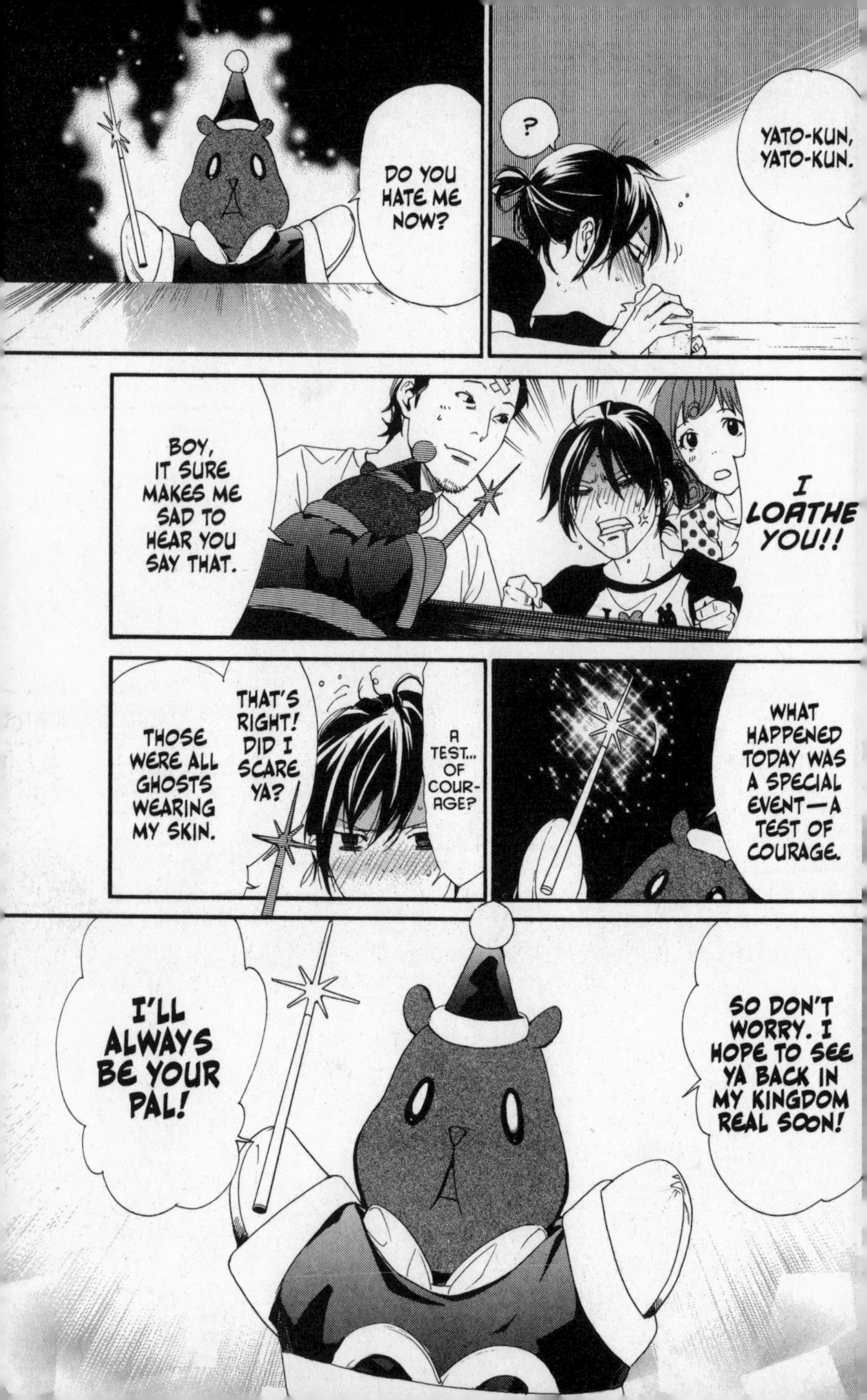
YATO-KUN, YATO-KUN.
?
DO YOU HATE ME NOW?
I LOATHE YOU!!
BOY, IT SURE MAKES ME SAD TO HEAR YOU SAY THAT.
WHAT HAPPENED TODAY WAS A SPECIAL EVENT—A TEST OF COURAGE.
A TEST... OF COURAGE?
THAT'S RIGHT! DID I SCARE YA?
THOSE WERE ALL GHOSTS WEARING MY SKIN.
SO DON'T WORRY. I HOPE TO SEE YA BACK IN MY KINGDOM REAL SOON!
I'LL ALWAYS BE YOUR PAL!

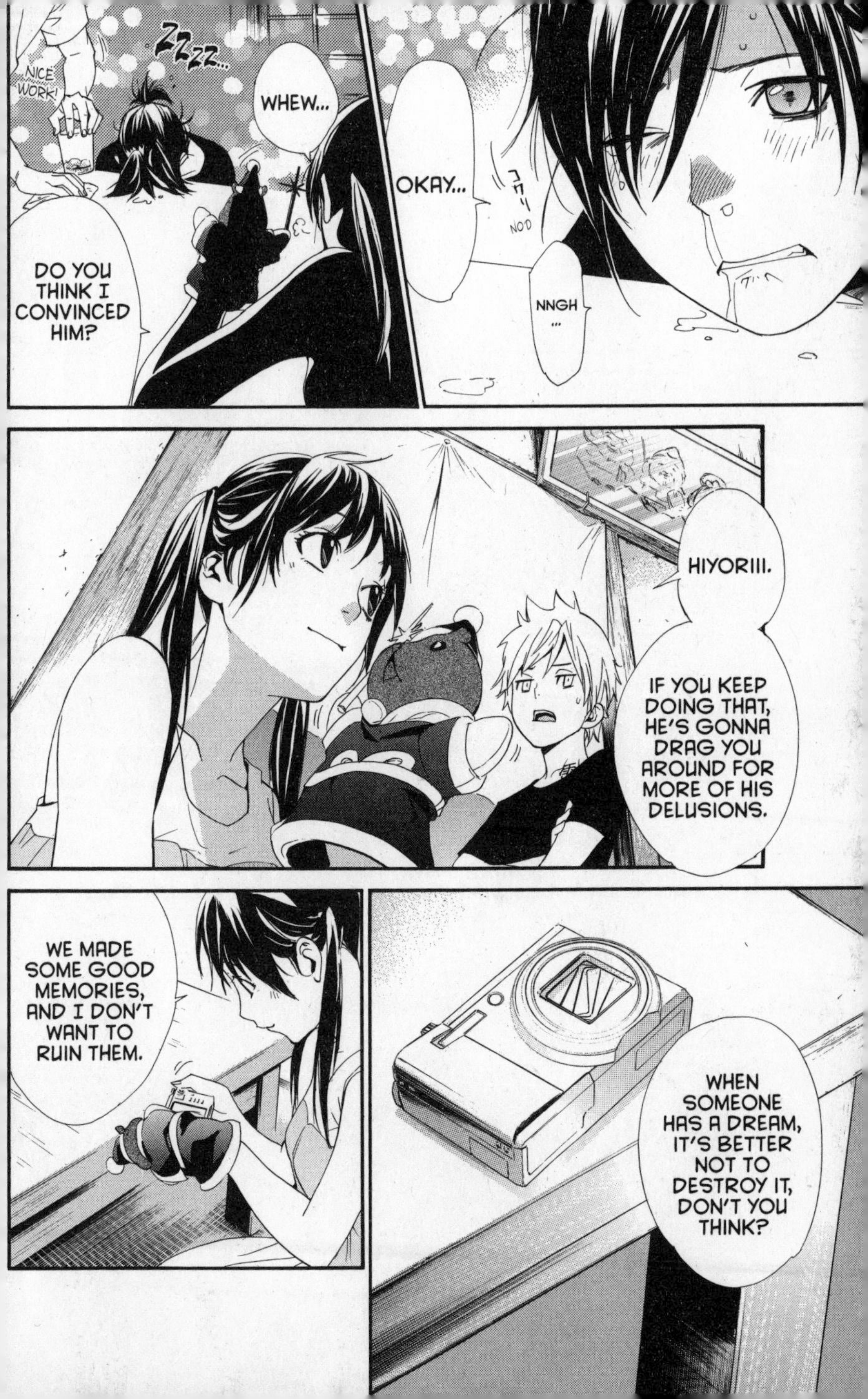
OKAY...
コクリ
NOD
NNGH ...
ZZZZ...
NICE WORK!
WHEW...
DO YOU THINK I CONVINCED HIM?
HIYORIII.
IF YOU KEEP DOING THAT, HE'S GONNA DRAG YOU AROUND FOR MORE OF HIS DELUSIONS.
WHEN SOMEONE HAS A DREAM, IT'S BETTER NOT TO DESTROY IT, DON'T YOU THINK?
WE MADE SOME GOOD MEMORIES, AND I DON'T WANT TO RUIN THEM.

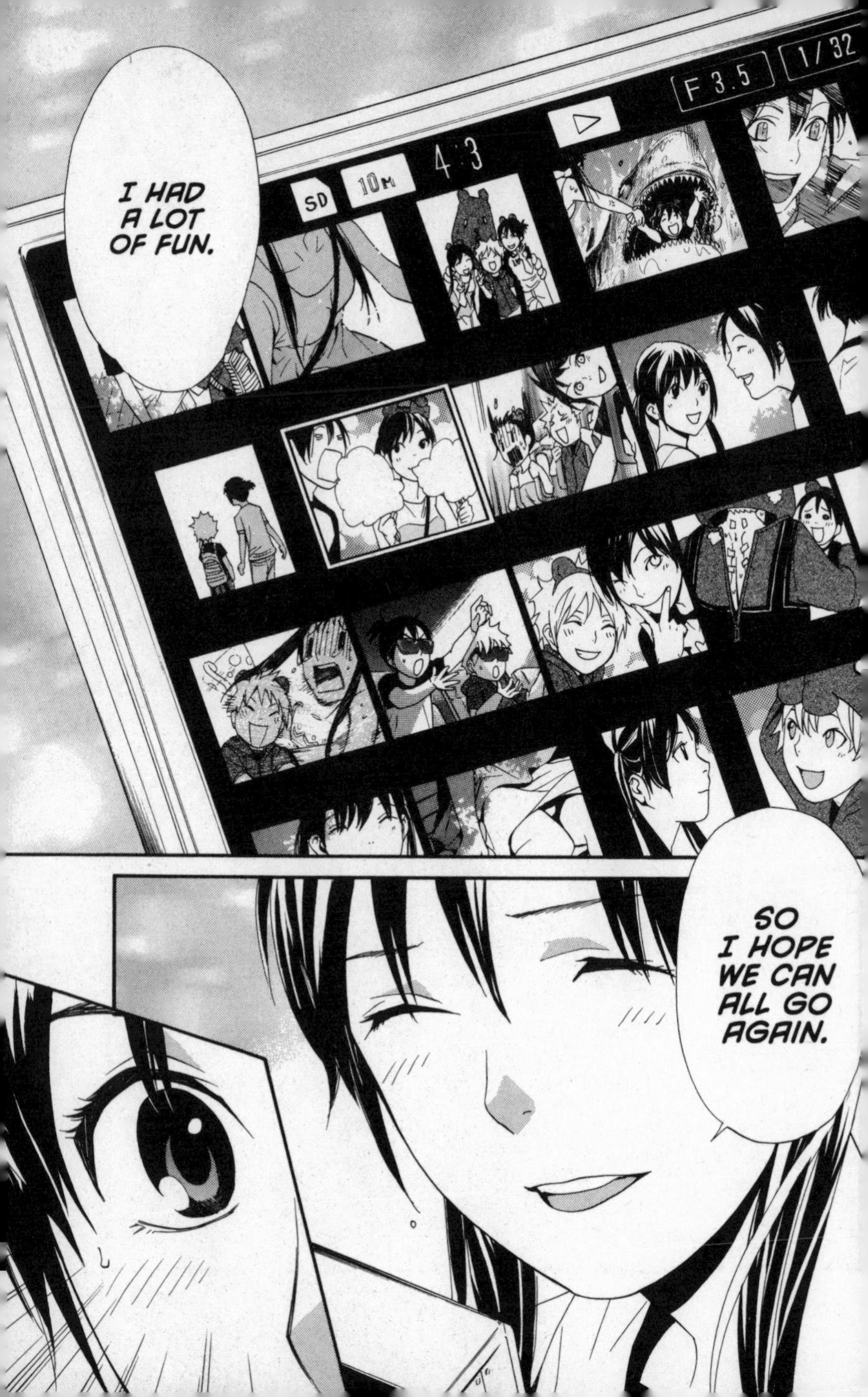
I HAD A LOT OF FUN.
F 3.5
1/32
SD
10M
4:3
SO I HOPE WE CAN ALL GO AGAIN.

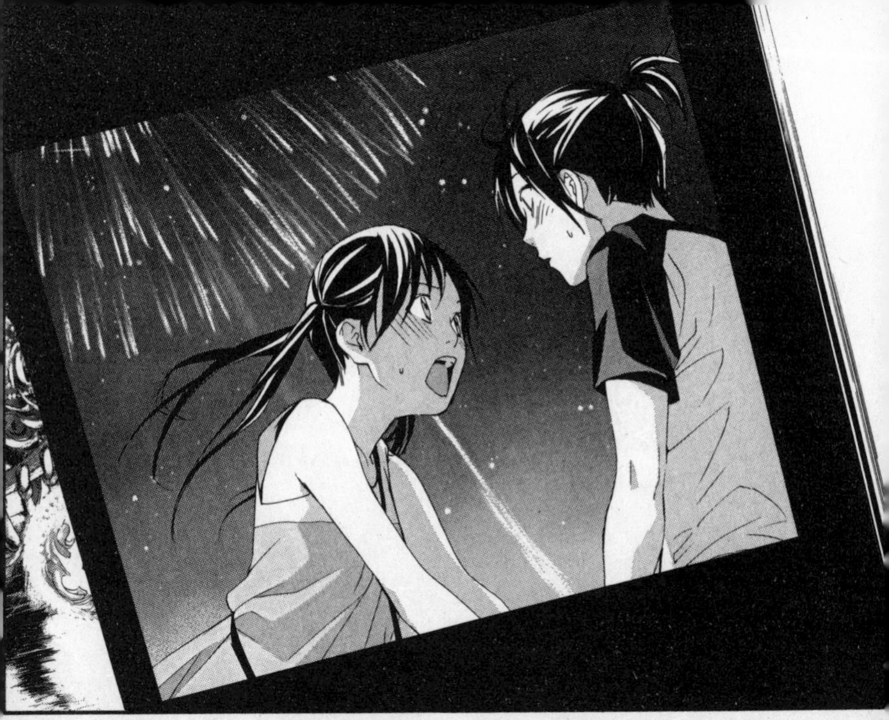

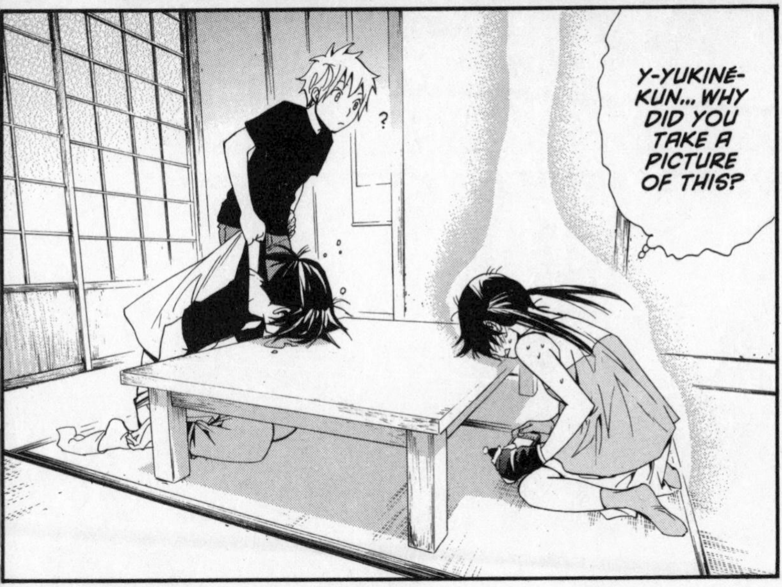
Y-YUKINÉ-KUN... WHY DID YOU TAKE A PICTURE OF THIS?
?

CHAPTER 41 / END

野

草

神

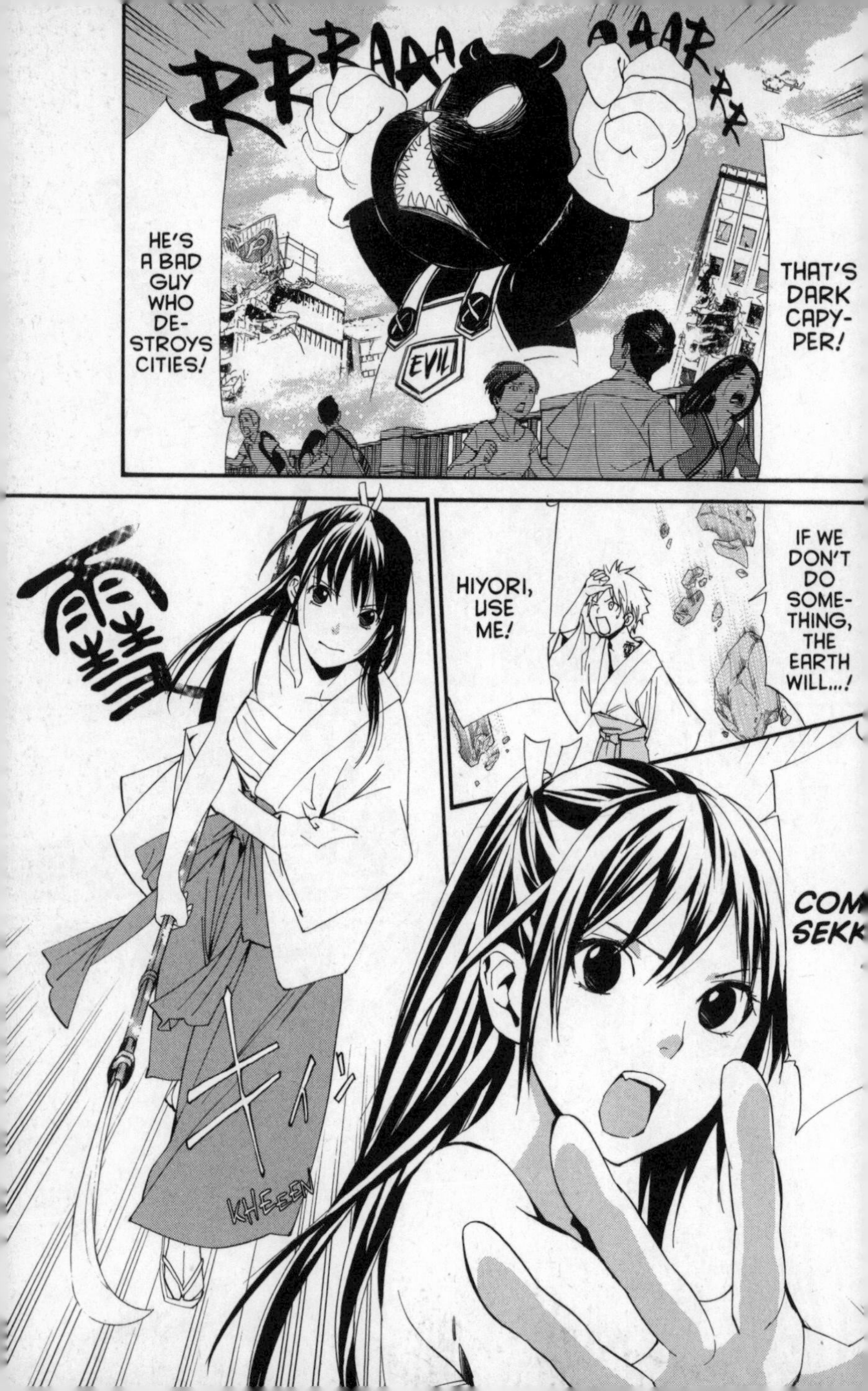
RRRAAAA AAARRR
THAT'S DARK CAPY-PER!
HE'S A BAD GUY WHO DE-STROYS CITIES!
IF WE DON'T DO SOME-THING, THE EARTH WILL...!
HIYORI, USE ME!
COM
SEKK
雪
KHE-EEN

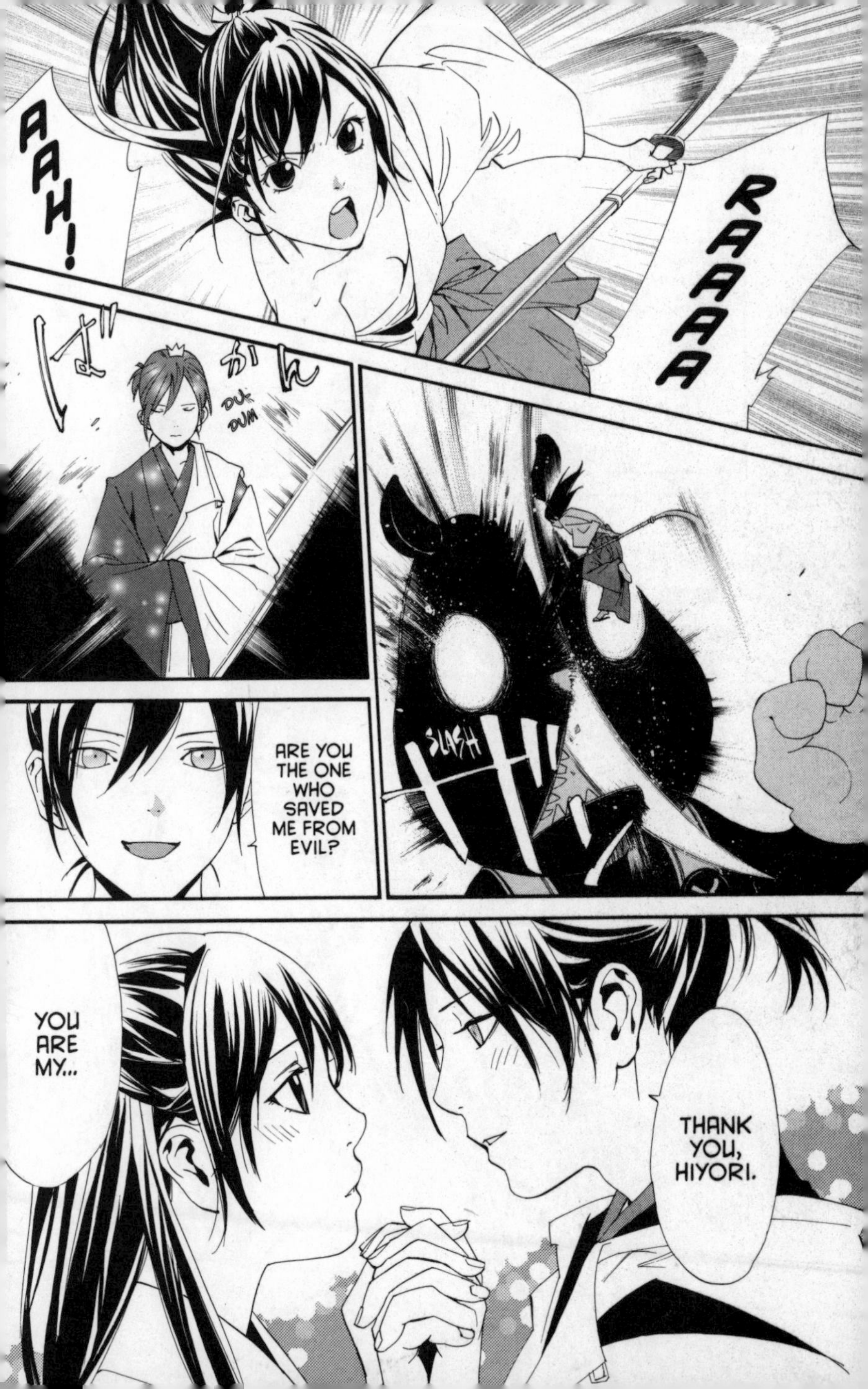
RAAAAA
AAH!
SLASH
ばかん
DU-DUM
ARE YOU THE ONE WHO SAVED ME FROM EVIL?
THANK YOU, HIYORI.
YOU ARE MY...

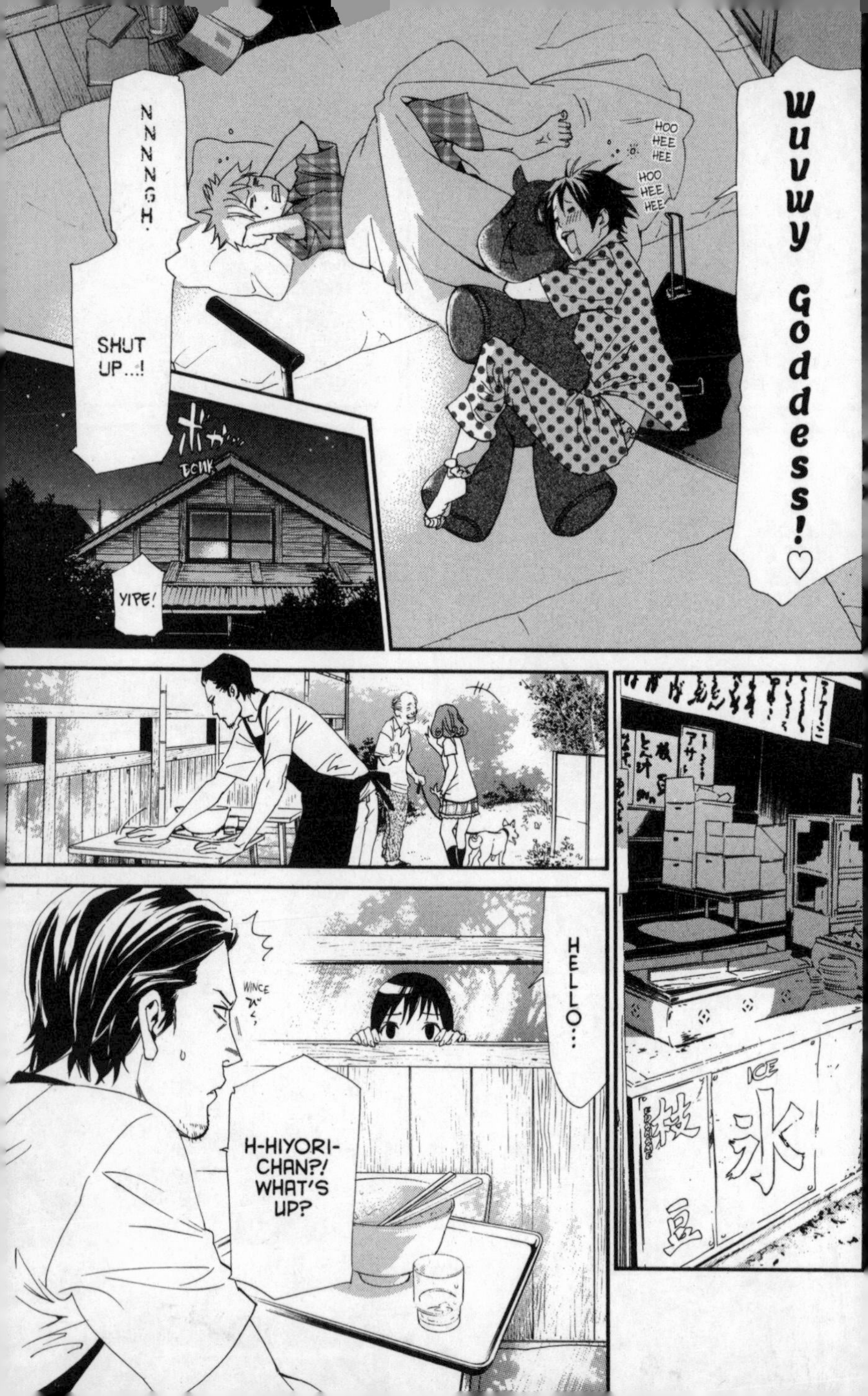

Wuvwy Goddess!♡
HOO HEE HEE
HOO HEE HEE
NNNNGH.
SHUT UP...!
ボガ…
TONK
YIPE!
ICE
氷
HELLO...
WINCE
H-HIYORI-CHAN?! WHAT'S UP?

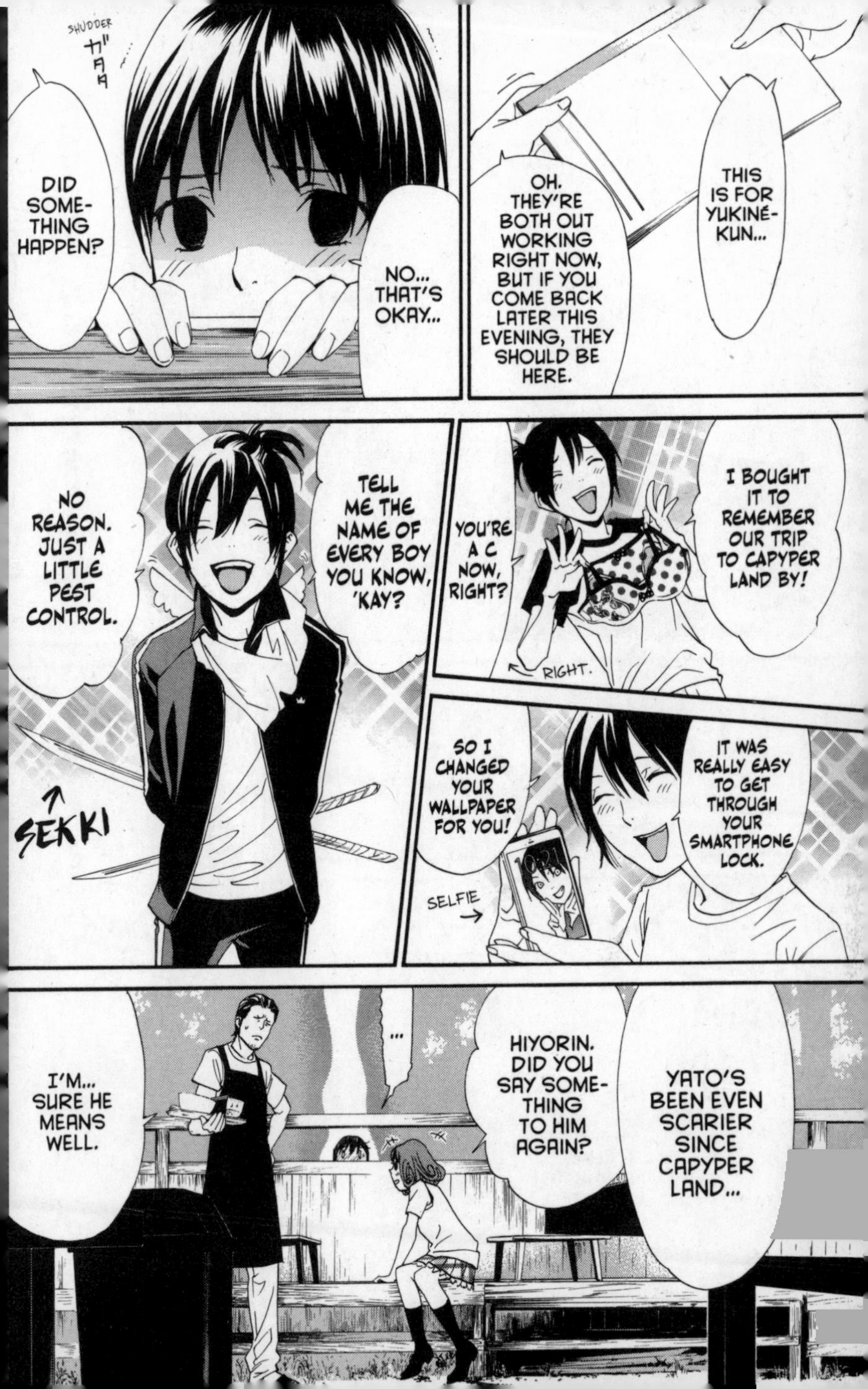
THIS IS FOR YUKINÉ-KUN...
OH. THEY'RE BOTH OUT WORKING RIGHT NOW, BUT IF YOU COME BACK LATER THIS EVENING, THEY SHOULD BE HERE.
NO... THAT'S OKAY...
SHUDDER
ガタタ
DID SOME-THING HAPPEN?
I BOUGHT IT TO REMEMBER OUR TRIP TO CAPYPER LAND BY!
YOU'RE A C NOW, RIGHT?
RIGHT.
IT WAS REALLY EASY TO GET THROUGH YOUR SMARTPHONE LOCK.
SO I CHANGED YOUR WALLPAPER FOR YOU!
SELFIE
TELL ME THE NAME OF EVERY BOY YOU KNOW, 'KAY?
NO REASON. JUST A LITTLE PEST CONTROL.
SEKKI
YATO'S BEEN EVEN SCARIER SINCE CAPYPER LAND...
HIYORIN. DID YOU SAY SOME-THING TO HIM AGAIN?
...
I'M... SURE HE MEANS WELL.

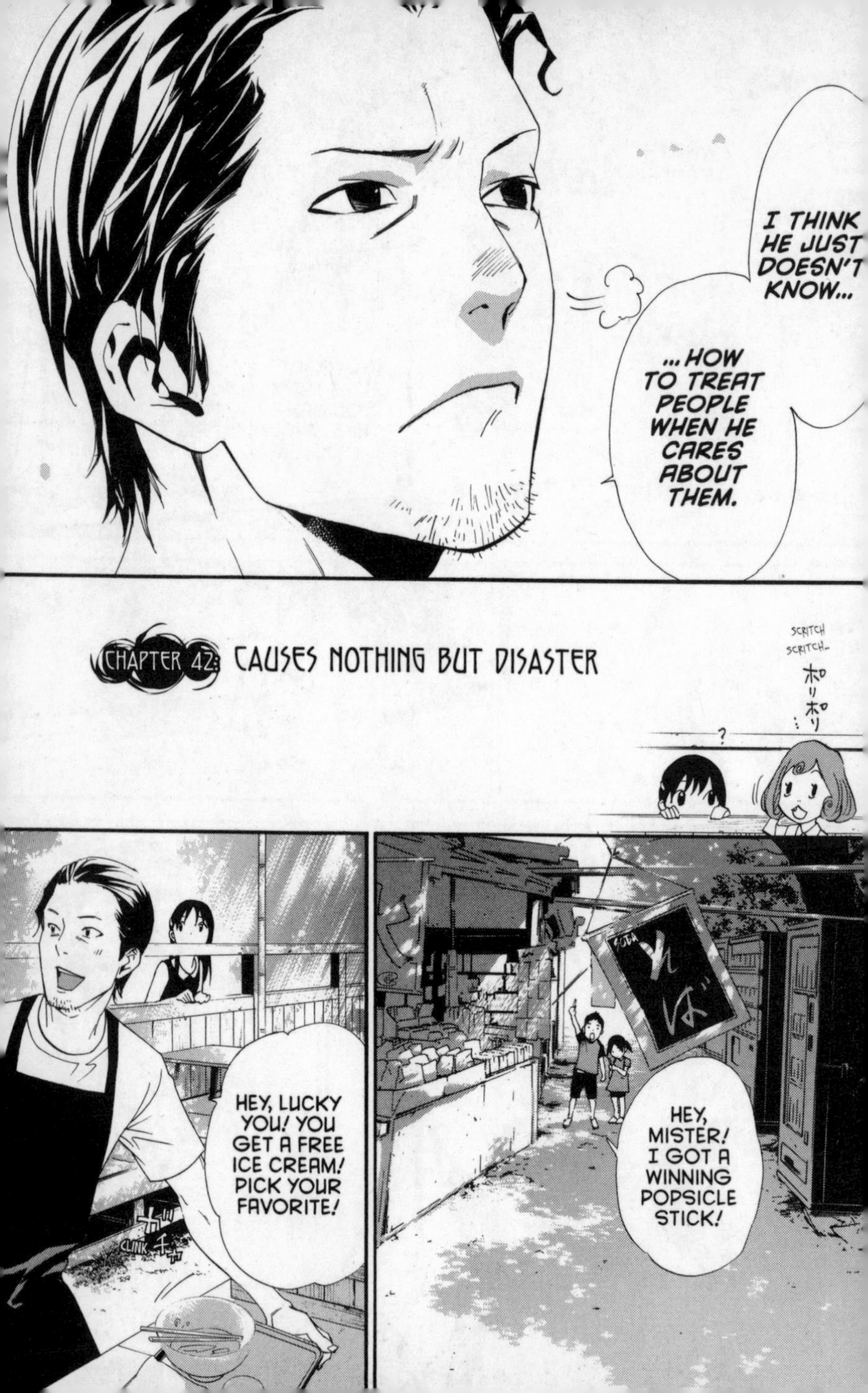

I THINK HE JUST DOESN'T KNOW...
...HOW TO TREAT PEOPLE WHEN HE CARES ABOUT THEM.
SCRITCH SCRITCH...
ポリポリ
?
CHAPTER 42: CAUSES NOTHING BUT DISASTER
HEY, MISTER! I GOT A WINNING POPSICLE STICK!
HEY, LUCKY YOU! YOU GET A FREE ICE CREAM! PICK YOUR FAVORITE!
CLINK

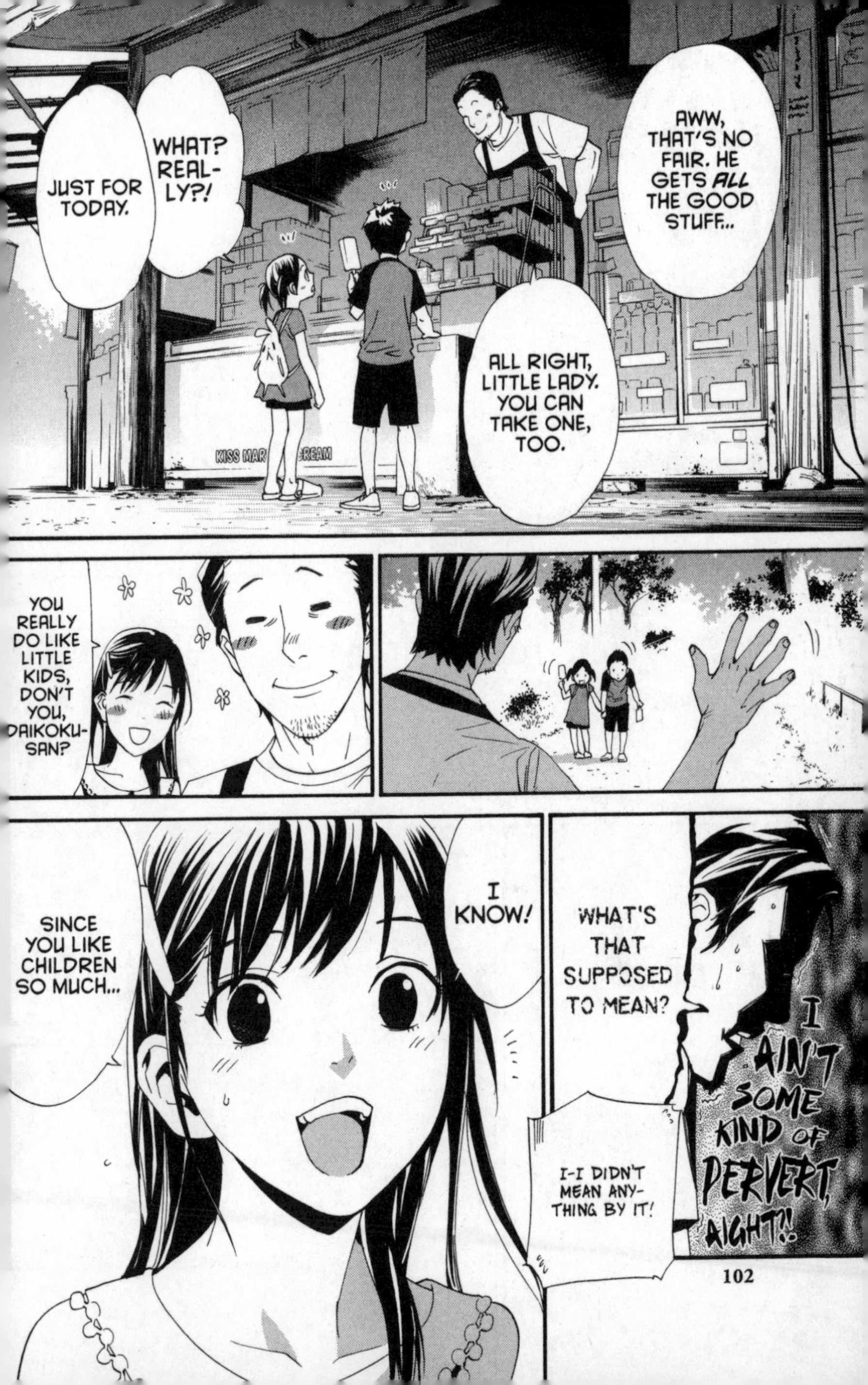
AWW, THAT'S NO FAIR. HE GETS ALL THE GOOD STUFF...
ALL RIGHT, LITTLE LADY. YOU CAN TAKE ONE, TOO.
WHAT? REAL-LY?!
JUST FOR TODAY.
YOU REALLY DO LIKE LITTLE KIDS, DON'T YOU, DAIKOKU-SAN?
WHAT'S THAT SUPPOSED TO MEAN?
I AIN'T SOME KIND OF PERVERT, AIGHT?!
I-I DIDN'T MEAN ANY-THING BY IT!
I KNOW!
SINCE YOU LIKE CHILDREN SO MUCH...

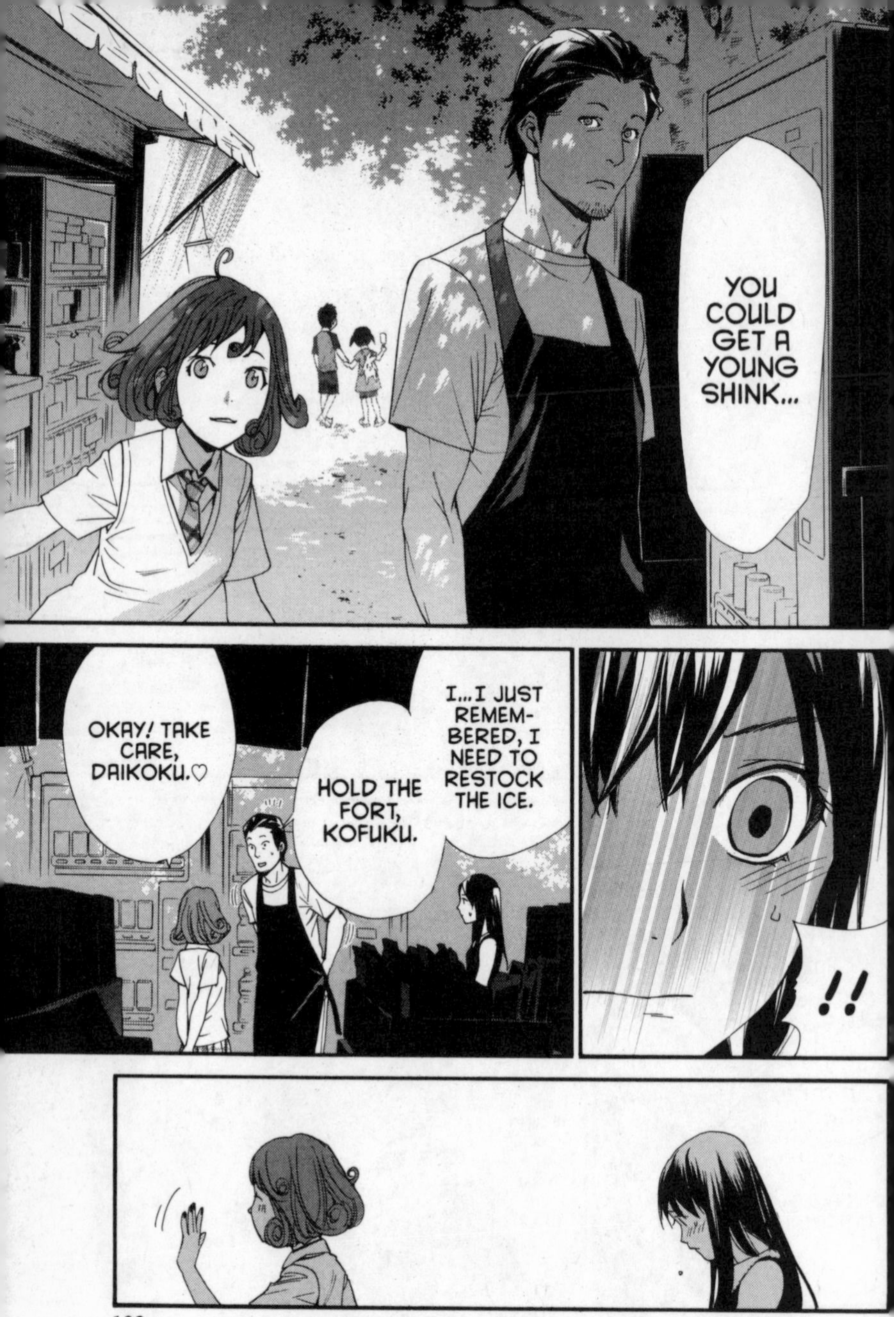
YOU COULD GET A YOUNG SHINK...
!!
I...I JUST REMEMBERED, I NEED TO RESTOCK THE ICE.
HOLD THE FORT, KOFUKU.
OKAY! TAKE CARE, DAIKOKU.♡

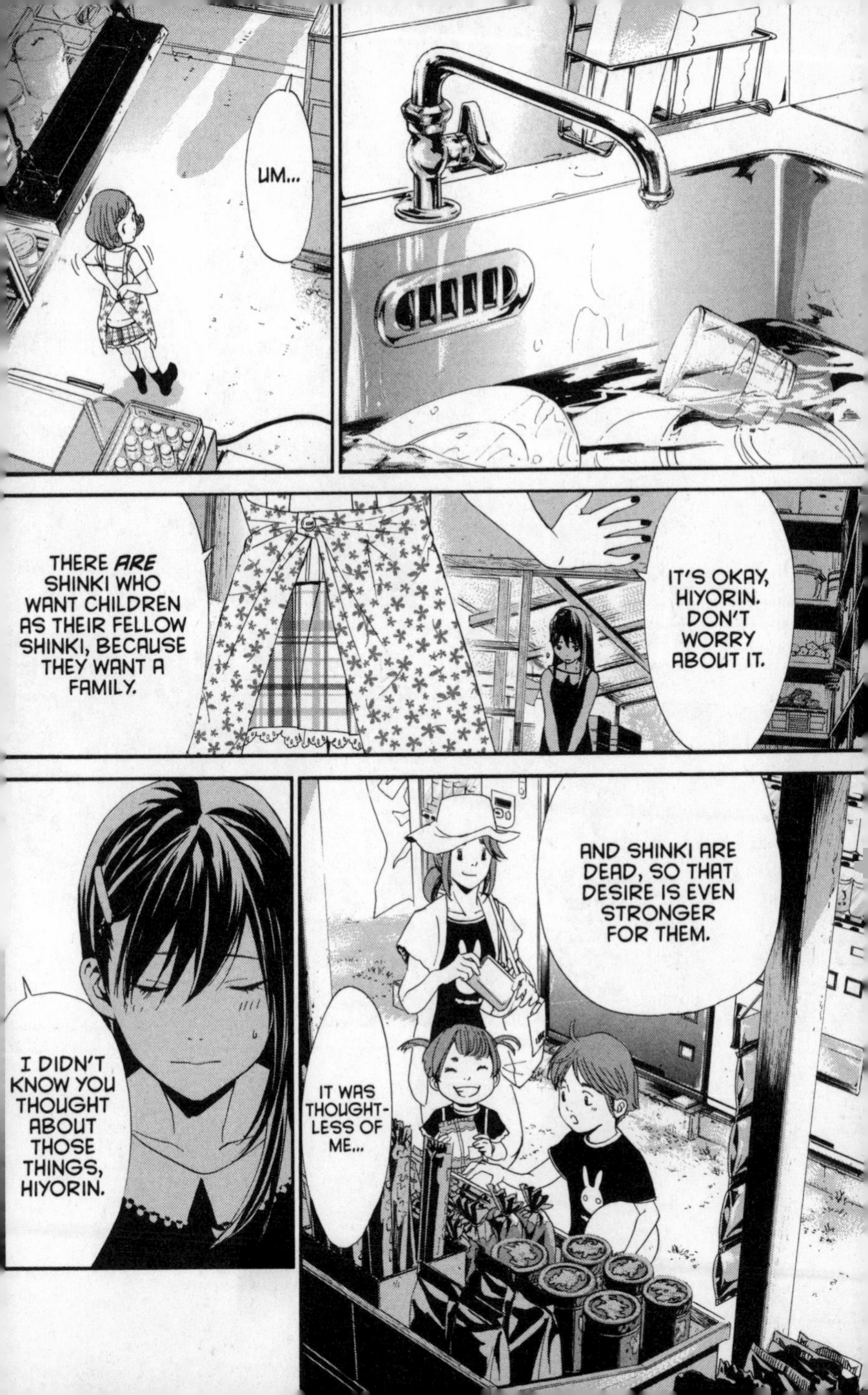
UM...
IT'S OKAY, HIYORIN. DON'T WORRY ABOUT IT.
THERE *ARE* SHINKI WHO WANT CHILDREN AS THEIR FELLOW SHINKI, BECAUSE THEY WANT A FAMILY.
AND SHINKI ARE DEAD, SO THAT DESIRE IS EVEN STRONGER FOR THEM.
IT WAS THOUGHT-LESS OF ME...
I DIDN'T KNOW YOU THOUGHT ABOUT THOSE THINGS, HIYORIN.

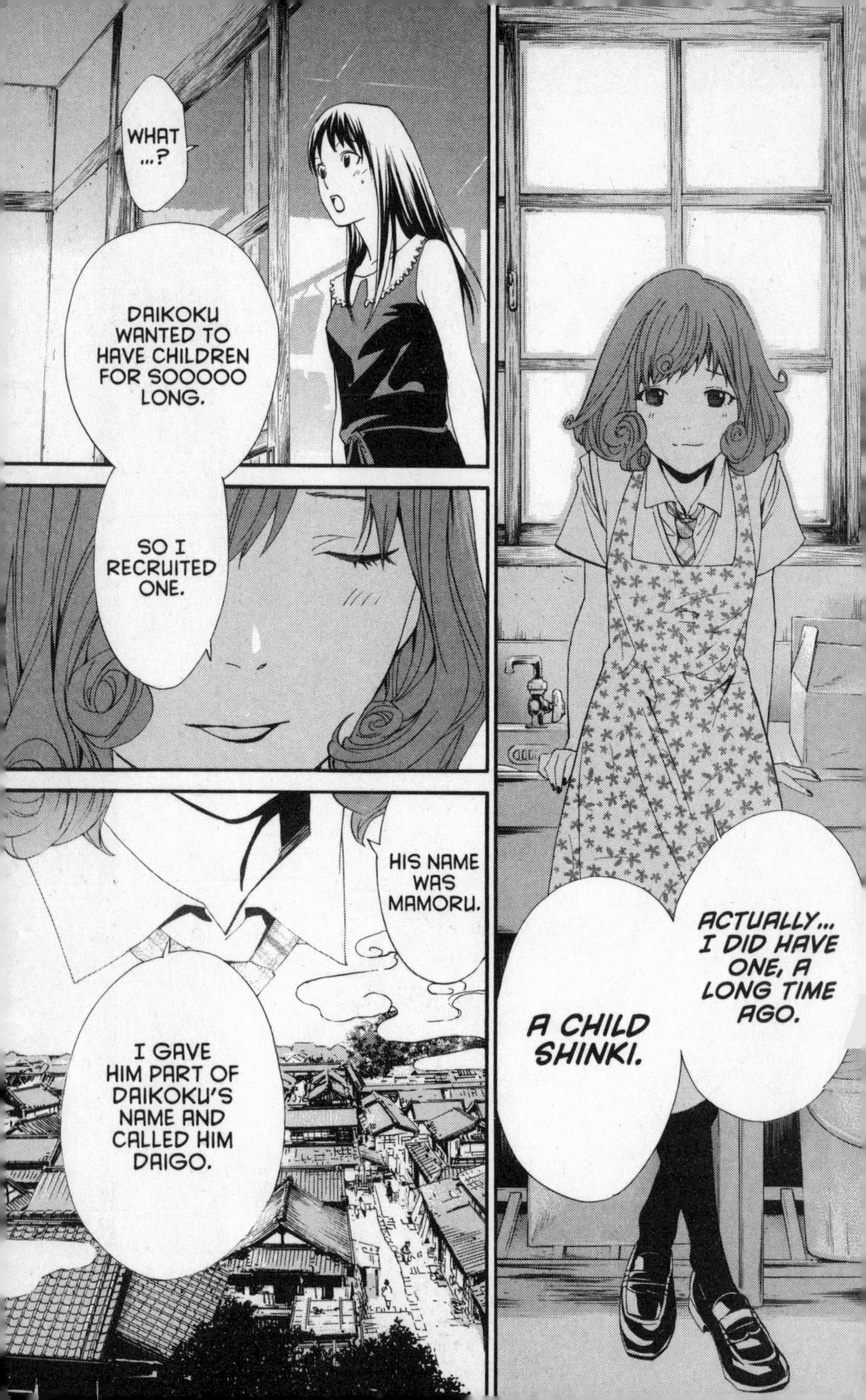
ACTUALLY... I DID HAVE ONE, A LONG TIME AGO.
A CHILD SHINKI.
WHAT ...?
DAIKOKU WANTED TO HAVE CHILDREN FOR SOOOOO LONG.
SO I RECRUITED ONE.
HIS NAME WAS MAMORU.
I GAVE HIM PART OF DAIKOKU'S NAME AND CALLED HIM DAIGO.

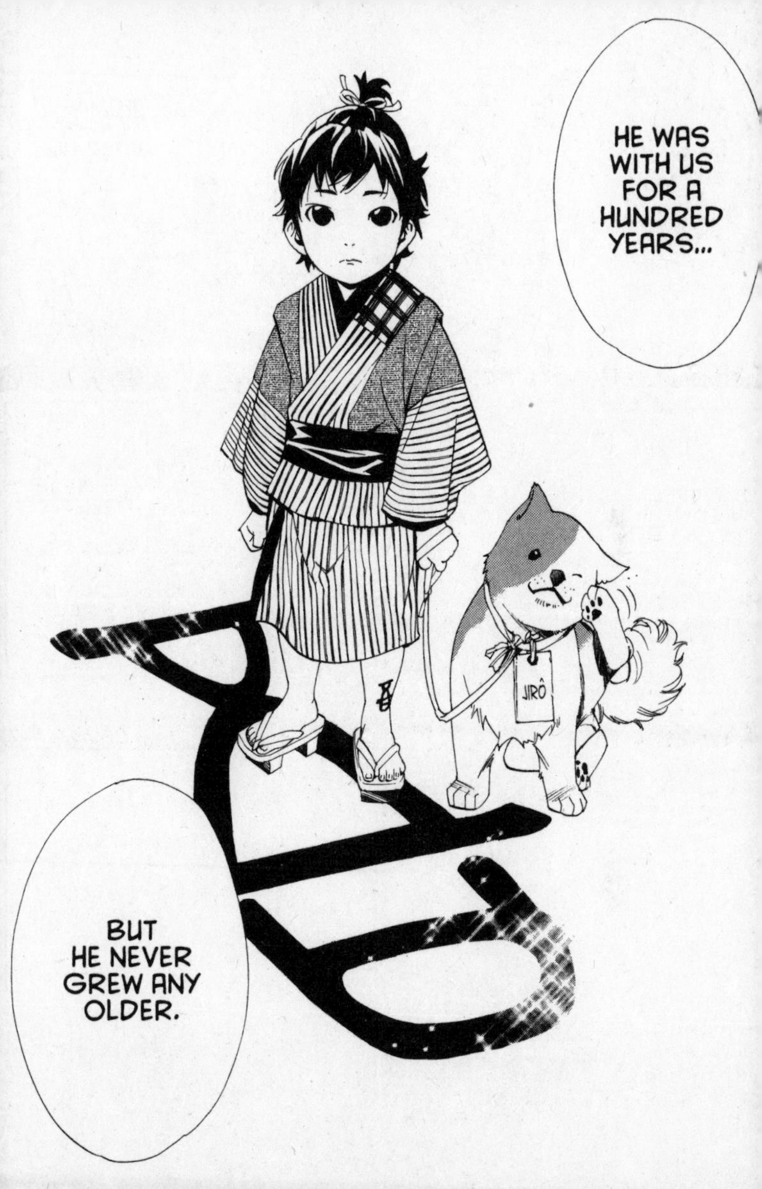
HE WAS WITH US FOR A HUNDRED YEARS...
JIRÔ
BUT HE NEVER GREW ANY OLDER.

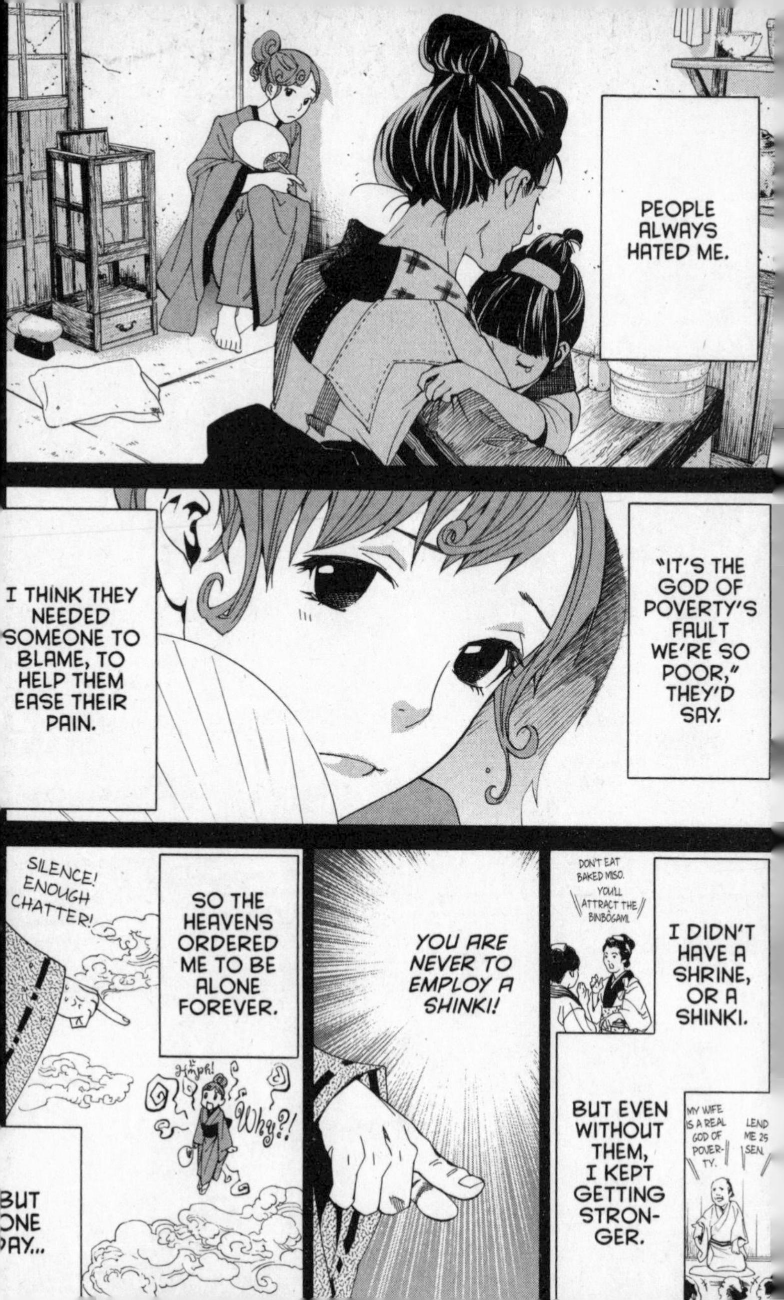
PEOPLE ALWAYS HATED ME.
"IT'S THE GOD OF POVERTY'S FAULT WE'RE SO POOR," THEY'D SAY.
I THINK THEY NEEDED SOMEONE TO BLAME, TO HELP THEM EASE THEIR PAIN.
I DIDN'T HAVE A SHRINE, OR A SHINKI.
DON'T EAT BAKED MISO. YOU'LL ATTRACT THE BINBŌGAMI.
LEND ME 25 SEN.
MY WIFE IS A REAL GOD OF POVER-TY.
BUT EVEN WITHOUT THEM, I KEPT GETTING STRON-GER.
YOU ARE NEVER TO EMPLOY A SHINKI!
SO THE HEAVENS ORDERED ME TO BE ALONE FOREVER.
SILENCE! ENOUGH CHATTER!
Hmph!
Why?!
BUT ONE DAY...

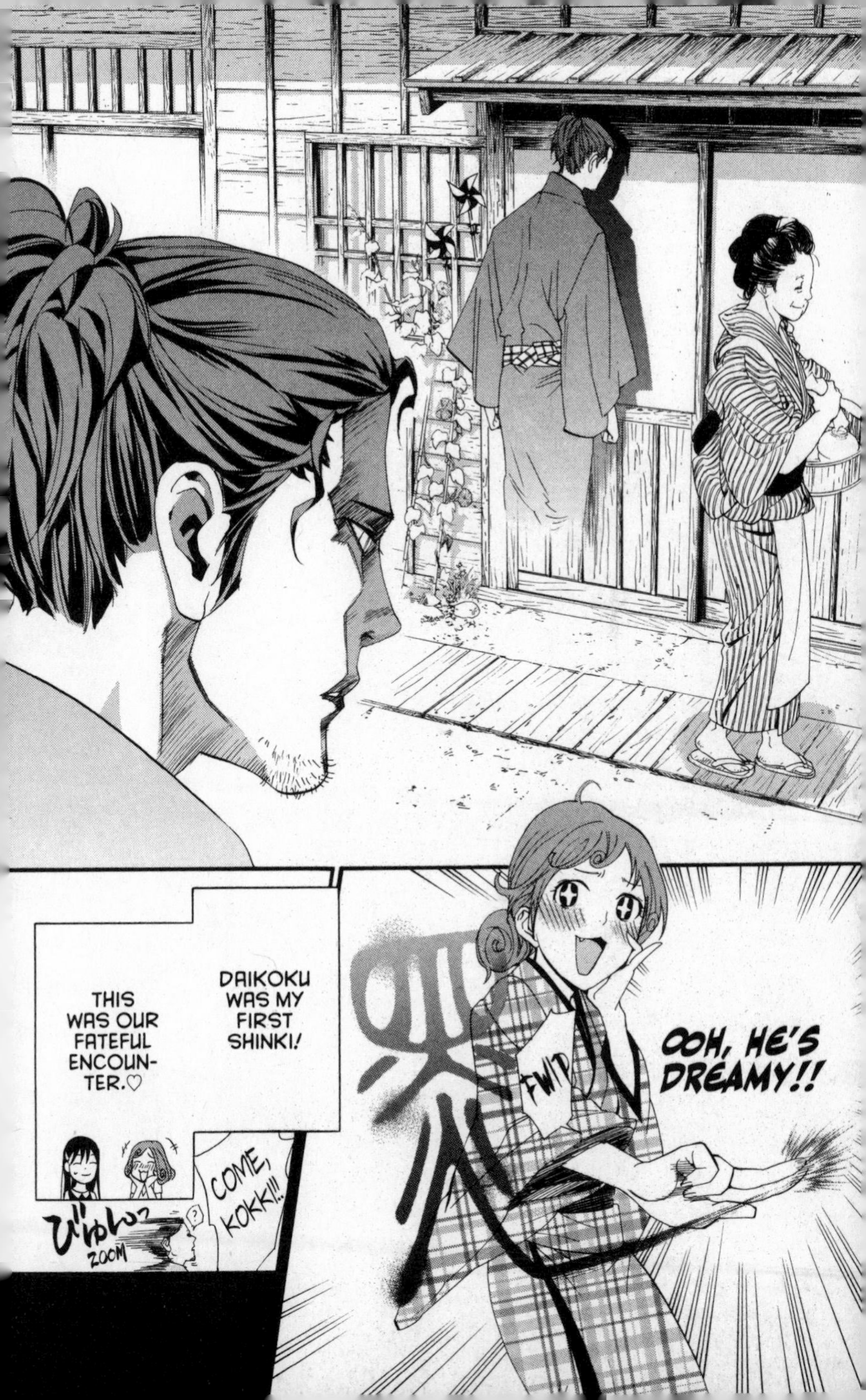
OOH, HE'S DREAMY!!
FWIP
DAIKOKU WAS MY FIRST SHINKI!
THIS WAS OUR FATEFUL ENCOUNTER.♡
COME, KOKKI!!
?
びゅんっ
ZOOM

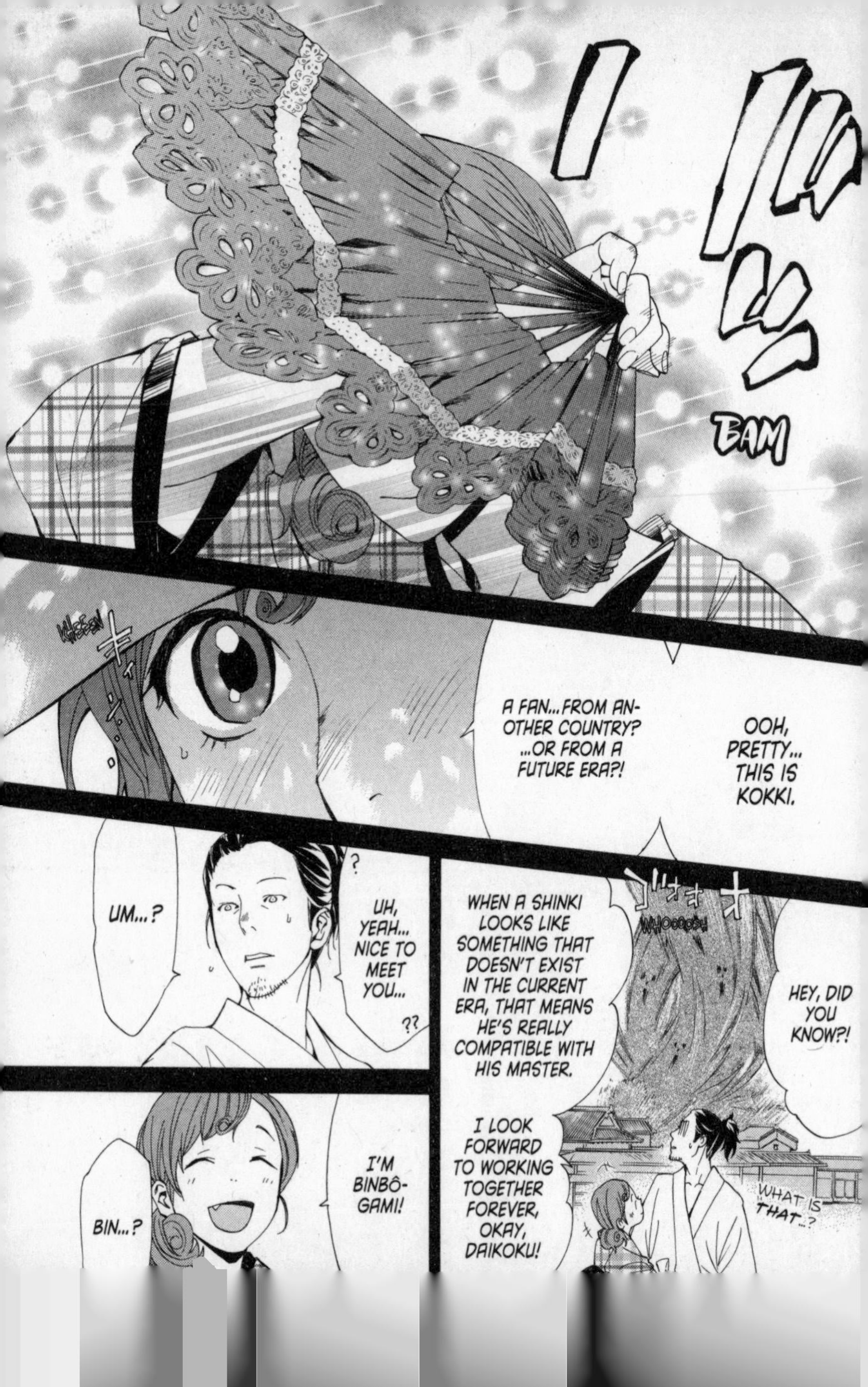
BAM
KWEEEN
OOH, PRETTY... THIS IS KOKKI.
A FAN...FROM AN-OTHER COUNTRY? ...OR FROM A FUTURE ERA?!
HEY, DID YOU KNOW?!
WHOOOOSH
WHEN A SHINKI LOOKS LIKE SOMETHING THAT DOESN'T EXIST IN THE CURRENT ERA, THAT MEANS HE'S REALLY COMPATIBLE WITH HIS MASTER.
I LOOK FORWARD TO WORKING TOGETHER FOREVER, OKAY, DAIKOKU!
WHAT IS THAT...?
UH, YEAH... NICE TO MEET YOU...
UM...?
I'M BINBÔ-GAMI!
BIN...?

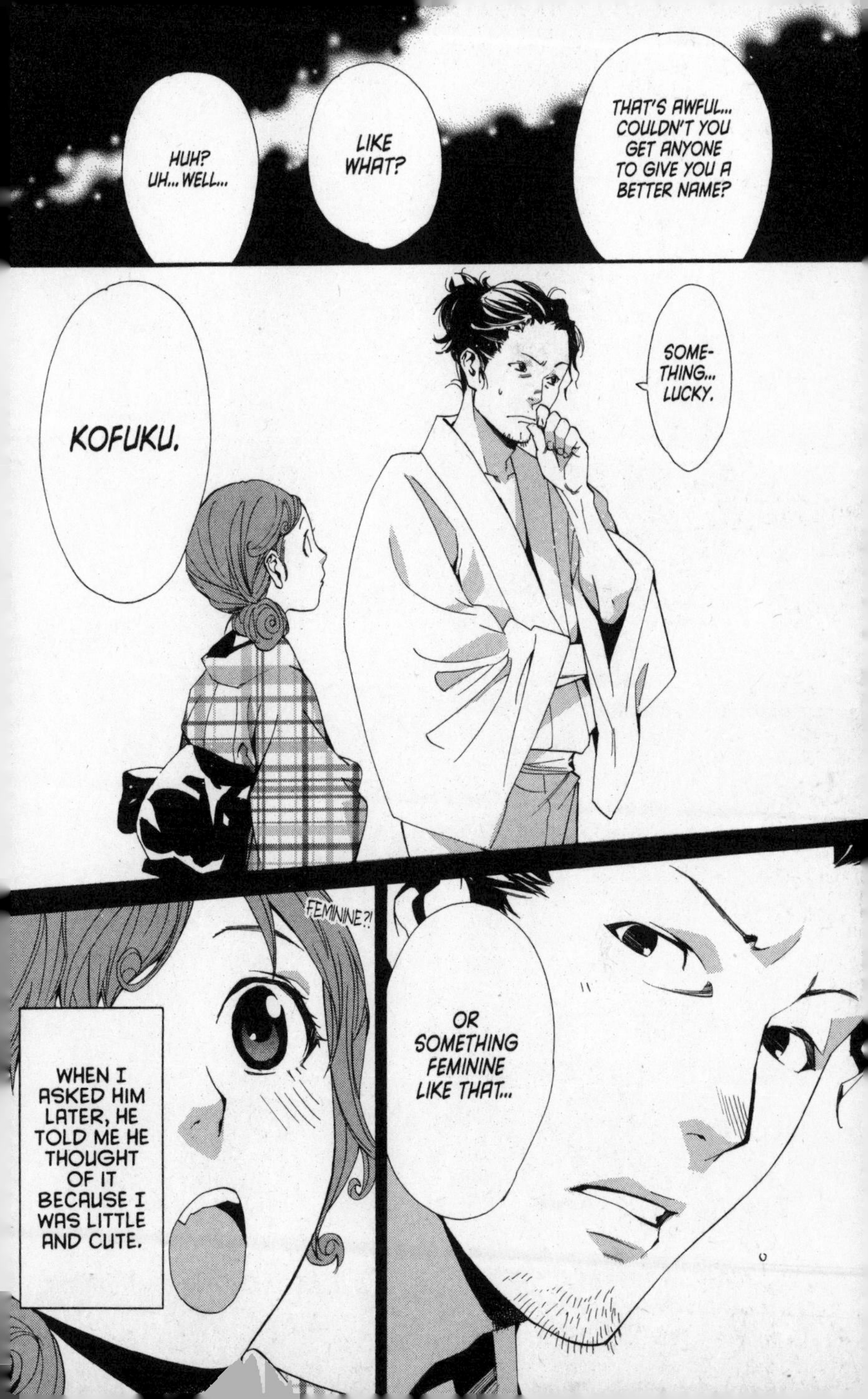
THAT'S AWFUL... COULDN'T YOU GET ANYONE TO GIVE YOU A BETTER NAME?
LIKE WHAT?
HUH? UH...WELL...
SOME-THING... LUCKY.
KOFUKU.
OR SOMETHING FEMININE LIKE THAT...
FEMININE?!
WHEN I ASKED HIM LATER, HE TOLD ME HE THOUGHT OF IT BECAUSE I WAS LITTLE AND CUTE.

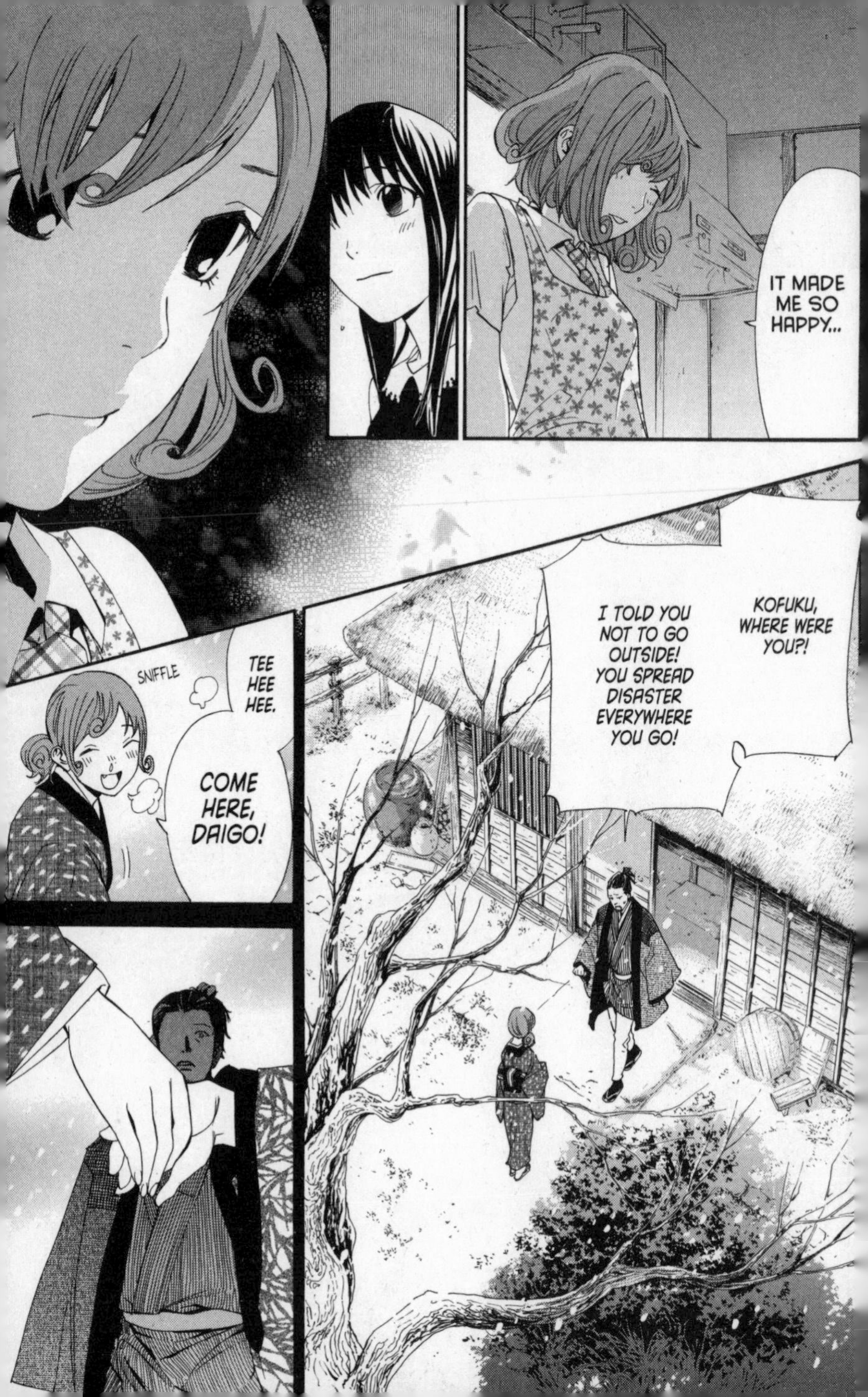
IT MADE ME SO HAPPY...
KOFUKU, WHERE WERE YOU?!
I TOLD YOU NOT TO GO OUTSIDE! YOU SPREAD DISASTER EVERYWHERE YOU GO!
TEE HEE HEE.
SNIFFLE
COME HERE, DAIGO!

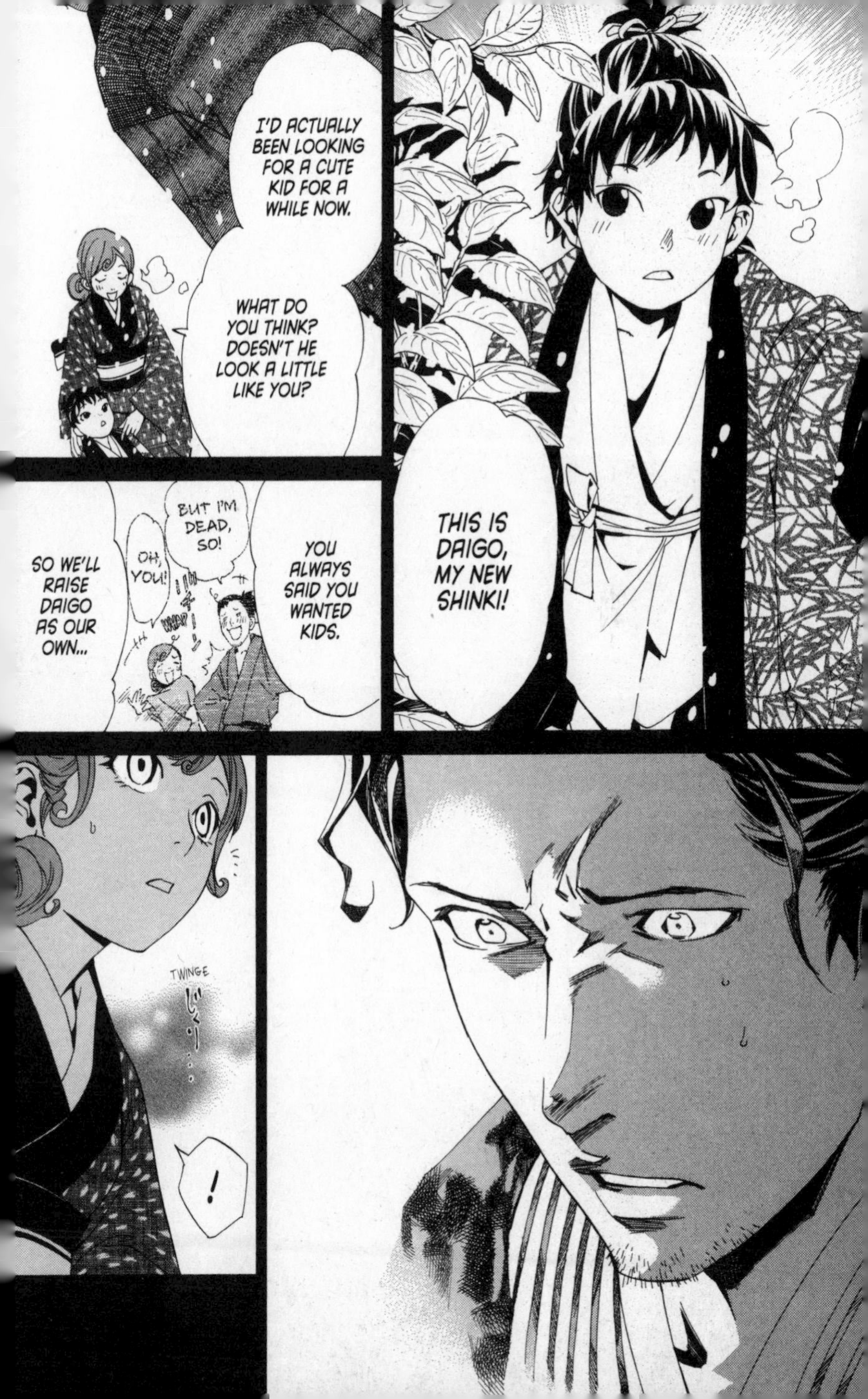
THIS IS DAIGO, MY NEW SHINKI!
I'D ACTUALLY BEEN LOOKING FOR A CUTE KID FOR A WHILE NOW.
WHAT DO YOU THINK? DOESN'T HE LOOK A LITTLE LIKE YOU?
YOU ALWAYS SAID YOU WANTED KIDS.
BUT I'M DEAD, SO!
OH, YOU!
WHAP
SO WE'LL RAISE DAIGO AS OUR OWN...
TWINGE
!

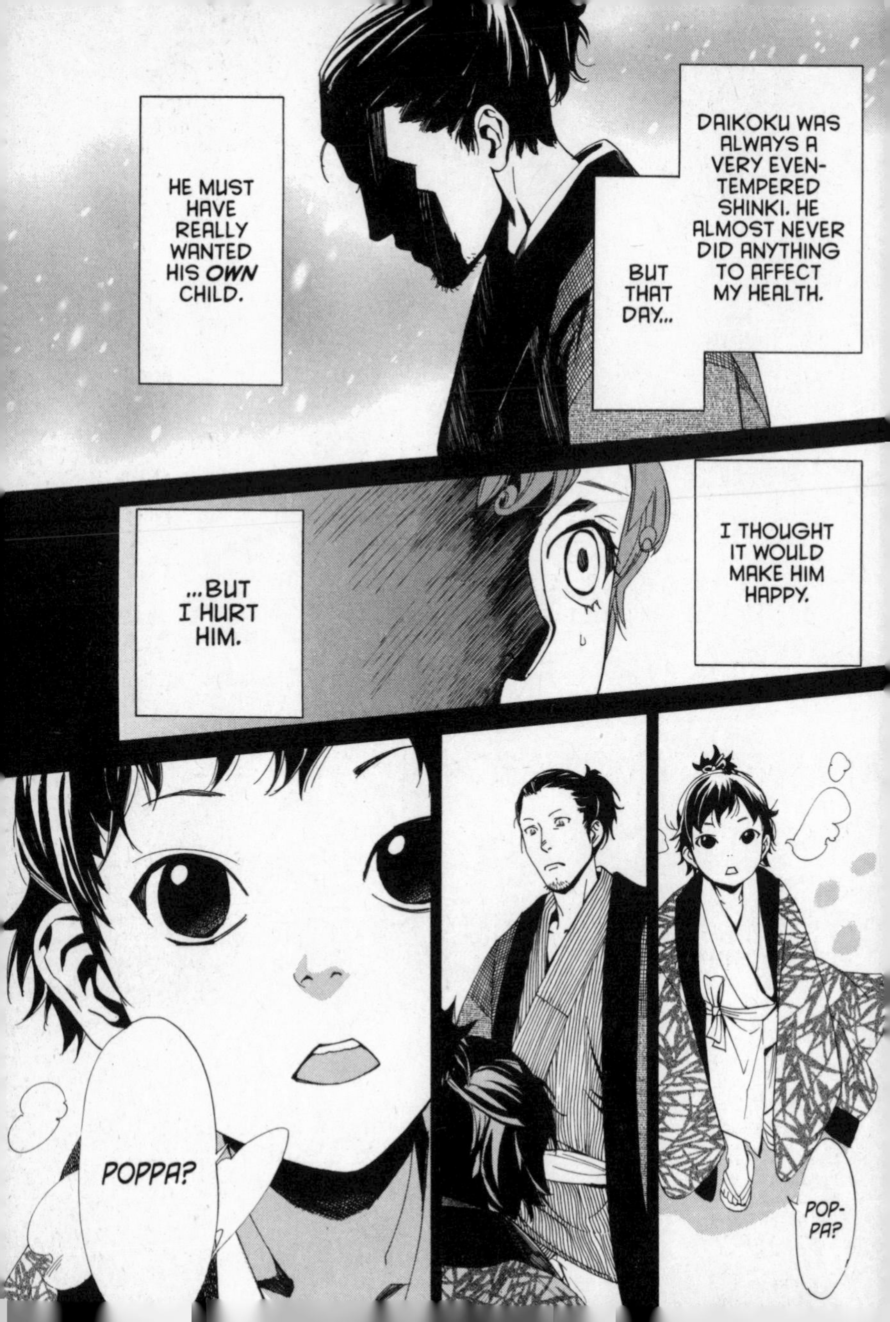
DAIKOKU WAS ALWAYS A VERY EVEN-TEMPERED SHINKI. HE ALMOST NEVER DID ANYTHING TO AFFECT MY HEALTH.
BUT THAT DAY...
HE MUST HAVE REALLY WANTED HIS *OWN* CHILD.
I THOUGHT IT WOULD MAKE HIM HAPPY.
...BUT I HURT HIM.
POP-PA?
POPPA?

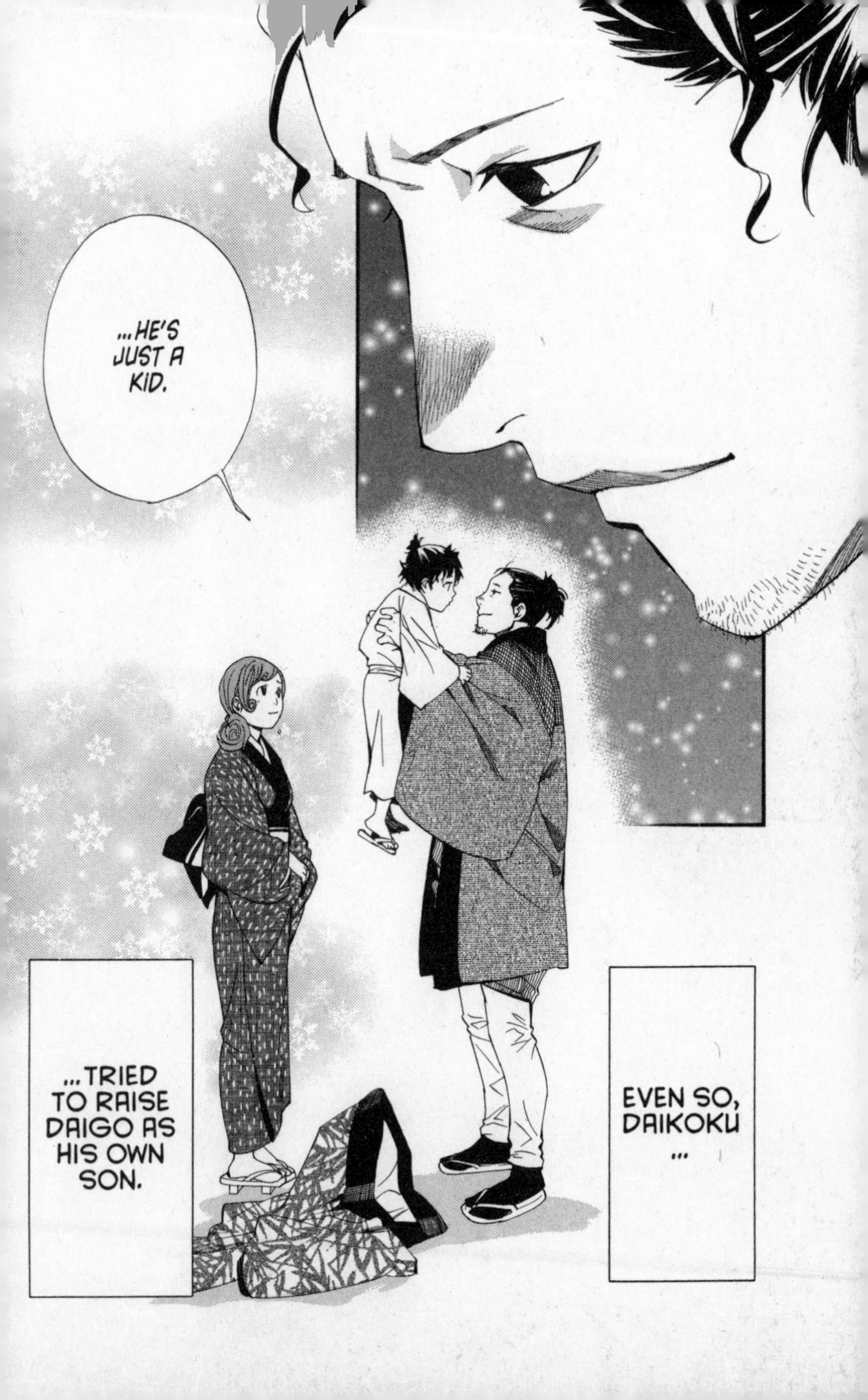
...HE'S JUST A KID.
EVEN SO, DAIKOKU ...
...TRIED TO RAISE DAIGO AS HIS OWN SON.

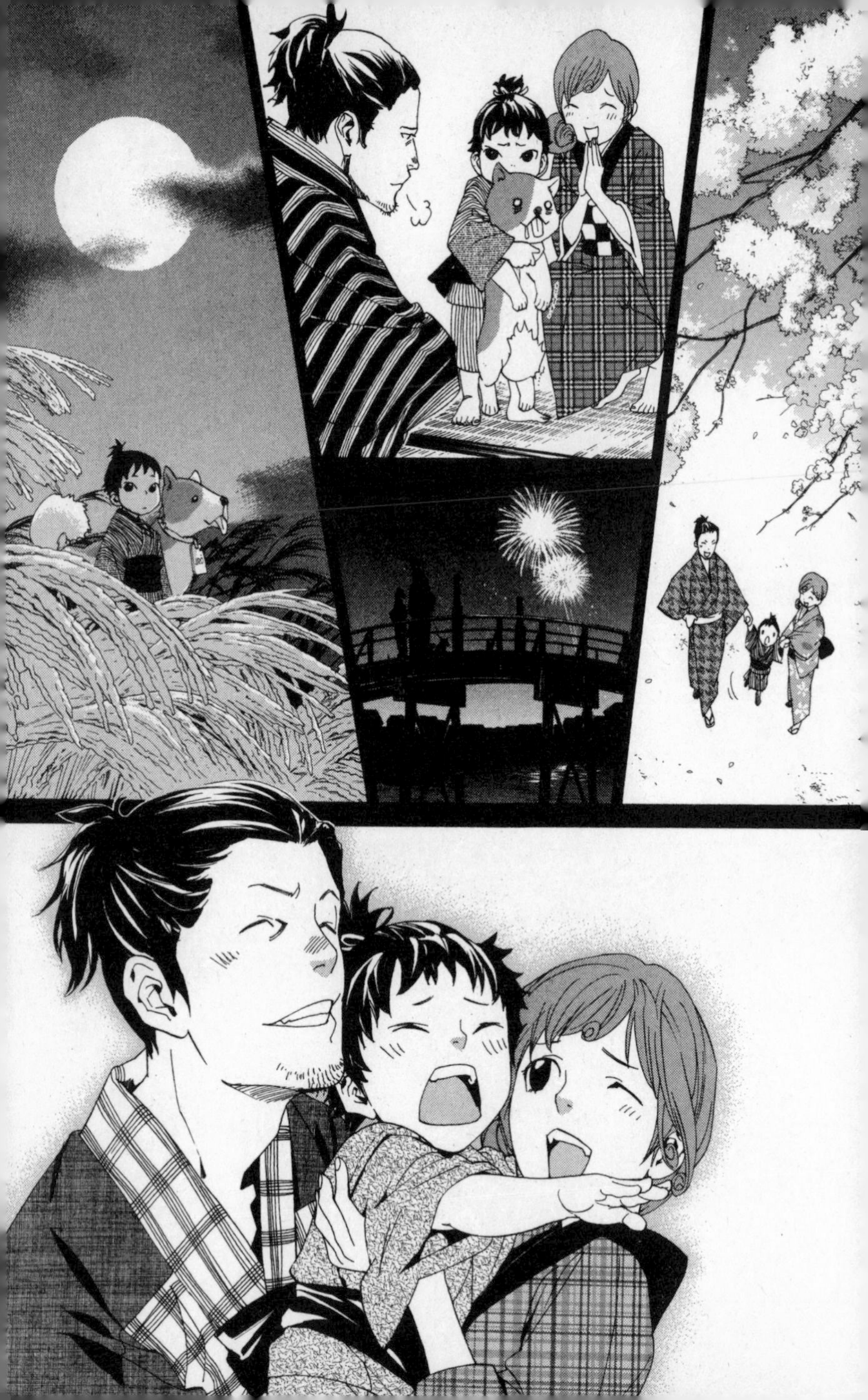

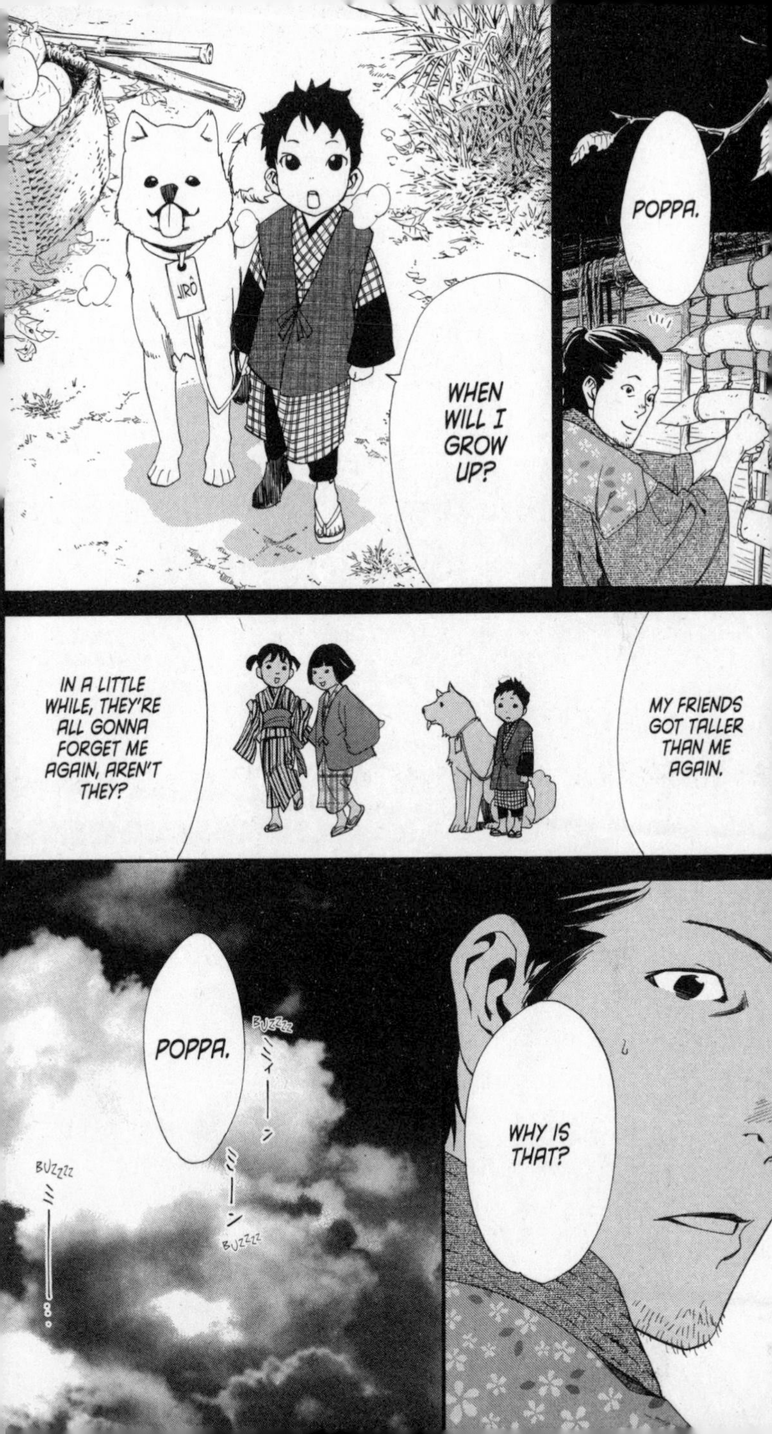
POPPA.
JIRÔ
WHEN WILL I GROW UP?
MY FRIENDS GOT TALLER THAN ME AGAIN.
IN A LITTLE WHILE, THEY'RE ALL GONNA FORGET ME AGAIN, AREN'T THEY?
WHY IS THAT?
POPPA.
BUZZZZ
BUZZZZ
BUZZZZ

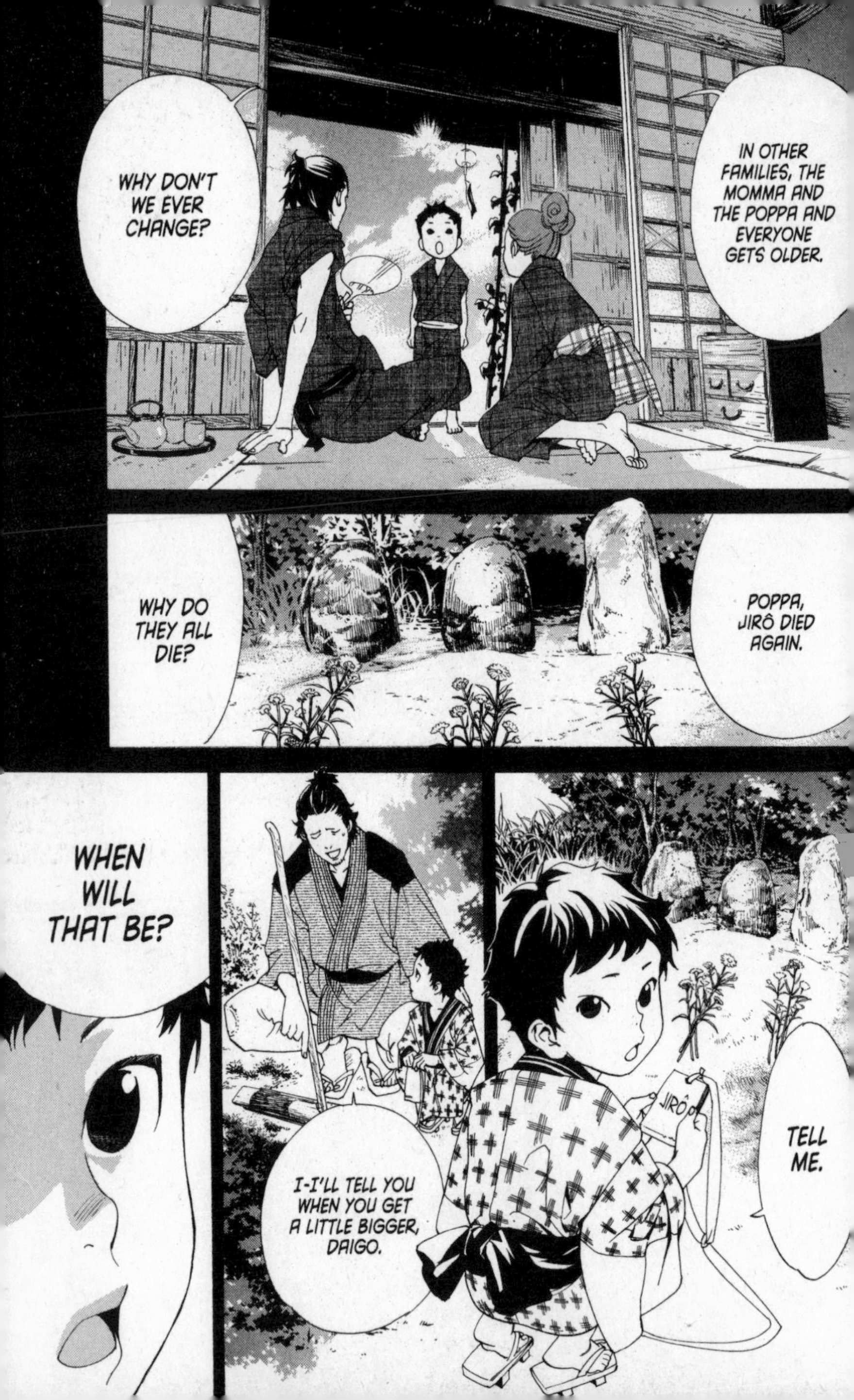
IN OTHER FAMILIES, THE MOMMA AND THE POPPA AND EVERYONE GETS OLDER.
WHY DON'T WE EVER CHANGE?
POPPA, JIRÔ DIED AGAIN.
WHY DO THEY ALL DIE?
TELL ME.
JIRÔ
I-I'LL TELL YOU WHEN YOU GET A LITTLE BIGGER, DAIGO.
WHEN WILL THAT BE?

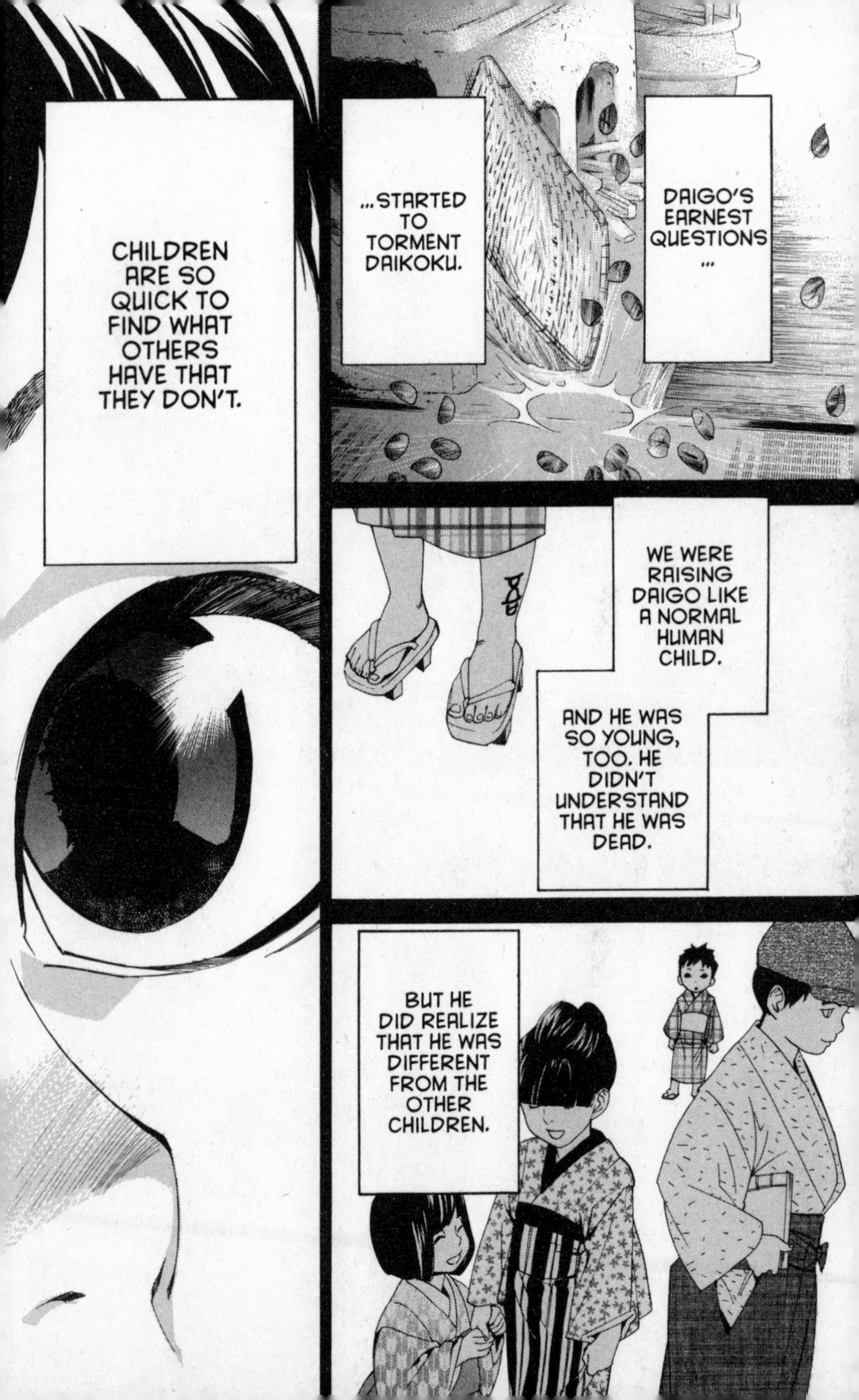
DAIGO'S EARNEST QUESTIONS ...
...STARTED TO TORMENT DAIKOKU.
WE WERE RAISING DAIGO LIKE A NORMAL HUMAN CHILD.
AND HE WAS SO YOUNG, TOO. HE DIDN'T UNDERSTAND THAT HE WAS DEAD.
BUT HE DID REALIZE THAT HE WAS DIFFERENT FROM THE OTHER CHILDREN.
CHILDREN ARE SO QUICK TO FIND WHAT OTHERS HAVE THAT THEY DON'T.

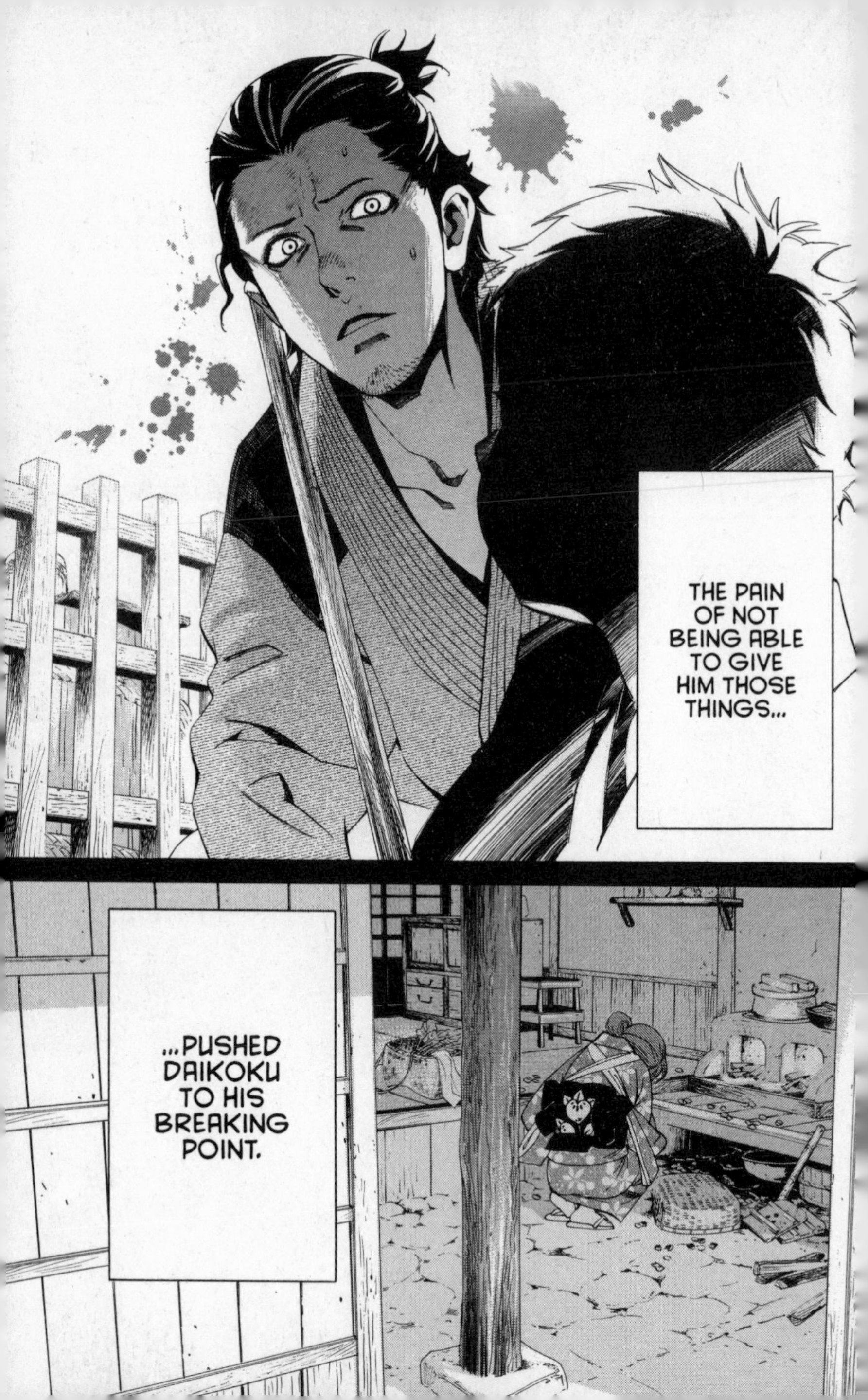
THE PAIN OF NOT BEING ABLE TO GIVE HIM THOSE THINGS...
...PUSHED DAIKOKU TO HIS BREAKING POINT.

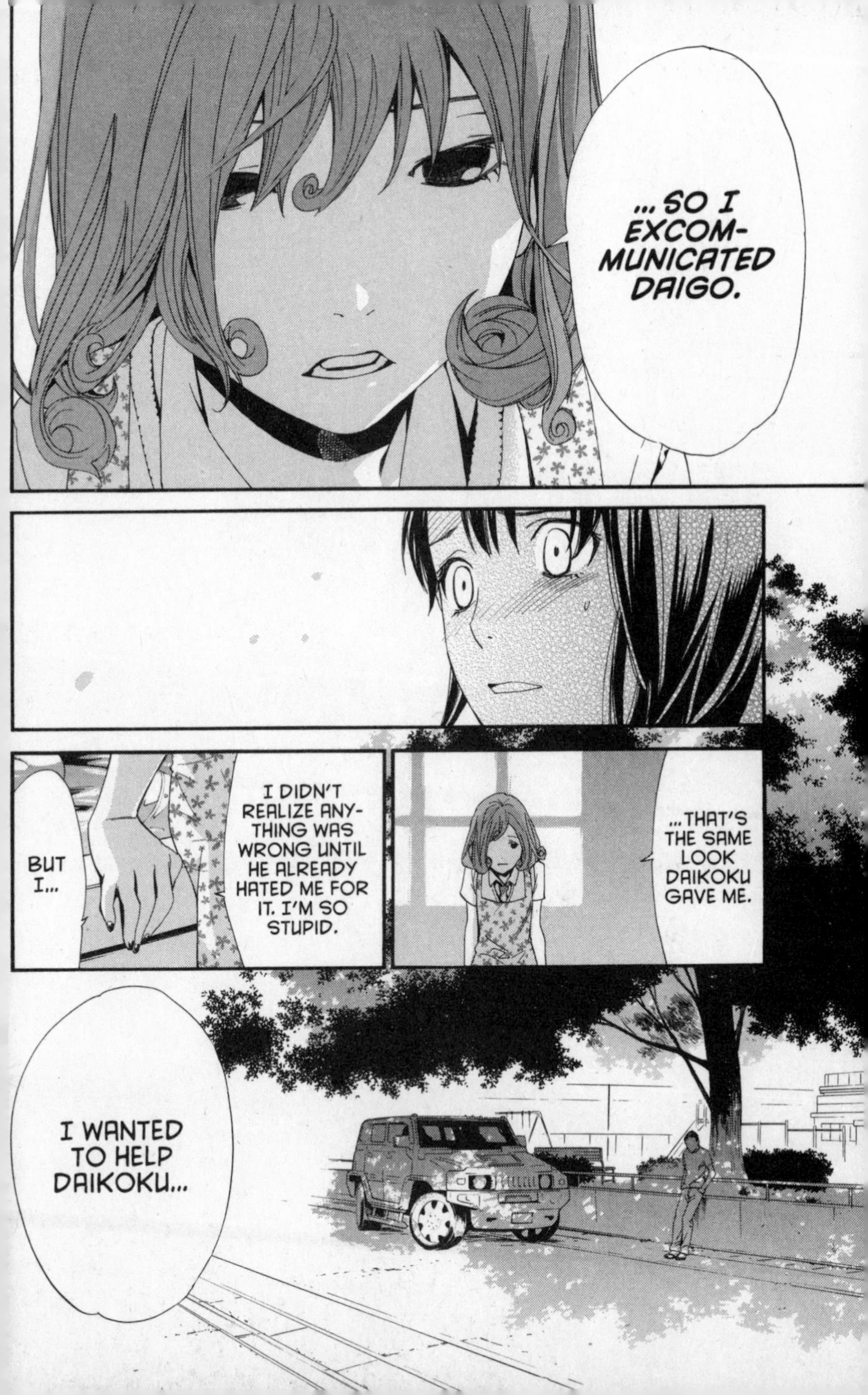
...SO I EXCOM-MUNICATED DAIGO.
...THAT'S THE SAME LOOK DAIKOKU GAVE ME.
I DIDN'T REALIZE ANY-THING WAS WRONG UNTIL HE ALREADY HATED ME FOR IT. I'M SO STUPID.
BUT I...
I WANTED TO HELP DAIKOKU...

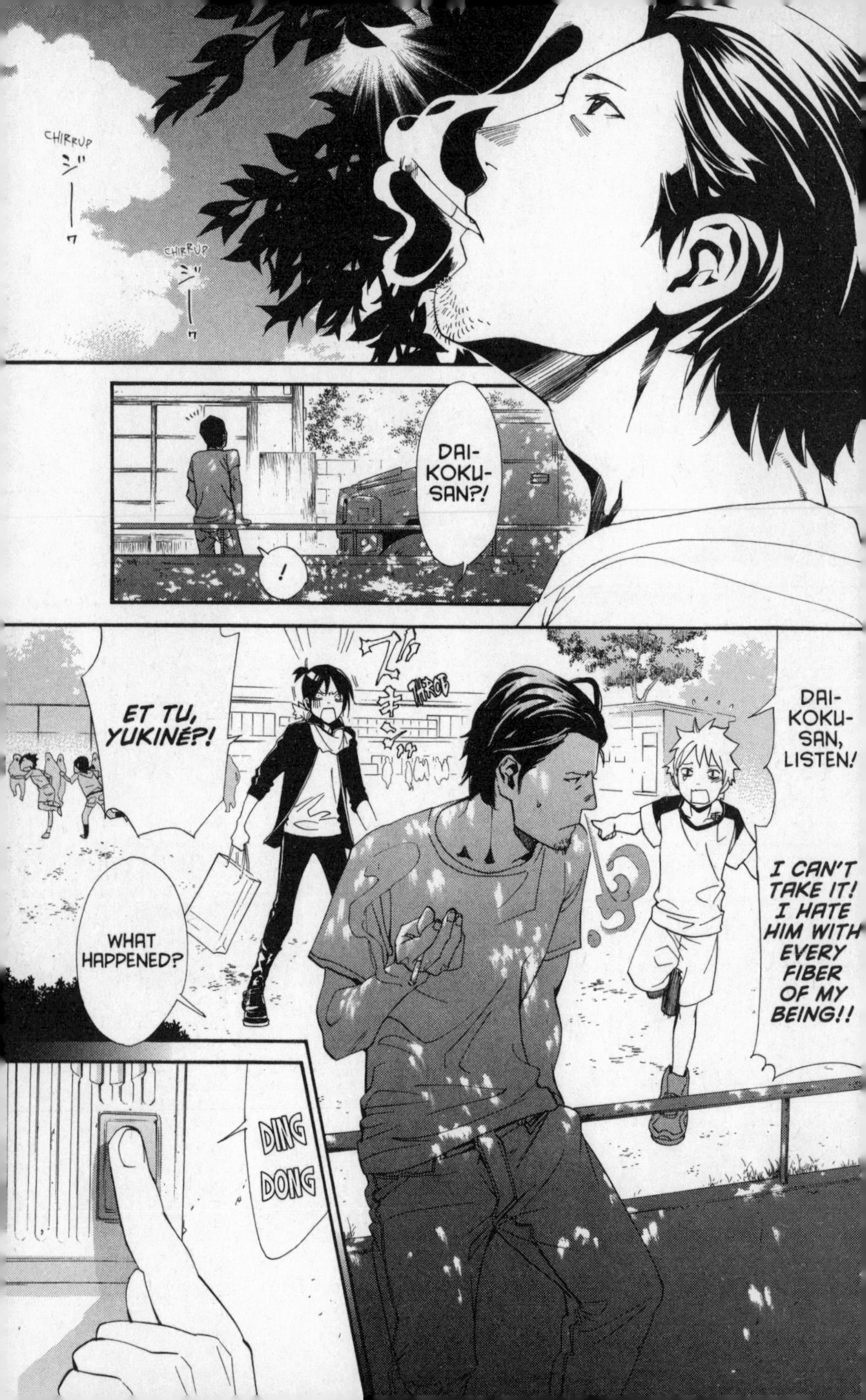
CHIRRUP
CHIRRUP
DAI-KOKU-SAN?!
!
DAI-KOKU-SAN, LISTEN!
I CAN'T TAKE IT! I HATE HIM WITH EVERY FIBER OF MY BEING!!
THROB
ET TU, YUKINÉ?!
WHAT HAPPENED?
DING DONG

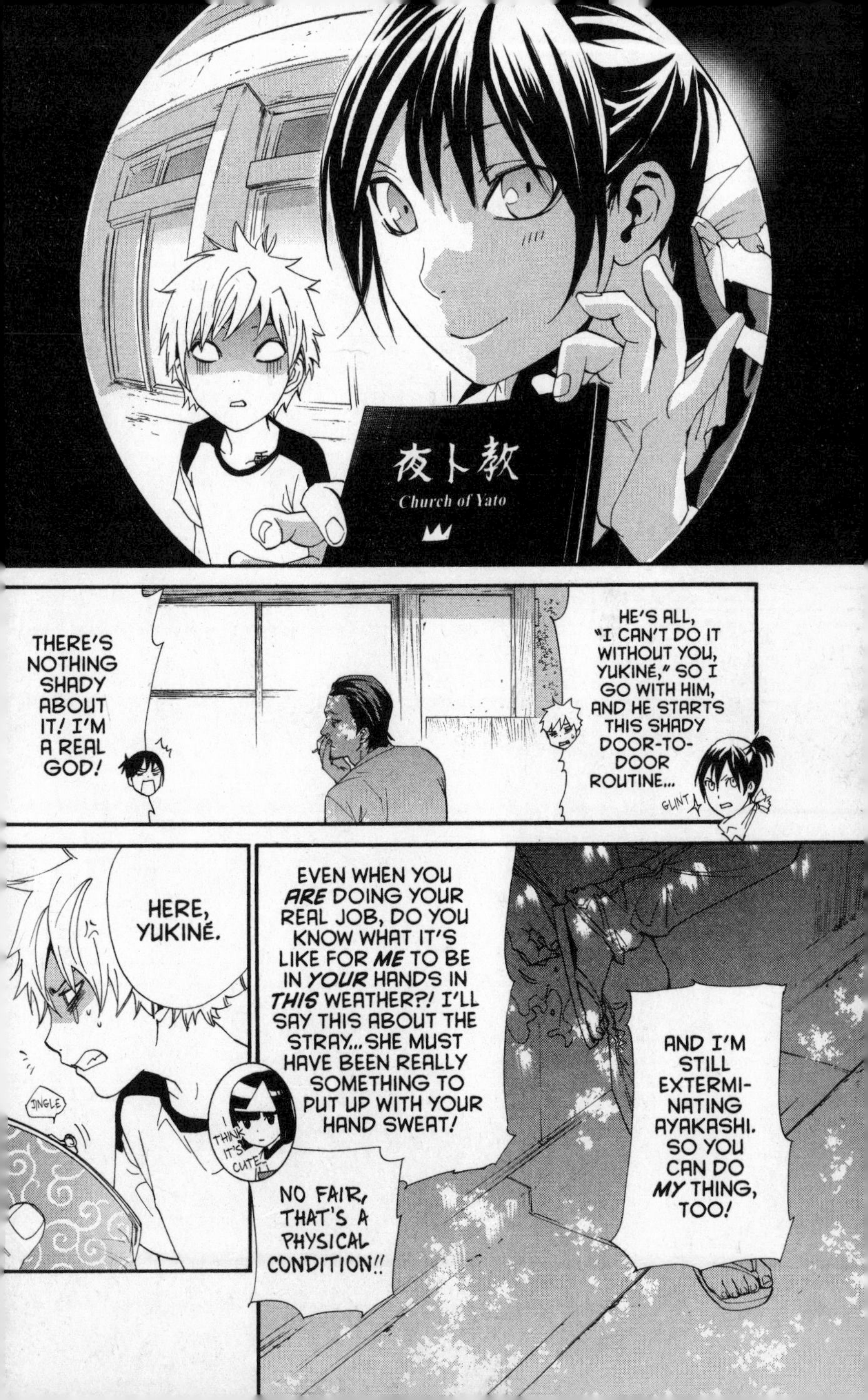

夜卜教
Church of Yato
HE'S ALL, "I CAN'T DO IT WITHOUT YOU, YUKINÉ," SO I GO WITH HIM, AND HE STARTS THIS SHADY DOOR-TO-DOOR ROUTINE...
GLINT
THERE'S NOTHING SHADY ABOUT IT! I'M A REAL GOD!
AND I'M STILL EXTERMINATING AYAKASHI. SO YOU CAN DO *MY* THING, TOO!
EVEN WHEN YOU *ARE* DOING YOUR REAL JOB, DO YOU KNOW WHAT IT'S LIKE FOR *ME* TO BE IN *YOUR* HANDS IN *THIS* WEATHER?! I'LL SAY THIS ABOUT THE STRAY... SHE MUST HAVE BEEN REALLY SOMETHING TO PUT UP WITH YOUR HAND SWEAT!
NO FAIR, THAT'S A PHYSICAL CONDITION!!
HERE, YUKINÉ.
JINGLE
I THINK IT'S CUTE

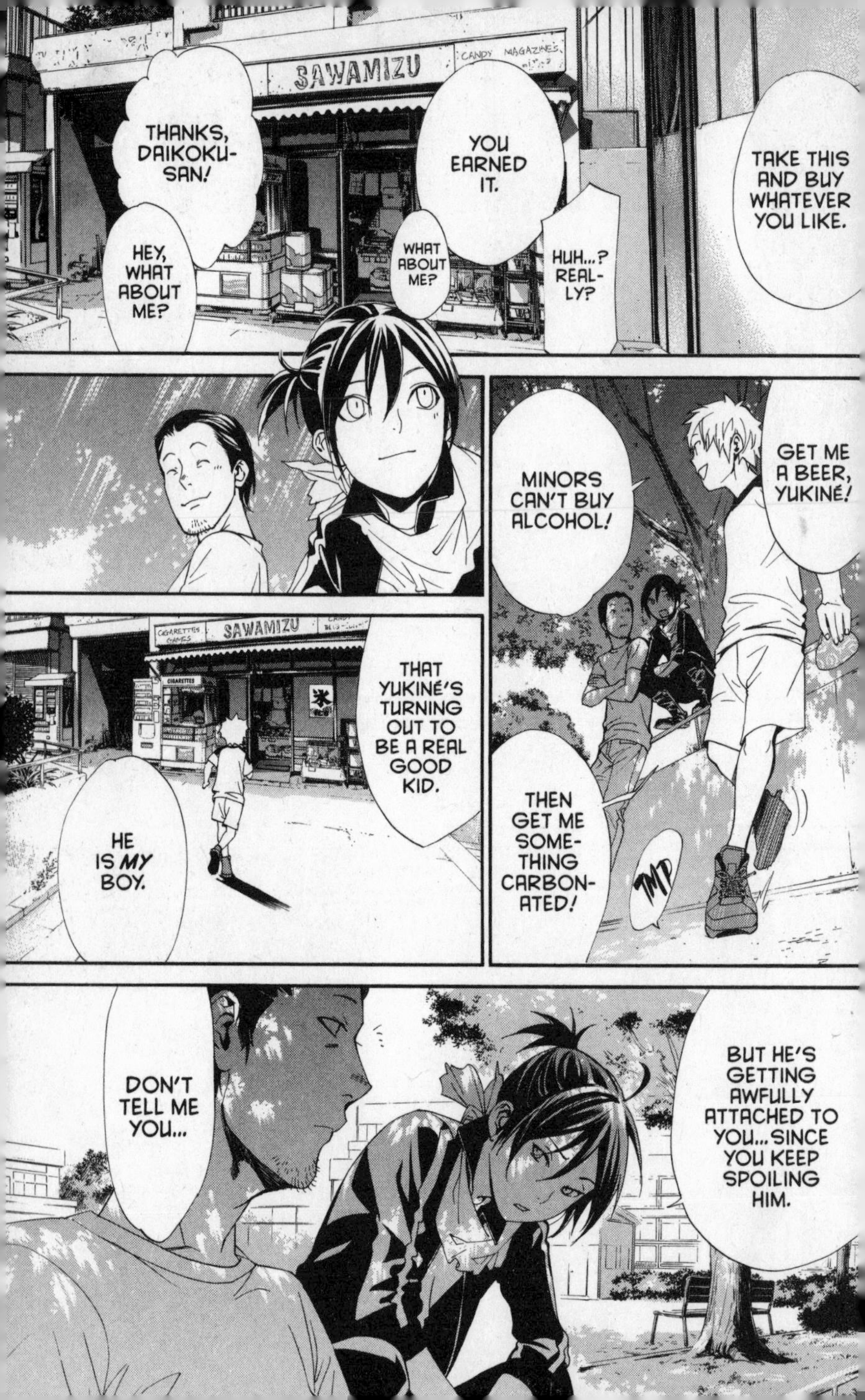
SAWAMIZU
CANDY MAGAZINES
TAKE THIS AND BUY WHATEVER YOU LIKE.
HUH...? REAL-LY?
YOU EARNED IT.
WHAT ABOUT ME?
THANKS, DAIKOKU-SAN!
HEY, WHAT ABOUT ME?
GET ME A BEER, YUKINÉ!
MINORS CAN'T BUY ALCOHOL!
THEN GET ME SOME-THING CARBON-ATED!
TMP
CIGARETTES GAMES
SAWAMIZU
CIGARETTES
THAT YUKINÉ'S TURNING OUT TO BE A REAL GOOD KID.
HE IS *MY* BOY.
BUT HE'S GETTING AWFULLY ATTACHED TO YOU...SINCE YOU KEEP SPOILING HIM.
DON'T TELL ME YOU...

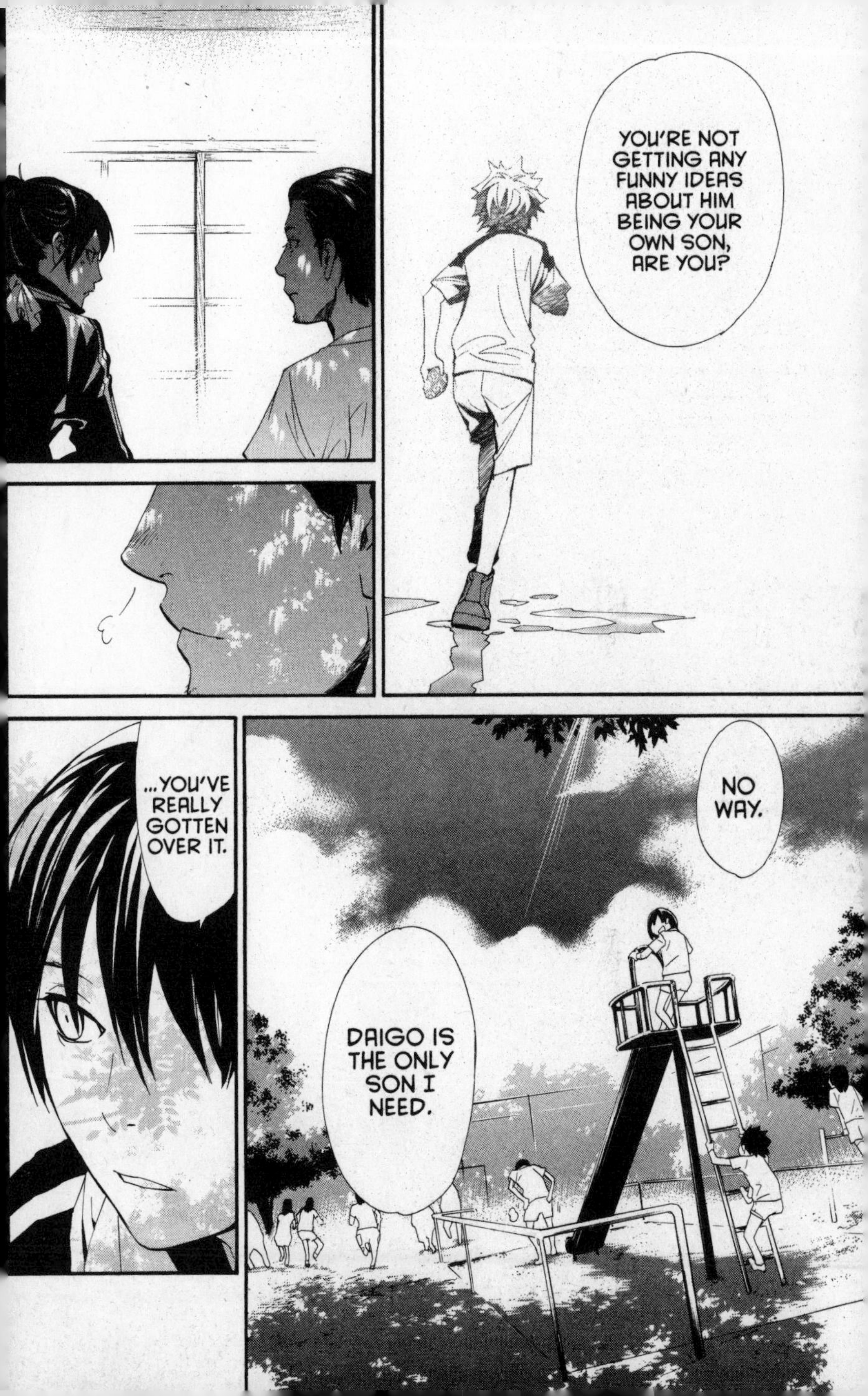
YOU'RE NOT GETTING ANY FUNNY IDEAS ABOUT HIM BEING YOUR OWN SON, ARE YOU?
NO WAY.
DAIGO IS THE ONLY SON I NEED.
...YOU'VE REALLY GOTTEN OVER IT.

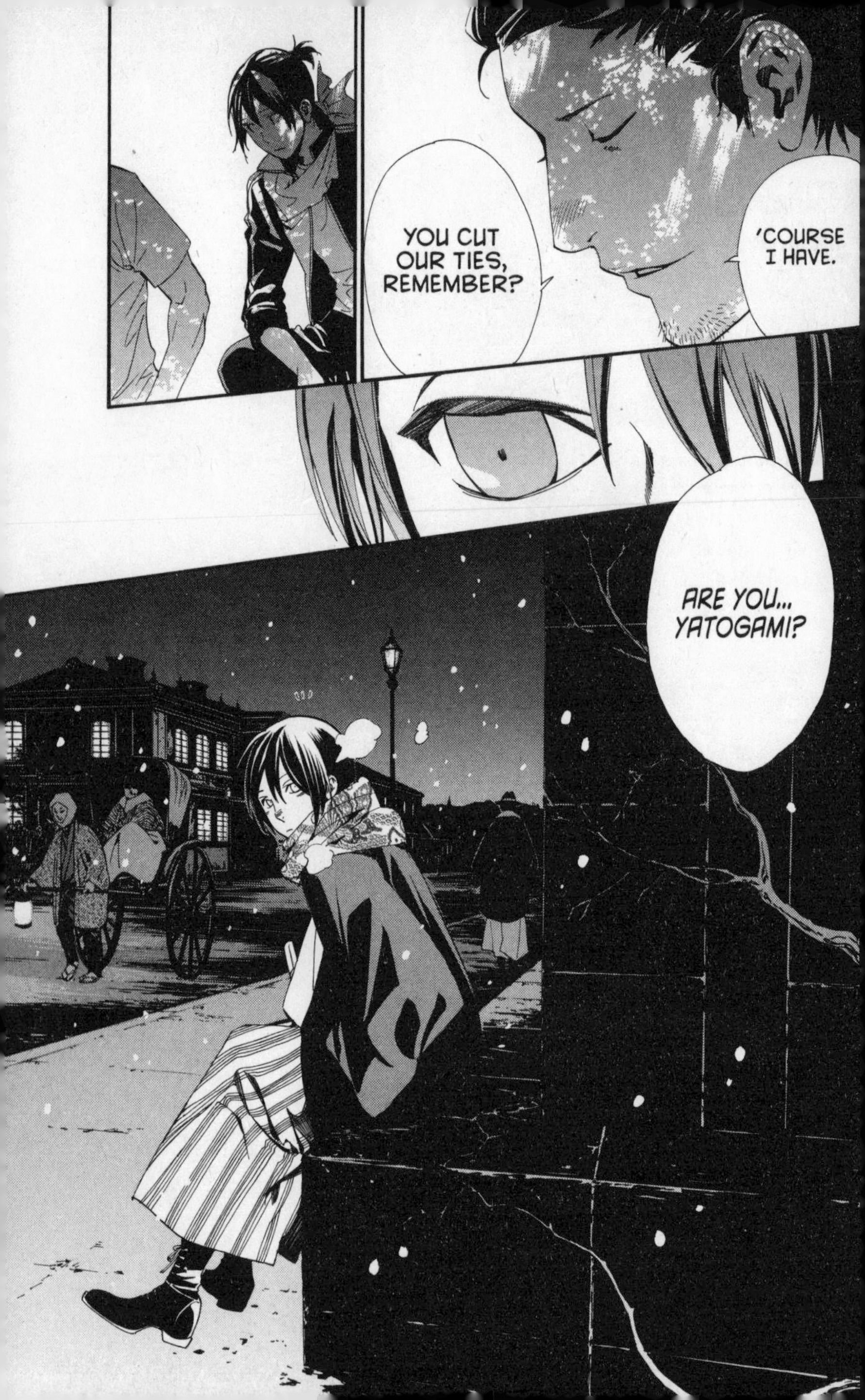
YOU CUT OUR TIES, REMEMBER?
'COURSE I HAVE.
ARE YOU... YATOGAMI?

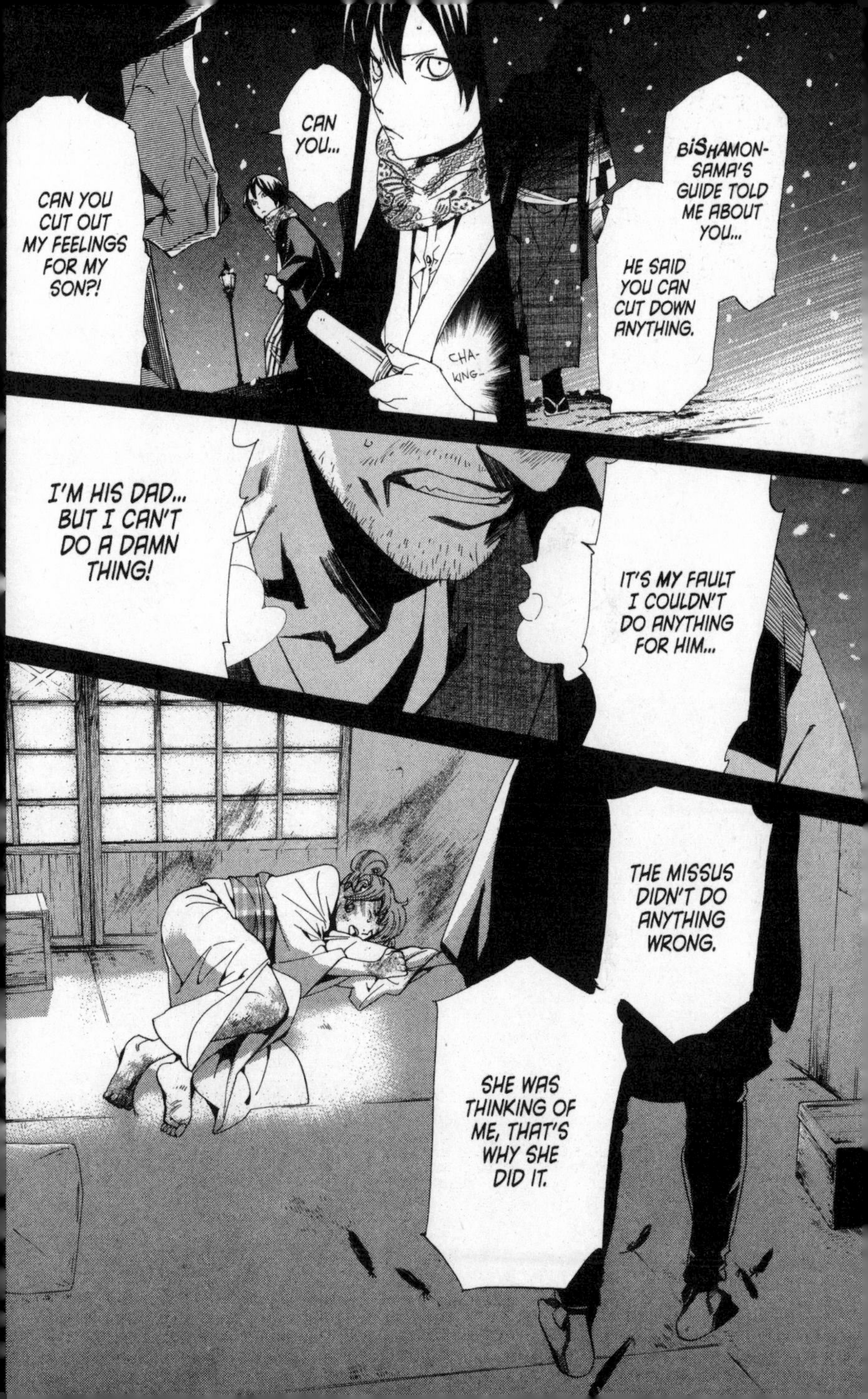
BISHAMON-SAMA'S GUIDE TOLD ME ABOUT YOU...
HE SAID YOU CAN CUT DOWN ANYTHING.
CHA-KING...
CAN YOU...
CAN YOU CUT OUT MY FEELINGS FOR MY SON?!
IT'S MY FAULT I COULDN'T DO ANYTHING FOR HIM...
I'M HIS DAD... BUT I CAN'T DO A DAMN THING!
THE MISSUS DIDN'T DO ANYTHING WRONG.
SHE WAS THINKING OF ME, THAT'S WHY SHE DID IT.

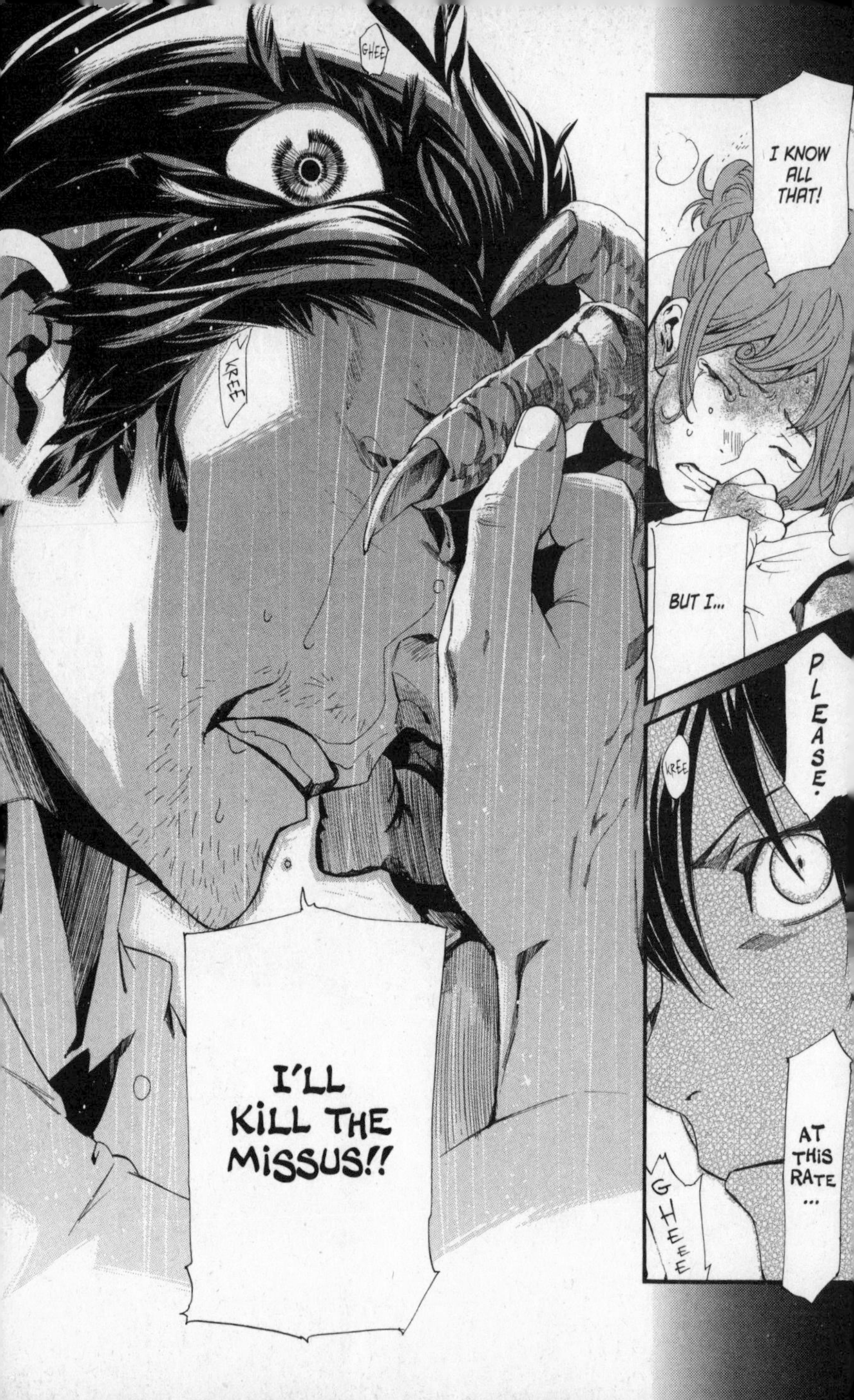
I KNOW ALL THAT!
BUT I...
PLEASE.
KREE
AT THIS RATE ...
GHEEE
GHEE
KREE
I'LL KILL THE MISSUS!!

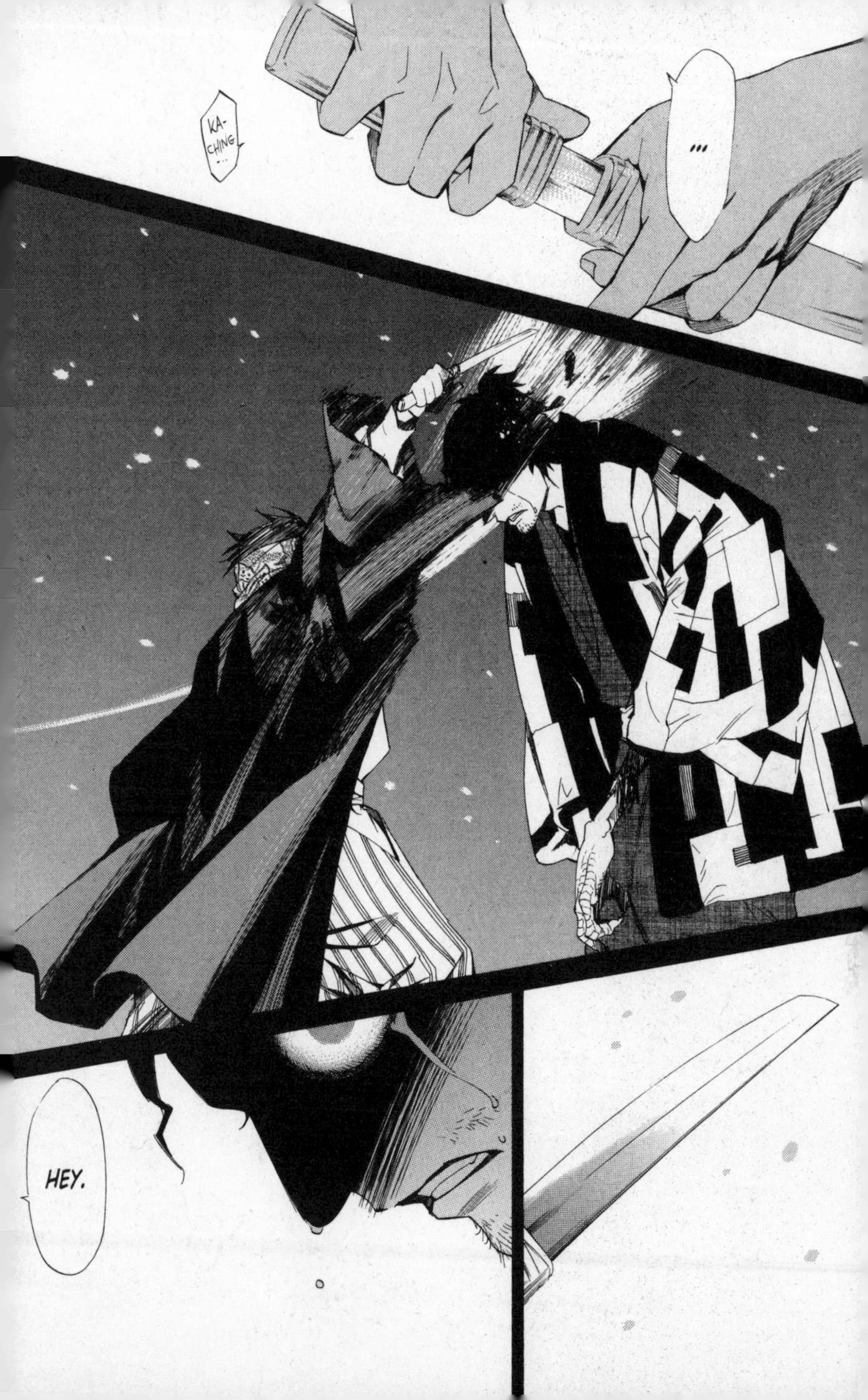
...
KA-CHING...
HEY.

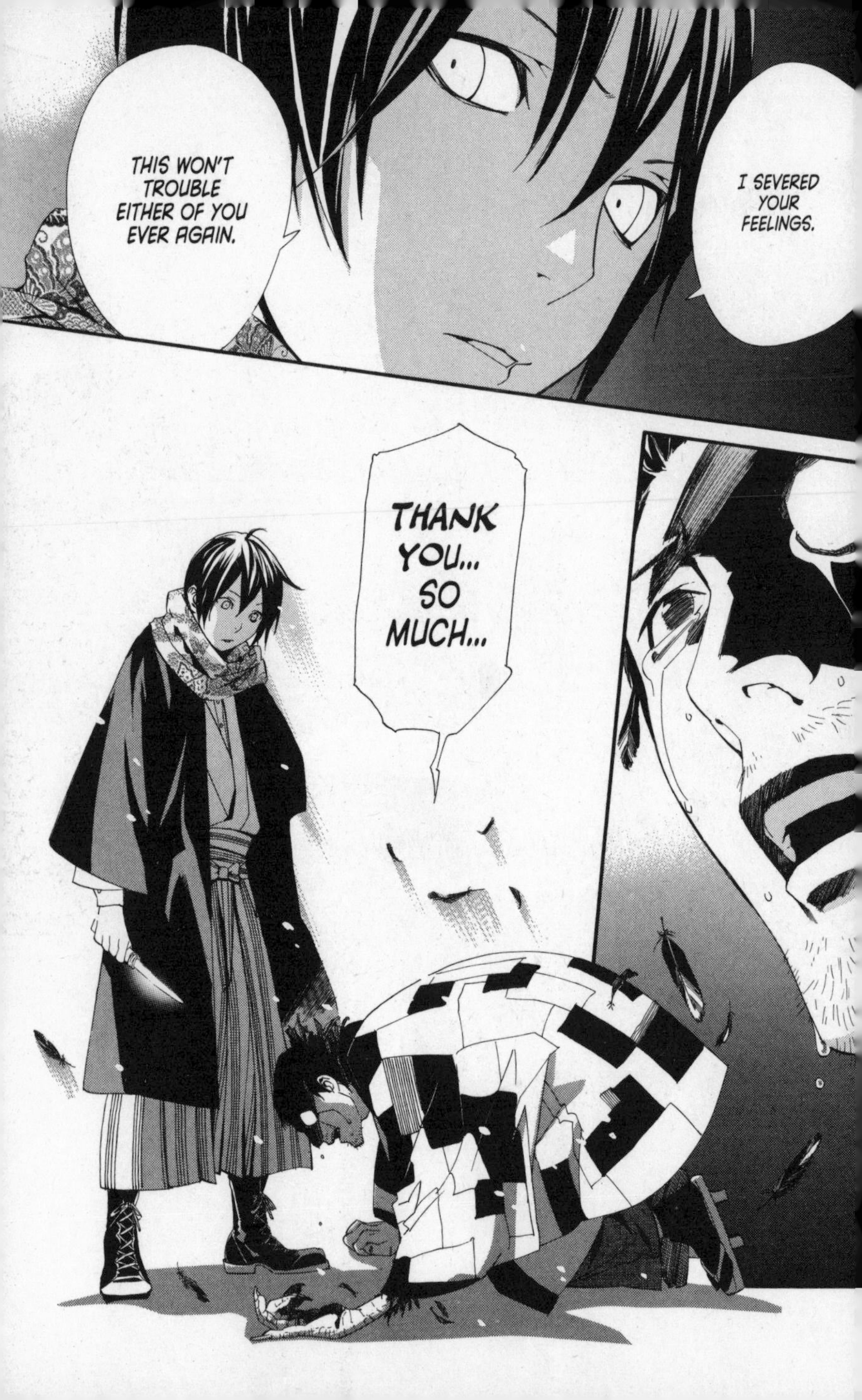
I SEVERED YOUR FEELINGS.
THIS WON'T TROUBLE EITHER OF YOU EVER AGAIN.
THANK YOU... SO MUCH...

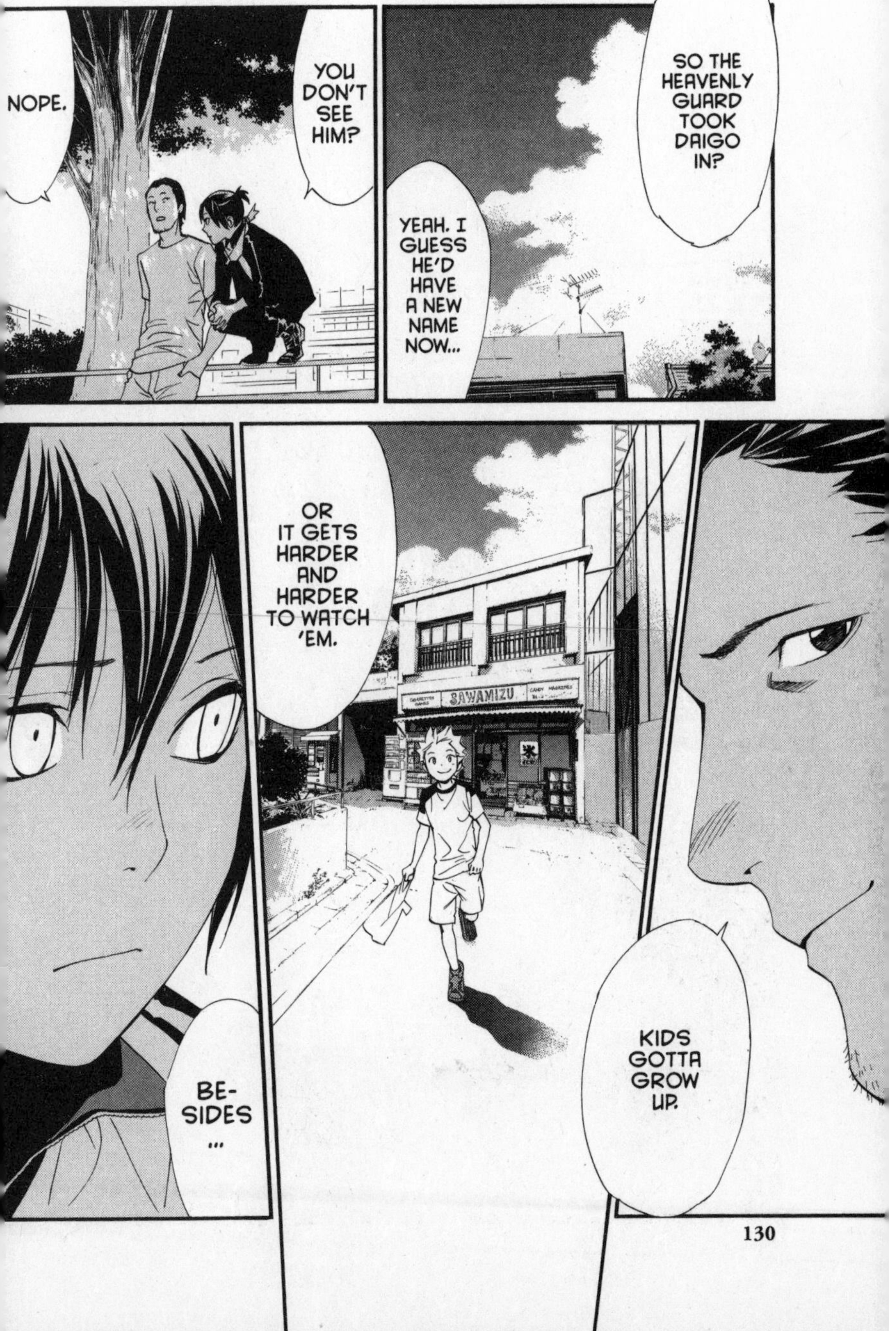
SO THE HEAVENLY GUARD TOOK DAIGO IN?
YEAH. I GUESS HE'D HAVE A NEW NAME NOW...
YOU DON'T SEE HIM?
NOPE.
KIDS GOTTA GROW UP.
OR IT GETS HARDER AND HARDER TO WATCH 'EM.
SAWAMIZU
BE-SIDES ...

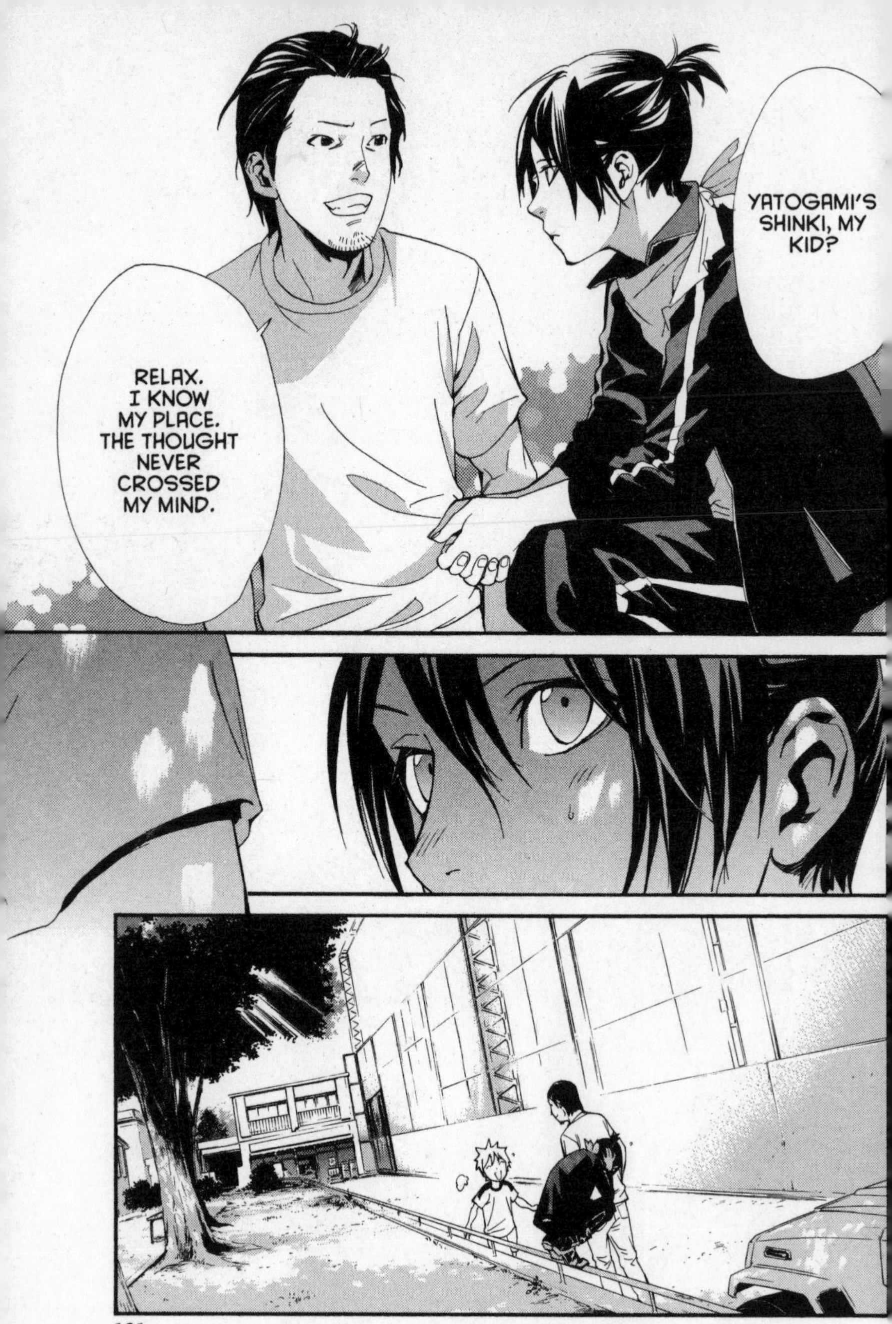
YATOGAMI'S SHINKI, MY KID?
RELAX. I KNOW MY PLACE. THE THOUGHT NEVER CROSSED MY MIND.

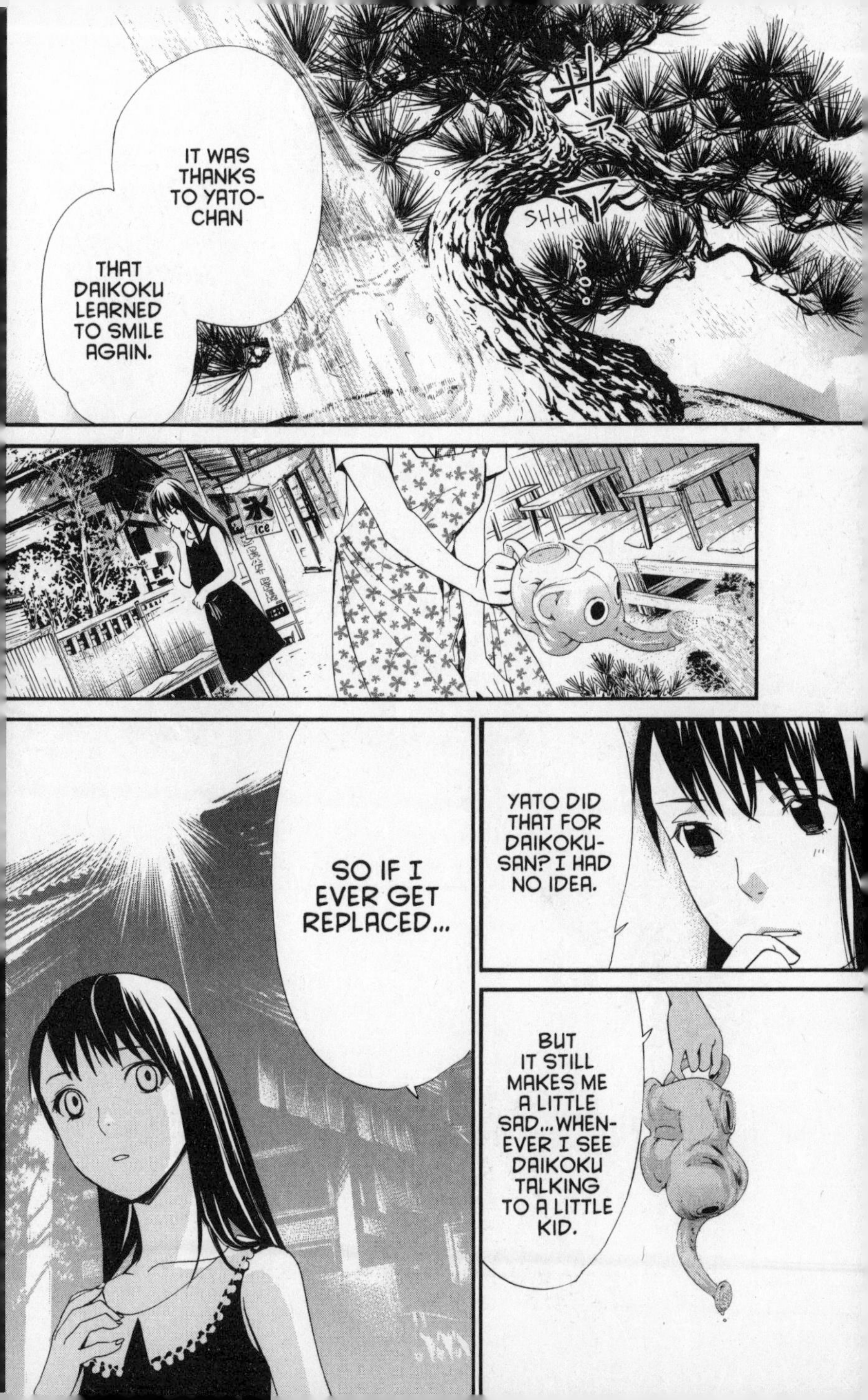
SHHH
IT WAS THANKS TO YATO-CHAN
THAT DAIKOKU LEARNED TO SMILE AGAIN.
Ice
YATO DID THAT FOR DAIKOKU-SAN? I HAD NO IDEA.
BUT IT STILL MAKES ME A LITTLE SAD...WHENEVER I SEE DAIKOKU TALKING TO A LITTLE KID.
SO IF I EVER GET REPLACED...

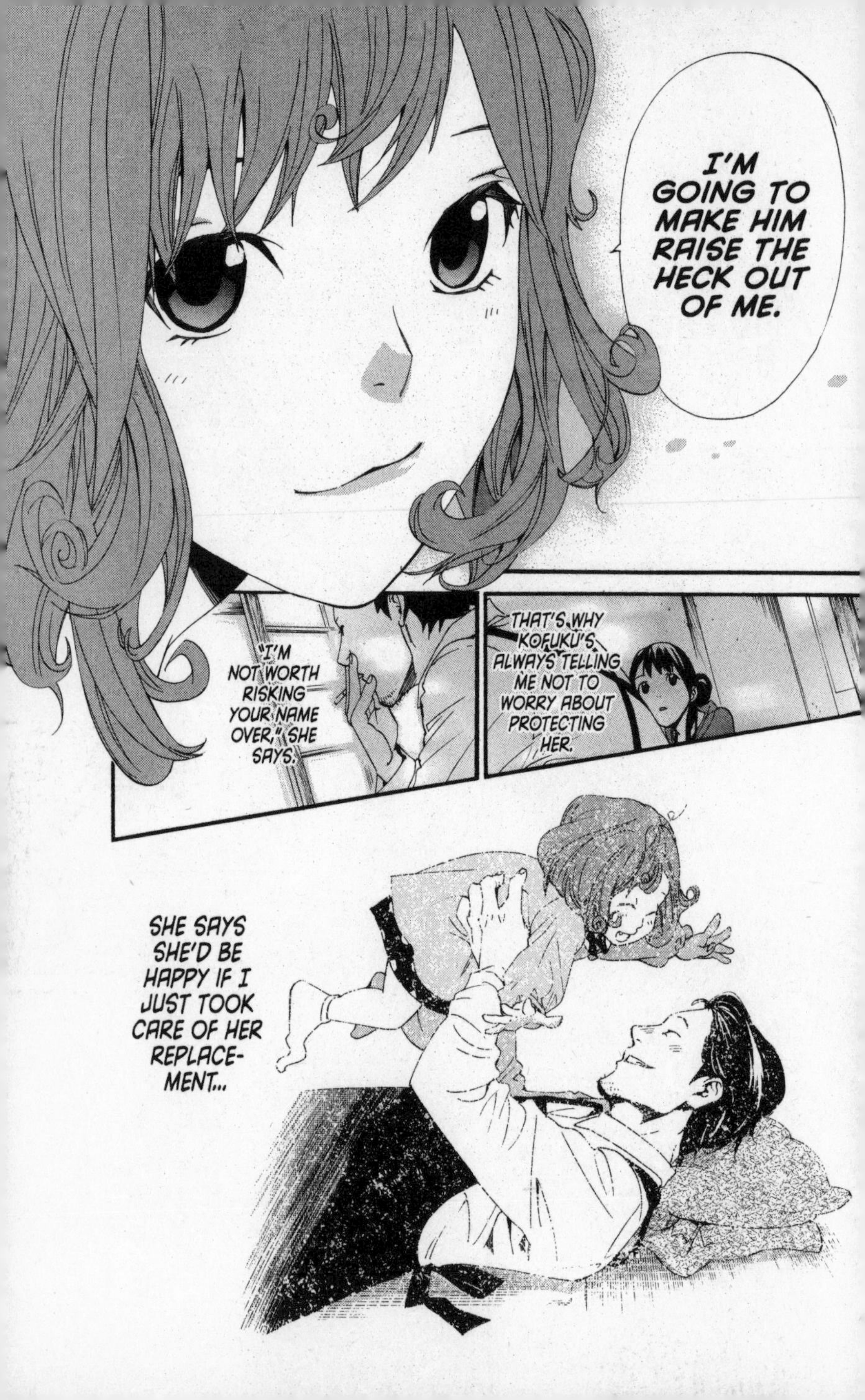
I'M GOING TO MAKE HIM RAISE THE HECK OUT OF ME.
THAT'S WHY KOFUKU'S ALWAYS TELLING ME NOT TO WORRY ABOUT PROTECTING HER.
"I'M NOT WORTH RISKING YOUR NAME OVER," SHE SAYS.
SHE SAYS SHE'D BE HAPPY IF I JUST TOOK CARE OF HER REPLACEMENT...

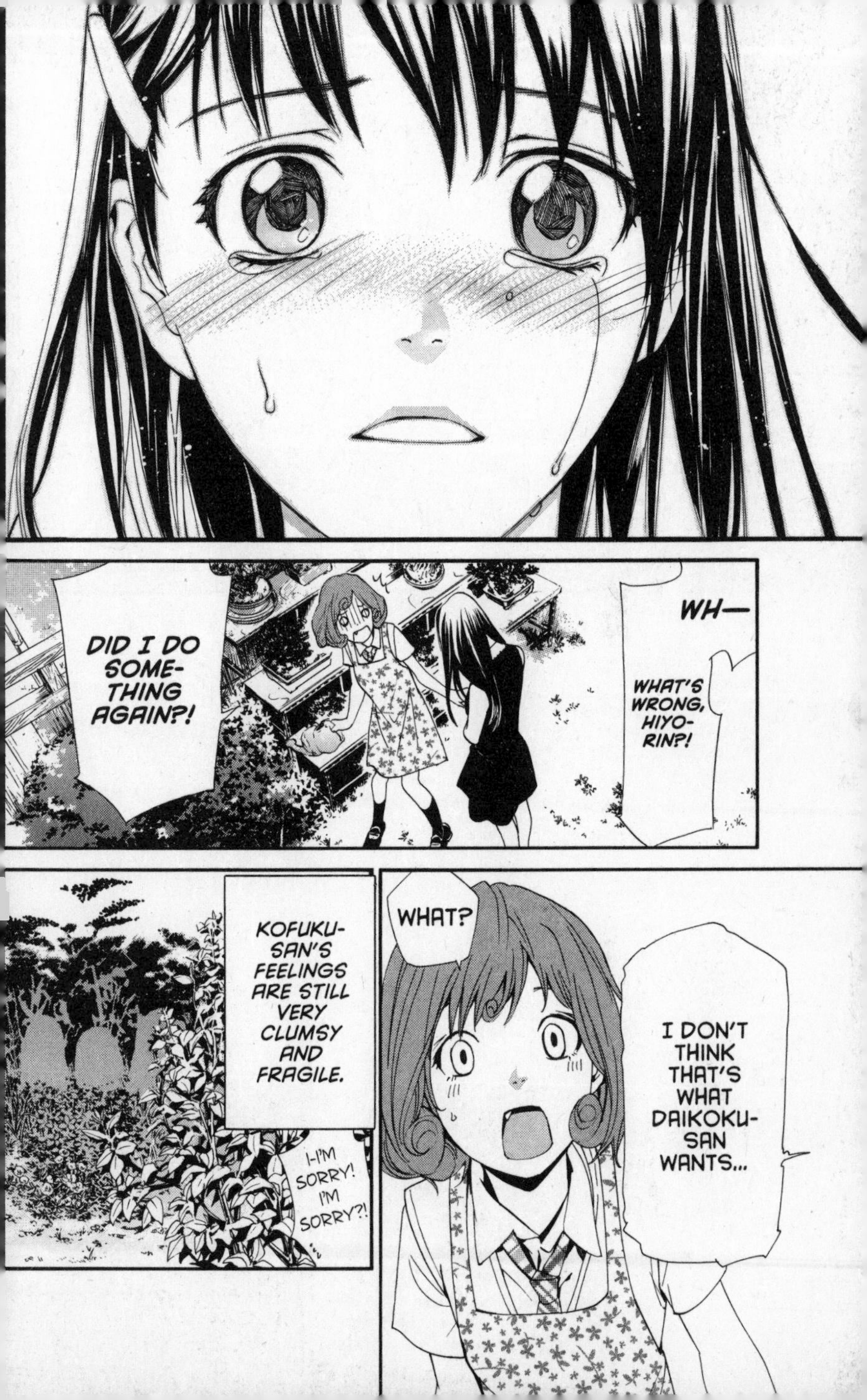
WH—
WHAT'S WRONG, HIYO-RIN?!
DID I DO SOME-THING AGAIN?!
WHAT?
I DON'T THINK THAT'S WHAT DAIKOKU-SAN WANTS...
KOFUKU-SAN'S FEELINGS ARE STILL VERY CLUMSY AND FRAGILE.
I-I'M SORRY! I'M SORRY?!

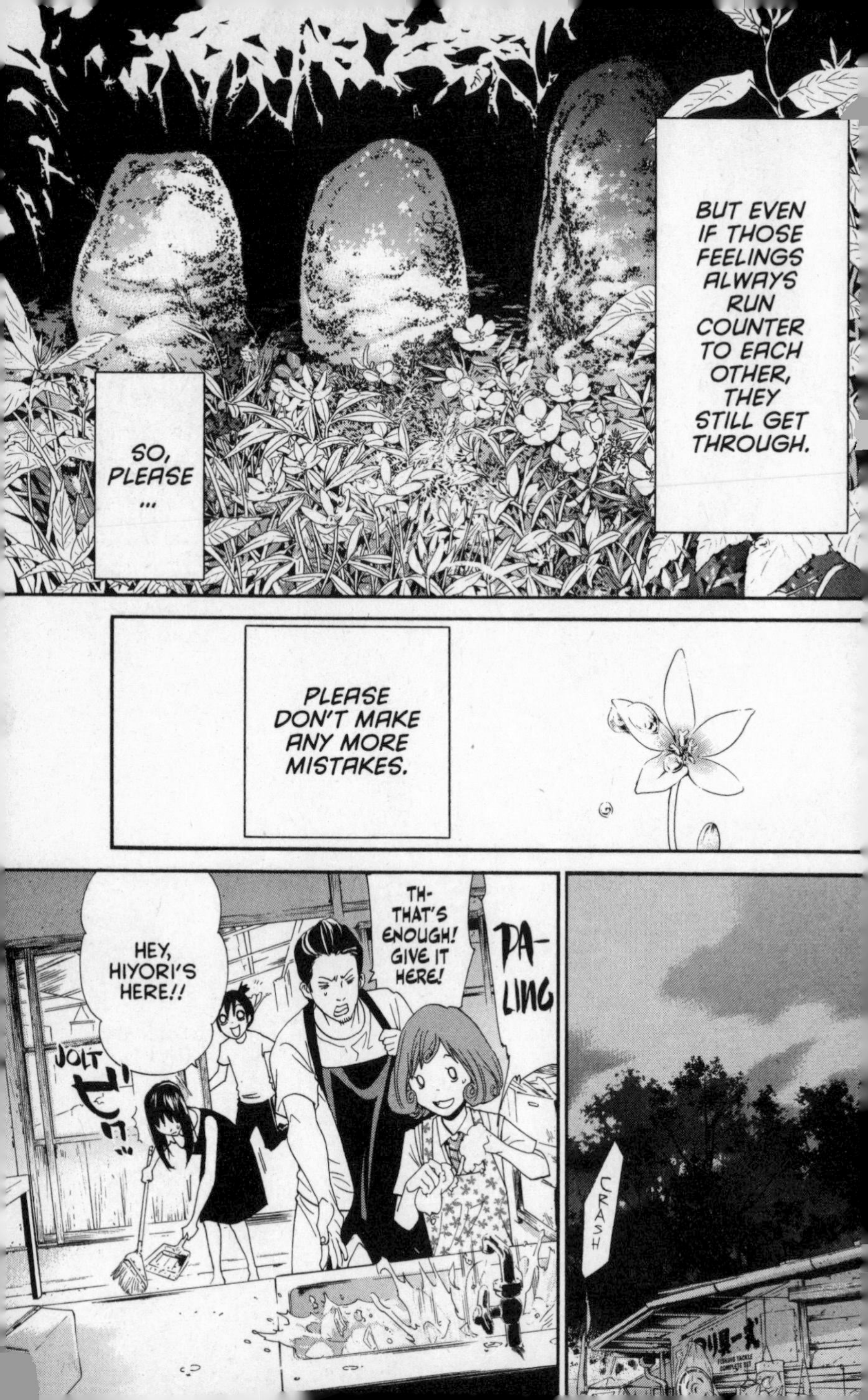
BUT EVEN IF THOSE FEELINGS ALWAYS RUN COUNTER TO EACH OTHER, THEY STILL GET THROUGH.
SO, PLEASE ...
PLEASE DON'T MAKE ANY MORE MISTAKES.
CRASH
PA-LING
TH-THAT'S ENOUGH! GIVE IT HERE!
HEY, HIYORI'S HERE!!
JOLT

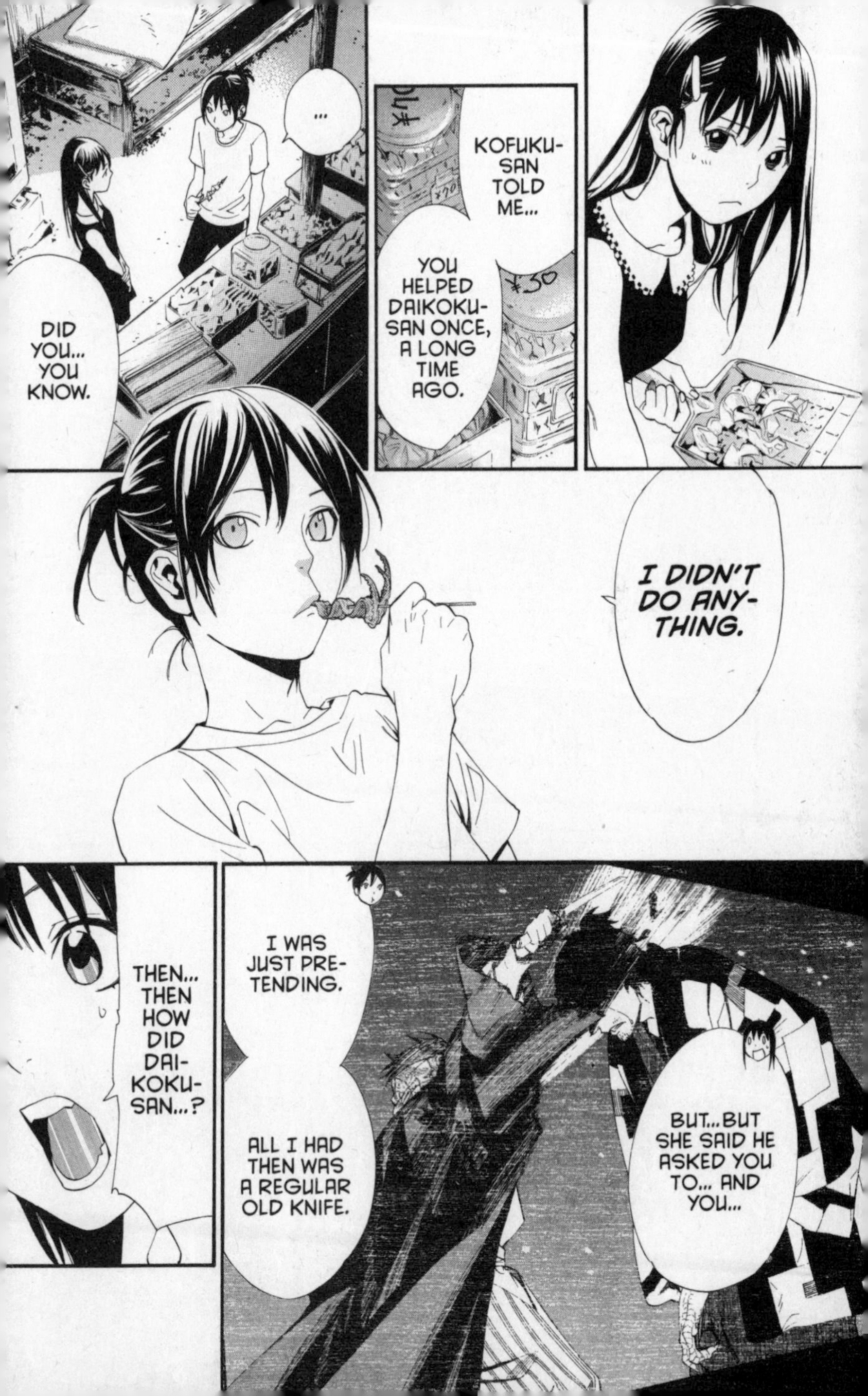
KOFUKU-SAN TOLD ME...
YOU HELPED DAIKOKU-SAN ONCE, A LONG TIME AGO.
...
DID YOU... YOU KNOW.
I DIDN'T DO ANYTHING.
BUT...BUT SHE SAID HE ASKED YOU TO... AND YOU...
I WAS JUST PRETENDING.
ALL I HAD THEN WAS A REGULAR OLD KNIFE.
THEN... THEN HOW DID DAIKOKU-SAN...?

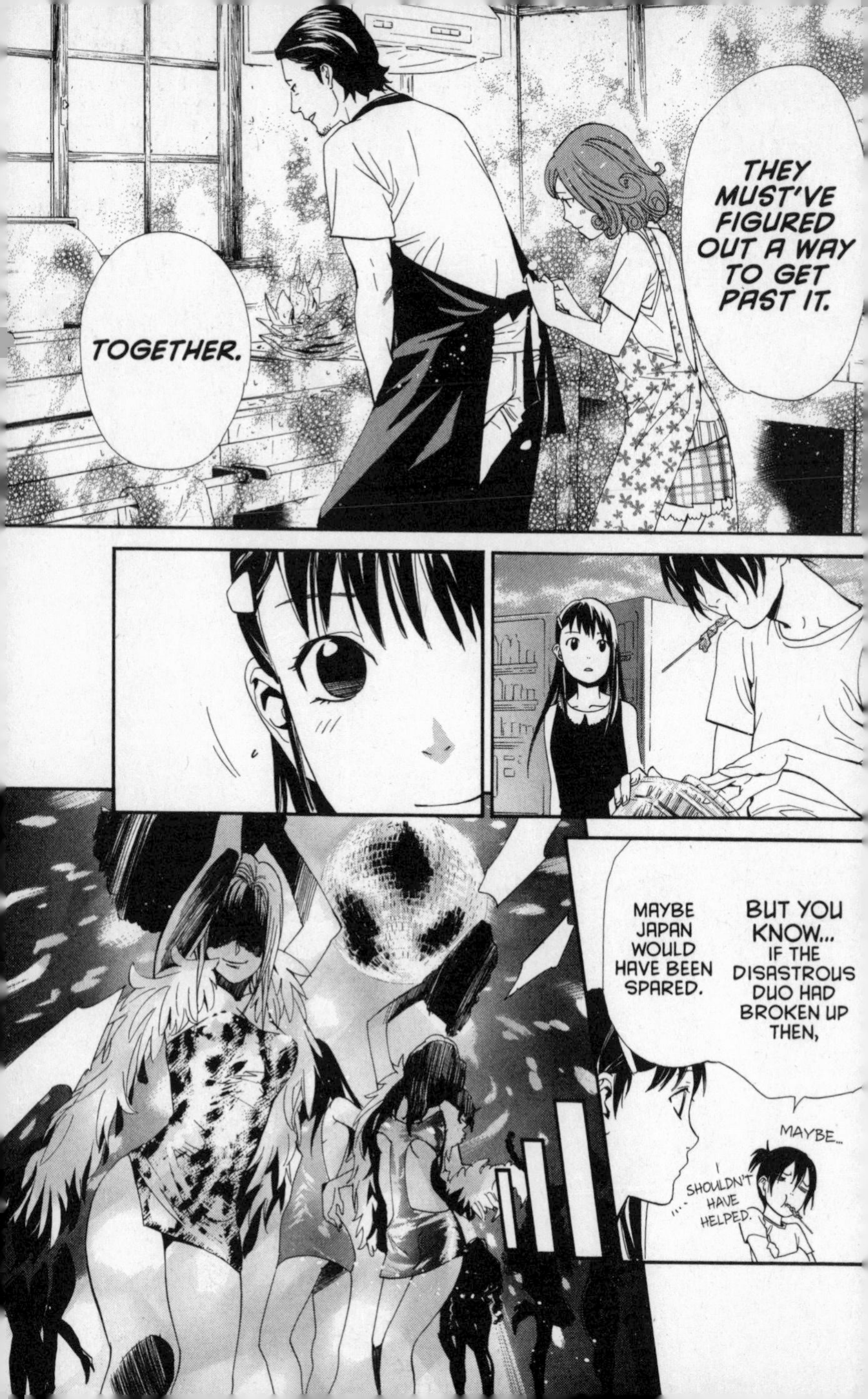
THEY MUST'VE FIGURED OUT A WAY TO GET PAST IT.
TOGETHER.
BUT YOU KNOW... IF THE DISASTROUS DUO HAD BROKEN UP THEN,
MAYBE JAPAN WOULD HAVE BEEN SPARED.
MAYBE...
I SHOULDN'T HAVE HELPED.

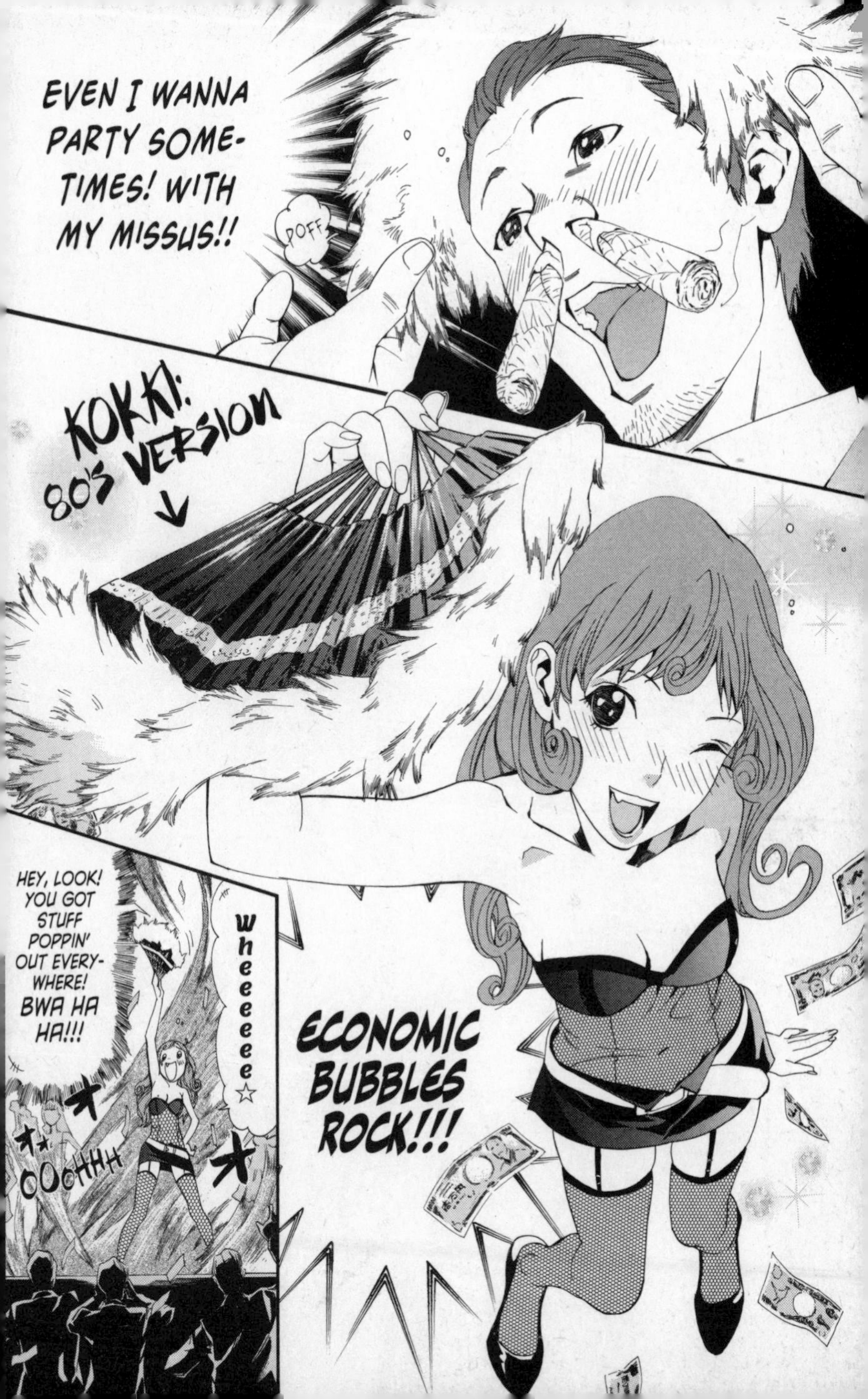
EVEN I WANNA PARTY SOME-TIMES! WITH MY MISSUS!!
POFF
KOKKI: 80's VERSION
ECONOMIC BUBBLES ROCK!!!
Wheeeeeee☆
HEY, LOOK! YOU GOT STUFF POPPIN' OUT EVERY-WHERE! BWA HA HA!!!
OOOHHH

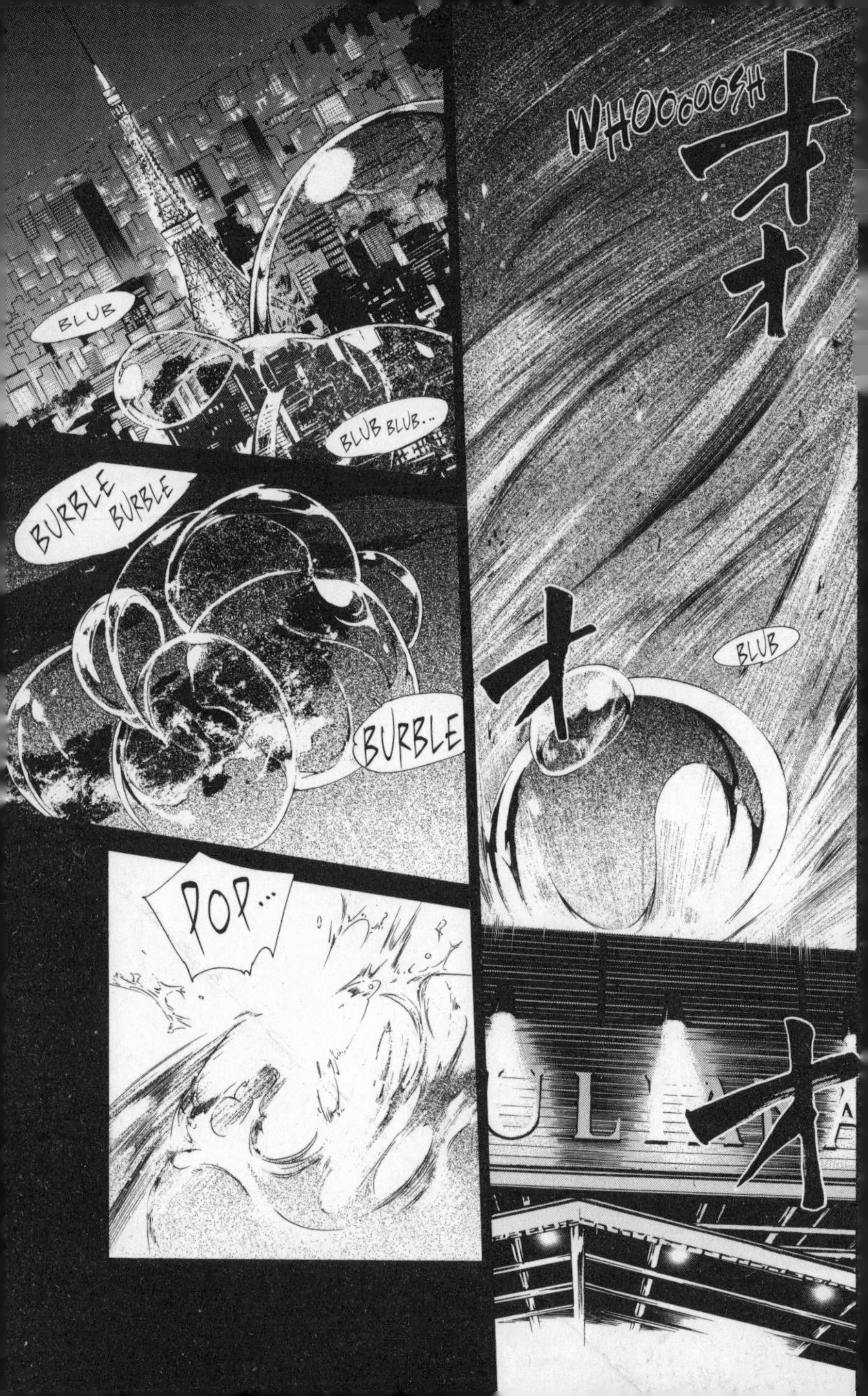
WHOOOOOSH
オオ
オ
BLUB
BLUB
BLUB BLUB...
BURBLE BURBLE
BURBLE
オ
POP...

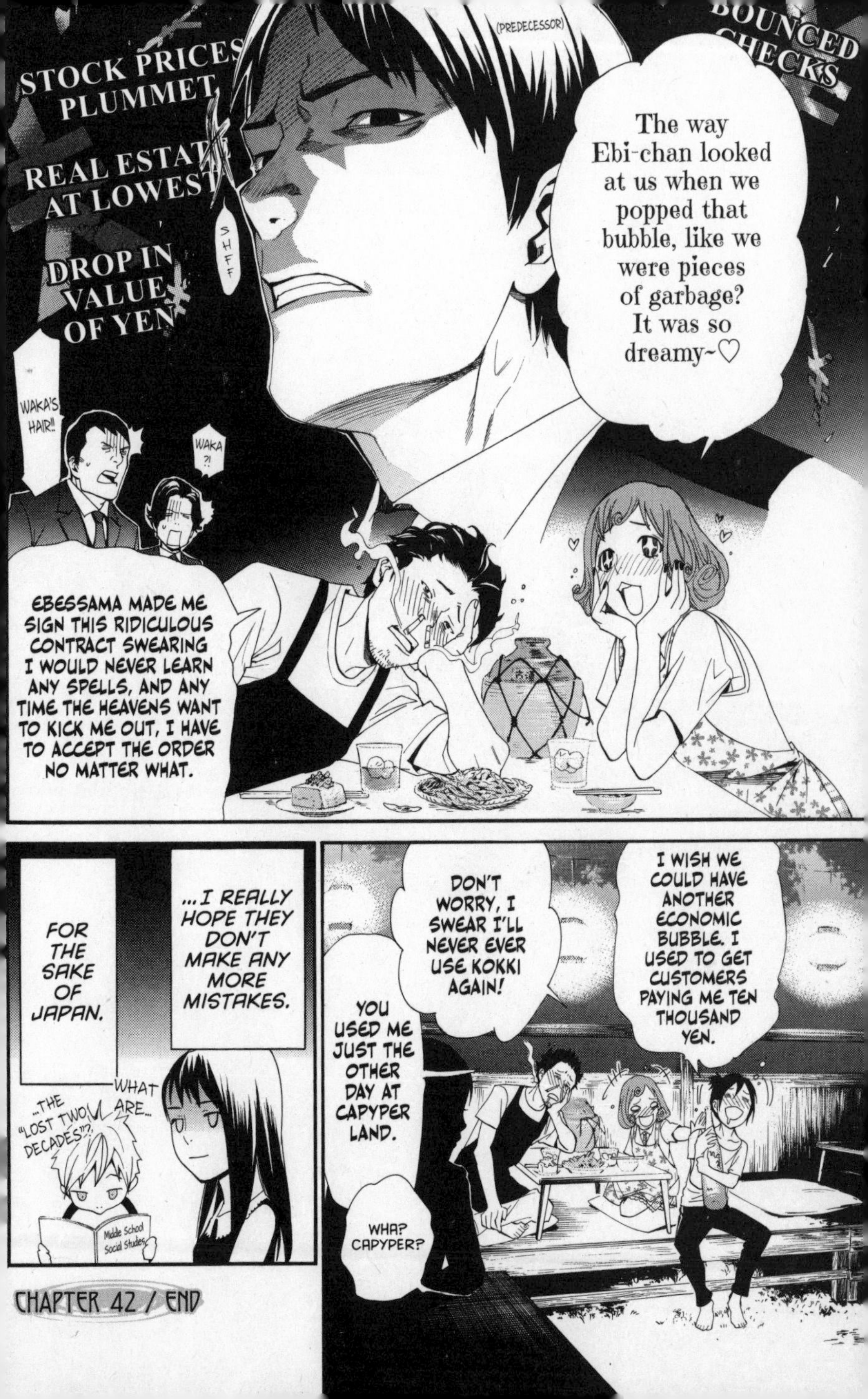
(PREDECESSOR)
BOUNCED CHECKS
The way Ebi-chan looked at us when we popped that bubble, like we were pieces of garbage? It was so dreamy~♡
STOCK PRICES PLUMMET
REAL ESTATE AT LOWEST
DROP IN VALUE OF YEN
SHFF
WAKA ?!
WAKA'S HAIR!!
EBESSAMA MADE ME SIGN THIS RIDICULOUS CONTRACT SWEARING I WOULD NEVER LEARN ANY SPELLS, AND ANY TIME THE HEAVENS WANT TO KICK ME OUT, I HAVE TO ACCEPT THE ORDER NO MATTER WHAT.
I WISH WE COULD HAVE ANOTHER ECONOMIC BUBBLE. I USED TO GET CUSTOMERS PAYING ME TEN THOUSAND YEN.
DON'T WORRY, I SWEAR I'LL NEVER EVER USE KOKKI AGAIN!
YOU USED ME JUST THE OTHER DAY AT CAPYPER LAND.
WHA? CAPYPER?
...I REALLY HOPE THEY DON'T MAKE ANY MORE MISTAKES.
FOR THE SAKE OF JAPAN.
WHAT ARE...
...THE "LOST TWO DECADES"!?
Middle School Social Studies
CHAPTER 42 / END

野

㿟

禪

聖

㝵

祡

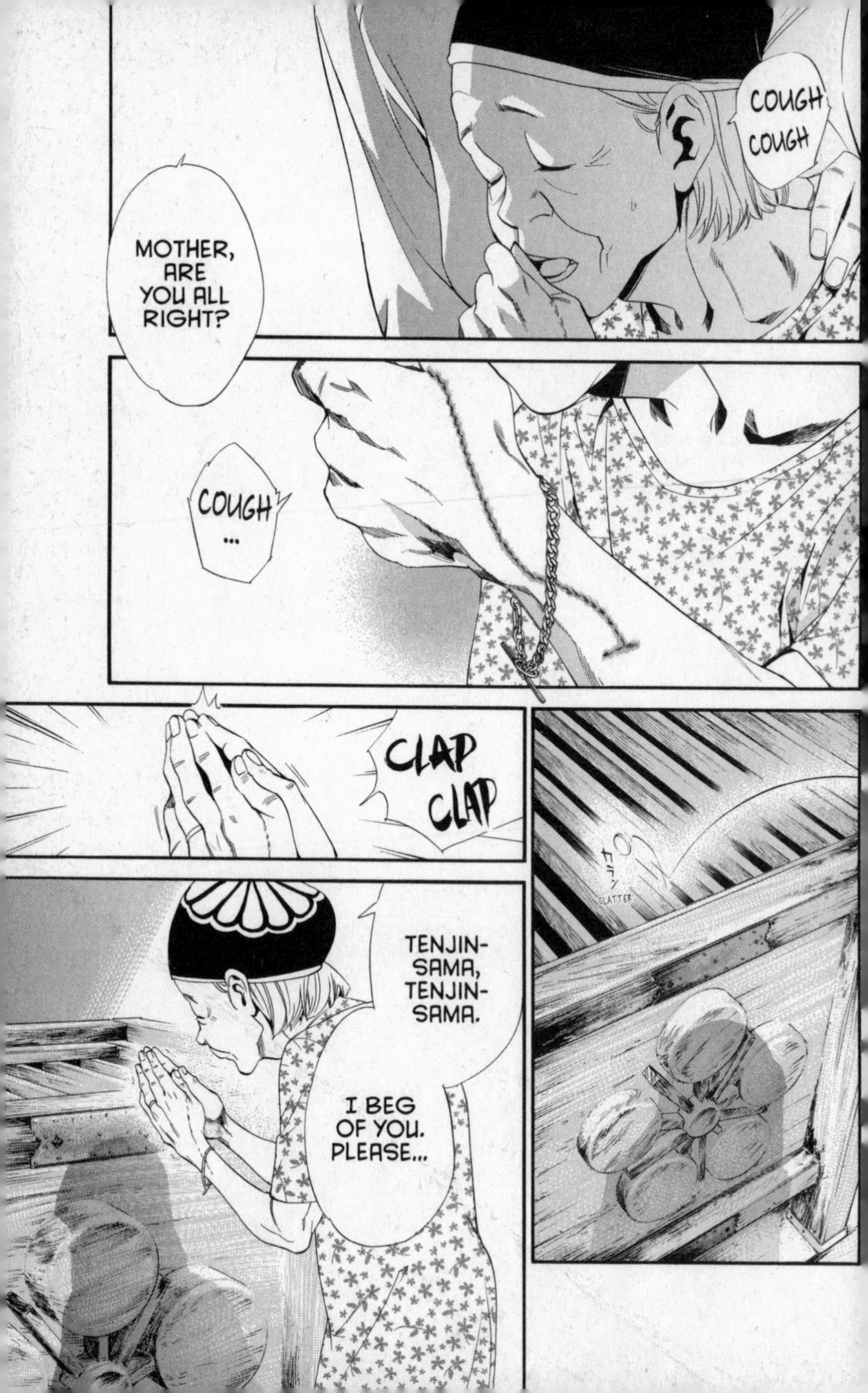
COUGH COUGH
MOTHER, ARE YOU ALL RIGHT?
COUGH ...
カラン
CLATTER
CLAP CLAP
TENJIN-SAMA, TENJIN-SAMA.
I BEG OF YOU. PLEASE...

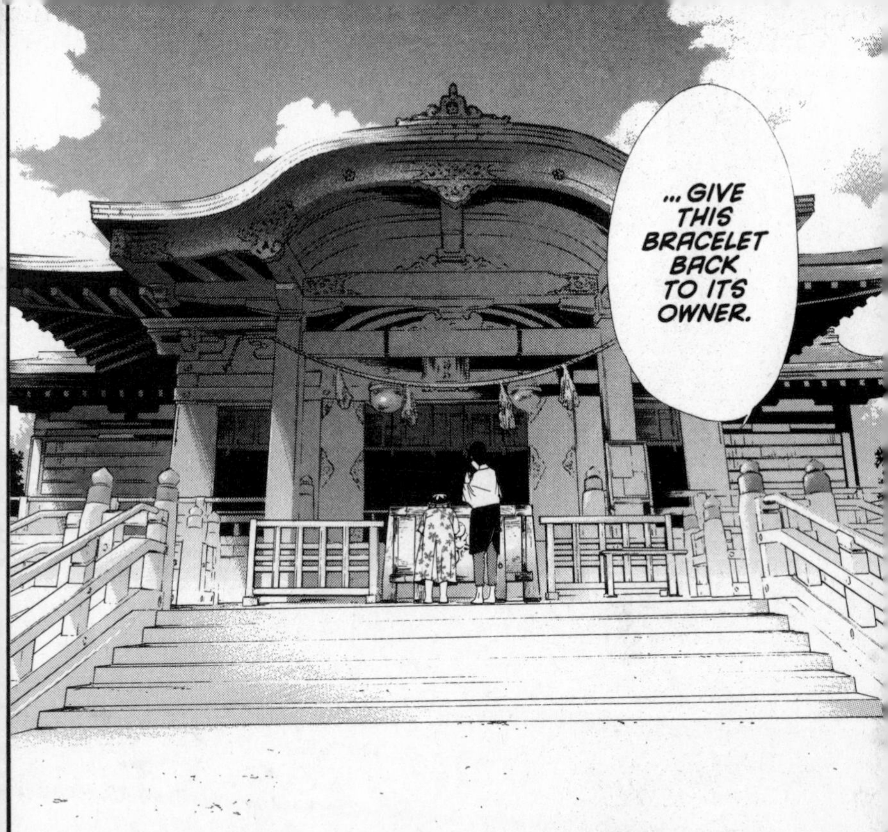
...GIVE THIS BRACELET BACK TO ITS OWNER.

CHAPTER 43: SECRETS

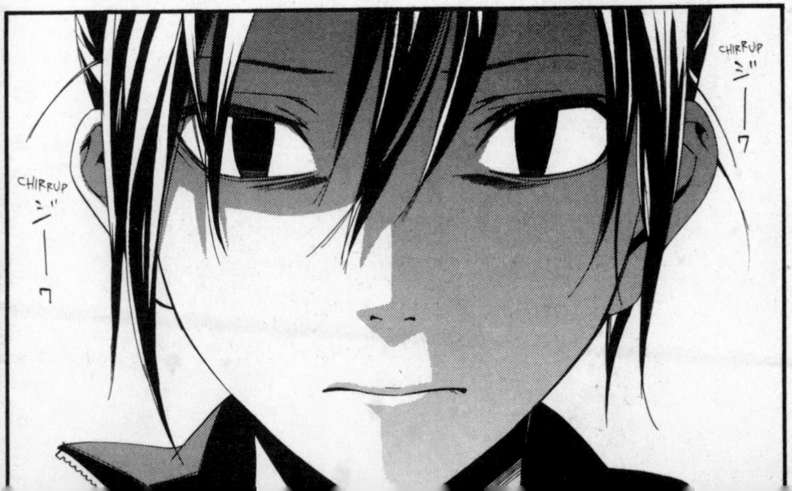
CHIRRUP
CHIRRUP

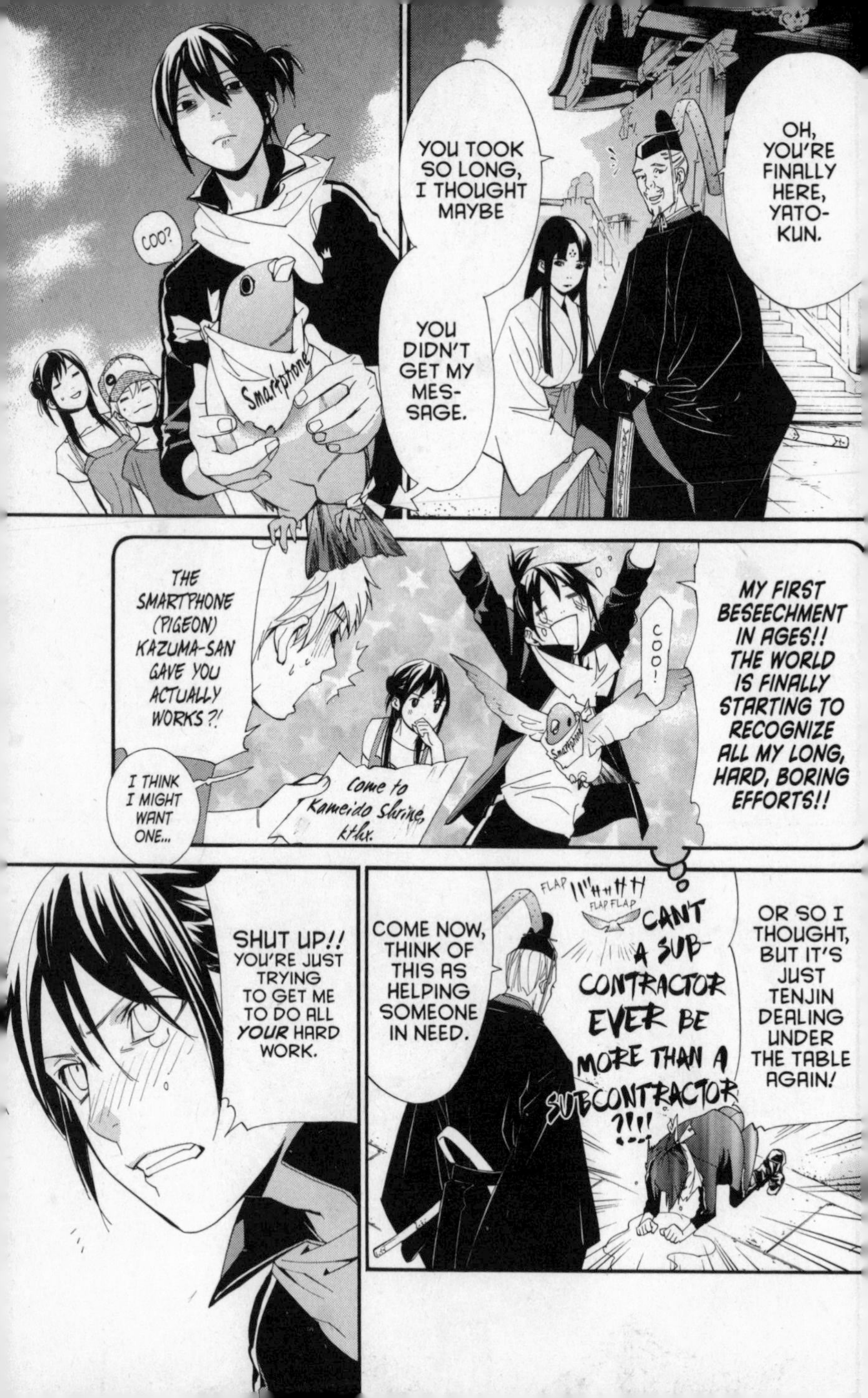
OH, YOU'RE FINALLY HERE, YATO-KUN.
YOU TOOK SO LONG, I THOUGHT MAYBE
YOU DIDN'T GET MY MES-SAGE.
COO?
Smartphone
MY FIRST BESEECHMENT IN AGES!! THE WORLD IS FINALLY STARTING TO RECOGNIZE ALL MY LONG, HARD, BORING EFFORTS!!
COO!
Smartphone
THE SMARTPHONE (PIGEON) KAZUMA-SAN GAVE YOU ACTUALLY WORKS?!
Come to Kameido Shrine, kthx.
I THINK I MIGHT WANT ONE...
OR SO I THOUGHT, BUT IT'S JUST TENJIN DEALING UNDER THE TABLE AGAIN!
FLAP FLAP FLAP
CAN'T A SUB-CONTRACTOR EVER BE MORE THAN A SUBCONTRACTOR?!!!
COME NOW, THINK OF THIS AS HELPING SOMEONE IN NEED.
SHUT UP!! YOU'RE JUST TRYING TO GET ME TO DO ALL *YOUR* HARD WORK.

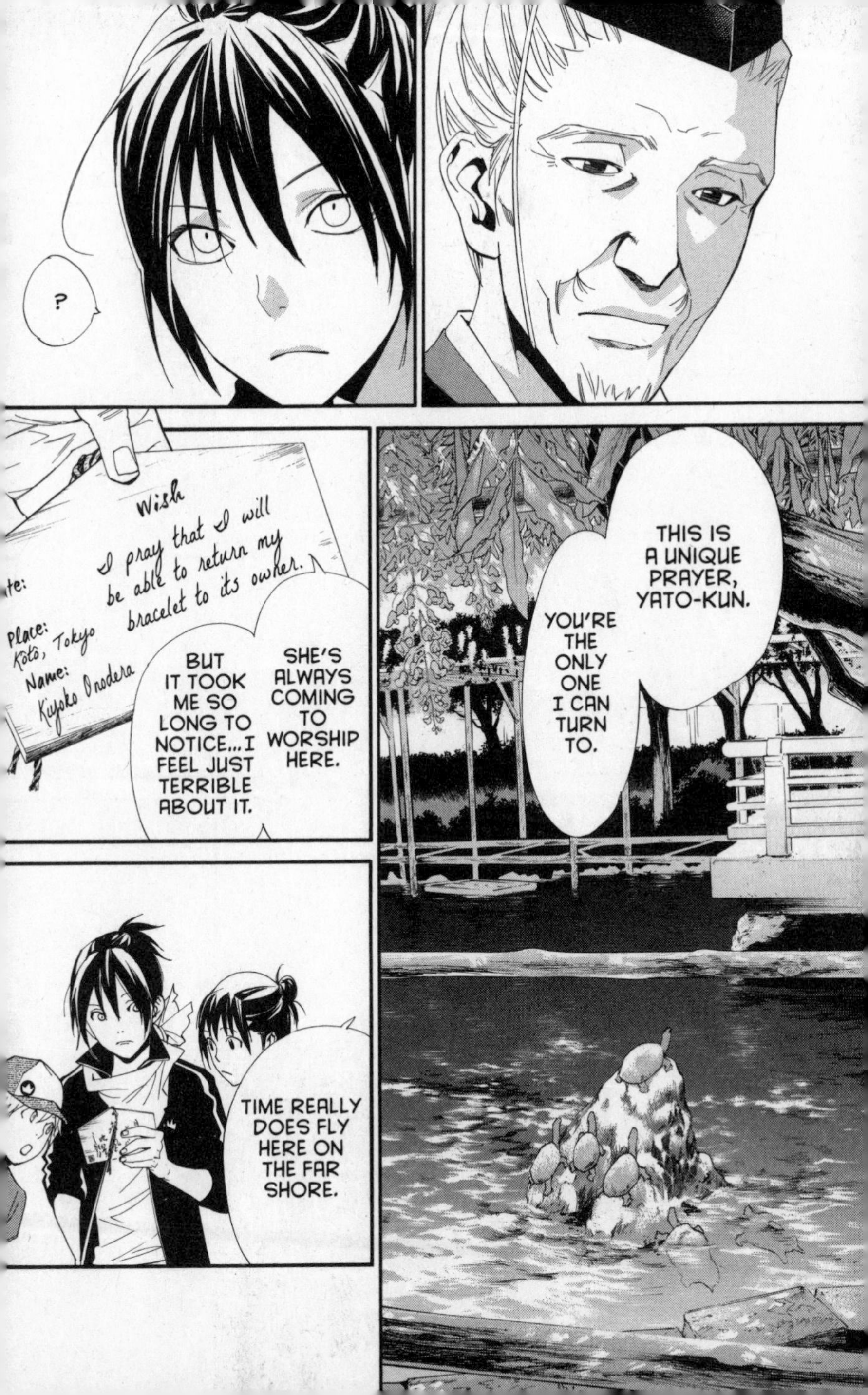
?
THIS IS A UNIQUE PRAYER, YATO-KUN.
YOU'RE THE ONLY ONE I CAN TURN TO.
Wish
I pray that I will be able to return my bracelet to its owner.
te:
Place: Kōtō, Tokyo
Name: Kiyoko Onodera
SHE'S ALWAYS COMING TO WORSHIP HERE.
BUT IT TOOK ME SO LONG TO NOTICE...I FEEL JUST TERRIBLE ABOUT IT.
TIME REALLY DOES FLY HERE ON THE FAR SHORE.

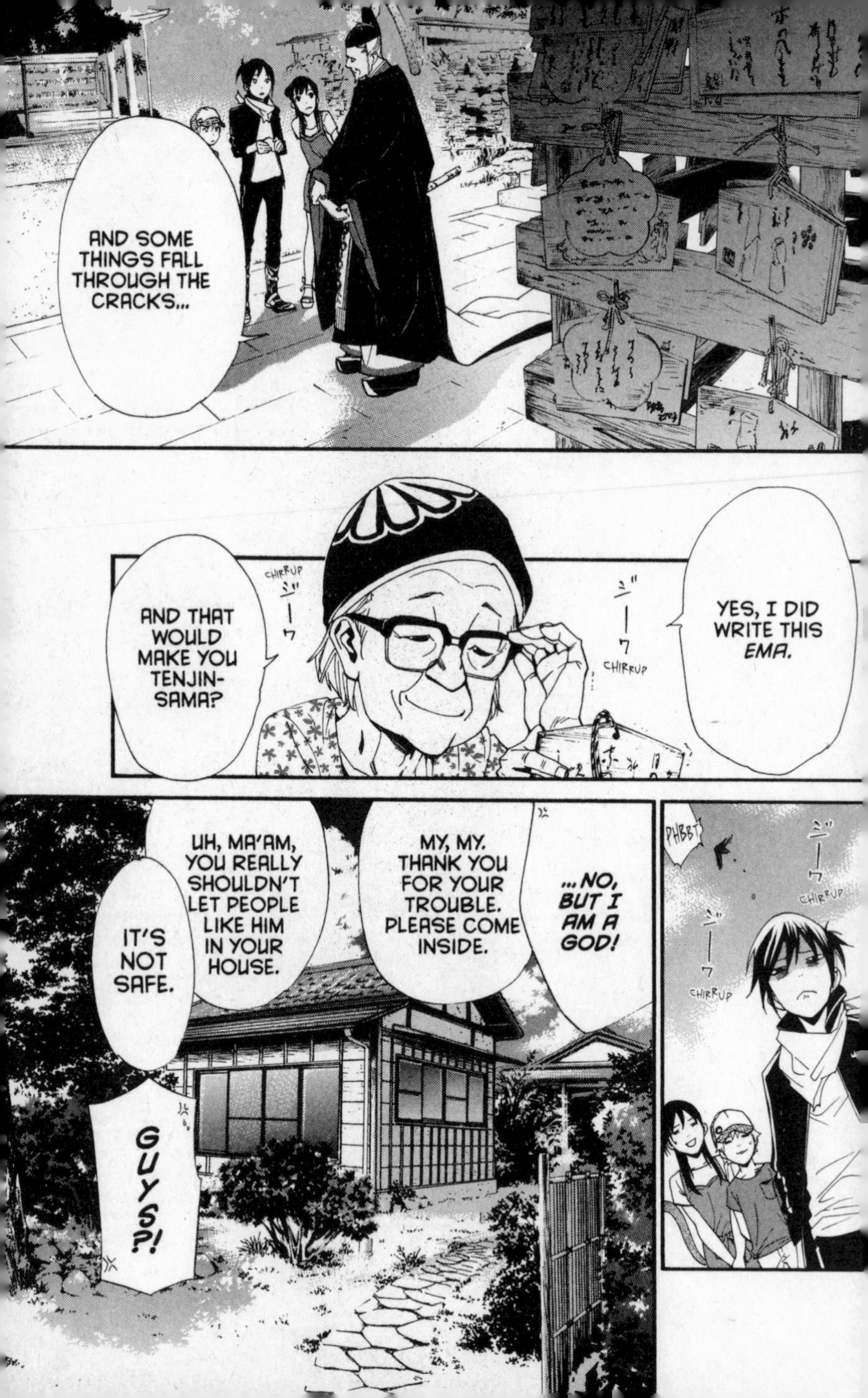
AND SOME THINGS FALL THROUGH THE CRACKS...
CHIRRUP
YES, I DID WRITE THIS *EMA*.
CHIRRUP
AND THAT WOULD MAKE YOU TENJIN-SAMA?
CHIRRUP
PHBBT
CHIRRUP
...NO, BUT I AM A GOD!
MY, MY. THANK YOU FOR YOUR TROUBLE. PLEASE COME INSIDE.
UH, MA'AM, YOU REALLY SHOULDN'T LET PEOPLE LIKE HIM IN YOUR HOUSE.
IT'S NOT SAFE.
GUYS?!

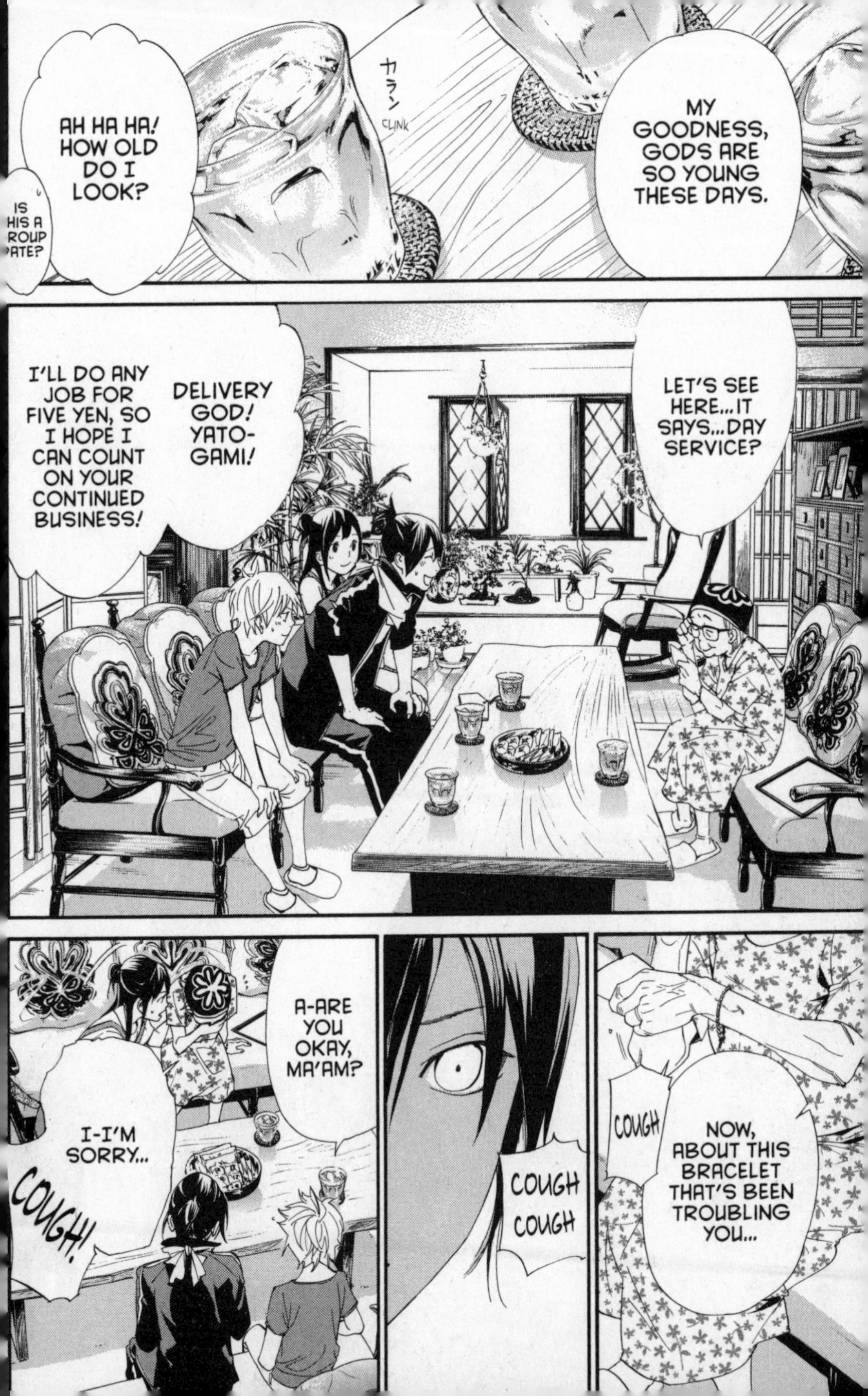
MY GOODNESS, GODS ARE SO YOUNG THESE DAYS.
カラン
CLINK
AH HA HA! HOW OLD DO I LOOK?
IS HIS A ROUP ATE?
LET'S SEE HERE...IT SAYS...DAY SERVICE?
DELIVERY GOD! YATO-GAMI!
I'LL DO ANY JOB FOR FIVE YEN, SO I HOPE I CAN COUNT ON YOUR CONTINUED BUSINESS!
NOW, ABOUT THIS BRACELET THAT'S BEEN TROUBLING YOU...
COUGH
COUGH
COUGH
A-ARE YOU OKAY, MA'AM?
I-I'M SORRY...
COUGH!

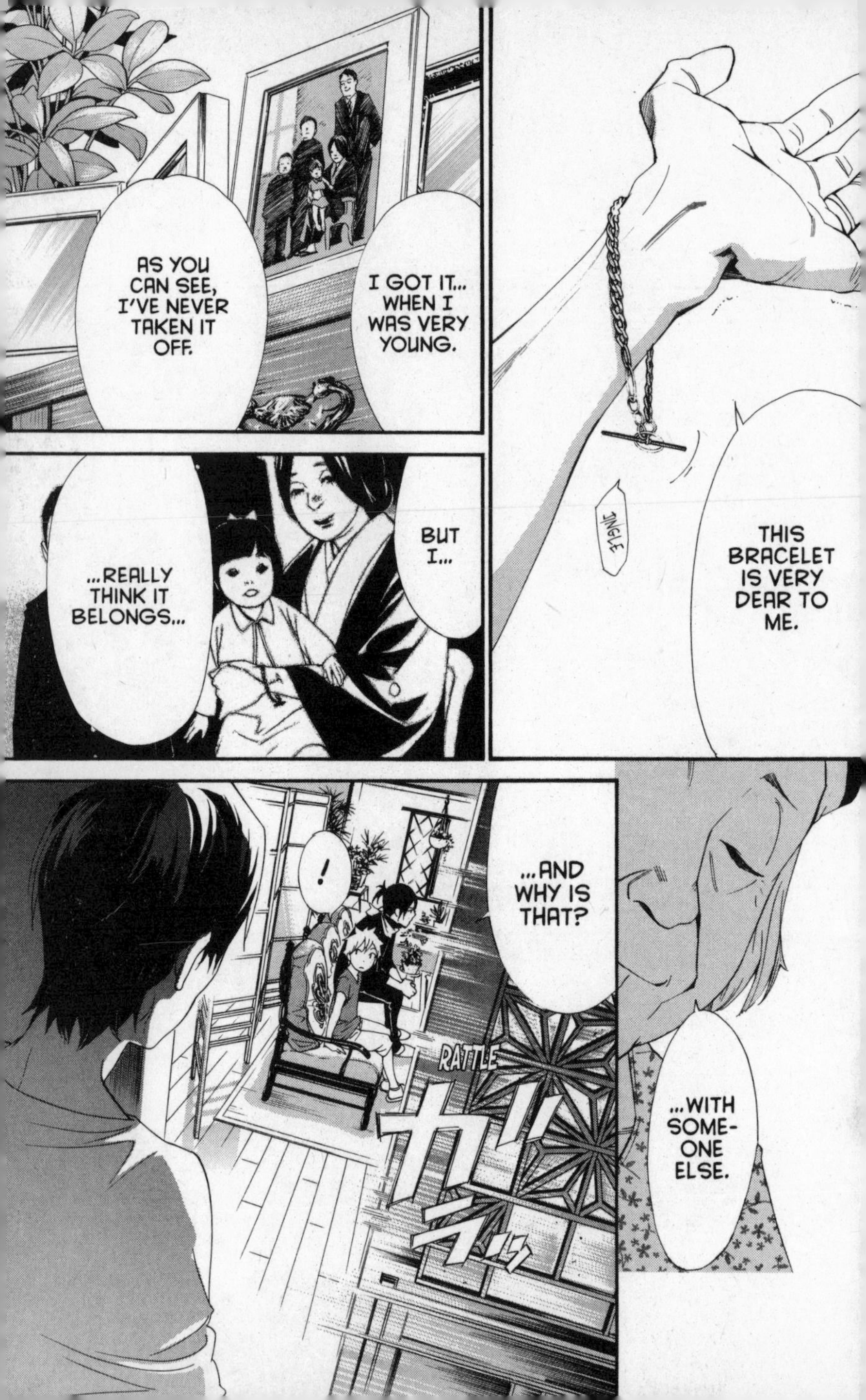
JINGLE
THIS BRACELET IS VERY DEAR TO ME.
I GOT IT... WHEN I WAS VERY YOUNG.
AS YOU CAN SEE, I'VE NEVER TAKEN IT OFF.
BUT I...
...REALLY THINK IT BELONGS...
...WITH SOME-ONE ELSE.
...AND WHY IS THAT?
!
RATTLE
ガタッ

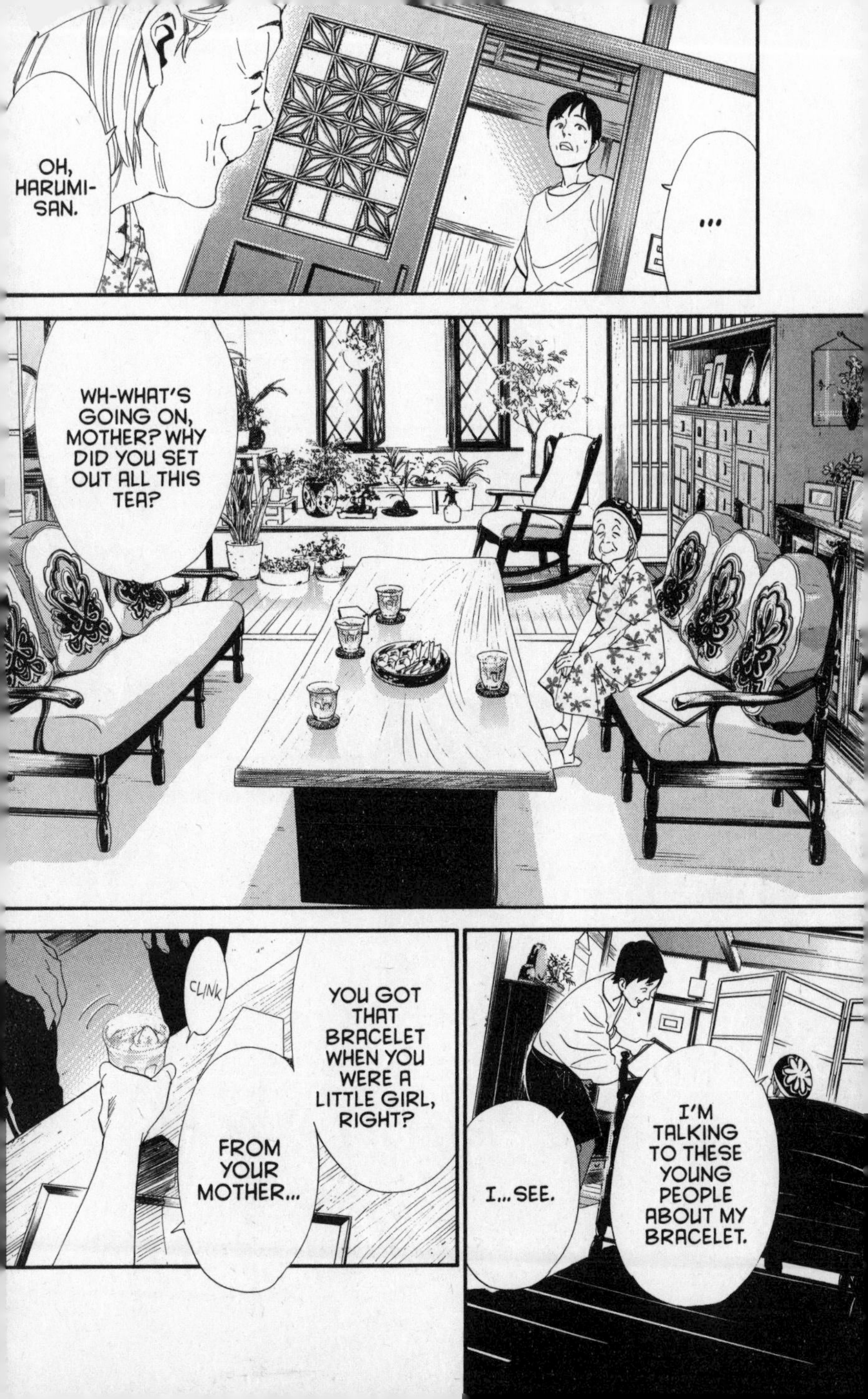
...
OH, HARUMI-SAN.
WH-WHAT'S GOING ON, MOTHER? WHY DID YOU SET OUT ALL THIS TEA?
I'M TALKING TO THESE YOUNG PEOPLE ABOUT MY BRACELET.
I...SEE.
YOU GOT THAT BRACELET WHEN YOU WERE A LITTLE GIRL, RIGHT?
CLINK
FROM YOUR MOTHER...

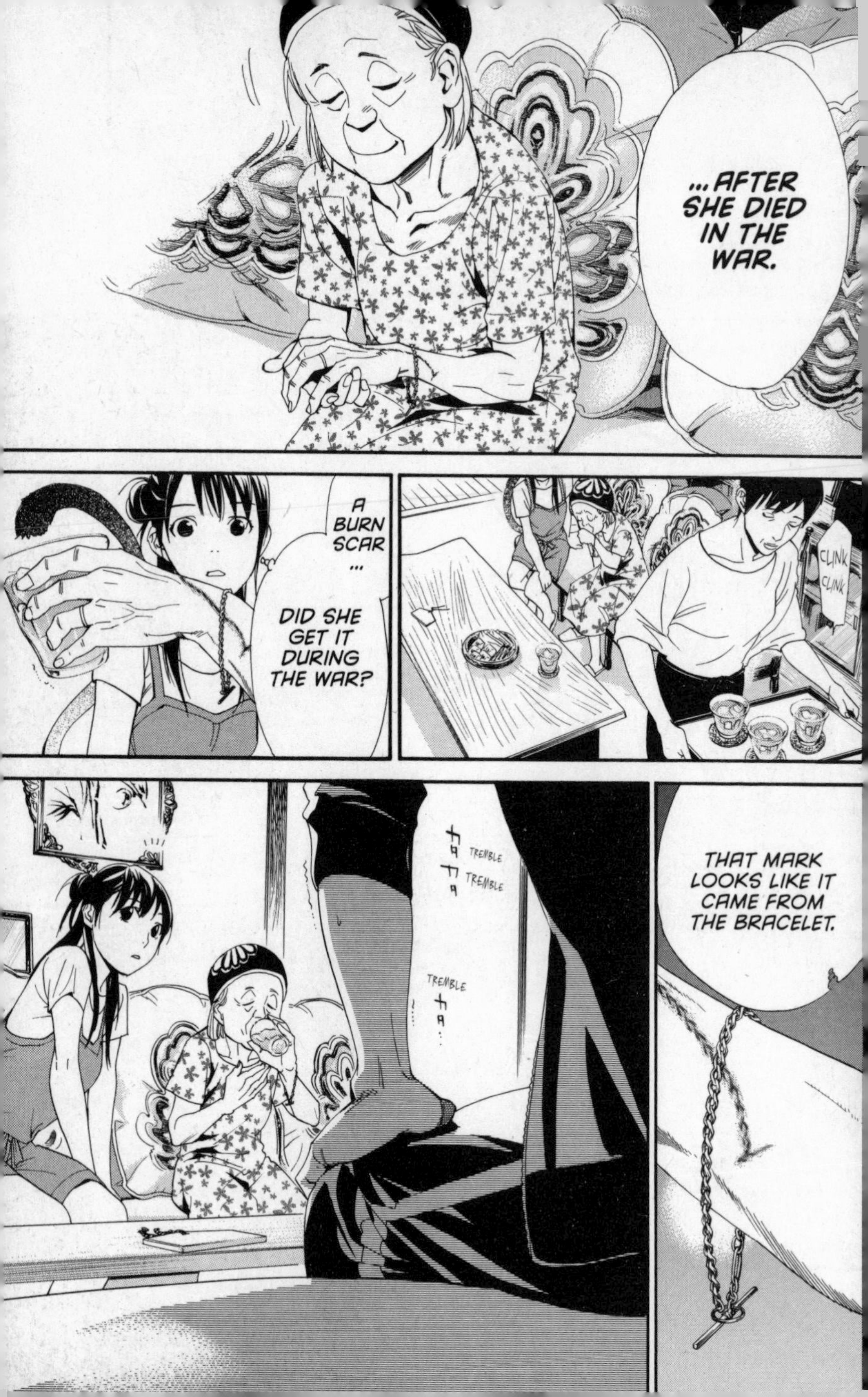
...AFTER SHE DIED IN THE WAR.
CLINK
CLINK
A BURN SCAR...
DID SHE GET IT DURING THE WAR?
THAT MARK LOOKS LIKE IT CAME FROM THE BRACELET.
TREMBLE
TREMBLE
TREMBLE

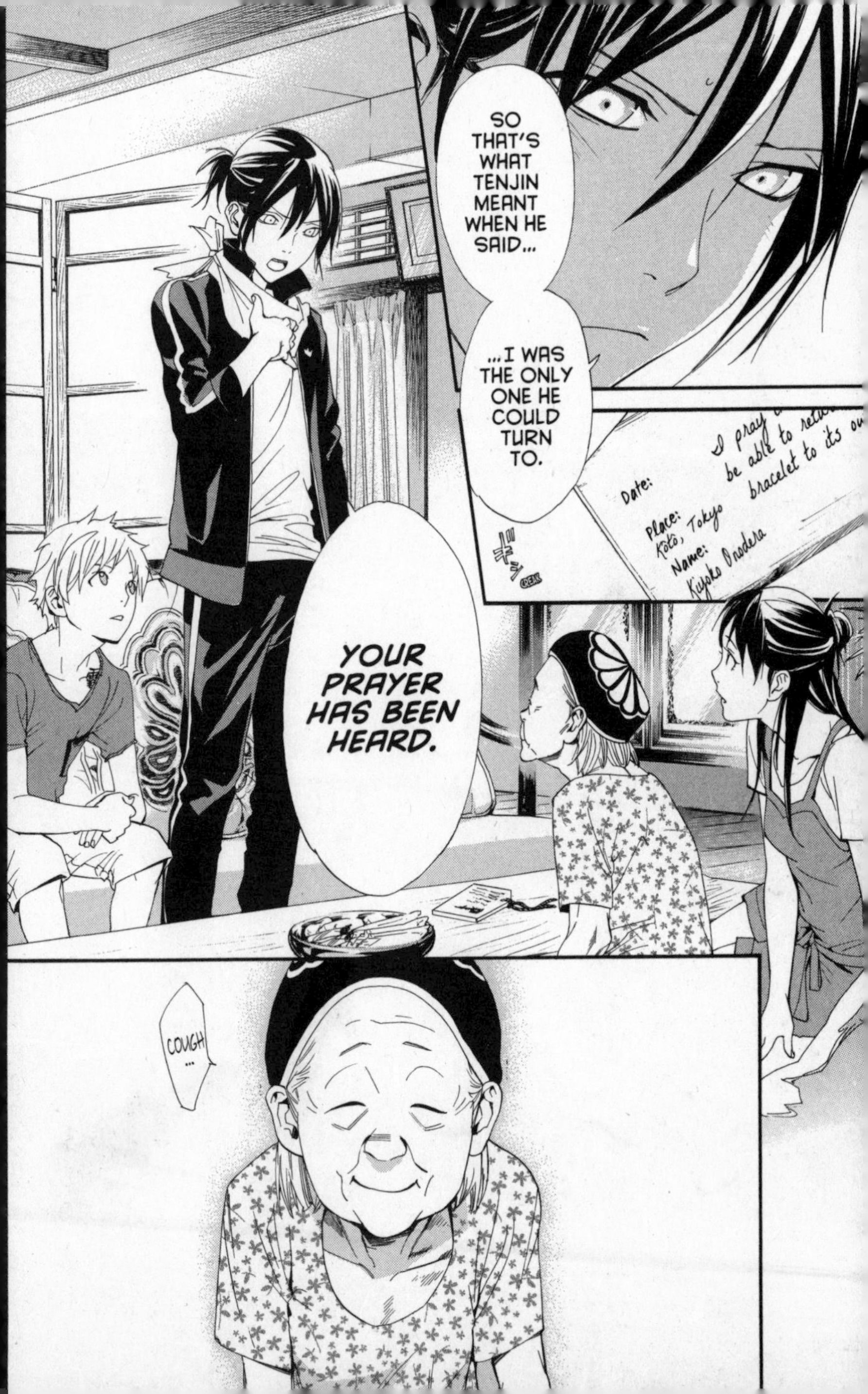
SO THAT'S WHAT TENJIN MEANT WHEN HE SAID...
...I WAS THE ONLY ONE HE COULD TURN TO.
Date:
Place: Koto, Tokyo
Name: Kiyoko Onodera
CREAK
YOUR PRAYER HAS BEEN HEARD.
COUGH ...

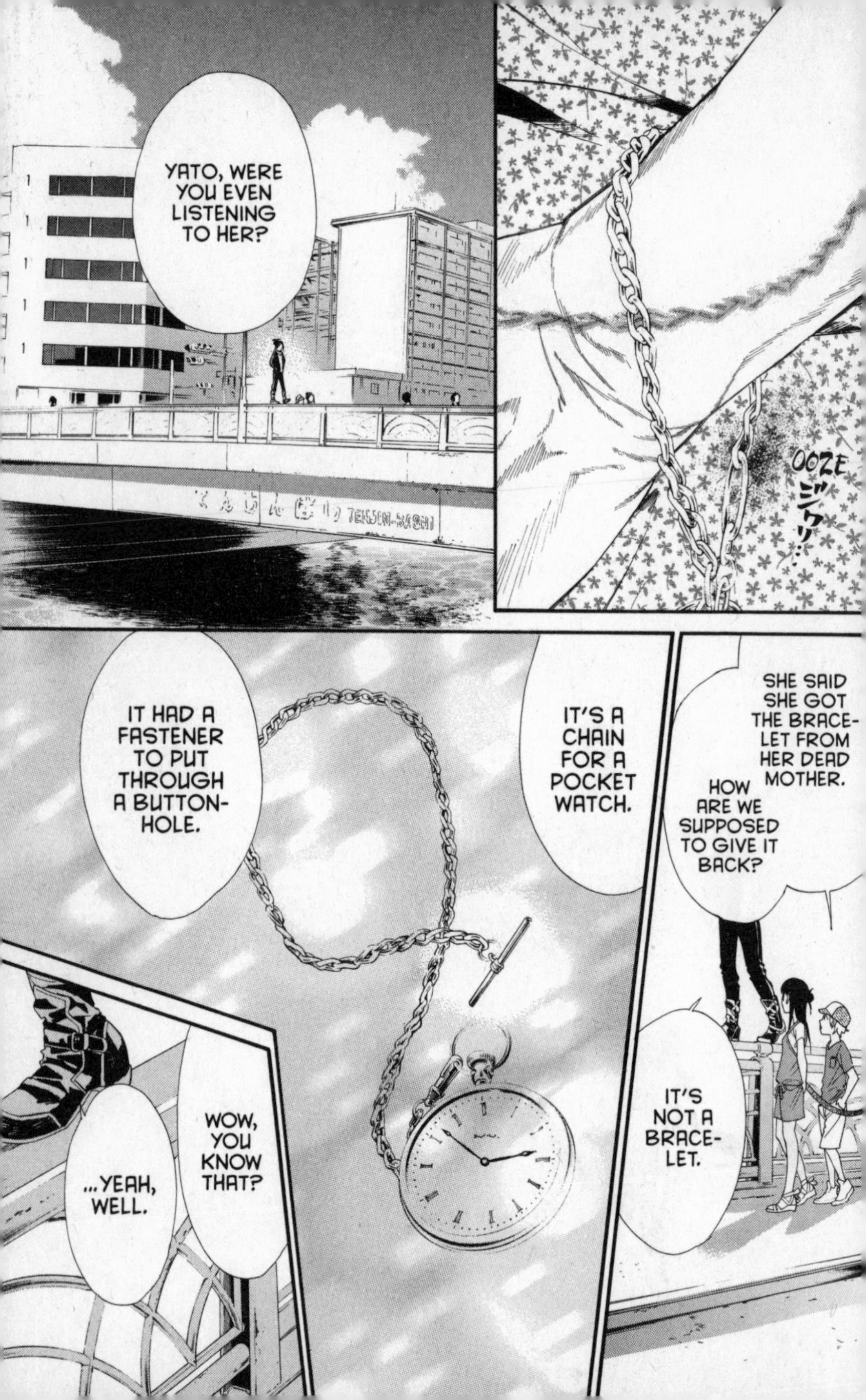
OOZE
ジワリ…
YATO, WERE YOU EVEN LISTENING TO HER?
TENJIN-BASHI
SHE SAID SHE GOT THE BRACELET FROM HER DEAD MOTHER.
HOW ARE WE SUPPOSED TO GIVE IT BACK?
IT'S NOT A BRACELET.
IT'S A CHAIN FOR A POCKET WATCH.
IT HAD A FASTENER TO PUT THROUGH A BUTTONHOLE.
WOW, YOU KNOW THAT?
...YEAH, WELL.

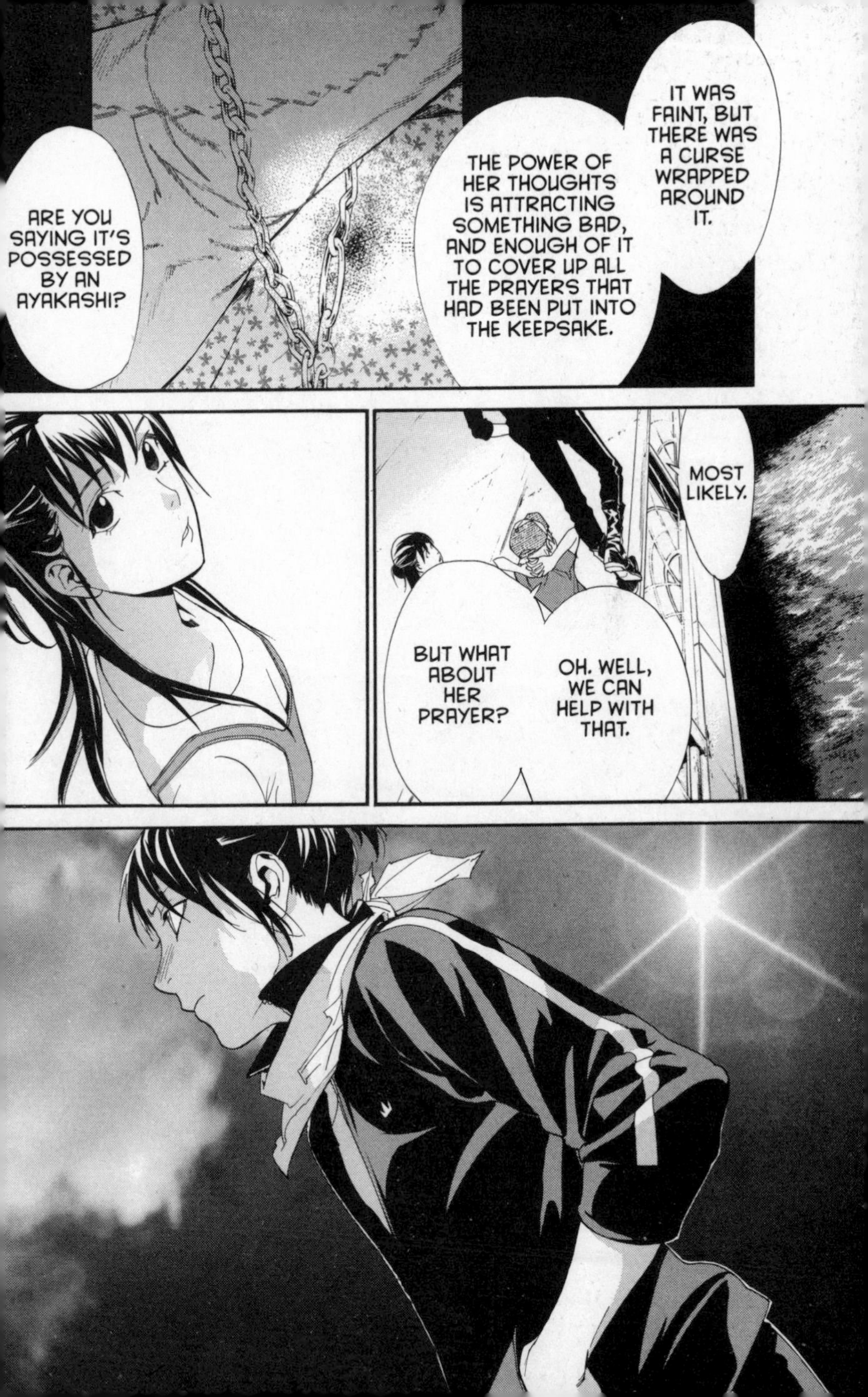

IT WAS FAINT, BUT THERE WAS A CURSE WRAPPED AROUND IT.
THE POWER OF HER THOUGHTS IS ATTRACTING SOMETHING BAD, AND ENOUGH OF IT TO COVER UP ALL THE PRAYERS THAT HAD BEEN PUT INTO THE KEEPSAKE.
ARE YOU SAYING IT'S POSSESSED BY AN AYAKASHI?
MOST LIKELY.
BUT WHAT ABOUT HER PRAYER?
OH. WELL, WE CAN HELP WITH THAT.

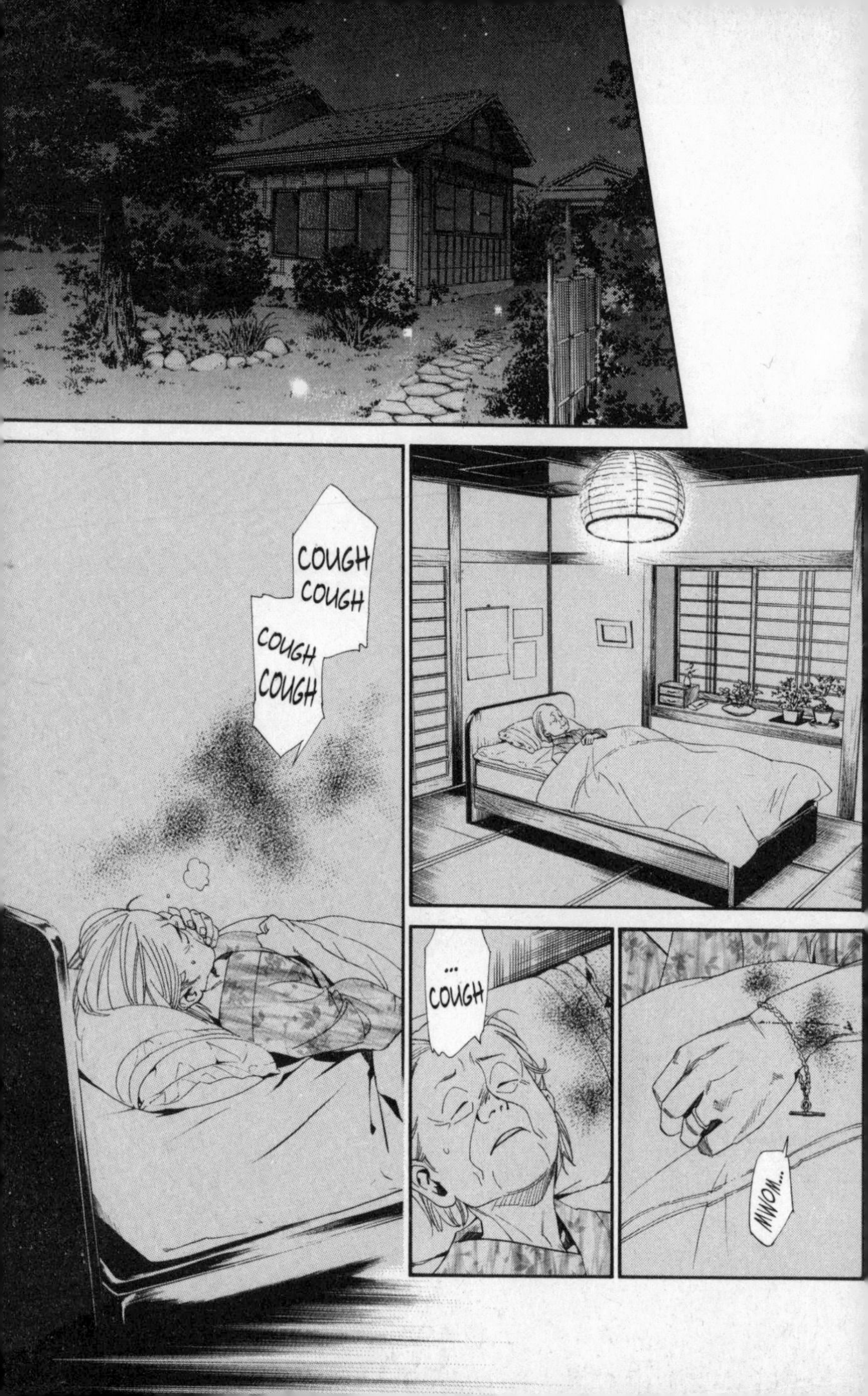
MOM...
...COUGH
COUGH COUGH
COUGH COUGH

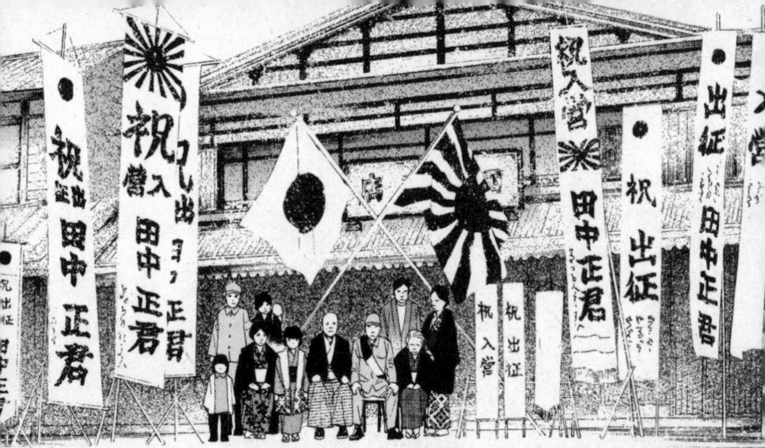
祝出征
田中正君
祝入營
祝出征
田中正君

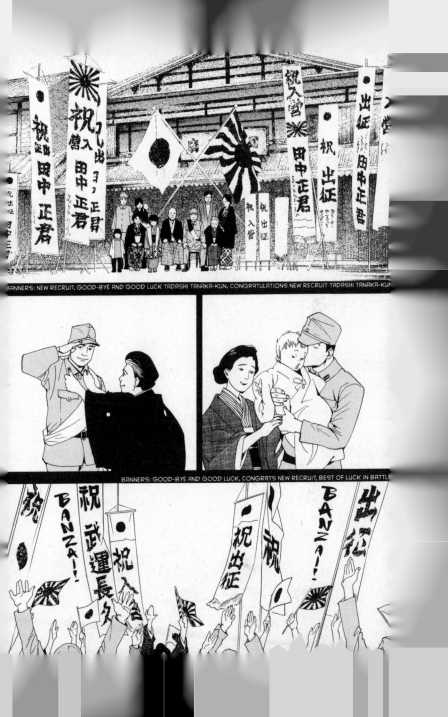

BANNERS: NEW RECRUIT, GOOD-BYE AND GOOD LUCK TADASHI TANAKA-KUN, CONGRATULATIONS NEW RECRUIT TADASHI TANAKA-KUN

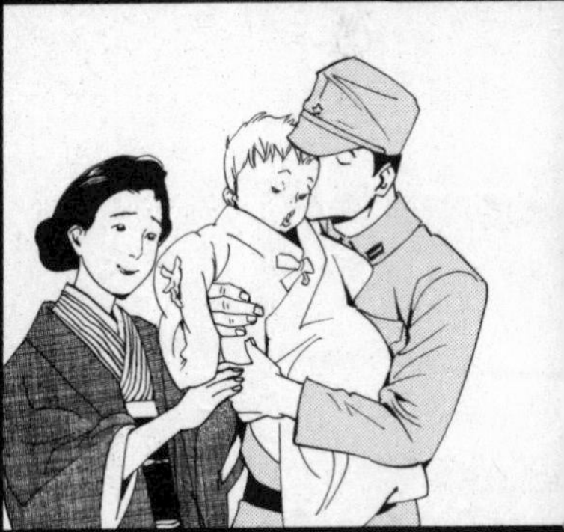

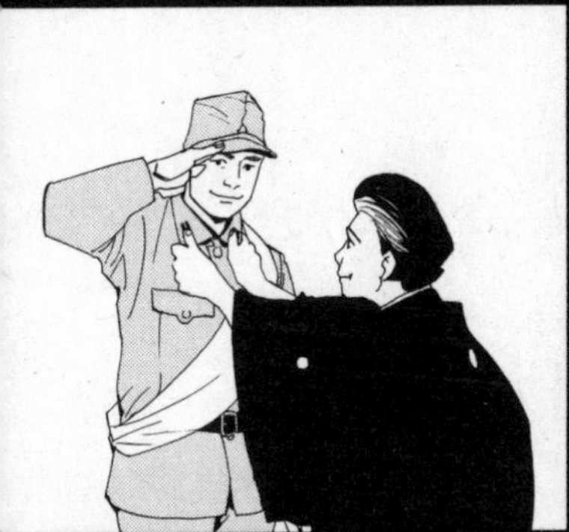

BANNERS: GOOD-BYE AND GOOD LUCK, CONGRATS NEW RECRUIT, BEST OF LUCK IN BATTLE

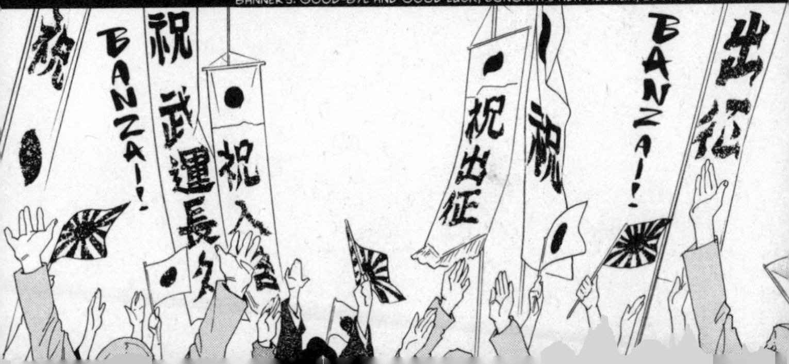
BANZAI!
祝出征
祝入營
祝武運長久
BANZAI!

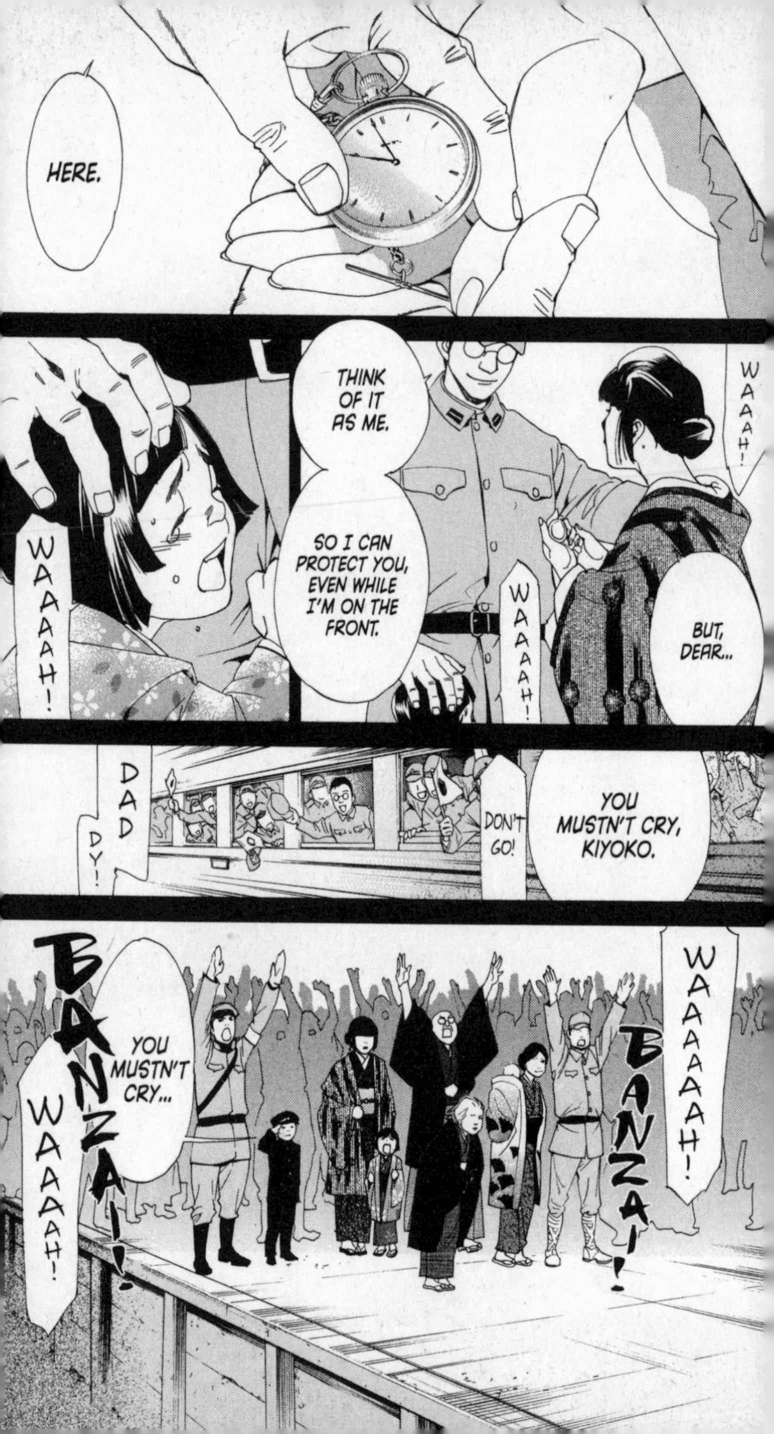
HERE.
WAAAH!
BUT, DEAR...
WAAAAAH!
THINK OF IT AS ME.
SO I CAN PROTECT YOU, EVEN WHILE I'M ON THE FRONT.
WAAAAAH!
YOU MUSTN'T CRY, KIYOKO.
DON'T GO!
DADDY!
WAAAAAAH!
BANZAI!
YOU MUSTN'T CRY...
BANZAI!
WAAAAAH!

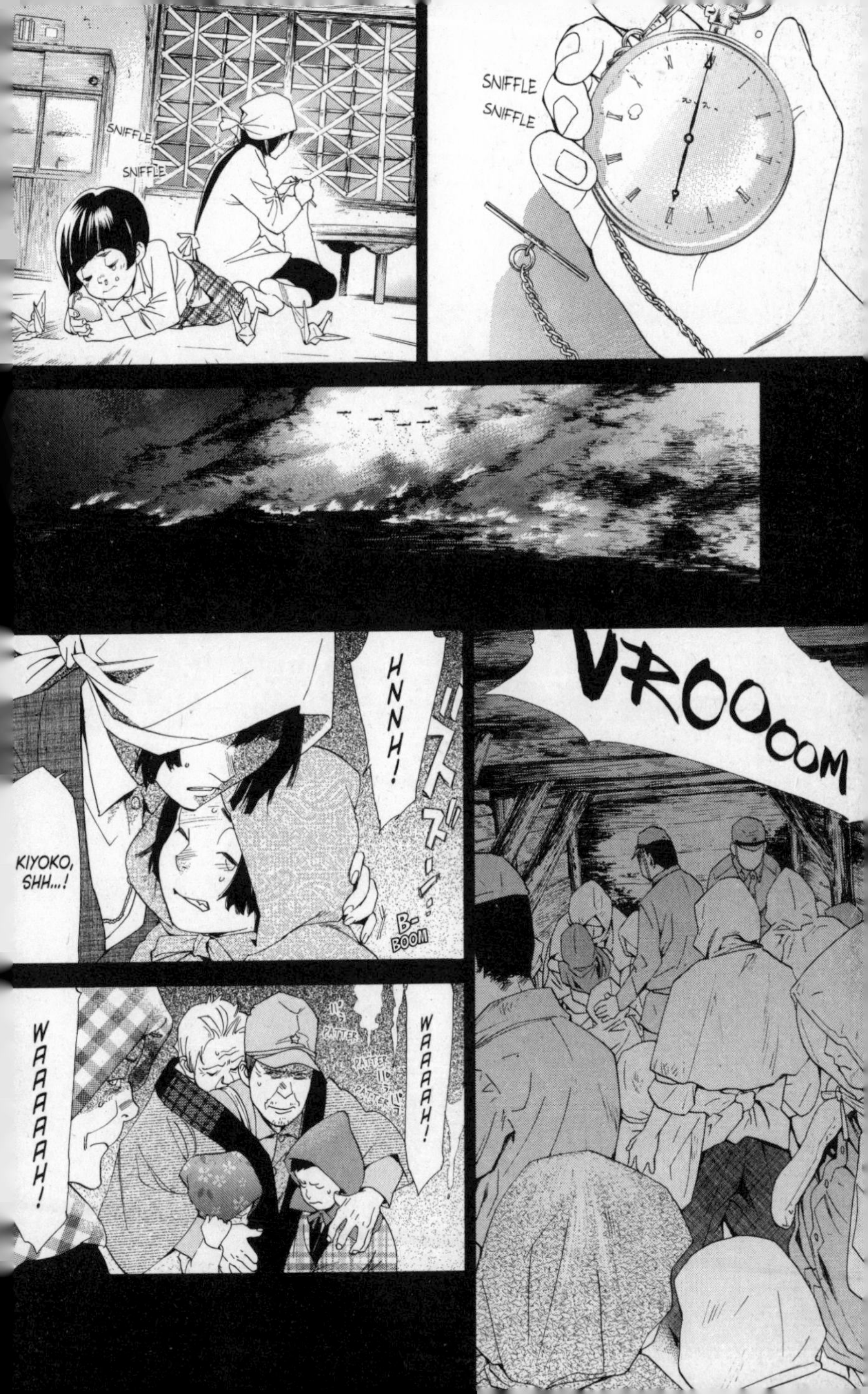
SNIFFLE
SNIFFLE
SNIFFLE
SNIFFLE
VROOOOOM
HNNNH!
B-BOOM
KIYOKO, SHH...!
WAAAAAH!
PATTER
PATTER
PATTER
WAAAAAAH!

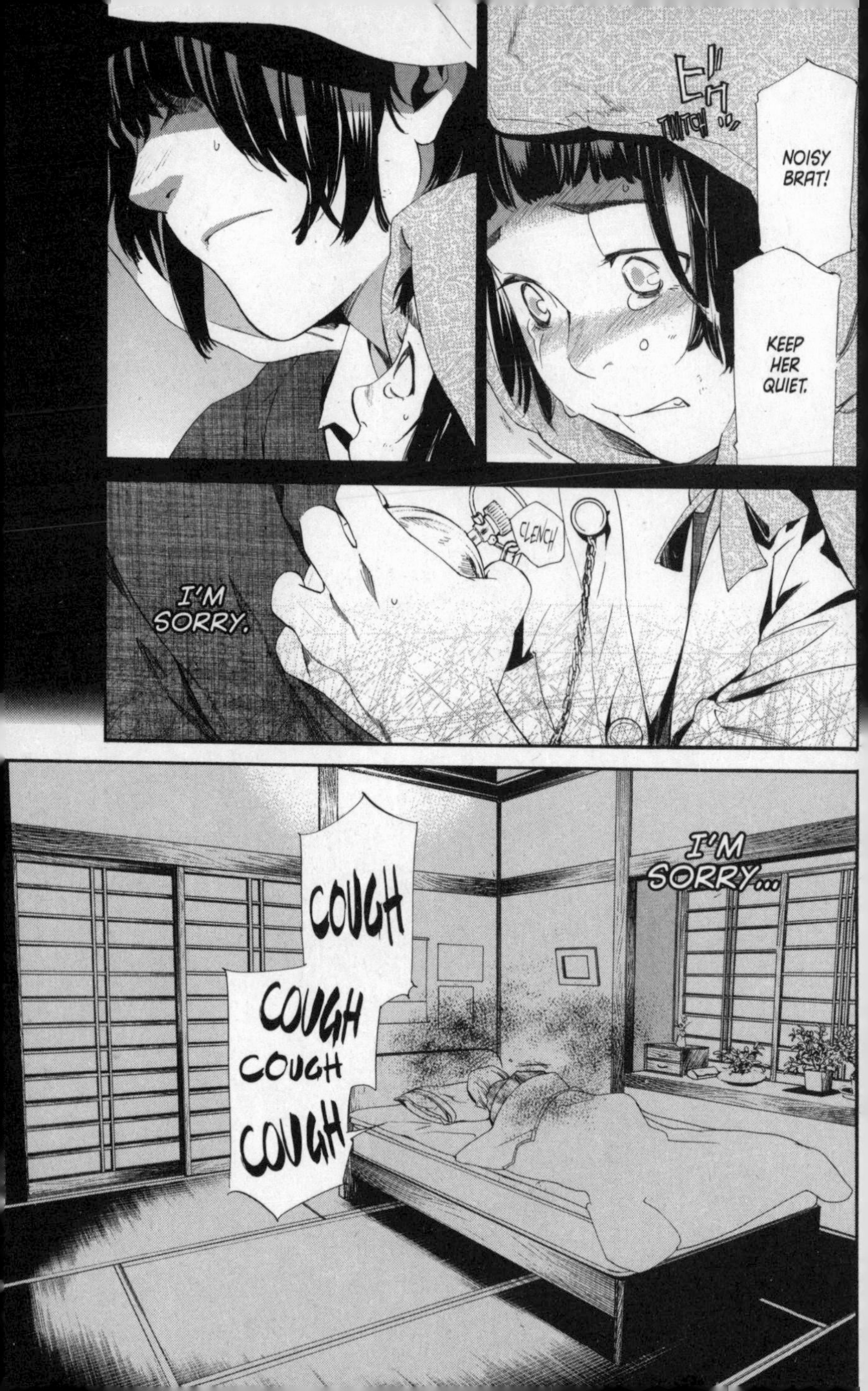
TWITCH
NOISY BRAT!
KEEP HER QUIET.
CLENCH
I'M SORRY.
I'M SORRY...
COUGH
COUGH
COUGH
COUGH

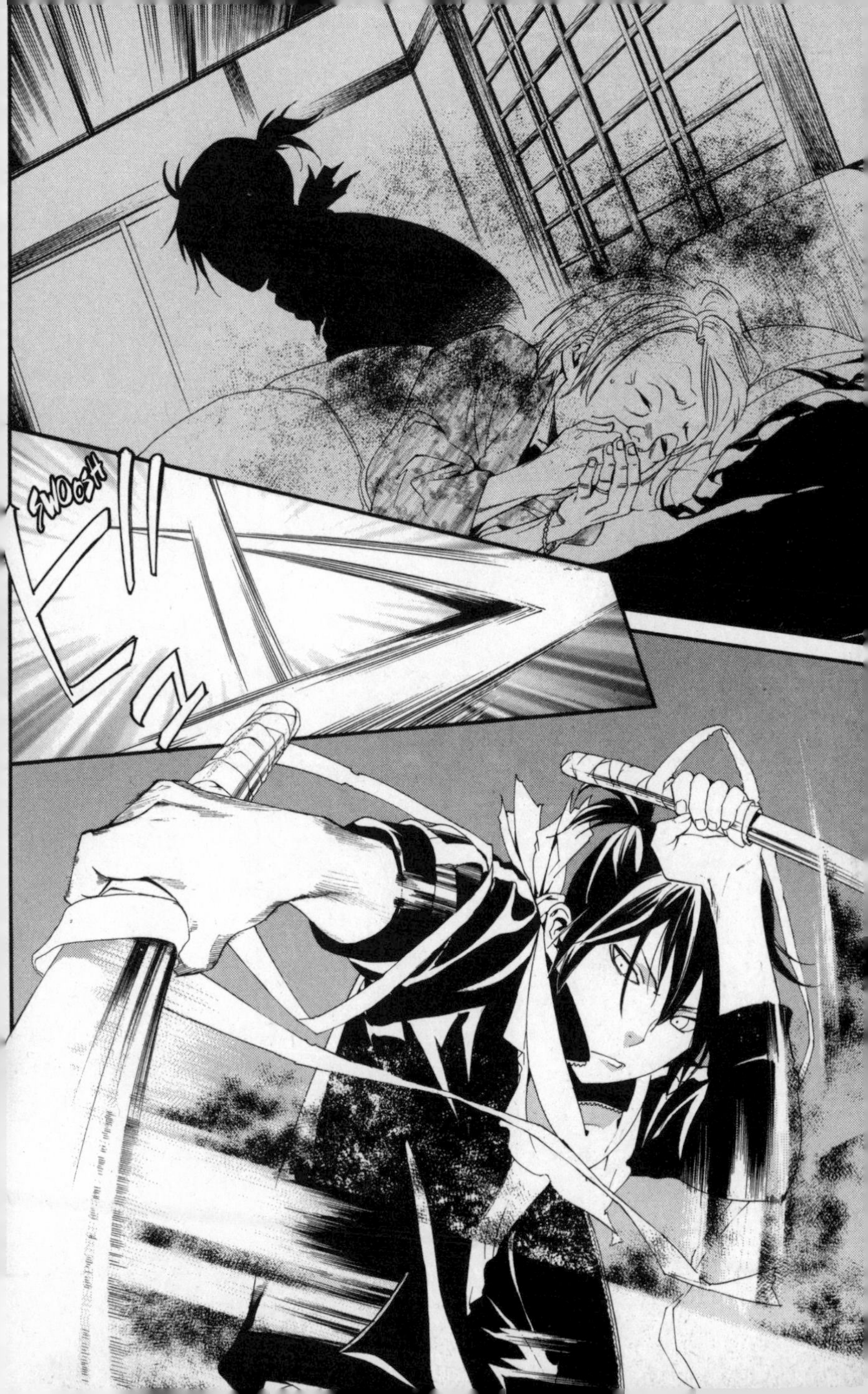
SWOOSH

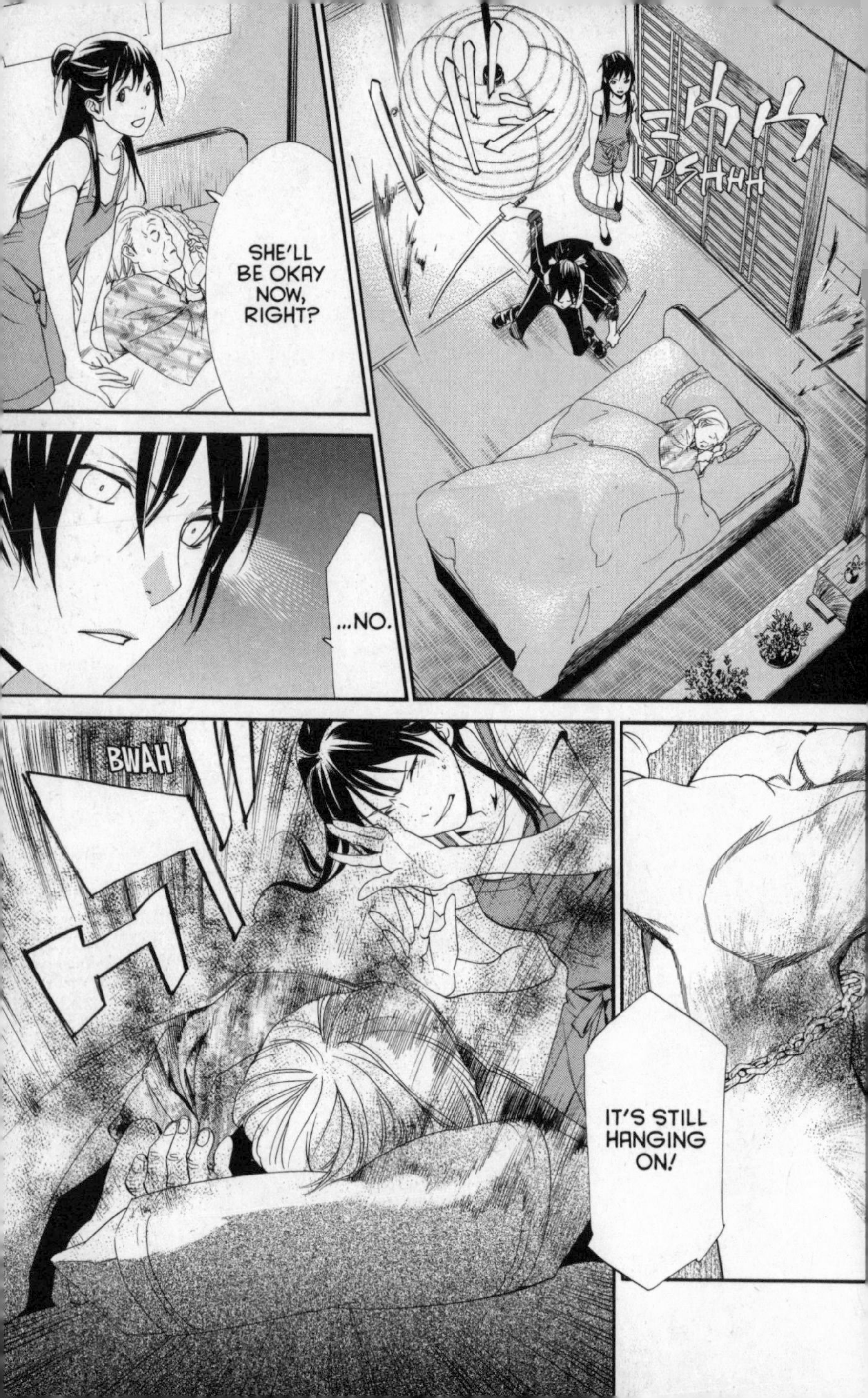
DSHHH
SHE'LL BE OKAY NOW, RIGHT?
...NO.
IT'S STILL HANGING ON!
BWAH

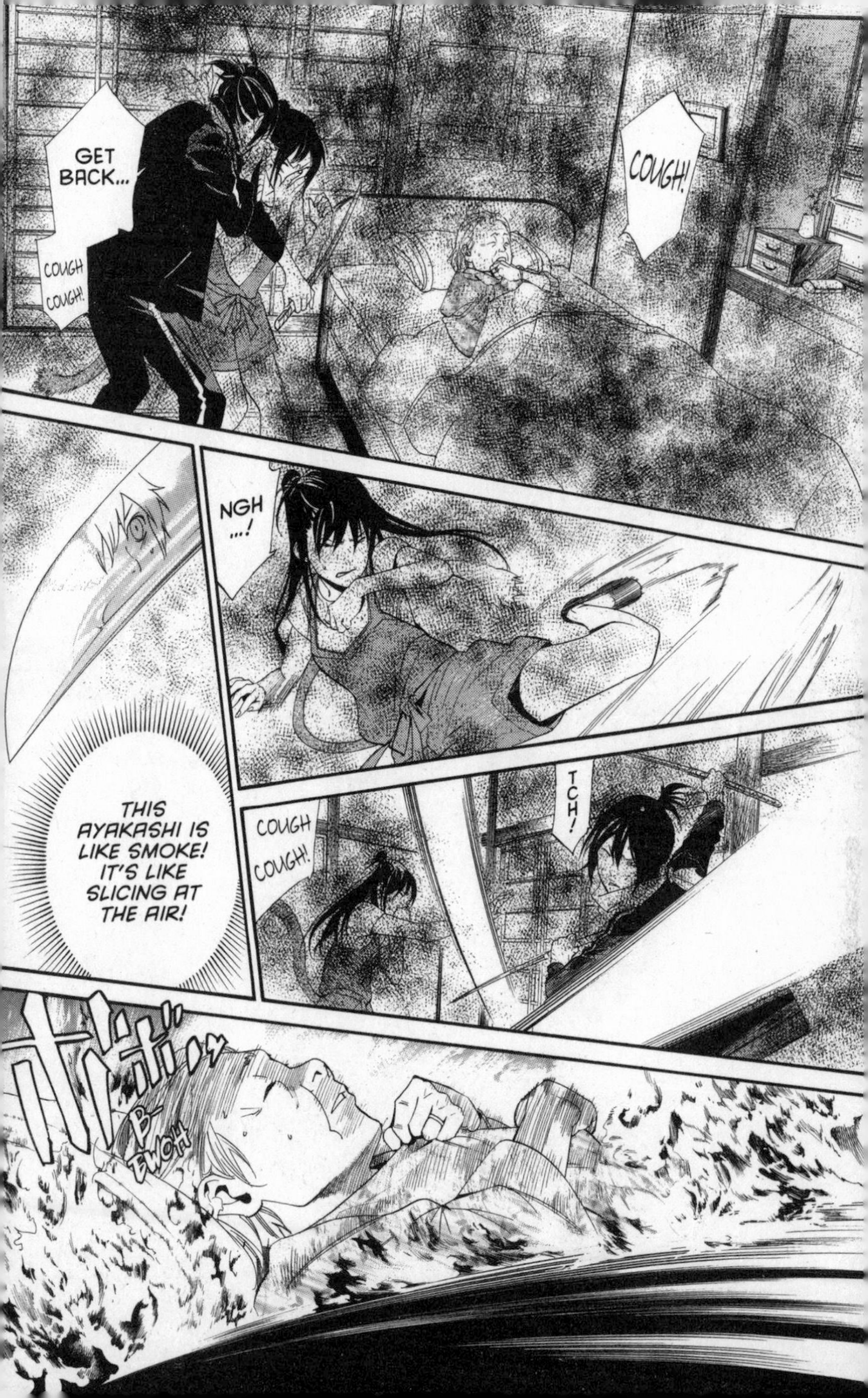
COUGH!
GET BACK...
COUGH COUGH!
NGH ...!
TCH!
COUGH COUGH!
THIS AYAKASHI IS LIKE SMOKE! IT'S LIKE SLICING AT THE AIR!
B-EWOH

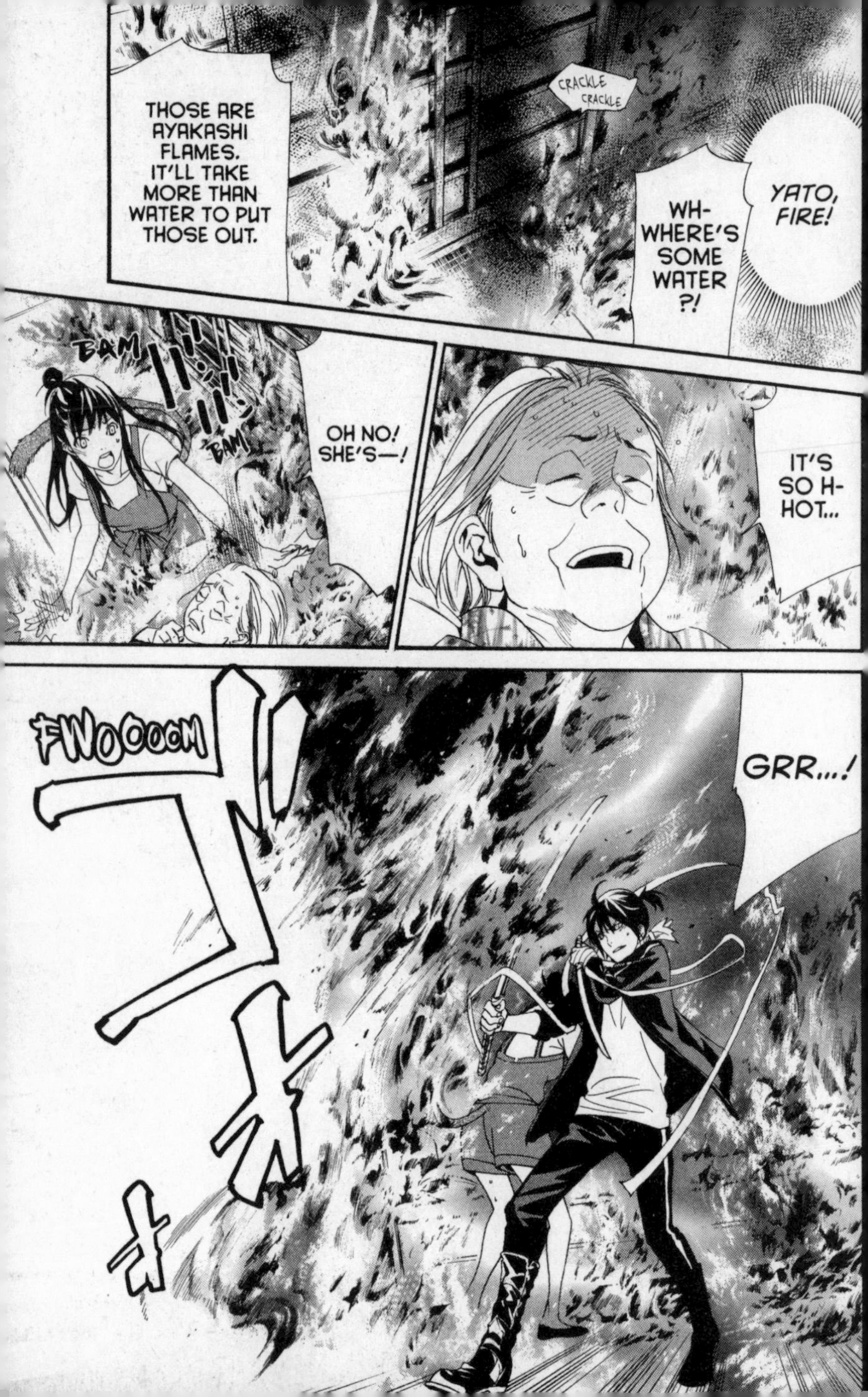
YATO, FIRE!
WH- WHERE'S SOME WATER ?!
CRACKLE CRACKLE
THOSE ARE AYAKASHI FLAMES. IT'LL TAKE MORE THAN WATER TO PUT THOSE OUT.
IT'S SO H-HOT...
OH NO! SHE'S—!
BAM
BAM
GRR...!
FWOOOOM

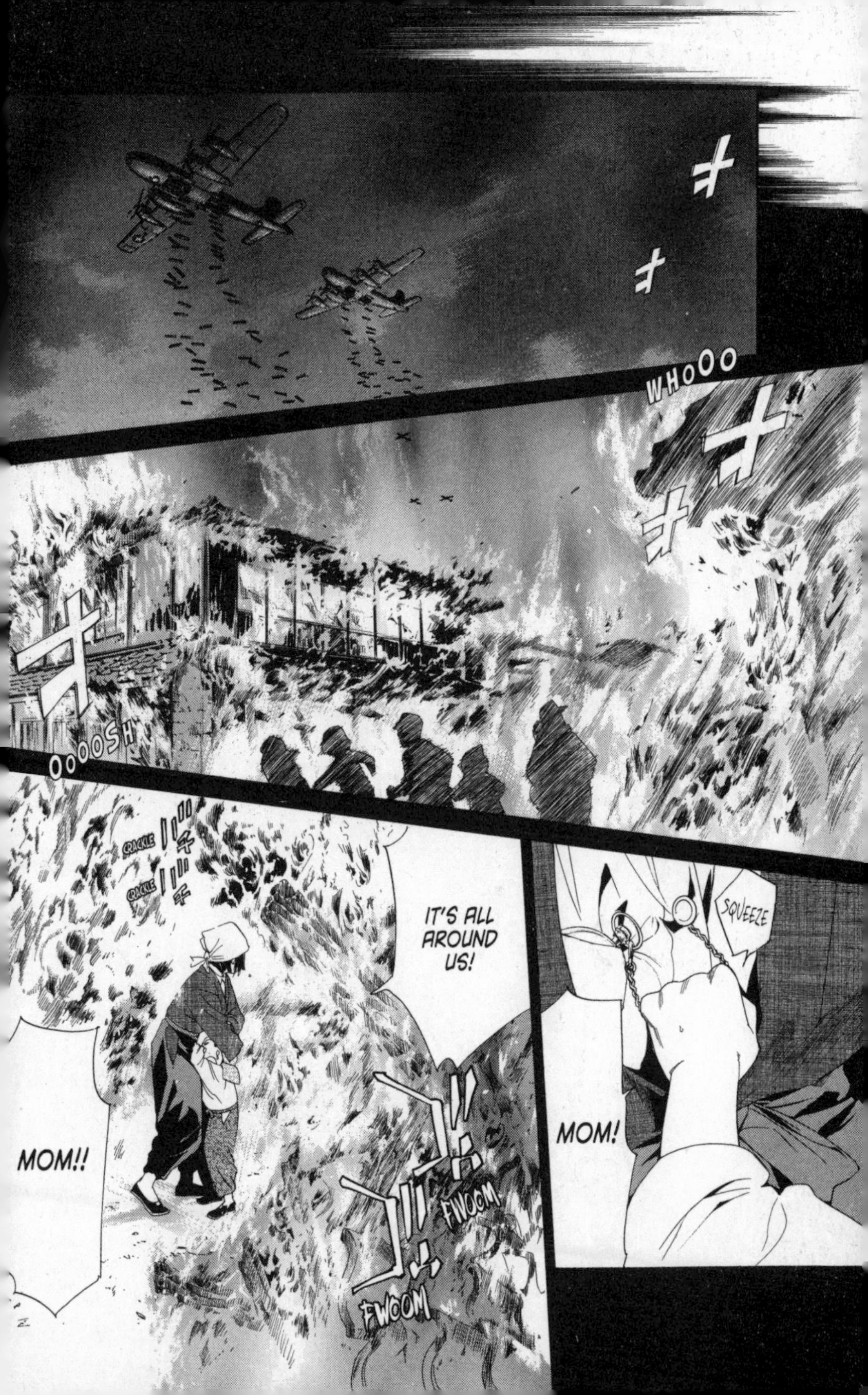

WHoOO
OOOOSH
SQUEEZE
MOM!
IT'S ALL AROUND US!
CRACKLE
CRACKLE
FWOOM
FWOOM
MOM!!

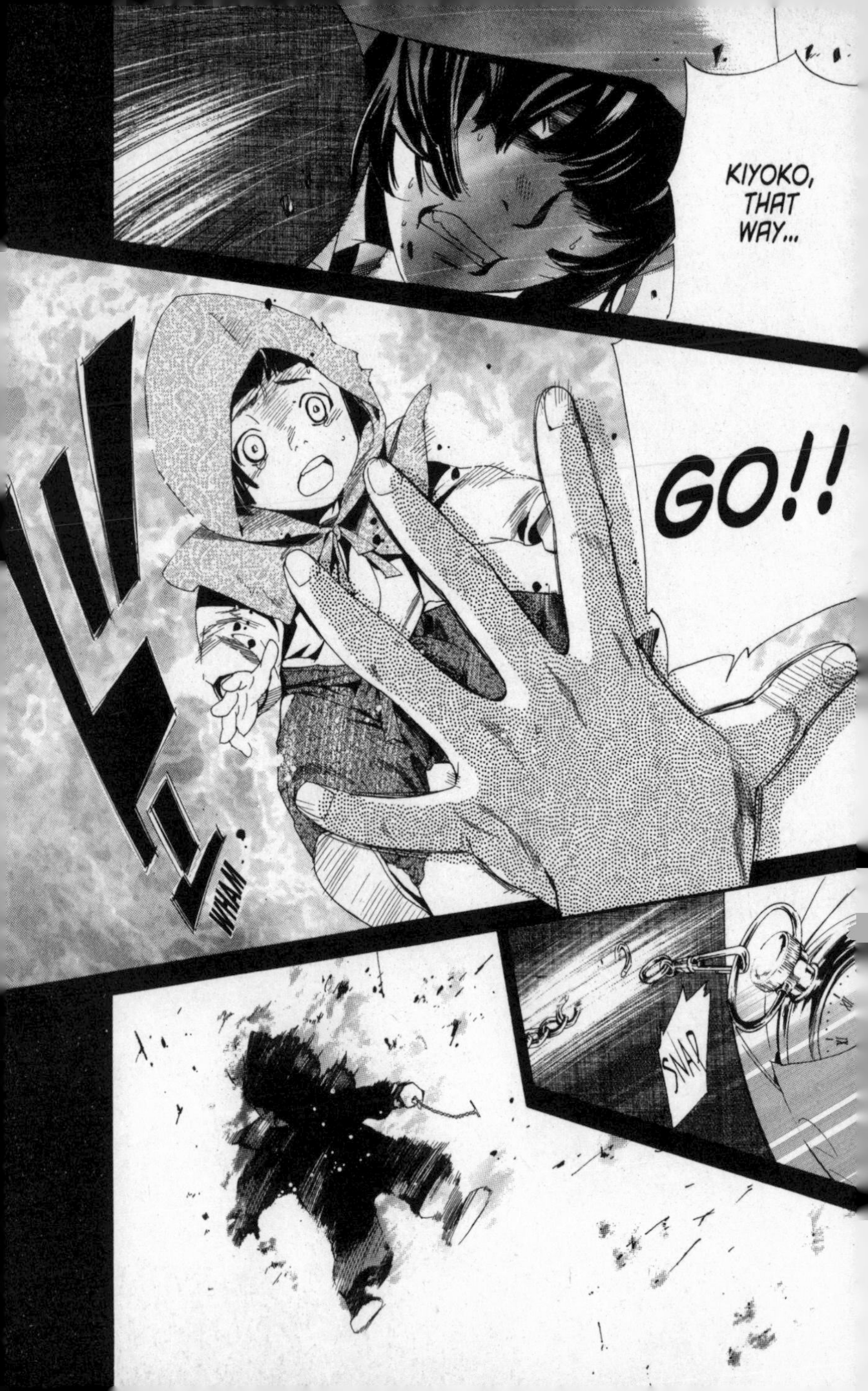
KIYOKO, THAT WAY...
GO!!
WHAM
SNAP

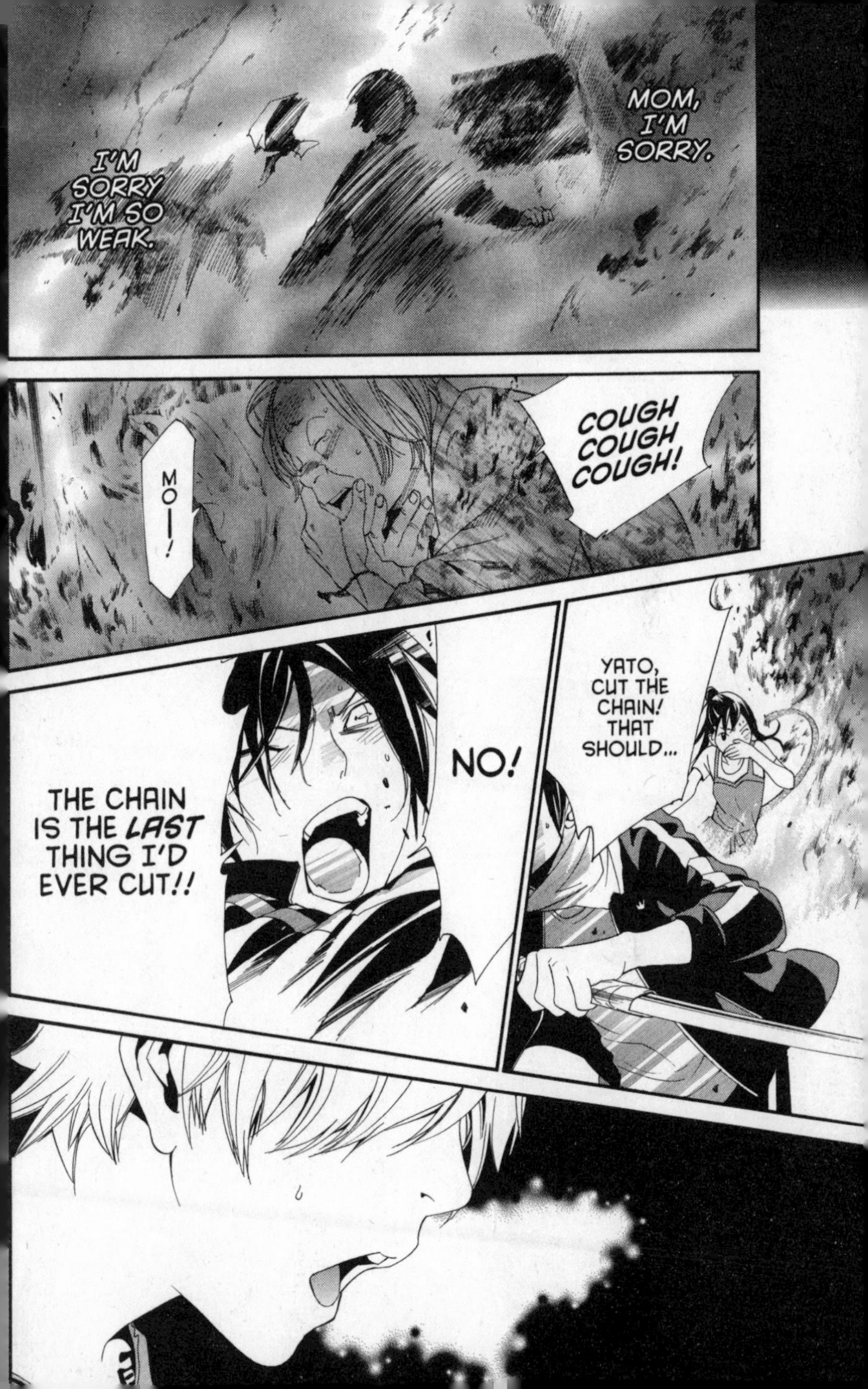
MOM, I'M SORRY.
I'M SORRY I'M SO WEAK.
COUGH COUGH COUGH!
MO—!
YATO, CUT THE CHAIN! THAT SHOULD...
NO!
THE CHAIN IS THE *LAST* THING I'D EVER CUT!!

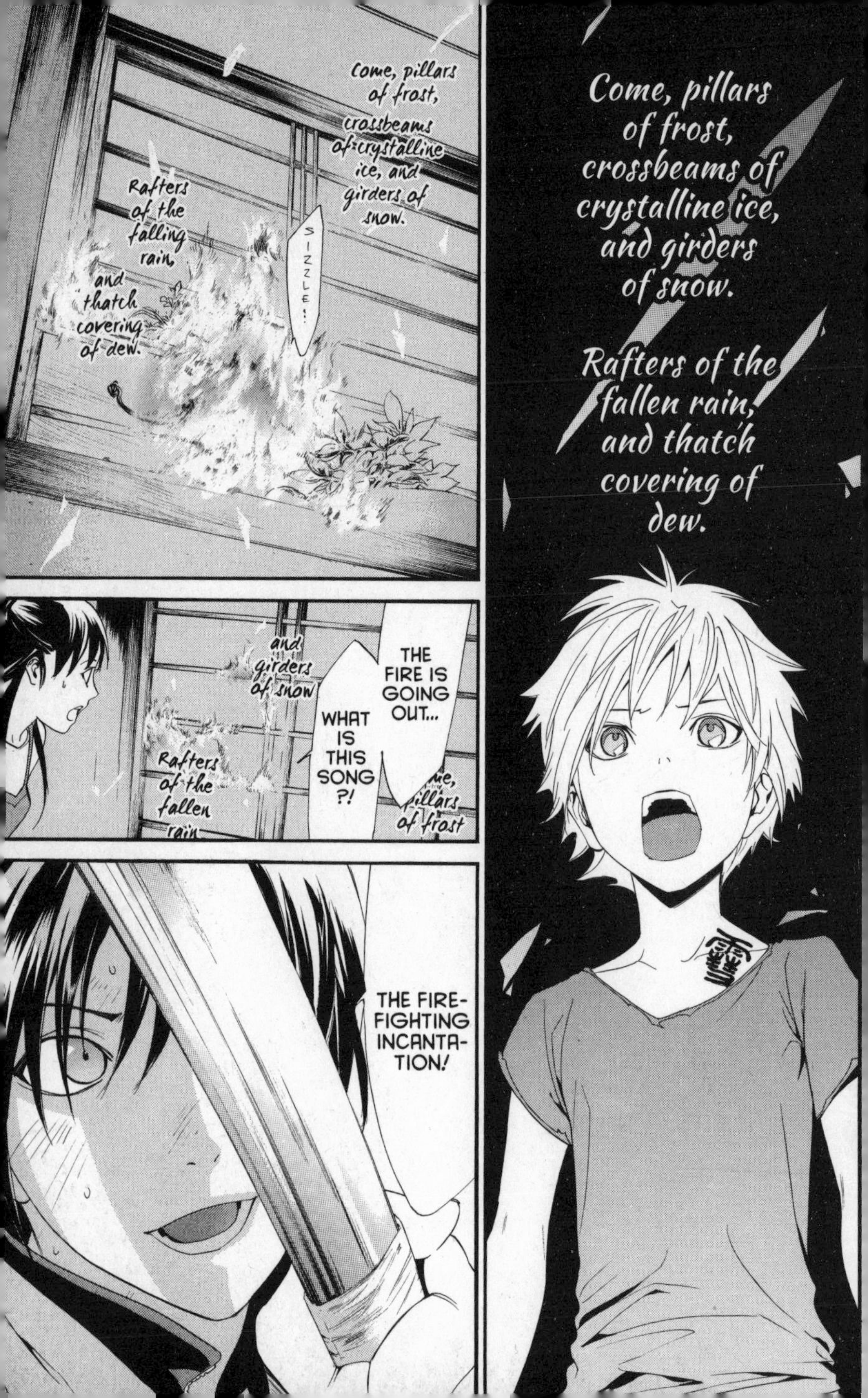
Come, pillars of frost, crossbeams of crystalline ice, and girders of snow.
Rafters of the fallen rain, and thatch covering of dew.
Come, pillars of frost, crossbeams of crystalline ice, and girders of snow.
SIZZLE...
Rafters of the falling rain, and thatch covering of dew.
THE FIRE IS GOING OUT...
me, pillars of frost
WHAT IS THIS SONG?!
and girders of snow
Rafters of the fallen rain
THE FIRE-FIGHTING INCANTATION!

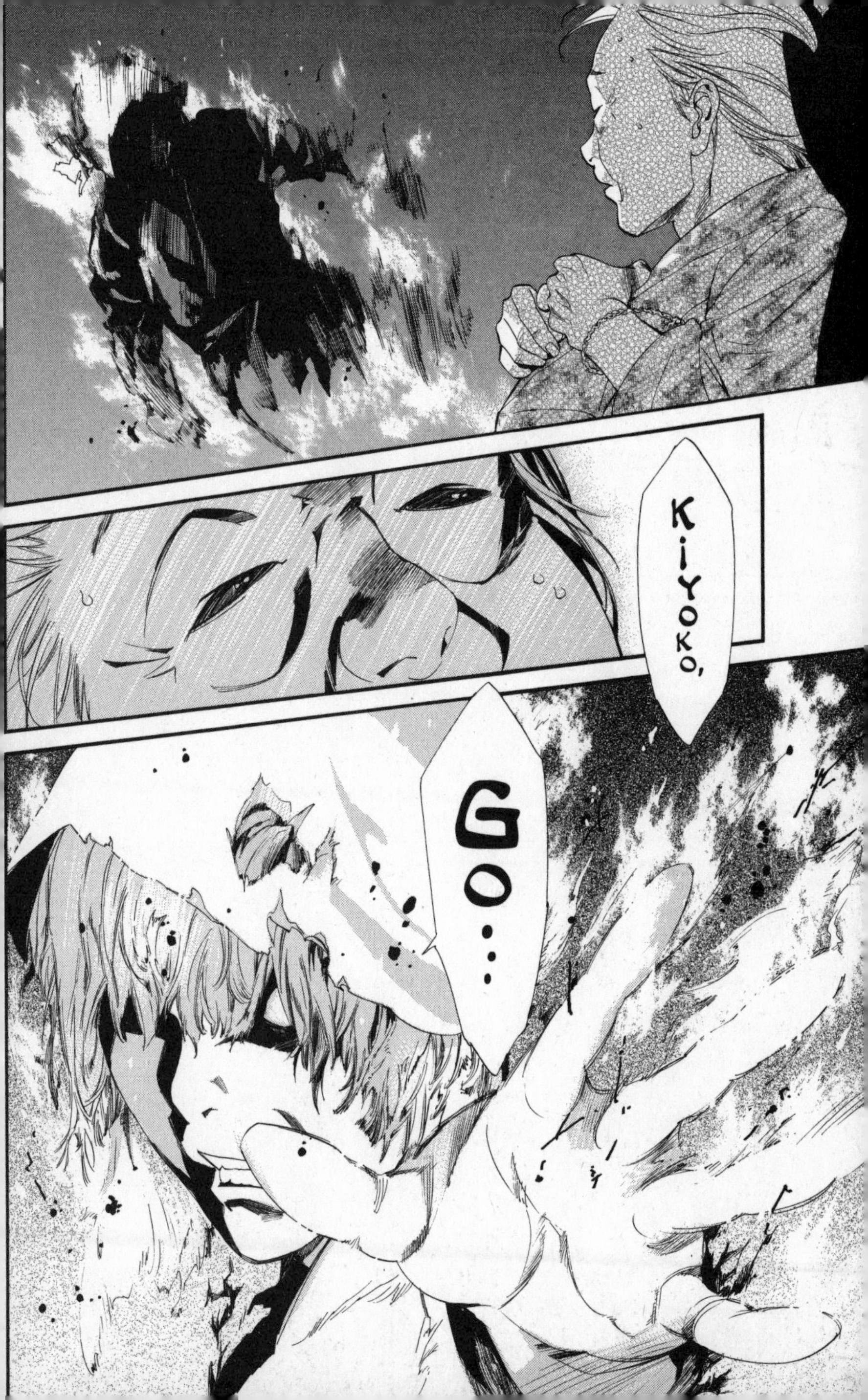
KIYOKO,
GO...

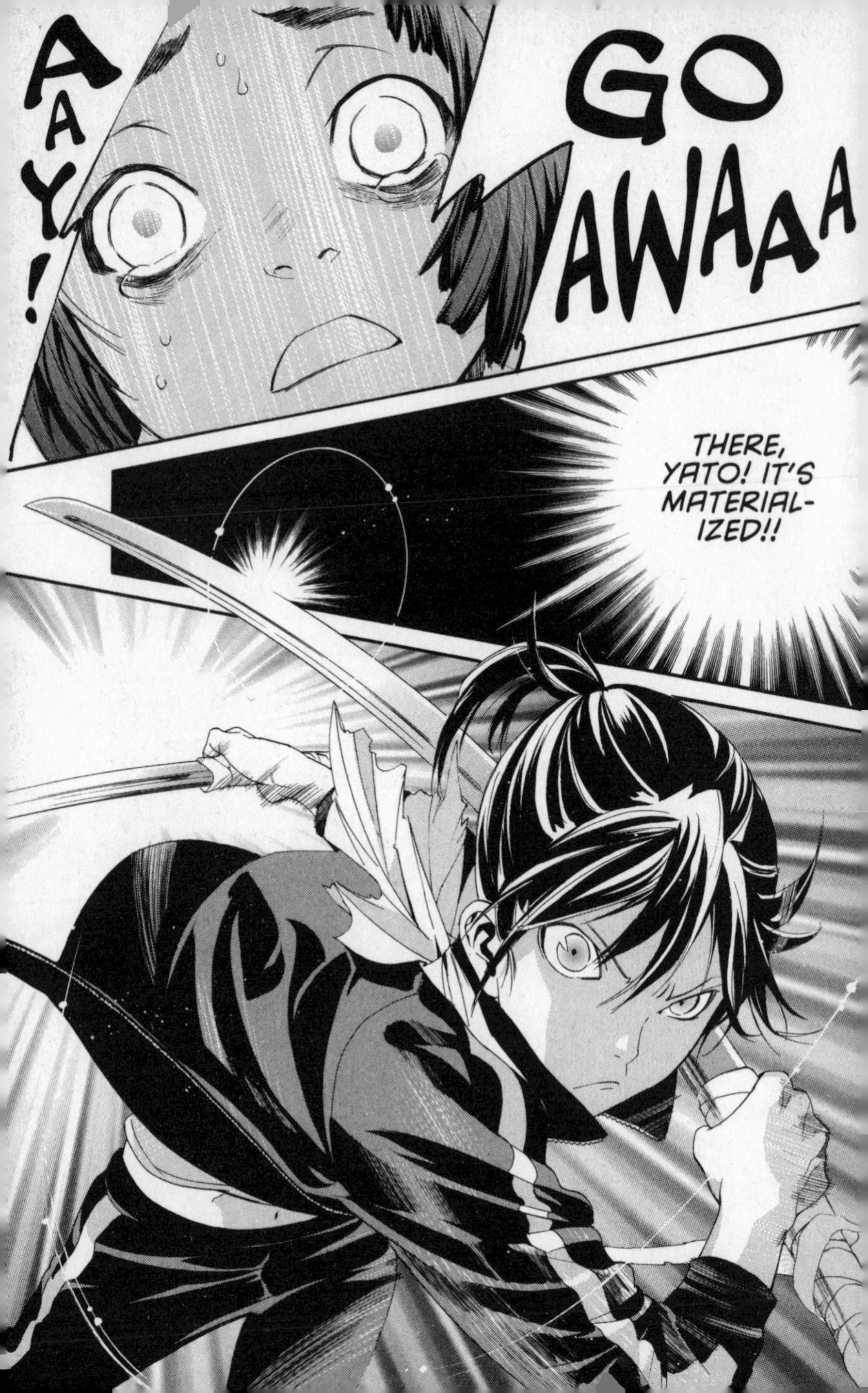
GO AWAAAA
AAY!
THERE, YATO! IT'S MATERIAL-IZED!!

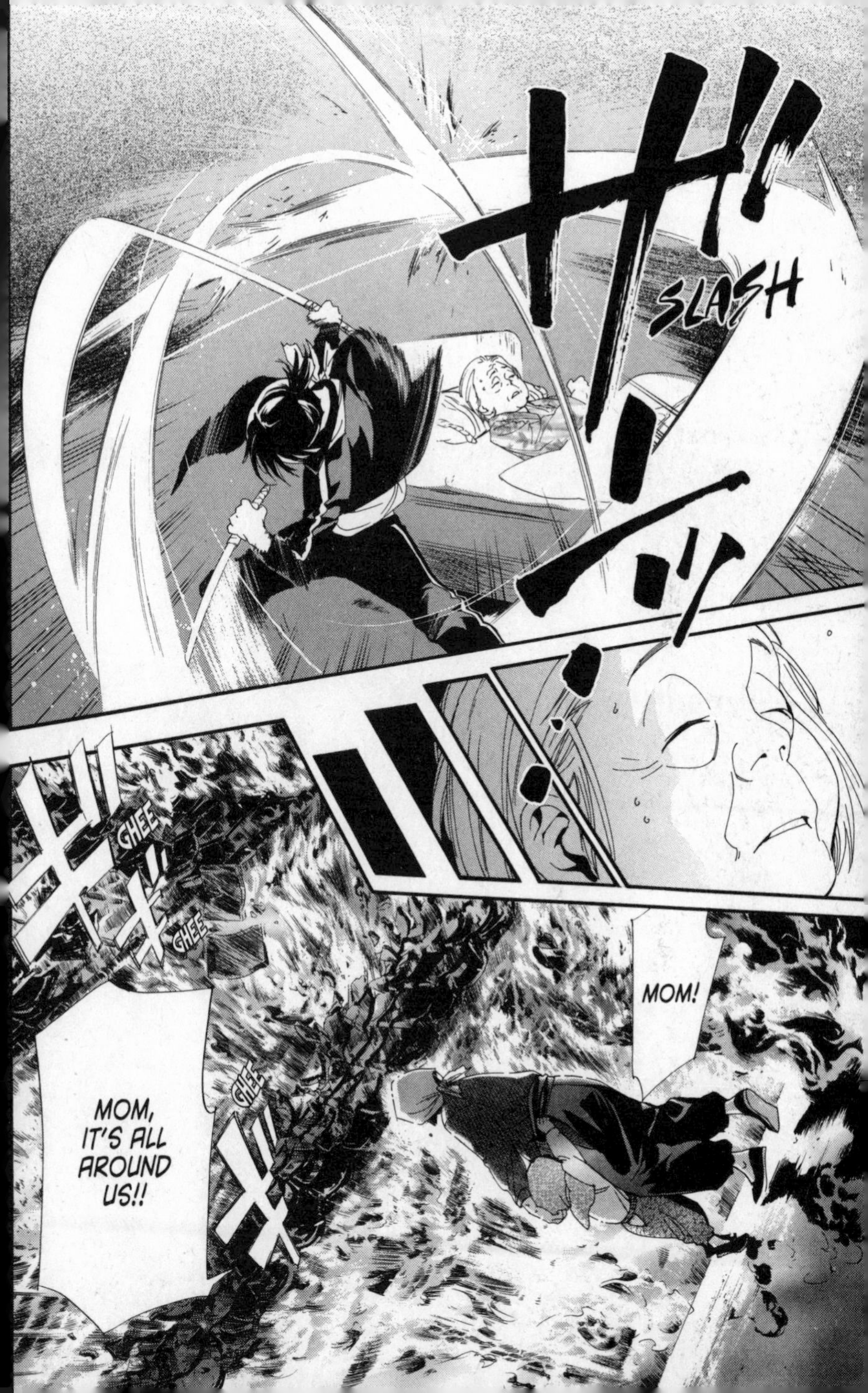
SLASH
GHEE
GHEE
MOM!
GHEE
MOM, IT'S ALL AROUND US!!

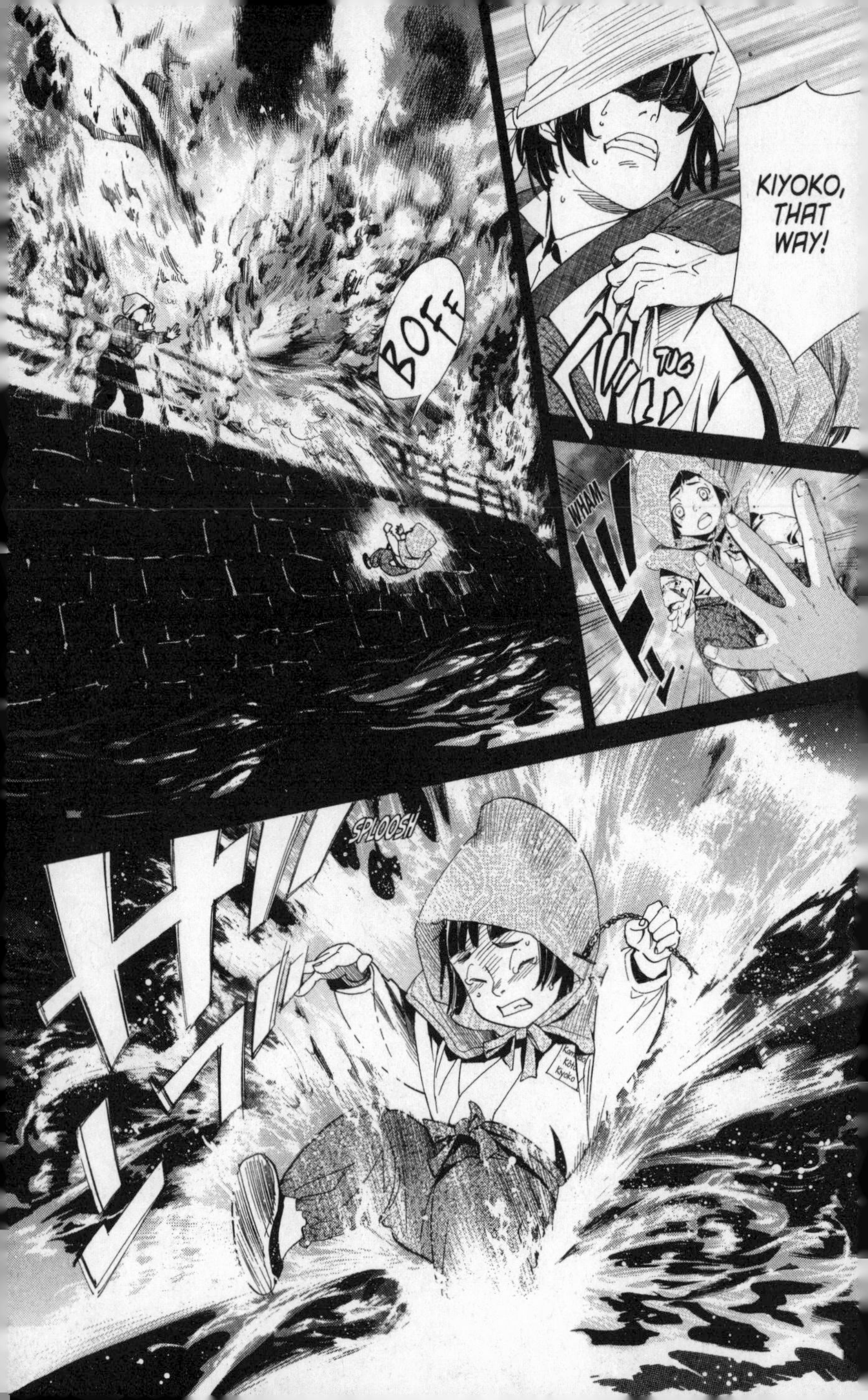
KIYOKO, THAT WAY!
TUG
WHAM
BOFF
SPLOOSH

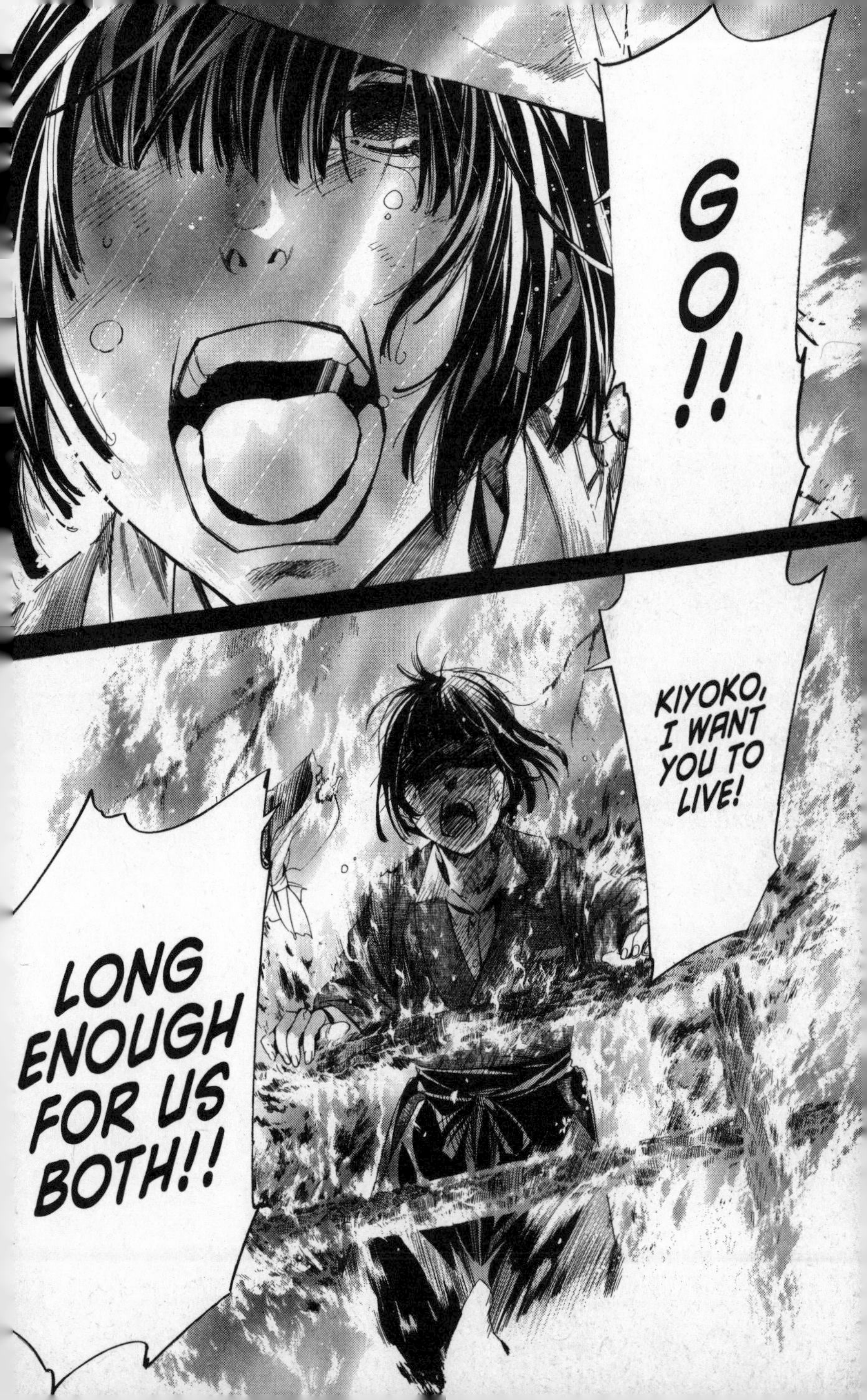
GO!!
KIYOKO, I WANT YOU TO LIVE!
LONG ENOUGH FOR US BOTH!!

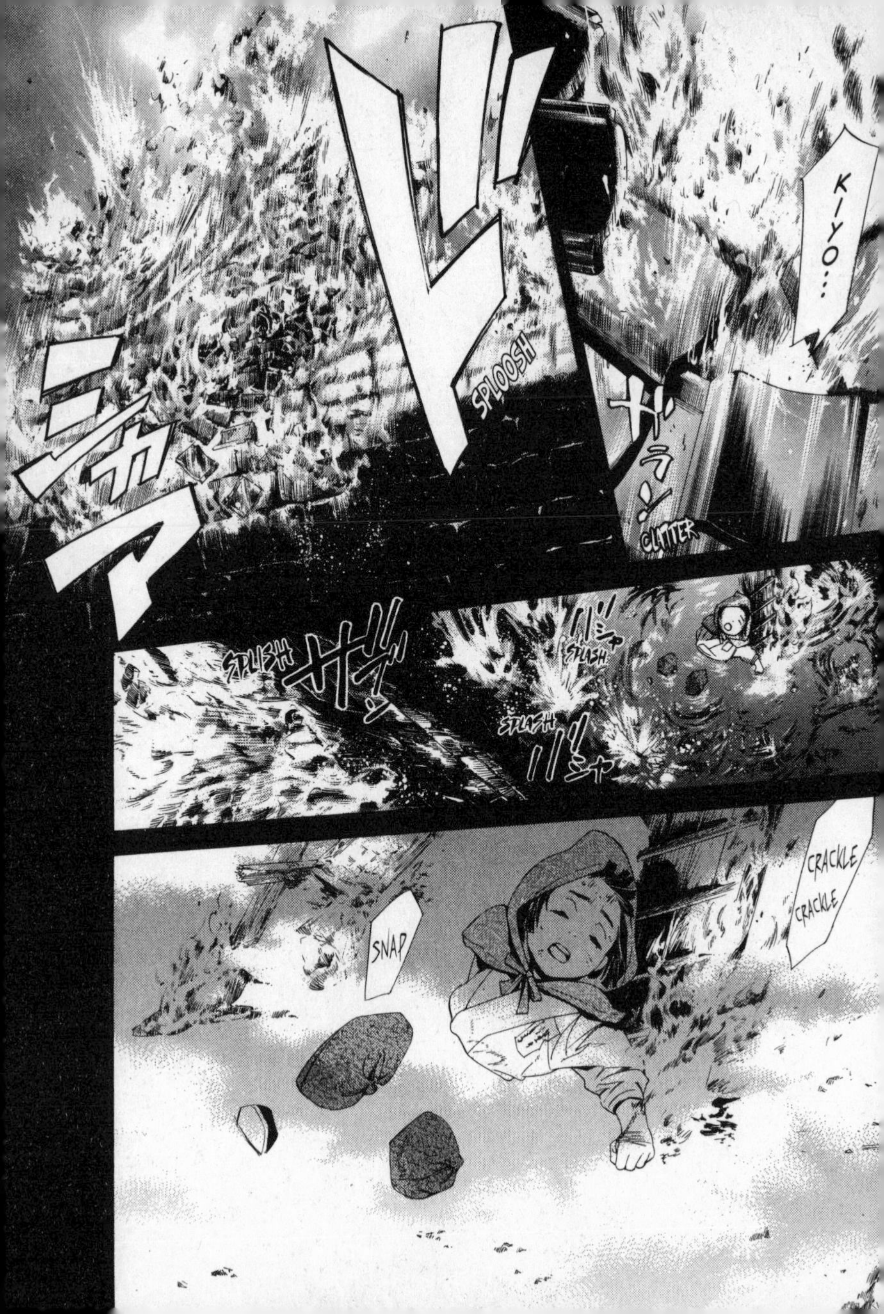

KIYO...
SPLOOSH
CLATTER
SPLASH
SPLASH
SPLISH
CRACKLE CRACKLE
SNAP

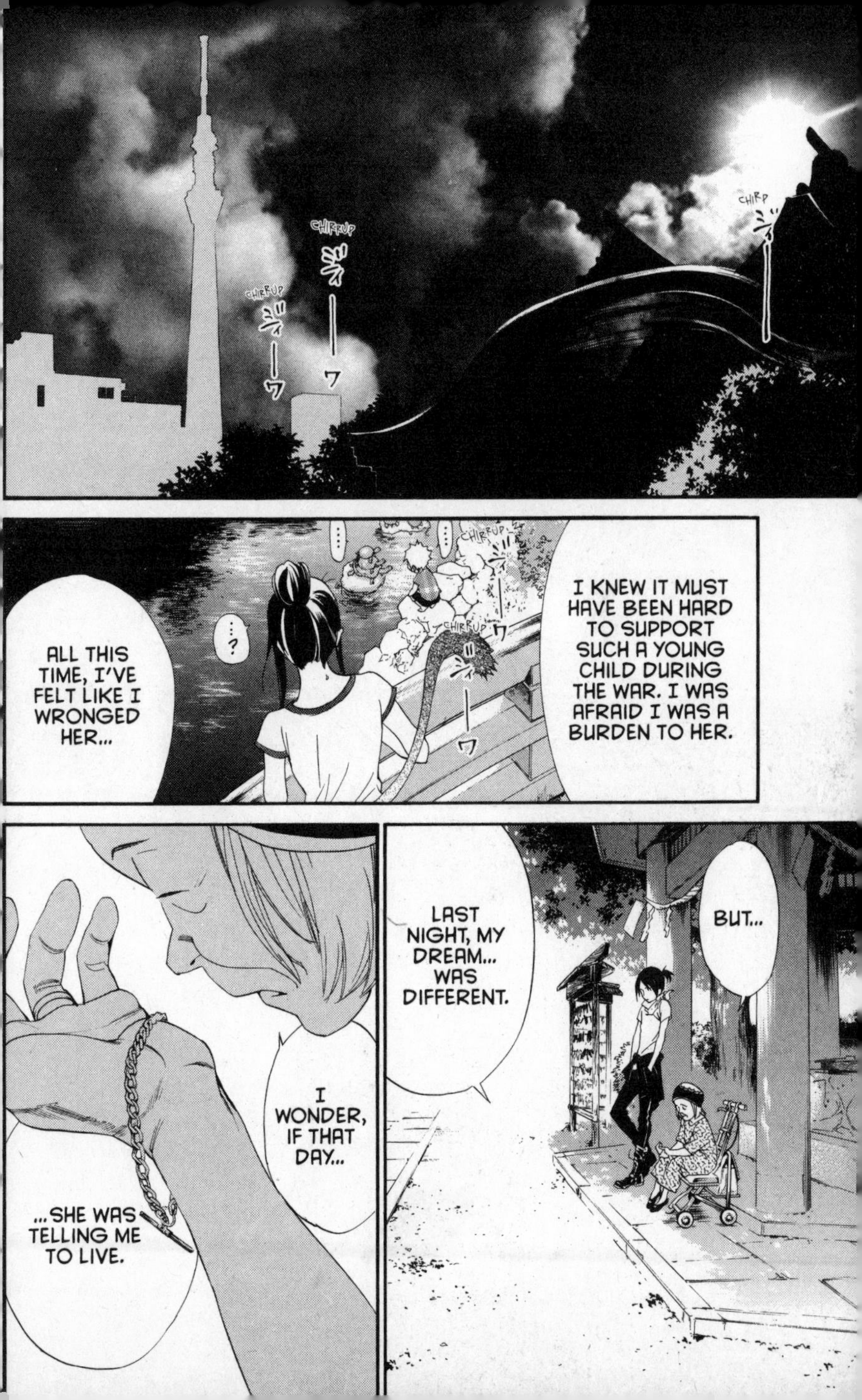
CHIRP
CHIRRUP
CHIRRUP
I KNEW IT MUST HAVE BEEN HARD TO SUPPORT SUCH A YOUNG CHILD DURING THE WAR. I WAS AFRAID I WAS A BURDEN TO HER.
CHIRRUP
CHIRRUP
...
...
...?
ALL THIS TIME, I'VE FELT LIKE I WRONGED HER...
BUT...
LAST NIGHT, MY DREAM... WAS DIFFERENT.
I WONDER, IF THAT DAY...
...SHE WAS TELLING ME TO LIVE.

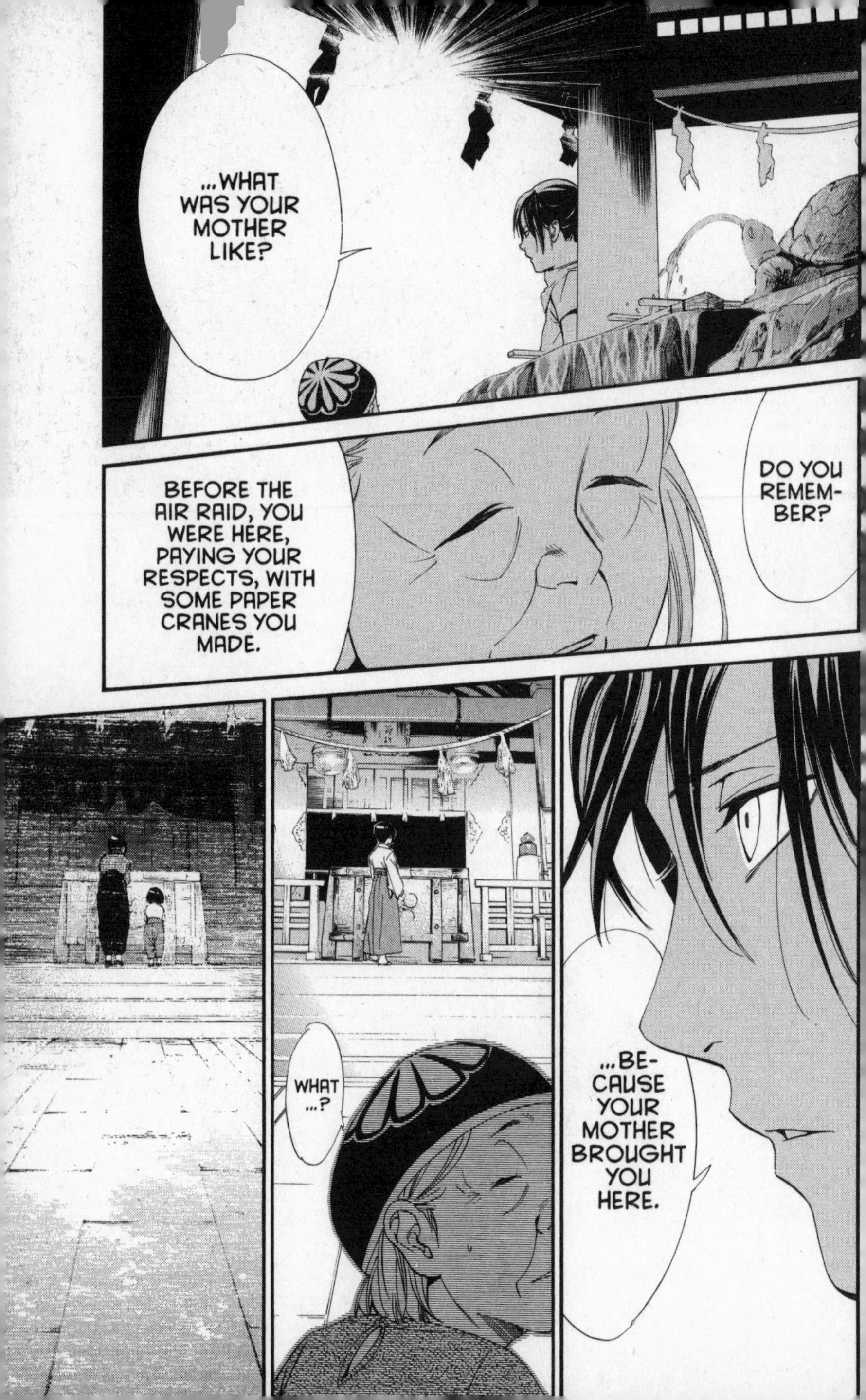
...WHAT WAS YOUR MOTHER LIKE?
DO YOU REMEM- BER?
BEFORE THE AIR RAID, YOU WERE HERE, PAYING YOUR RESPECTS, WITH SOME PAPER CRANES YOU MADE.
...BE- CAUSE YOUR MOTHER BROUGHT YOU HERE.
WHAT ...?

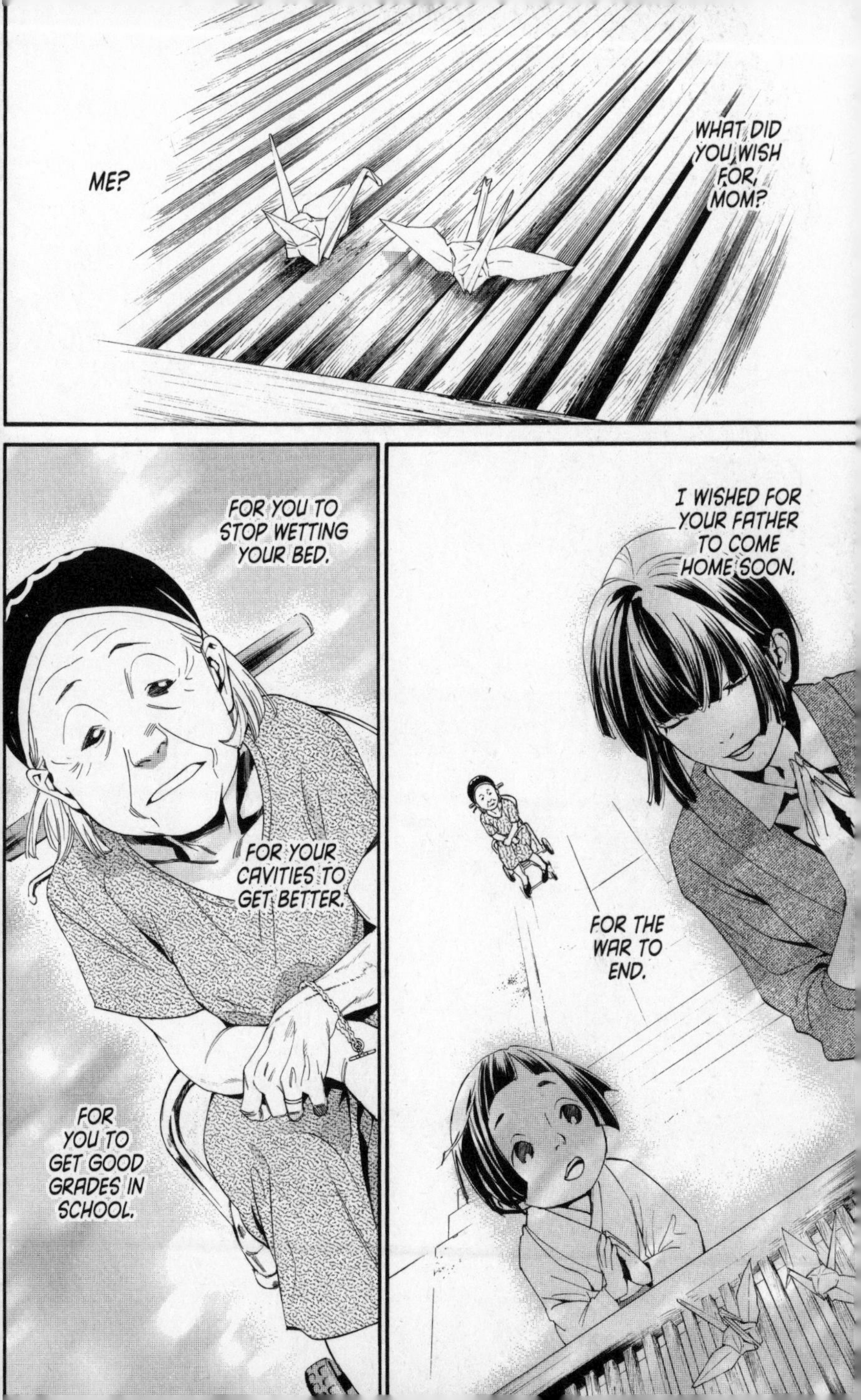
WHAT DID YOU WISH FOR, MOM?
ME?
I WISHED FOR YOUR FATHER TO COME HOME SOON.
FOR THE WAR TO END.
FOR YOU TO STOP WETTING YOUR BED.
FOR YOUR CAVITIES TO GET BETTER.
FOR YOU TO GET GOOD GRADES IN SCHOOL.

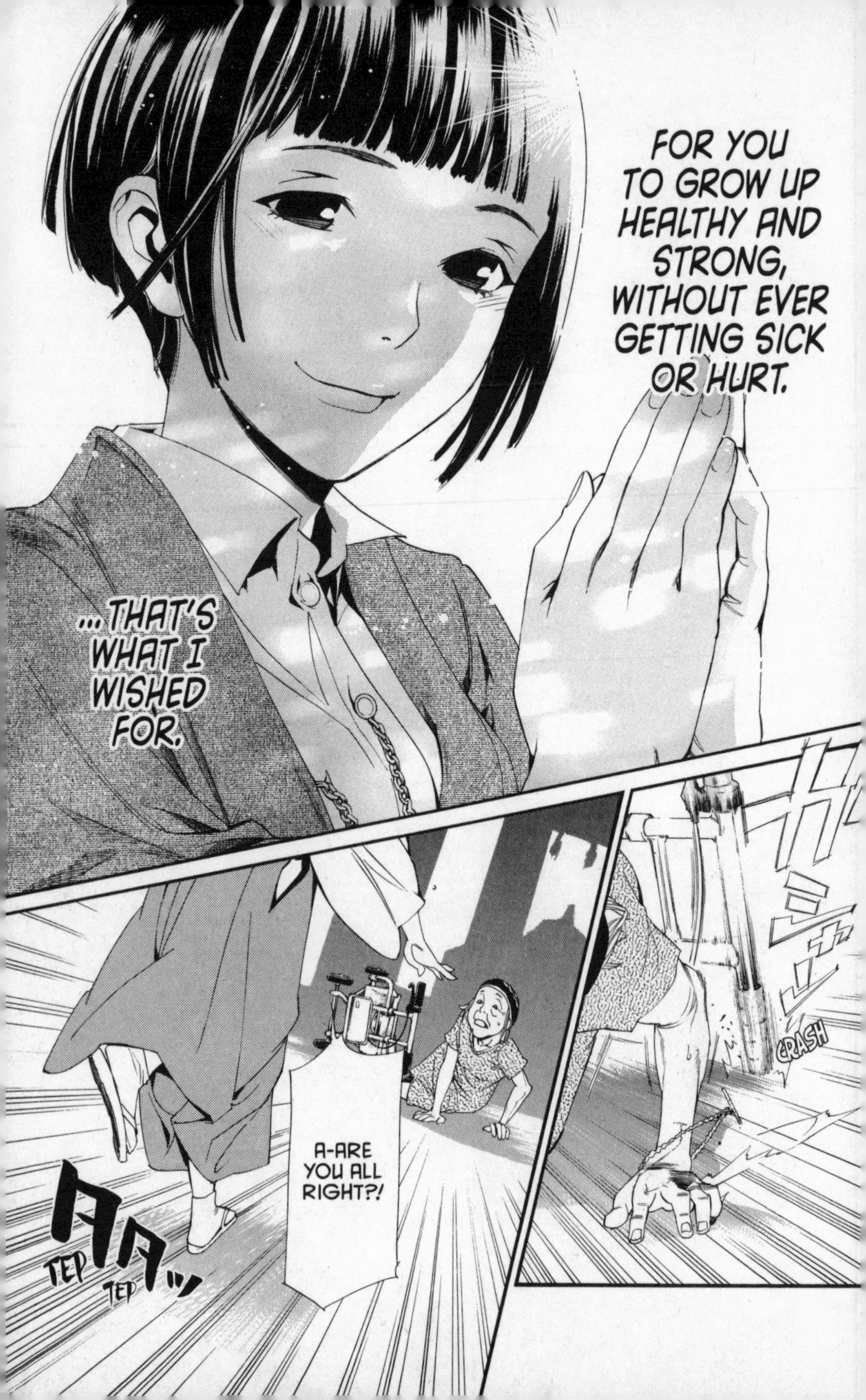
FOR YOU TO GROW UP HEALTHY AND STRONG, WITHOUT EVER GETTING SICK OR HURT.
...THAT'S WHAT I WISHED FOR.
CRASH
A-ARE YOU ALL RIGHT?!
TEP TEP

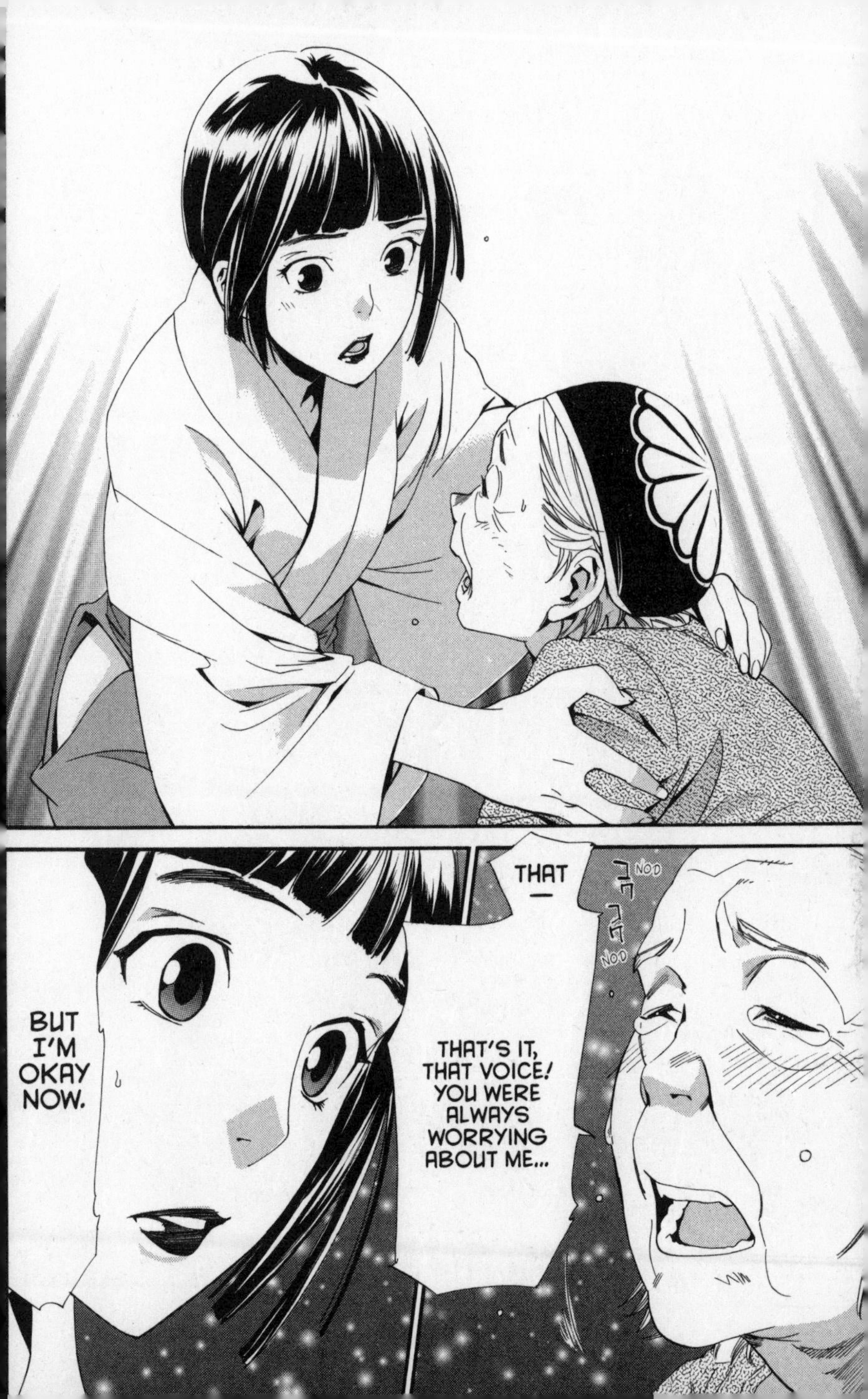
NOD
THAT —
NOD
THAT'S IT, THAT VOICE! YOU WERE ALWAYS WORRYING ABOUT ME...
BUT I'M OKAY NOW.

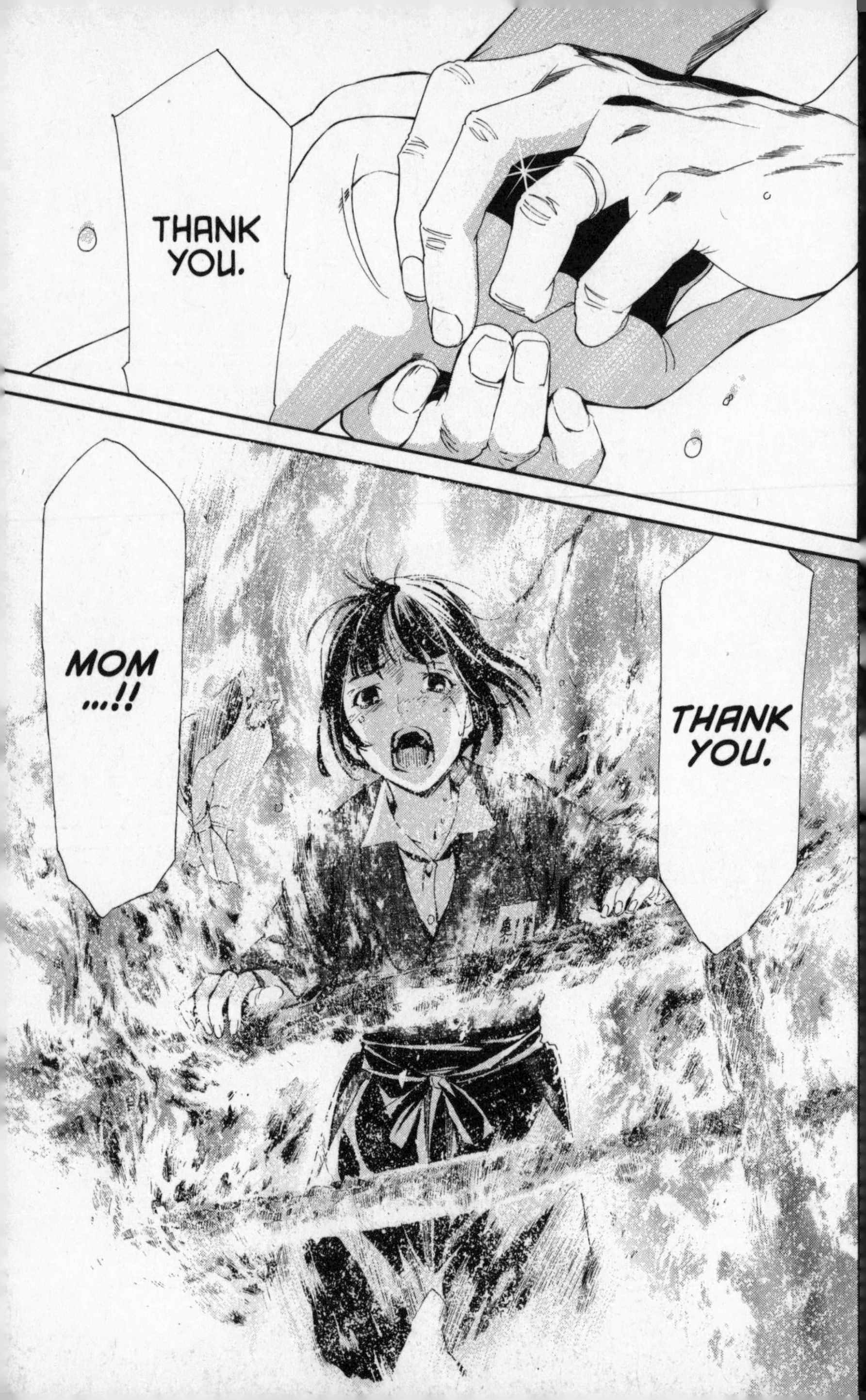
THANK YOU.
THANK YOU.
MOM ...!!

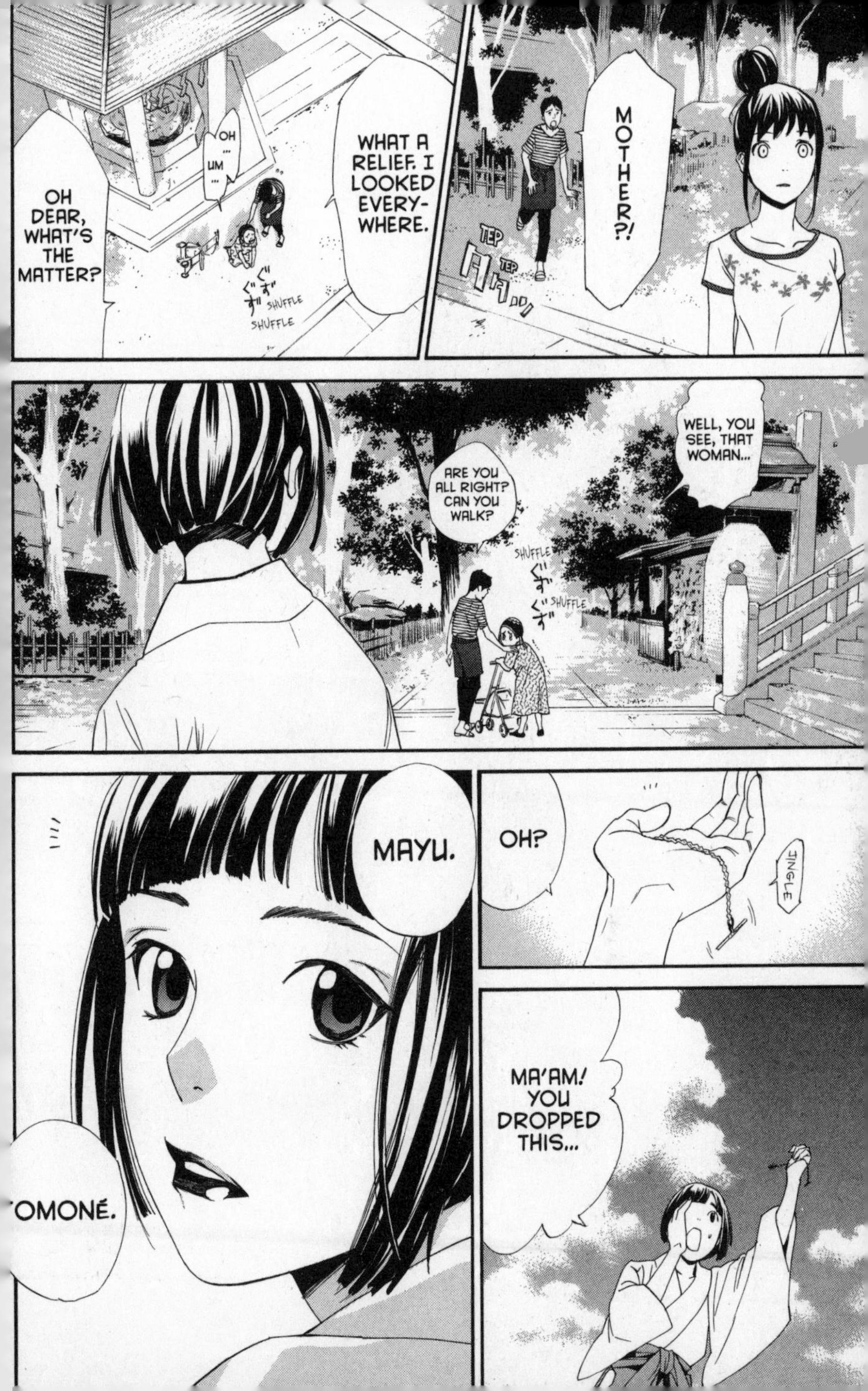
MOTHER?!
TEP TEP
WHAT A RELIEF. I LOOKED EVERYWHERE.
OH ... UM ...
OH DEAR, WHAT'S THE MATTER?
ぐずぐず SHUFFLE SHUFFLE
WELL, YOU SEE, THAT WOMAN...
ARE YOU ALL RIGHT? CAN YOU WALK?
SHUFFLE ぐずぐず SHUFFLE
OH?
JINGLE
MA'AM! YOU DROPPED THIS...
MAYU.
TOMONÉ.

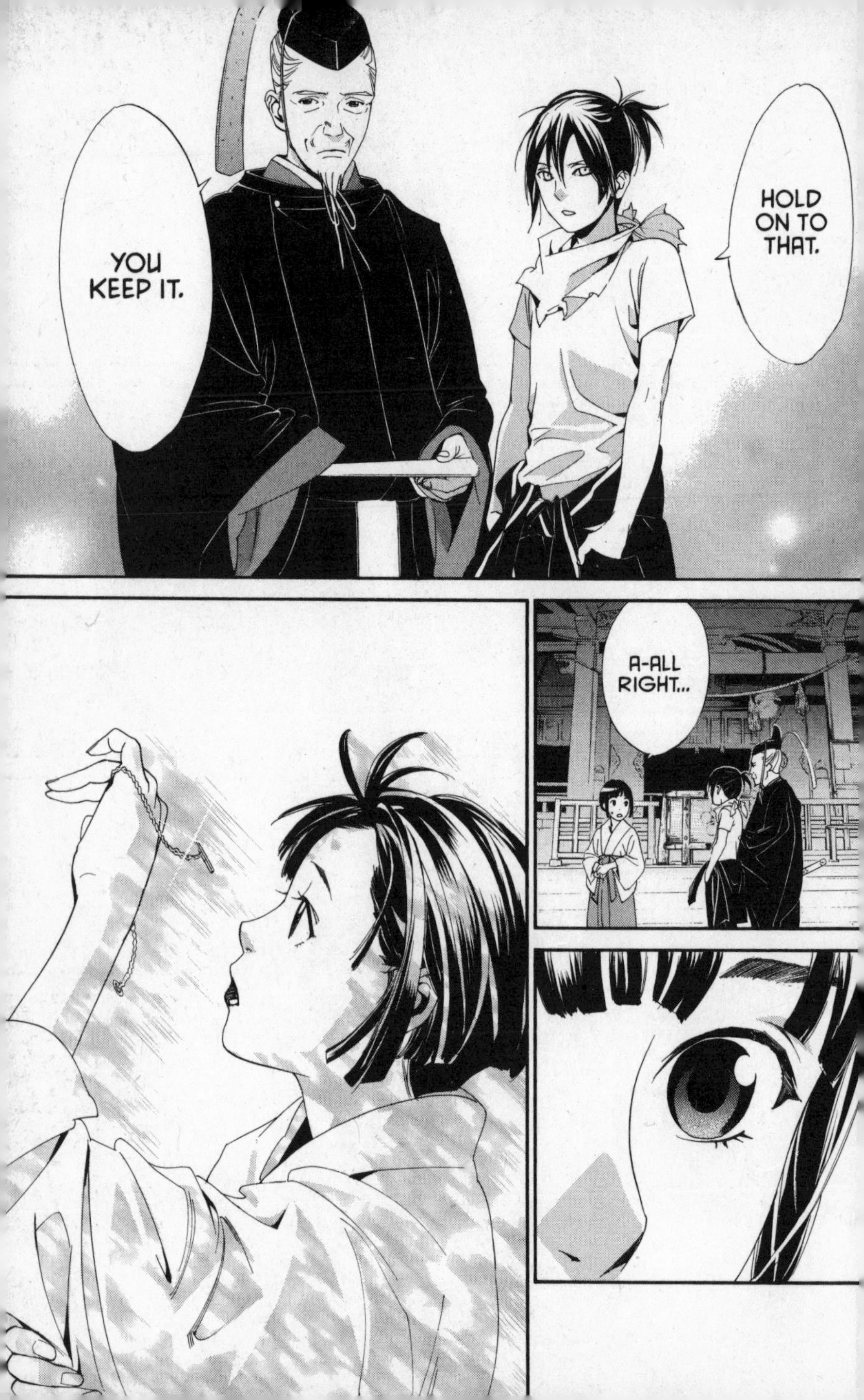
HOLD ON TO THAT.
YOU KEEP IT.
A-ALL RIGHT...

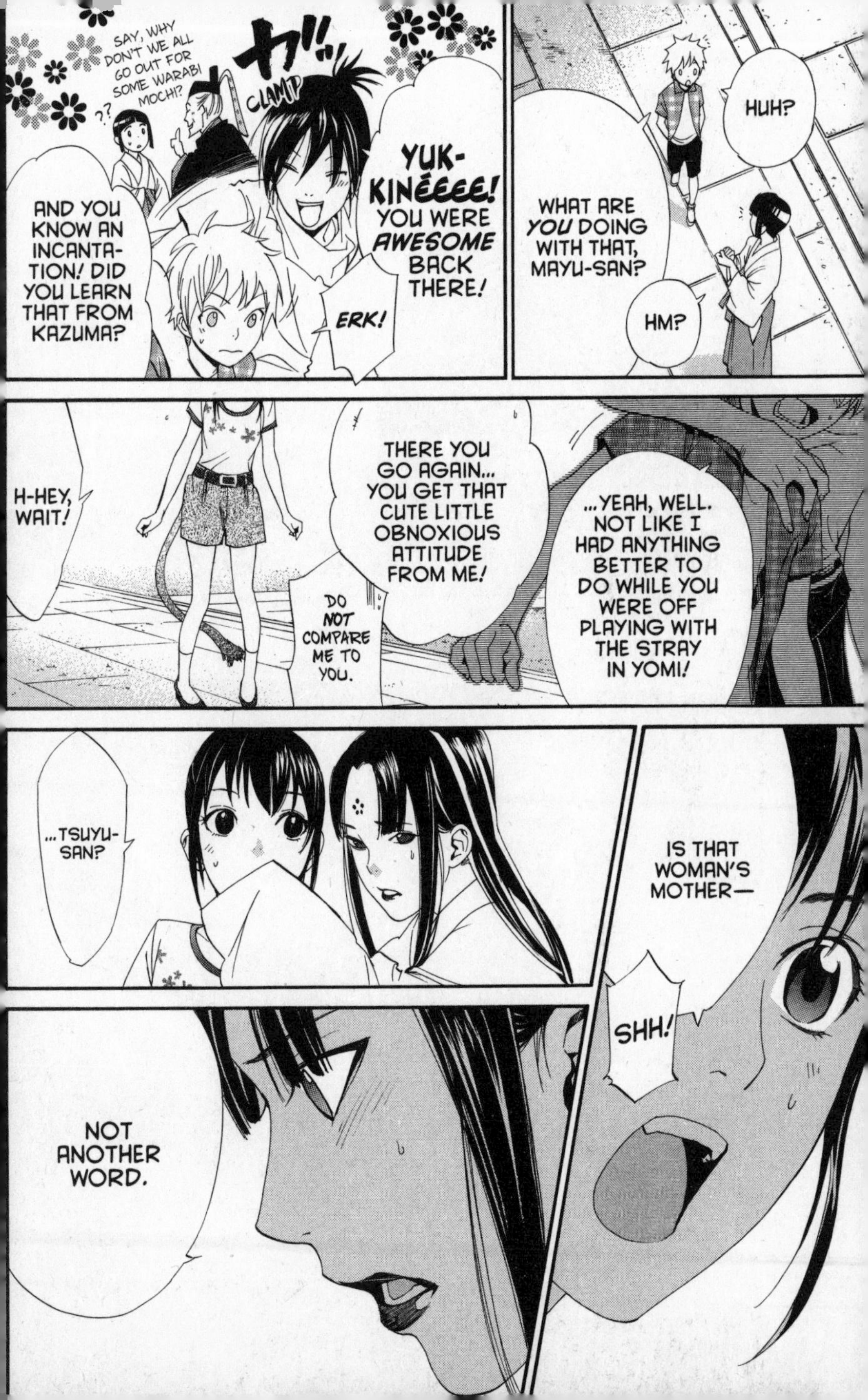
HUH?
WHAT ARE YOU DOING WITH THAT, MAYU-SAN?
HM?
YUK-KINÉÉÉÉ! YOU WERE AWESOME BACK THERE!
CLAMP
SAY, WHY DON'T WE ALL GO OUT FOR SOME WARABI MOCHI?
??
ERK!
AND YOU KNOW AN INCANTA-TION! DID YOU LEARN THAT FROM KAZUMA?
...YEAH, WELL. NOT LIKE I HAD ANYTHING BETTER TO DO WHILE YOU WERE OFF PLAYING WITH THE STRAY IN YOMI!
THERE YOU GO AGAIN... YOU GET THAT CUTE LITTLE OBNOXIOUS ATTITUDE FROM ME!
DO NOT COMPARE ME TO YOU.
H-HEY, WAIT!
IS THAT WOMAN'S MOTHER—
SHH!
...TSUYU-SAN?
NOT ANOTHER WORD.

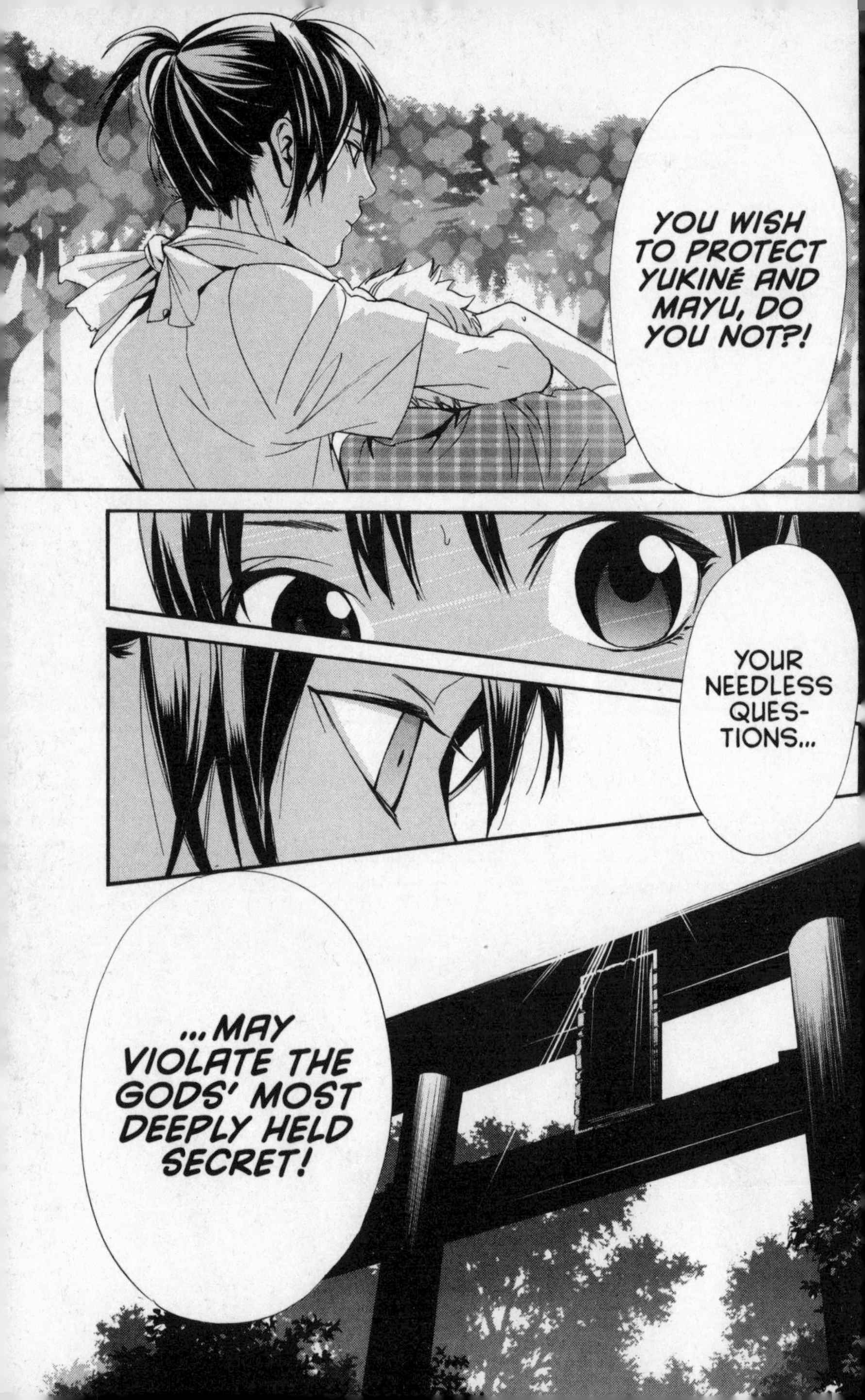
YOU WISH TO PROTECT YUKINÉ AND MAYU, DO YOU NOT?!
YOUR NEEDLESS QUES-TIONS...
...MAY VIOLATE THE GODS' MOST DEEPLY HELD SECRET!

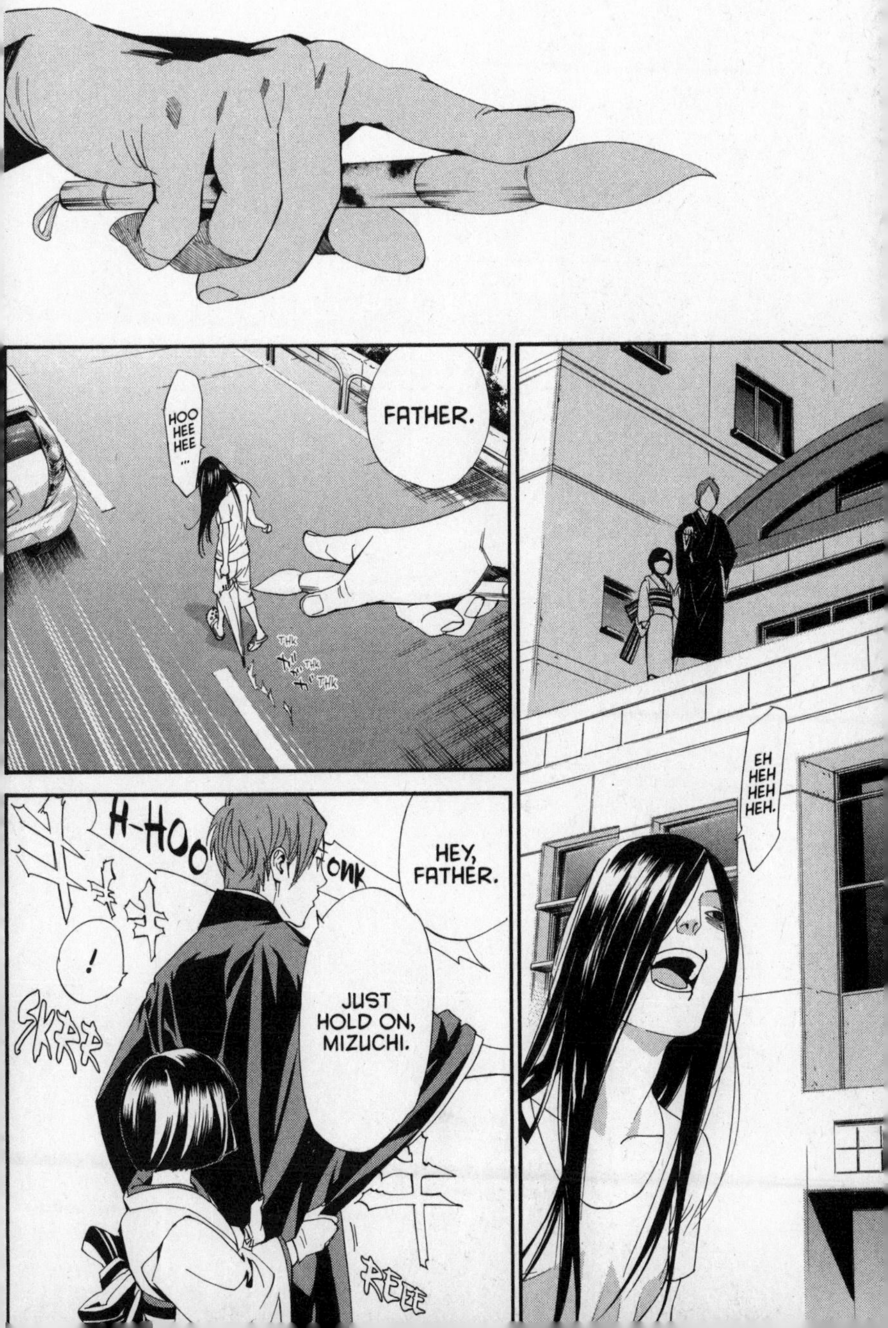
EH HEH HEH HEH.
FATHER.
HOO HEE HEE ...
THK THK THK THK
HEY, FATHER.
JUST HOLD ON, MIZUCHI.
H-HOONK
!
SKRR
REEE

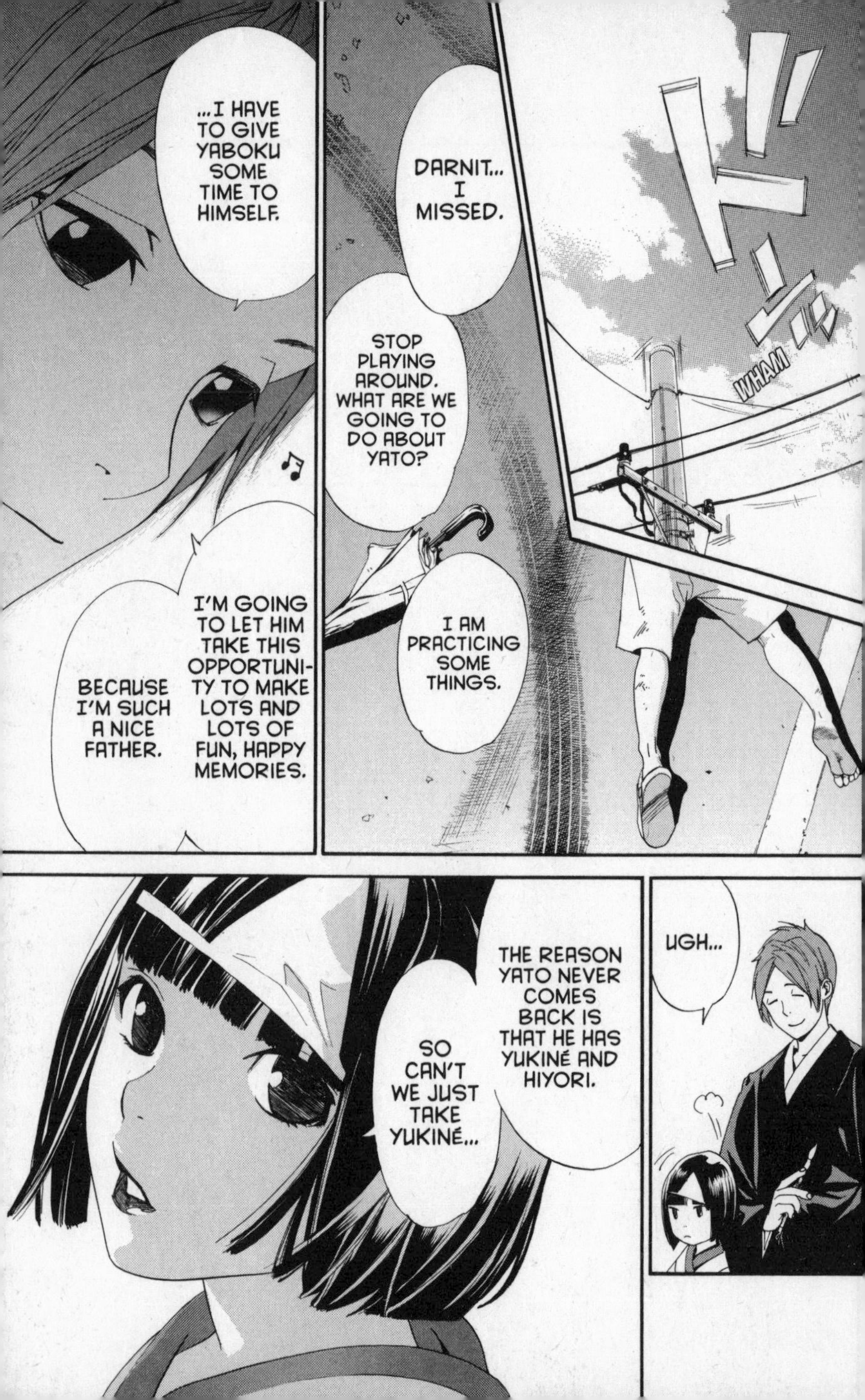
ドン
WHAM
DARNIT... I MISSED.
STOP PLAYING AROUND. WHAT ARE WE GOING TO DO ABOUT YATO?
I AM PRACTICING SOME THINGS.
...I HAVE TO GIVE YABOKU SOME TIME TO HIMSELF.
I'M GOING TO LET HIM TAKE THIS OPPORTUNITY TO MAKE LOTS AND LOTS OF FUN, HAPPY MEMORIES.
BECAUSE I'M SUCH A NICE FATHER.
UGH...
THE REASON YATO NEVER COMES BACK IS THAT HE HAS YUKINÉ AND HIYORI.
SO CAN'T WE JUST TAKE YUKINÉ...

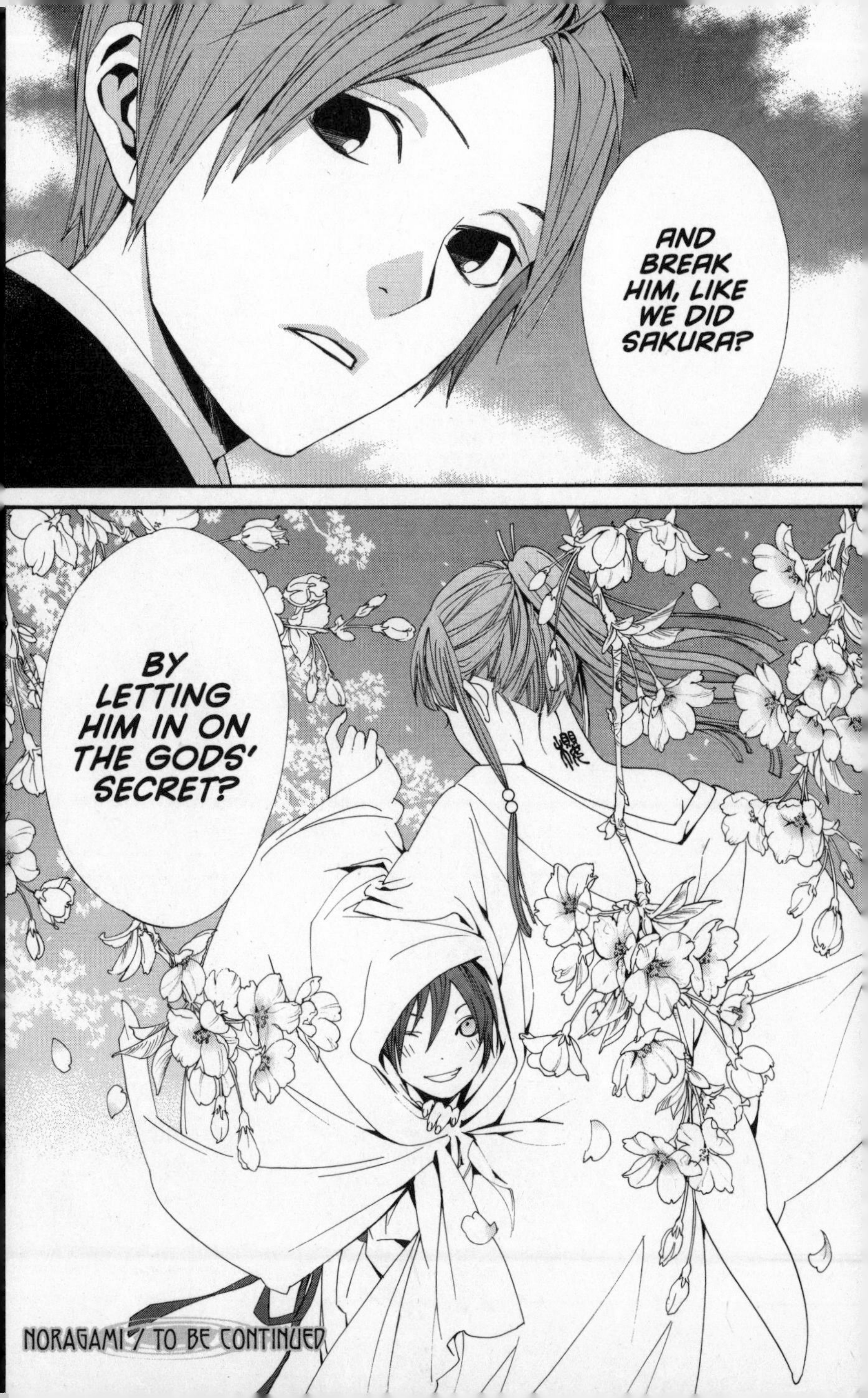
AND BREAK HIM, LIKE WE DID SAKURA?
BY LETTING HIM IN ON THE GODS' SECRET?
NORAGAMI / TO BE CONTINUED

野

𠄔

神

ATROCIOUS MANGA

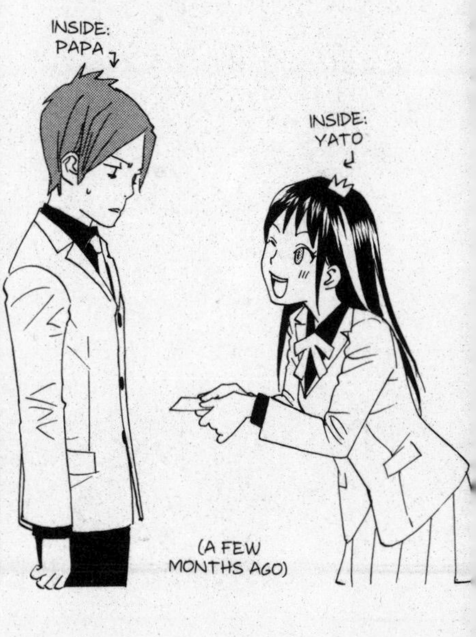
INSIDE: PAPA
INSIDE: YATO
(A FEW MONTHS AGO)

JK WALKING

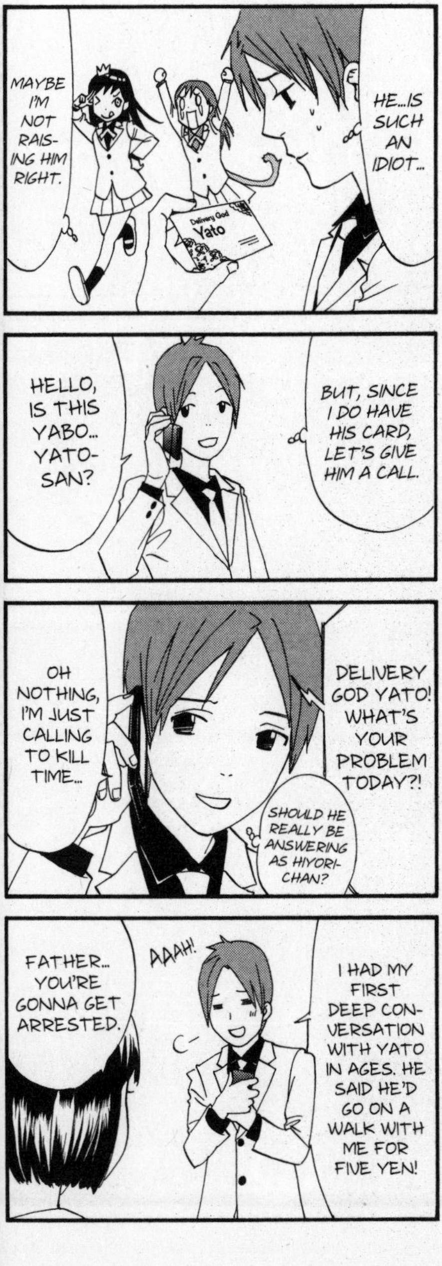
HE...IS SUCH AN IDIOT...
Delivery God Yato
MAYBE I'M NOT RAISING HIM RIGHT.
BUT, SINCE I DO HAVE HIS CARD, LET'S GIVE HIM A CALL.
HELLO, IS THIS YABO... YATO-SAN?
DELIVERY GOD YATO! WHAT'S YOUR PROBLEM TODAY?!
OH NOTHING, I'M JUST CALLING TO KILL TIME...
SHOULD HE REALLY BE ANSWERING AS HIYORI-CHAN?
I HAD MY FIRST DEEP CONVERSATION WITH YATO IN AGES. HE SAID HE'D GO ON A WALK WITH ME FOR FIVE YEN!
AAAH!
FATHER... YOU'RE GONNA GET ARRESTED.

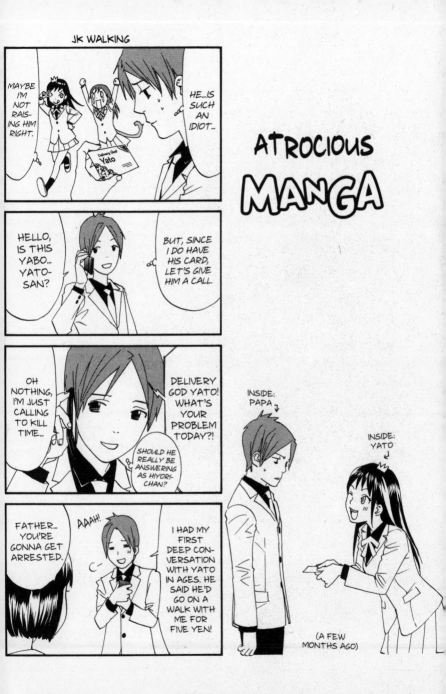

BIRD CONTROL SPIKES

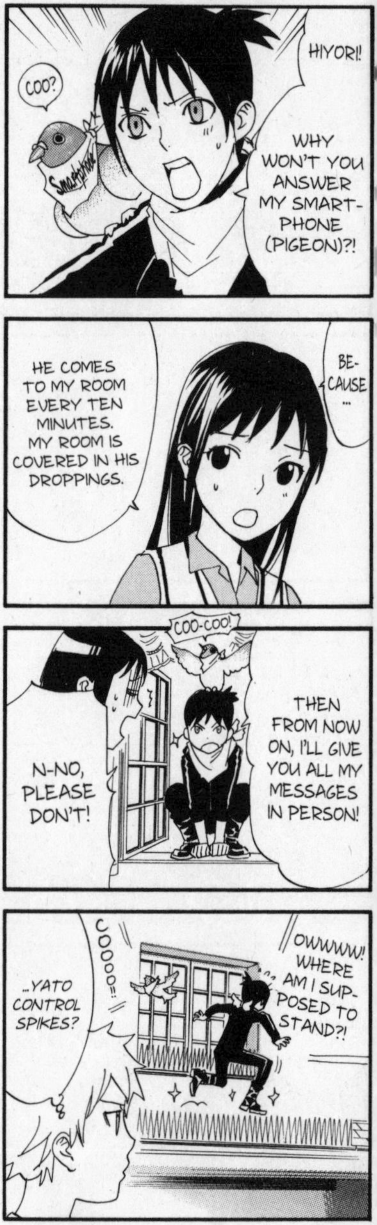
HIYORI!
WHY WON'T YOU ANSWER MY SMARTPHONE (PIGEON)?!
COO?
BECAUSE...
HE COMES TO MY ROOM EVERY TEN MINUTES. MY ROOM IS COVERED IN HIS DROPPINGS.
COO-COO!
THEN FROM NOW ON, I'LL GIVE YOU ALL MY MESSAGES IN PERSON!
N-NO, PLEASE DON'T!
OWWWW! WHERE AM I SUPPOSED TO STAND?!
COOOO!!
...YATO CONTROL SPIKES?

SAME OLD WAKA

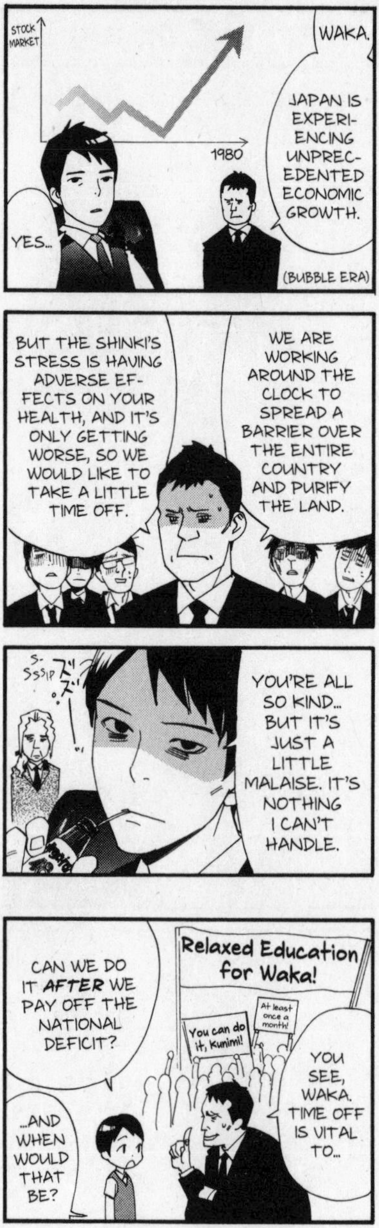
WAKA.
JAPAN IS EXPERIENCING UNPRECEDENTED ECONOMIC GROWTH.
STOCK MARKET
1980
(BUBBLE ERA)
YES...
WE ARE WORKING AROUND THE CLOCK TO SPREAD A BARRIER OVER THE ENTIRE COUNTRY AND PURIFY THE LAND.
BUT THE SHINKI'S STRESS IS HAVING ADVERSE EFFECTS ON YOUR HEALTH, AND IT'S ONLY GETTING WORSE, SO WE WOULD LIKE TO TAKE A LITTLE TIME OFF.
YOU'RE ALL SO KIND... BUT IT'S JUST A LITTLE MALAISE. IT'S NOTHING I CAN'T HANDLE.
S-SSSIP
YOU SEE, WAKA. TIME OFF IS VITAL TO...
Relaxed Education for Waka!
At least once a month!
You can do it, Kunimi!
CAN WE DO IT *AFTER* WE PAY OFF THE NATIONAL DEFICIT?
...AND WHEN WOULD THAT BE?

KAZUMA RISES TO GREATER HEIGHTS

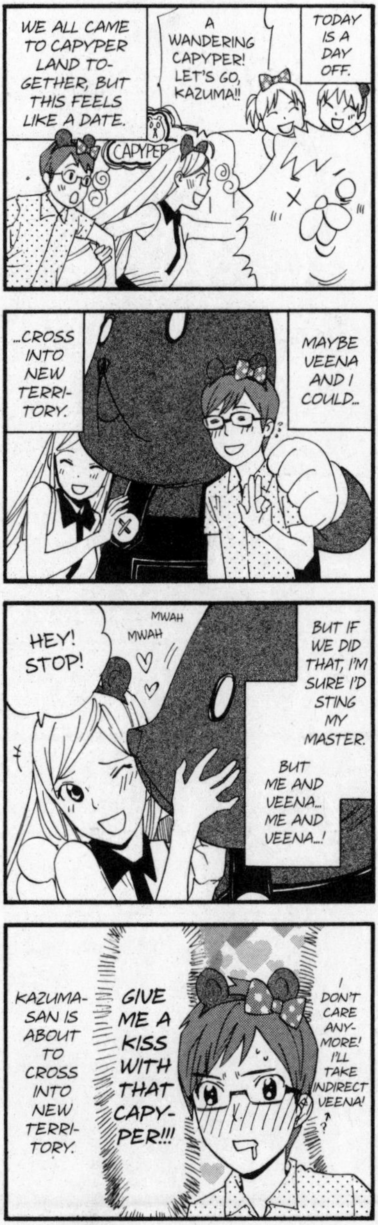
TODAY IS A DAY OFF.
A WANDERING CAPYPER! LET'S GO, KAZUMA!!
WE ALL CAME TO CAPYPER LAND TOGETHER, BUT THIS FEELS LIKE A DATE.
CAPYPER
MAYBE VEENA AND I COULD...
...CROSS INTO NEW TERRITORY.
BUT IF WE DID THAT, I'M SURE I'D STING MY MASTER.
BUT ME AND VEENA... ME AND VEENA...!
MWAH
MWAH
HEY! STOP!
I DON'T CARE ANYMORE! I'LL TAKE INDIRECT VEENA!
GIVE ME A KISS WITH THAT CAPYPER!!!
KAZUMA-SAN IS ABOUT TO CROSS INTO NEW TERRITORY.

SAME OLD WAKA

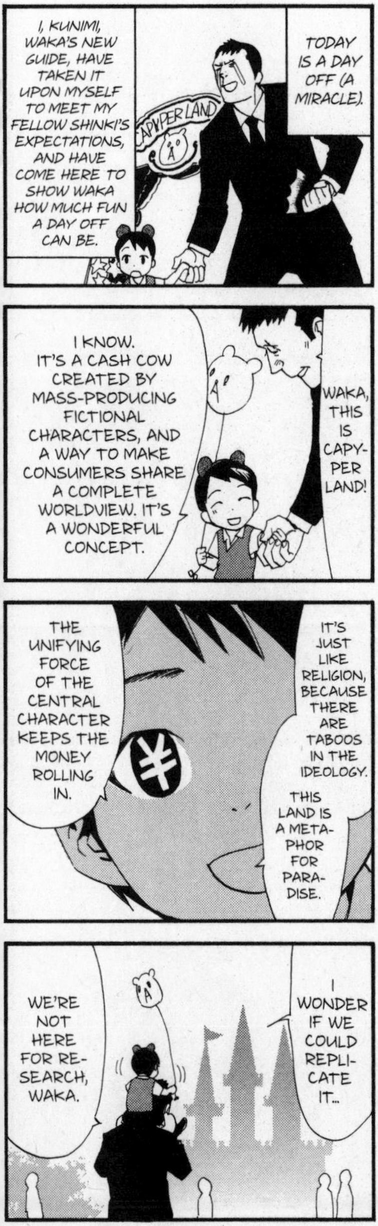
TODAY IS A DAY OFF (A MIRACLE).
I, KUNIMI, WAKA'S NEW GUIDE, HAVE TAKEN IT UPON MYSELF TO MEET MY FELLOW SHINKI'S EXPECTATIONS, AND HAVE COME HERE TO SHOW WAKA HOW MUCH FUN A DAY OFF CAN BE.
CAPYPER LAND
WAKA, THIS IS CAPYPER LAND!
I KNOW. IT'S A CASH COW CREATED BY MASS-PRODUCING FICTIONAL CHARACTERS, AND A WAY TO MAKE CONSUMERS SHARE A COMPLETE WORLDVIEW. IT'S A WONDERFUL CONCEPT.
IT'S JUST LIKE RELIGION, BECAUSE THERE ARE TABOOS IN THE IDEOLOGY.
THIS LAND IS A METAPHOR FOR PARADISE.
THE UNIFYING FORCE OF THE CENTRAL CHARACTER KEEPS THE MONEY ROLLING IN.
I WONDER IF WE COULD REPLICATE IT...
WE'RE NOT HERE FOR RESEARCH, WAKA.

THE BENEFACTOR

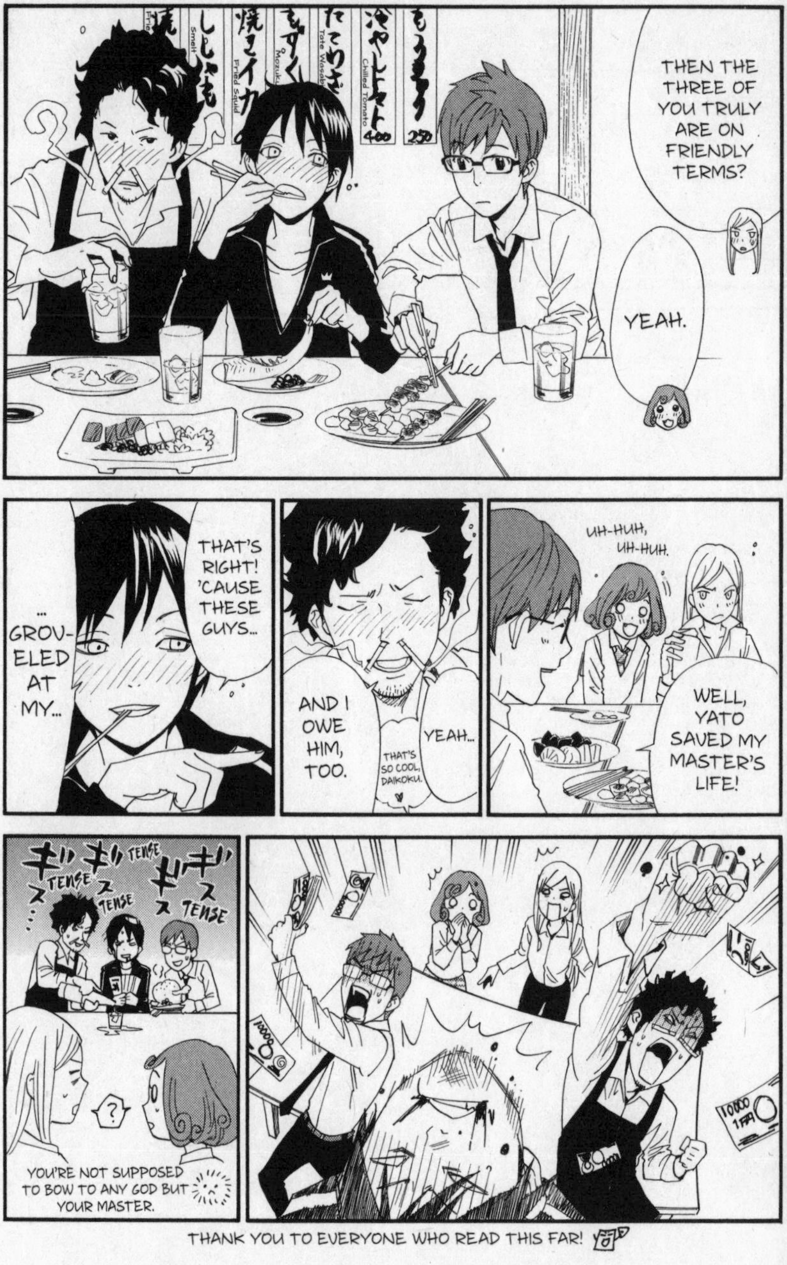
250
Chilled Tomato
400
Tote Wasabi
Mozuku
Fried Squid
Smelt
THEN THE THREE OF YOU TRULY ARE ON FRIENDLY TERMS?
YEAH.
UH-HUH, UH-HUH.
WELL, YATO SAVED MY MASTER'S LIFE!
AND I OWE HIM, TOO.
YEAH...
THAT'S SO COOL, DAIKOKU.
THAT'S RIGHT! 'CAUSE THESE GUYS...
... GROVELED AT MY...
10000
ギスギス
TENSE
TENSE
TENSE
TENSE
TENSE
?
YOU'RE NOT SUPPOSED TO BOW TO ANY GOD BUT YOUR MASTER.

THANK YOU TO EVERYONE WHO READ THIS FAR!

野

叟

曝

TRANSLATION NOTES

Japanese is a tricky language for most Westerners, and translation is often more art than science. For your edification and reading pleasure, here are notes on some of the places where we could have gone in a different direction in our translation of the work, or where a Japanese cultural reference is used.

BUBBLE REVOLUTIONARY
HIKARU GENSHI YATO
YOU AND JINJA
now on sale!!
¥5
LIKE, NO WAY
SALE!
¥5
CASSETTE SINGLE
¥5

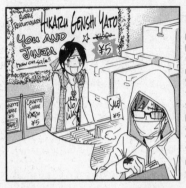

You and Jinja, page 22

For our younger readers, before we had mp3s, before we even had CDs, we recorded music on little boxes with magnetic tape inside called cassettes. Since Yato was a pop star in the '80s, that was the recording format for his songs. The one he's advertising most prominently at this booth is called "You and Jinja," which is a play on words. "Jinja" can sound like the girl's name "Ginger," but it also sounds like Yato's most cherished wish, his own *jinja*, or shrine.

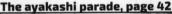

The ayakashi parade, page 42

JUST MAKES YOU WANT TO MESS WITH HER.
HUH?
...NOTHING.

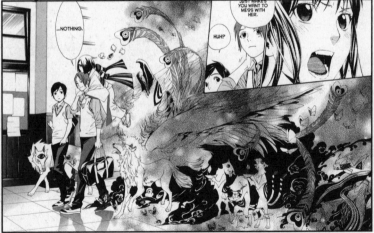

Some readers may remember that Hiyori's friend Yama-chan was originally attracted to Kôto because he reminded her of the vocalist from her favorite band, Hyakki Yakô. Kôto's friend didn't see it, but apparently she wasn't too far off in associating him with the term, which, as you may recall, refers to a parade of a hundred or so demons.

Boozing, betting, and buying, page 53
One Japanese phrase for three of a man's worst vices is *nomu utsu kau*, meaning "to drink, to gamble, to buy." Usually the unspoken object of purchase is the services of a prostitute, but for better or worse, Yato's depravity has taken him in a different direction.

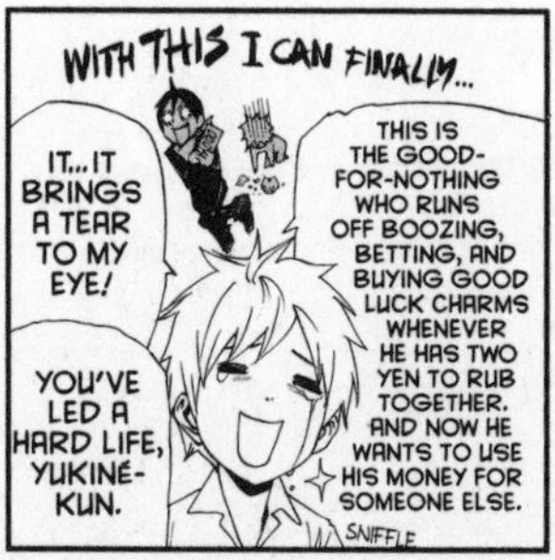
WITH THIS I CAN FINALLY...
THIS IS THE GOOD-FOR-NOTHING WHO RUNS OFF BOOZING, BETTING, AND BUYING GOOD LUCK CHARMS WHENEVER HE HAS TWO YEN TO RUB TOGETHER. AND NOW HE WANTS TO USE HIS MONEY FOR SOMEONE ELSE.
IT...IT BRINGS A TEAR TO MY EYE!
YOU'VE LED A HARD LIFE, YUKINÉ-KUN.
SNIFFLE

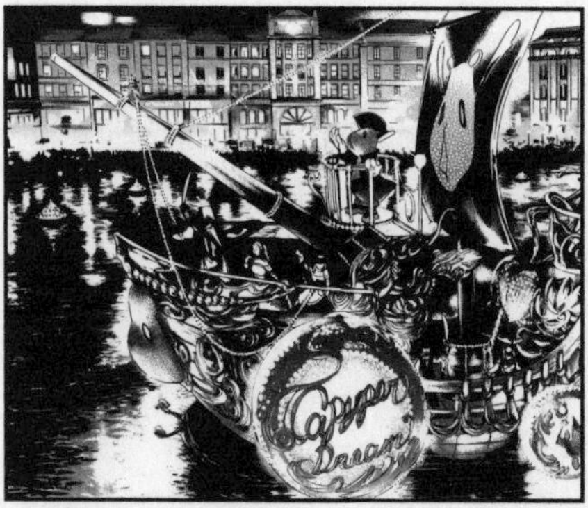

Elekiter Parade, page 77
Readers may or may not find it interesting to note that an elekiter, while sounding very much like the word used in the name of another famous light parade, is also an 18th-century Japanese invention that could store static electricity. The word derives from the Dutch word for electricity, *elektriciteit*, and, as such, can refer to the device or electricity itself.

We're in Chiba, page 88
As everyone in Tokyo surely knows, despite having Tokyo in the name, the most famous Japanese theme park associated with a rodent of unusual size is actually located in the neighboring prefecture of Chiba. But the important thing to remember is, Tokyo or Chiba, the odds of seeing an iceberg are extremely small. On the other hand, it is a magical kingdom.

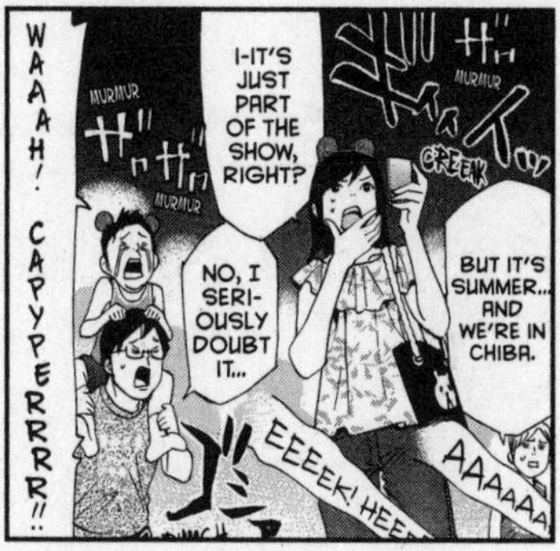
MURMUR
BUT IT'S SUMMER... AND WE'RE IN CHIBA.
I-IT'S JUST PART OF THE SHOW, RIGHT?
NO, I SERIOUSLY DOUBT IT...
MURMUR
MURMUR
WAAAH! CAPYPERRRR!!
EEEEK!
AAAAAA

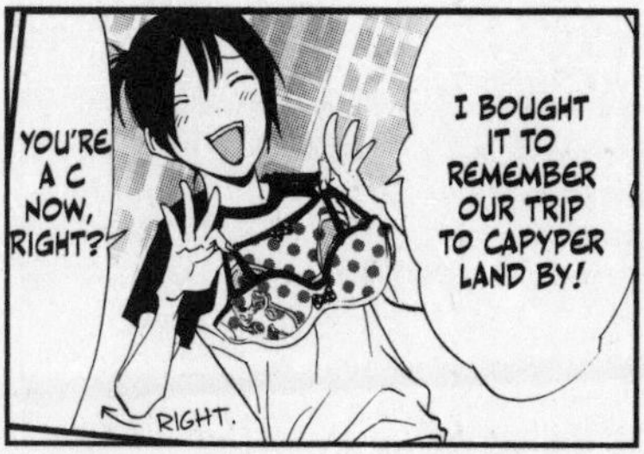
I BOUGHT IT TO REMEMBER OUR TRIP TO CAPYPER LAND BY!
YOU'RE A C NOW, RIGHT?
RIGHT.

You're a C now, right?, page 100
Not that anyone really needs to know this unless you want to go shopping for intimates in Japan, but cup sizes are smaller there, so a C cup is actually a B here in North America.

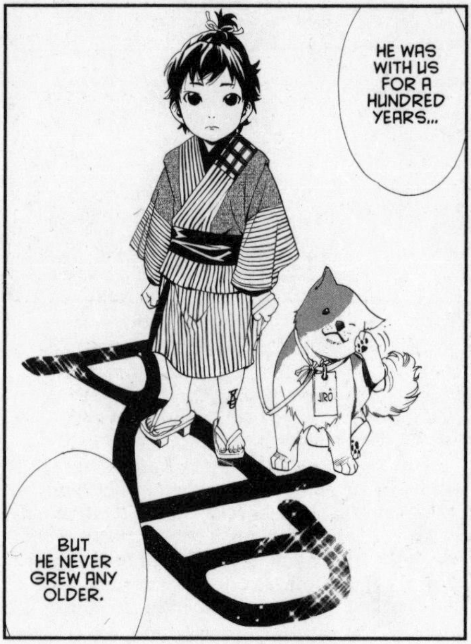
HE WAS WITH US FOR A HUNDRED YEARS...
JIRÔ
BUT HE NEVER GREW ANY OLDER.

Mamoru and Daigo, page 105

As we all know by now, all shinki have multiple names, so Mamoru is the child's true name, while Daigo is the *yobina* or "called name." We also know that gods tend to give their shinki similar names to mark them as family, which might make it seem strange that Kofuku would specifically point this out. But in her case, since she isn't in the market for a large shinki family, she had a different reason to make sure her shinki shared part of their name. In Japanese culture, it's not uncommon to name a son after his father—not by giving him the same name, but by giving him *part* of the name. Kofuku gave her shinki the name Daigo as a way of creating a father-son bond between him and Daikoku.

Baked miso and 25 *sen*, page 107

As described in this panel, superstition has it that gods of poverty are fond of baked miso. The *binbôgami* is often depicted holding a fan, which he uses to fan the miso's aroma to him, so he can enjoy it all the more. One way to get rid of them is to lure them out of the house with baked miso, then throw the baked miso into the river.

The man who is asking for 25 *sen* is a *rakugo* storyteller. *Rakugo* is an old form of Japanese comedy in which a storyteller retells a conversation between two people, playing both parts. Several of these stories are about the god of poverty. *Sen* is an old form of Japanese currency.

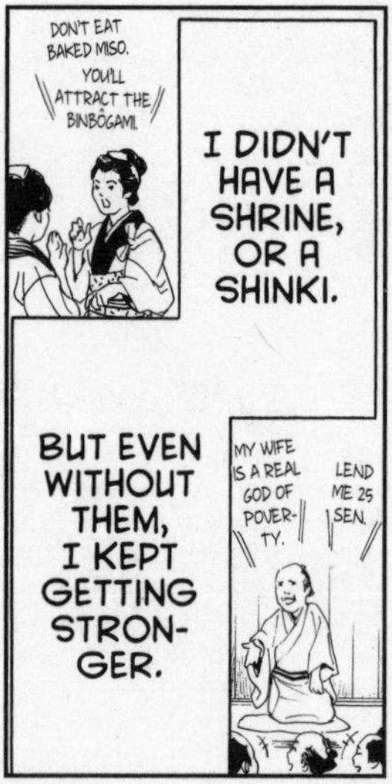
I DIDN'T HAVE A SHRINE, OR A SHINKI.
DON'T EAT BAKED MISO. YOU'LL ATTRACT THE BINBÔGAMI.
LEND ME 25 SEN.
MY WIFE IS A REAL GOD OF POVERTY.
BUT EVEN WITHOUT THEM, I KEPT GETTING STRONGER.

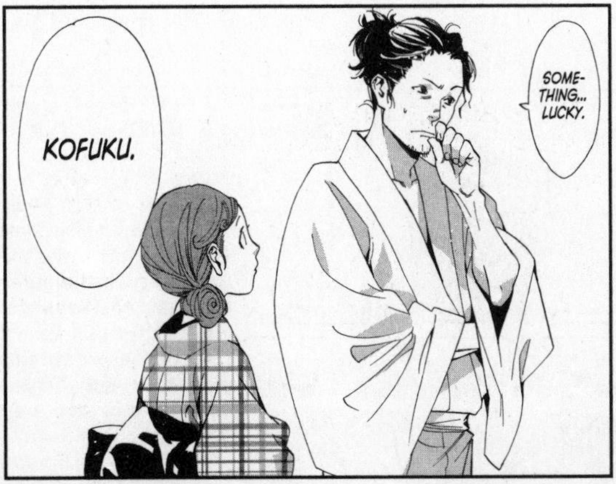
SOME-THING... LUCKY.
KOFUKU.

Lucky Kofuku, page 110

In case you're wondering what makes Kofuku a lucky name, it's the *fuku*, which means "good fortune." *Ko* means "little," so the name Kofuku means "little good fortune," and makes Kofuku sound like a cute little goddess of happiness. Looking at it another way, it also suggests that if you let her stick around, your good fortune will shrink, thus making the name Kofuku very appropriate.

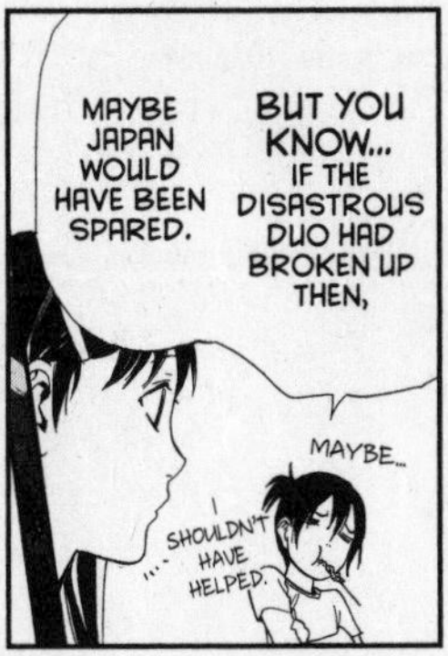
BUT YOU KNOW... IF THE DISASTROUS DUO HAD BROKEN UP THEN,
MAYBE JAPAN WOULD HAVE BEEN SPARED.
MAYBE...
I SHOULDN'T HAVE HELPED.

The Disastrous Duo, page 137

Here, Yato refers to Kofuku and Daikoku as a *saikyô* combo. This is a play on words—usually when someone calls something *saikyô*, they're talking about how it's the most powerful of all powerful things. But Yato replaces the "powerful" *kanji* with the character meaning "bad luck," so they're the "greatest bad luck combo." The translators attempted to recapture the fun in the epithet by using alliteration.

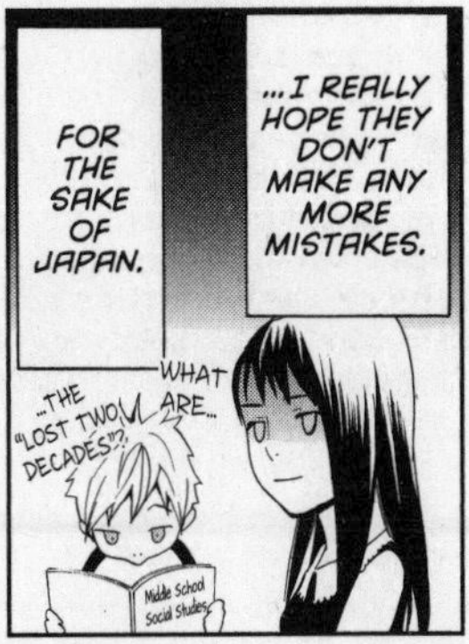
...I REALLY HOPE THEY DON'T MAKE ANY MORE MISTAKES.
FOR THE SAKE OF JAPAN.
WHAT ARE...
...THE "LOST TWO DECADES"!?
Middle School Social Studies

What are the "Lost Two Decades"?, page 140

Thanks, Yukiné! We're so glad you asked. Some readers may remember a note about the "bubble period," referring to the Japanese economic bubble that existed from 1986 to 1991. When the bubble popped, it led to years of financial stagnation in Japan, which have come to be known as the Lost Decade (from 1991 to 2000), or as the Lost Two Decades (from 1991 to 2010).

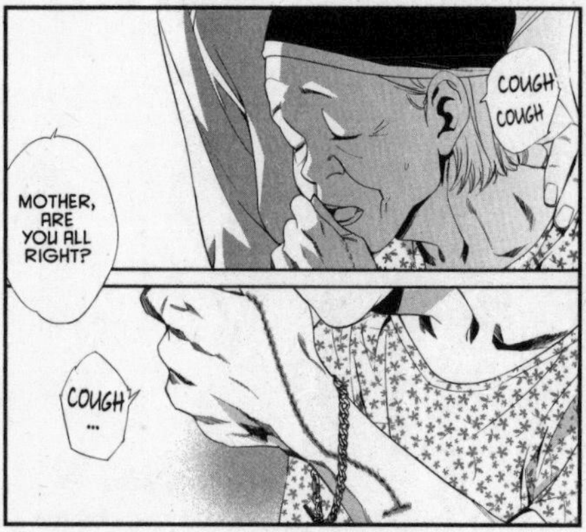
COUGH COUGH
MOTHER, ARE YOU ALL RIGHT?
COUGH ...

Mother, page 143

The reader may be interested to know that while the woman calls the older woman "mother," the *kanji* characters indicate that she is actually a stepmother, adopted mother, or mother-in-law. The specifics of their relationship are not made clear.

The firefighting incantation, page 167

This is a *tanka*, or Japanese poem like a haiku but a little longer—haiku consist of three lines of five, seven, and five syllables, while *tanka* have five lines of five, seven, five, seven, and seven syllables. The author of this particular poem is unknown, but it has been used for years as a way of warding off fires, through such methods as displaying it as calligraphy in the home, and writing it on the house's rafters. Here, Yukiné chants the words, which then take form to extinguish the supernatural flames. Yato refers to the incantation as a *juka*, which means roughly "spell song."

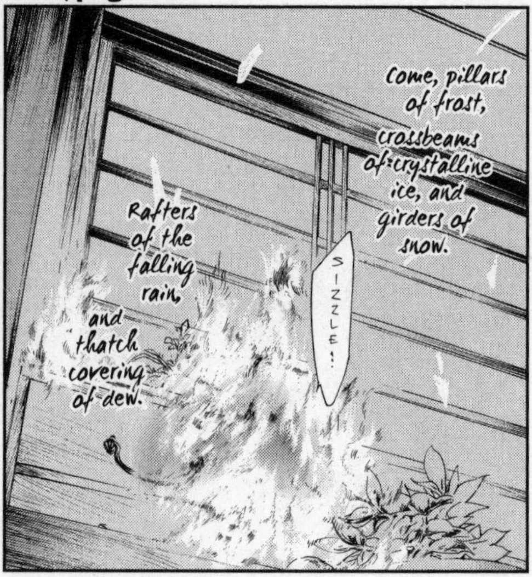
Come, pillars of frost, crossbeams of crystalline ice, and girders of snow.
SIZZLE!!
Rafters of the falling rain,
and thatch covering of dew.

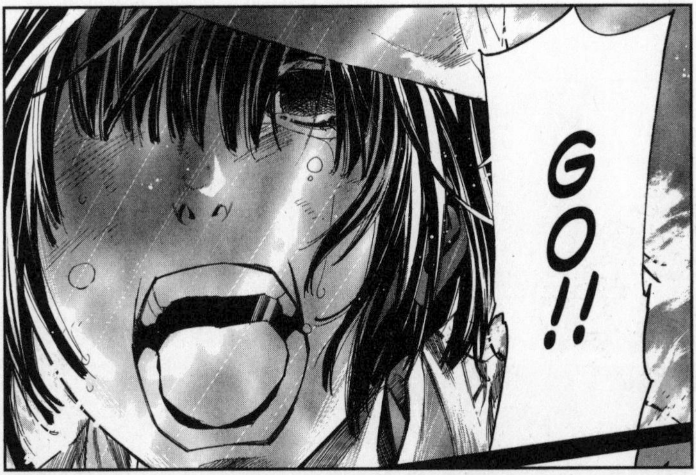
GO!!

Go, page 172
This phrase from Kiyoko's memories lends itself to greater ambiguity in Japanese. What her mother said was *ikinasai*, which could mean either "go" or "live." Kiyoko always remembered it as "go," as her mother commanded her to go away to safety. Unfortunately for her, "go that way" is what they say in Japanese to mean "go away," as in, "Get lost; I don't want to see you anymore," and this is part of what has been tormenting her, lo these many years. Fortunately for the translators, in the accurate memory, Kiyoko's mother was kind enough to elaborate on her meaning, so the translators didn't have to come up with an English word or phrase that means both "go away" and "stay alive."

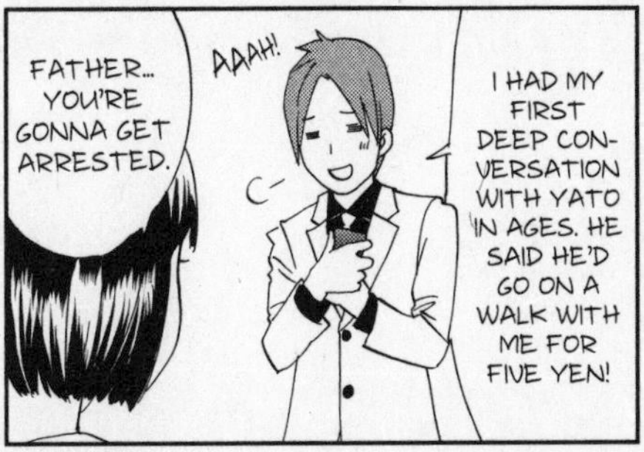
I HAD MY FIRST DEEP CONVERSATION WITH YATO IN AGES. HE SAID HE'D GO ON A WALK WITH ME FOR FIVE YEN!
AAAH!
FATHER... YOU'RE GONNA GET ARRESTED.

JK Walking, page 188
JK walking, where the JK stands for *joshi kôsei* (high school girl), is a form of subsi-date. The "walk" may be just that, but sometimes girls provide other services for more money.

野 N O R A 良 G A M I 神

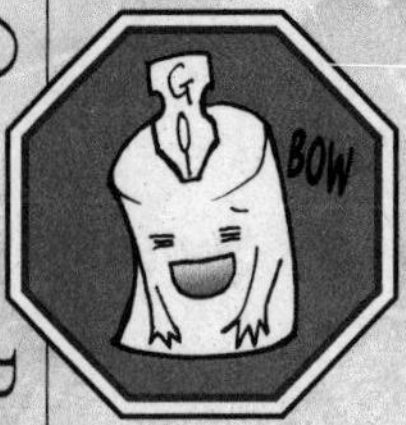
BOW

Tenjin: "The name of the *fuji* flower [the Japanese wisteria] can also mean 'incurable disease'..."

The Kameido Tenjin Shrine is famous for its wisteria flowers. When I went there, an image flashed across my mind of Lord Michizane's grumpy face, cursing his political enemies in the Fujiwara family with reckless abandon, while Tsuyu sighed at having to deal with his rants again.

No one can match My Lord in scariness.

Adachitoka

Noragami: Stray God volume 11 is a work of fiction. Names, characters, places, and incidents are the products of the author's imagination or are used fictitiously. Any resemblance to actual events, locales, or persons, living or dead, is entirely coincidental.

A Kodansha Comics Trade Paperback Original.

Published in the United States by Kodansha Comics, an imprint of Kodansha USA Publishing, LLC, New York.

Publication rights for this English edition arranged through Kodansha Ltd., Tokyo.

First published in Japan in 2014 by Kodansha Ltd., Tokyo.

ISBN 978-1-63236-252-0

Printed in the United States of America.

www.kodanshacomics.com

9 8 7 6 5 4 3 2 1

Translator: Alethea Nibley & Athena Nibley
Lettering: Lys Blakeslee
Editing: Lauren Scanlan